THE CANADIAN MOUNTAINEERING ANTHOLOGY

edited by **Bruce Fairley**

foreword by **Sid Marty**

LONE
PINE

The Publisher
Lone Pine Publishing

202A – 1110 Seymour Street	206, 10426 – 81 Ave.	16149 Redmond Way, #180
Vancouver, British Columbia	Edmonton, Alberta	Redmond, Washington 98052
Canada V6B 3N3	Canada T6E 1X5	USA

Canadian Cataloguing in Publication Data
Main entry under title:
The Canadian mountaineering anthology

    ISBN 1-55105-041-2

    1. Mountaineering—Canada. 2. Rock climbing—Canada 3.
Mountaineering. I. Fairley, Bruce, 1951-
GV199.44.C2C2 1994   796.5'22'0971   C94-910813-8

    Editor-in-Chief: Glenn Rollans
    Editor: Roland Lines
    Cover Design: Beata Kurpinski
    Design: David Harris, Bruce Timothy Keith
    Layout and Production: Bruce Timothy Keith, Greg Brown
    Copyediting: Vivian Elias
    Printing: Jasper Printing Group Ltd., Edmonton, Alberta, Canada
    Cover Background Photo: Ken Legg
    Cover Inset Photo: Don Serl

Reprinted materials and photographs in this book are used with the generous permission of
their copyright holders. Pages ix, xi and xii of this book, which list reprinted material and
photo credits and permissions, constitute an extension of this copyright page.

"To Bear Creek" and "Mount Murchison" are reprinted from *Climbs and Explorations in the
Canadian Rockies* by Hugh E.M. Stutfield and J. Norman Collie. Copyright © 1903 by
Longman's, London. Reprinted with permission of the publishers.

All footnotes appearing in this book are by Bruce Fairley, except those appearing with "The
Centenary of David Douglas' Ascent of Mount Brown," which are by J. Monroe Thorington,
and those appearing with "Mounts Brown and Hooker" and "Mounts Brown and Hooker—
A Reply," which are by Alex McCoubrey, the editor of the *Canadian Alpine Journal* at the time
those articles were first printed.

The publisher gratefully acknowledges the assistance of Alberta Community Development
and the Department of Canadian Heritage, the support of the Canada/Alberta Agreement
on the cultural industries, and the financial support provided by the Alberta Foundation
for the Arts.

The publisher also thanks The Alpine Club of Canada
for its enabling support for this publication.

Table of Contents

List of Illustrations

Acknowledgements

David Harris was a kind of unofficial editor, consultant, critic and prod throughout the ordeal of creating *The Canadian Mountaineering Anthology*—a keen supporter from the moment he first heard of the project. In the last three years of putting the book together he has acted as a thoughtful sounding board for many issues and has contributed many fine introductions for pieces he was mainly responsible for choosing. He is due thanks on numerous other counts, not the least of which was steering us through the rigours of securing financial backing from the Alpine Club of Canada. As the most recent editor of the *Canadian Alpine Journal* he has very carefully developed ideas about the direction and style in mountain writing, and as chairman of the Alpine Club of Canada publications committee he gave us a blanket permission to reprint material from the *Canadian Alpine Journal*.

Moira Irvine did not live to see this volume in print; she died of cancer about three years into the project. She and I came up with the idea at more or less about the same time, and it was the last thing we spoke of before I said good-bye to her two days before she died. She had a great love of mountain writing, especially from the earlier years of Canadian mountaineering, a discerning ear born of many years' service as editor of the *Canadian Alpine Journal*.

John Manuel was a friend of both Moira and me; he too had a keen interest in the history of Canadian mountaineering, especially as it developed on the coast. In the first couple of years of the project he read great numbers of articles and assisted us greatly in making our final selection. His imprint is also found on several of the introductions to the selections.

Each of these three has contributed introductory material to the anthology.

For proof reading assistance our thanks go to Anders Ourom and Stephanie Fairley.

For permission to reprint their articles, our thanks go to all the authors. We have attempted to contact each of the living authors personally, and succeeded in almost all cases. We would be interested in hearing from those we missed. Please contact the editor at: Box 989, Golden, British Columbia, V0A 1H0.

Likewise our thanks to the talented photographers who supplied us with the kind of pictures we all dream of taking, and to the Whyte Museum and Archives of the Canadian Rockies, in Banff, for permission to reprint photographs from their remarkable collection.

We would also like to thank the following who gave permission for authors who were deceased or unavailable: Mrs. B. Wickham of Whiterock for the writings of Don Munday; Franc De La Vega and the American Alpine Club for extracts from *Where the Clouds Can Go* on behalf of Dr. Monroe Thorington; Dr. John Wheeler for the writings of Arthur O. Wheeler; Peter Croft, Sr. for the writings of Peter Croft; and Mary Lauchlan for the writings of John Lauchlan.

The Alpine Club of Canada is Canada's national mountaineering club, and has published, since its inception in 1907, the *Canadian Alpine Journal*, which has recorded more mountain adventures, catastrophes and daring deeds than many would believe imaginable. Our thanks to the Alpine Club of Canada, its officers, employees and publications committee for their support of this endeavour.

Thanks also to those publishers who gave permission to reprint material over which they hold copyright. If there have been any errors or omissions, the publishers would be grateful if those concerned would contact the editor so that corrections can be made to any future editions.

"Glacier House," "A Surveying Escapade" and "The First Ascent of Mount Bonney" by William Spotswood Green, from *Among the Selkirk Glaciers* (London: Macmillan & Co., 1890).

"The First Ascent of Mount Hector" by Philip S. Abbot, from *Appalachia*, VIII, Journal of the Appalachian Mountain Club, 1896-1898. By permission of the Appalachian Mountain Club.

"The Discovery of Paradise Valley," "Camp Life" and "Bill Peyto" by Walter D. Wilcox, from *The Rockies of Canada* (New York: G. Putnam's Sons, 1900).

"To Bear Creek" and "Mount Murchison" by Hugh E.M. Stutfield and J. Norman Collie, from *Climbs and Explorations in the Canadian Rockies* (London: Longman's, 1903). By permission of the publisher.

"Mount Lefroy" by Charles S. Thompson, from *Sierra Club Bulletin*, II, 1897-1899. By permission of Sierra Club Books.

"Our Summer Camp at Lake O'Hara," "Hip-Hip Hurrah!" "The First Ascent of Mount Robson" and "The Millionaire Guide" by Conrad Kain, from *Where the Clouds Can Go* (New York: The American Alpine Club, 1935). By permission of Franc De La Vega and the American Alpine Club.

"Trials of the Campfire" by Kate McQueen and "Viscount Amery" by Edward Feuz, from *In the Western Mountains: Early Mountaineering in British Columbia* (Victoria: B.C. Provincial Archives, 1980). By permission of the B.C. Records and Archives Service, Sound Heritage Series.

"The Mightiest Hump of Nature" by Paddy Sherman, from *Cloudwalkers* (Toronto: Macmillan of Canada, 1965). By permission of the author.

"The Rediscovery of Athabasca Pass" by Arthur P. Coleman, from *The Canadian Rockies: New and Old Trails* (London: T. Fisher Unwin, 1911).

"The Iron Butterfly" by Jeff Marshall and "The Wild Thing" by Barry Blanchard and Peter Arbic, from *Alpinism* (Calgary: Apollo Publications, 1988). By permission of the authors and Chic Scott.

"High Anxiety" by Jeff Marshall, from *Polar Circus*, vol. 2 (Calgary: Summit Publishing, 1987). By permission of the author.

"Kellogs" by George Homer and "Eckhard Grassman" by Murray Toft, from *The Calgary Mountain Club Newsletter*, Newsletter of the Calgary Mountain Club. By permission of the authors.

"Introduction from *A Climber's Guide to the Coastal Ranges of British Columbia*" by Dick Culbert, from *A Climber's Guide to the Coastal Ranges of British Columbia* (Banff: The Alpine Club of Canada, 1965). By permission of the author.

"The Golden Hinde" by Ralph Hutchinson, "Misadventures in South America" and "Freight Christmas" by Dick Culbert and "The Old Camp of 1911 Revisited" (anon.), from *The B.C. Mountaineer*, Newsletter of the B.C. Mountaineering Club, by permission of the authors.

"Diedre in Winter" by Tami Knight, from *The Avalanche Echoes*, Newsletter of the Vancouver Section of the Alpine Club of Canada. By permission of the author.

"Coming Down" by Sharon Wood, originally published simultaneously in *Vancouver Magazine, Calgary Magazine* and *Edmonton Magazine*. By permission of the author and the publishers of *Vancouver Magazine*.

"Climbing Competitions" by Orvel Miskiw, from *The Chinook*, Newsletter of the Calgary Section of the Alpine Club of Canada. By permission of the author.

"Shattered Dreams" by Richard Howes, "Further Uses of an Ice Axe" by Steve Grant, "Air Drop" by Roland Burton, "Logan Bread" by Bill Lisett and "The Great Siwash Fiasco" by John Rance, from *The Varsity Outdoor Club Journal*, published annually by the Varsity Outdoor Club, University of British Columbia, Vancouver. By permission of the authors in each case.

"The Apex of the Coast Range" and "Mountain Troops, A Lighter View" by W.A. Don Munday (permission by Mrs. B. Wickham); "Jimmy and the Kid" by Steve DeMaio; "Rogers Pass at the Summit of the Selkirks," "Mounts Brown and Hooker" and "Some Memories of Edward Whymper" by Arthur O. Wheeler (permission by Dr. John Wheeler); "Gangapurna Stories" and "Aggressive Treatment" by John Lauchlan (permission by Mary Lauchlan); "The Centenary of David Douglas' Ascent of Mount Brown" and "Mounts Brown and Hooker—A Reply" by J.M. Thorington; "Turret's Way" by Michael Down; "Zodiac Wall" by Hugh Burton; "Oh, Canada" by Les MacDonald; "Mountaineering and the Ethics of Technique" by Bruce Fairley, "Small Wall" by Ben Gadd; "The Cat's Ears" by Paul Starr; "Tellot Lake to Knight Inlet" by Sara Golling; "The Traverse" by Don Serl; "Arctic Lobsters" by David Harris; "Huascaran—The First Ascent of the Western Spur" by Paddy Sherman; "Dhauligiri IV—An Attempt from the South" by Chic Scott; "Pickled in Yosemite" by Peter Croft; "Of Rurps and Nursery Rhymes" by Matt Scott; "Where Heathen Rage" by David Dornian; and "Sometimes You Know—Sometimes You Don't" by Jim Sinclair; all from the *Canadian Alpine Journal*, published annually by the Alpine Club of Canada. By permission of the authors except as noted.

Foreword

To live here is to know
The jagged arcs of glory
are at war with gravity

That spent footfalls
of giant lives still echo
among earth's frozen blue
pavilions, the heaped up
sharpened bones of history

And blood, though petrified
is singing in the stone

Under our feet the raised beds
of ancient seas remind us
that we only came here yesterday

What gives us our dominion?

That we soar and follow with the mind
anything the mind can cover
Until we think the eye can take in time

And the last thing we discover is humility
In the small, white petalled anemone
below the swooning, ice-carved tower

Seeing in that green kiss, what power!
To take this measure
that will take us
everywhere

What I sometimes remember first of the mountains I have climbed are
flowers, pink moss campion and yellow saxifrage, that led me and my
friends up beyond the timberline and back to the edge of winter in July. Or
I see again a goat run out of room above Lineham Ledge in Waterton park,
stand up on hind legs to pivot backwards, then hesitate—its front hooves
cupped to the rock—to bite green manna from the stone. And I turn away,
never as at home here as those white beasts are, my fingers brushing white
prayer flags of goat hair from a handhold. Peer around the corner now,
because it wouldn't be the first time—that was on Wiwaxy Peaks at

Lake O'Hara—that a jealous old billy rushed you off your holds. It forced me, that first time, to make a variation on the old Grassi route. But it had been climbed so many times anyway it was starting to feel like a staircase.

Mountains lifted me up, out of myself and into a bigger world, into a giant life where the elements contend like warring gods, and white-bearded judges peer down from towering benches in the clouds to watch my progress.

When you man the mountains, there is drama, tragedy and comedy among the peaks. And fortunately, since its earliest days, Canadian mountaineering has attracted devotees of a literary bent to record its vivid moments. From the pioneering contemporaries of John Muir (who saw the mountain in holistic terms, looking for the natural line that leads to the summit) to the gonzo generation of today (the minimalist solo climbers looking for the hard routes, the ones written off as unclimbable), this book offers a broad selection of their varied thoughts and experiences that is a good introduction for the general reader, and spice for the skilled mountaineer.

We start out with the Rev. William Spotswood Green back in the days of hemp climbing ropes, when hiking trails were just a futurist's pipedream. We find him sitting around the fire, "picking the bones of a marmot." W.D. Wilcox, a pioneer mountaineer in the Rockies, writes of his own adventures, and poses a fundamental question: "Why not stay home and be comfortable?" It is a phrase that echoes throughout the book.

Green and Wilcox were part of the first wave of climber-explorers, mostly of American or British stock, who ushered in the golden age of mountaineering in Canada, a time when many of the great peaks were first climbed—or at least those within close range of a good C.P.R. hotel. These pioneers were an accomplished and illustrious crew: J. Norman Collie, the discoverer of neon, was an explorer in several fields of endeavour; Wilcox was a distinguished writer; others were statesmen, professors, lawyers. They were led by an elite cadre of European guides and supported by a crusty bunch of Canadian outfitters. Their method of travel, the pack train, tied them to an even earlier generation of explorers and traders. Mountain mornings echoed with the bells of the lead mare ringing in the high meadow—and the cursing of the wrangler wrestling with a galled-up packhorse.

*   *   *   *   *

Each mountaineer carries a personal history of mountaineering in his or her head. It is good to remember those who came before us, who still climb with us, unseen. The history of mountaineering in Canada is brief—the Columbia Icefield, now a famous landmark for millions, was first seen by white men only 95 years ago—so some of us have been around long enough to have met, or climbed with, the old characters who are now historic figures of the sport.

Edward Feuz, Swiss guide, figures in my own history. I remember my teen-aged self running up the trail to Lake McArthur, and an ancient, be-knickered gnome smoking a Peterson Bent gripped in yellow teeth kept plodding along and passing me as I stopped to gasp for breath. Finally Edward stopped and glared at me through a wreath of Sail tobacco smoke. "How you going to climb zee PEAK," he demanded, "ven you don't know how to VALK?" And he gave me mountain walking lessons on the spot.

Edward represented the old, conservative school that climbed mountains via the classic routes, the less exposed gentler lines that seem mere alpine hikes to the kids of today, but that doesn't mean he was soft. A few years later, as a park warden at Lake O'Hara, I watched through a spotting scope, amazed, as he, a septuagenarian, led a rope of elderly women, day after day, up routes that younger folk bragged of doing. The women had been climbing with him since girlhood—women have been climbing mountains here for as long as the men have. (This book is not always a his-story, and includes Sharon Wood's account of the expedition that made her the first North American woman to climb Everest.)

After the accounts of the early years, the action switches to the sometimes dangerous process of capturing the more isolated peaks in North America and abroad. Paddy Sherman's record of the first ascent by MacCarthy, Taylor and Atkinson shows us a glimpse of a trip to Mt. Logan so hair raising that "it was twenty-five years before anybody even attempted the mountain again."

A more modern climber, Brian Greenwood, is another who stands out for me; he bridged between generations, perfecting the new approach, combining the techniques of rock and ice climbing to take the direct route to the top. Greenwood and his pals in the renegade Calgary Mountain Club were the admired outlaws of my generation, swilling beer in the King Edward Hotel by night and kicking sacred cows off the mountains by day. Greenwood sold me my first pair of Lowe boots in Calgary's first climbing store in the basement of his old house on Elbow drive. I remember the smell of leather, the bewitching jingle of pitons and 'biners, and the noise of kids squalling upstairs. Meeting him put a human face on the legends.

I'm well aware that the hard men and women who have come along these past two decades have pushed past the edge of what was once thought impossible. Their climbs are ruled by millimetres: their margin of escape is sometimes pared to the bone. Still I prefer the macro—the whole mountain—over the micro chip hold that can never be the crux of a mountain, though it may be the crux of an extreme route up it. The whole mountain presents a new crux every day for the next climber to discover. It has a glacial indifference to these esoteric accomplishments that should be bracing to the soul of rock-jock and alpinist alike.

For me, the flower, goat and human face stand out in living colour against the chiaroscuro of blackened limestone and white cornice that I see through these pages: each mountain its own country, and the passport just the will and wisdom to explore. The quest's the thing, and the motive behind each quest is fascinating, even when it's opposed to my own desires. Jeff Marshall's account of racking up doubles on frozen waterfalls—climbing two in one day, *solo*; or big wall climbing—hanging in a tent suspended by ropes somewhere in the back end of Patabeyondia, as told here by the late John Lauchlan—these fascinate me, but I remain a ridge rat, and prefer my ice in a glass of scotch, rather than underfoot.

The "Conquistadores of the Useless" met with in these pages are mostly of good cheer: their compensation for being so little known, so misunderstood by the masses. The masses don't bother much with poetry, either. There is no money in poetry, and so it, like mountaineering, becomes a refuge for truth. As a writer, I return to poetry, which is where I started, as I return to mountains: both are ends in themselves.

After all striving upward in this mortal clay is done, after the fear and the exultation, words are left to keep these memories alive. The words take us up to feel a bit of what was felt when that exhausted leader blew on his hands and shouted:

"On belay!"

"Climbing," his partner shouted back.

The words fragment in syllables of wind, and perhaps the climbers, sensing each other's moves through a perlon umbilicus, could not even hear themselves at that moment. But we are there with them now, and we have heard; so let the climb begin.

∿ Sid Marty

Introduction

In 1888 two reverend gentlemen from England spent some time in the Selkirk Mountains. Officially they were there to climb, but things being what they were in those days they spent much of their first weeks at Glacier House making surveys, sketching and recording botanical observations. When they finally did get down to serious climbing they settled on Mt. Bonney, a somewhat brooding summit with a massive, black north wall, which faces down onto Loop Brook. Despite the evils of Selkirk bush and unpredictable weather, the ascent was made, and Reverend William Spotswood Green and Reverend Henry Swanzy reached the summit on August 9, 1888. Many commentators adopt this date as "day one" of Canadian mountaineering.

Between 1888 and May 20, 1986, when Sharon Wood became the first North American woman to reach the summit of Mt. Everest, and continuing to the present, many dramatic changes have taken place in Canadian climbing, and untold numbers of remarkable ascents have been made. The purpose of this collection is to celebrate some of the greatest moments in that more than hundred-year history.

Undoubtedly, those who are familiar with the story that is Canadian mountaineering will be disappointed that some of the pieces they most prize have not been included here. We can almost hear them asking now: Where is Palmer? Why is Outram excluded? What of Frank Smythe's famous "piton incident" on Mt. Colin? Or the exploits of Gibson and Wates, Sterling Hendricks, Alice Purdey or Sean Dougherty?

To this we can only answer that this anthology does not seek to be representative. Our intention has been to present those selections from the hundreds available that we found to be most readable, not to canvas all periods or all regions of Canada equally. We selected articles which seemed to us to have intrinsic merit no matter who wrote them, or at what time they appeared. But we think that within these pages every reader will find tales to make the palms sweaty or the heart inspired.

Most mountaineering writers are amateurs, both at climbing and writing. The tendency for most of them is to start at the beginning and work their way through to the end. This chronological style has much to recommend it—it is difficult for a writer using this format to become lost in the jungles of disorganized verbiage. However, as in cooking or sex, one methodology can become tedious if applied with too little variation. The problem for mountain writers generally is to achieve originality. In making our selections we have tried to be alert for those writers who progressed beyond mere narrative and achieved a sense of drama in the telling of their tales.

Probably 95 percent of Canadian mountain writing is contained in articles of less than five thousand words, which appear in newsletters, magazines and journals. There are surprisingly few book-length depictions of climbing in Canada, and almost none published since the Second World War. The one source of overwhelming importance in recording the history of Canadian climbing and mountain exploration is the *Canadian Alpine Journal,* published annually by the Alpine Club of Canada. Everyone who loves Canadian mountaineering and its story should thank this worthy organization for their dedication over the years in publishing the *Canadian Alpine Journal,* without which most of the story of the discovery of Canada's mountain wildness would have been lost forever.

The Alpine Club of Canada also has probably the finest mountaineering library in North America. The collection is housed in the Whyte Museum of the Canadian Rockies, in Banff, Alberta. Those who love books about mountaineering should at some time make a pilgrimage to this shrine, if only to see and smell the old leather-bound volumes and the wonderful photographs of the early explorers of the hills. For some aspects of the Canadian mountaineering story, the archives in the Whyte Museum are the *only* practical source available. This is particularly so with respect to irregular publications or ones, such as outing club newsletters, that circulate in limited numbers.

One by-product of the publication of this work is that a stab has been made at establishing something like the beginnings of a criticism of Canadian mountain writing. It will be evident simply from the selections chosen that there are writers whom we prefer above others. No doubt personal taste enters into the choice. One pre-publication reader of the manuscript lamented the dearth of a "humanistic" outlook in all articles selected from the post-1945 period, urging us to reject the more "technical" thrust of this later writing for pieces that breathed more the spirit of the packtrain and campfire. Alas, the world has changed since the days of Wilcox and Collie, and in vain were our remonstrances that climbing had changed along with it. Others felt that the inclusion of material about climbs outside Canada weakened the focus of the book. But how can one omit from the story of Canadian climbing those deeds done by Canadian climbers in South America, Yosemite and the Himalayas?

"Here is God's plenty," wrote the poet John Dryden of another collection of tales—*The Canterbury Tales* of Geoffrey Chaucer. We think that this collection will reveal a cast of characters as diverse, eccentric, generous, improvident, scholarly, whimsical, good-hearted, bountiful, sanguine, philosophical, loveable and magnificent as Chaucer's celebrated pilgrims.

We had great fun putting the collection together and wish the reader all the best in his journey through the great story that unfolds in these pages.

∿ Bruce Fairley

I PIONEERS

The end of the Golden Era of climbing in the European Alps is taken to be 1865, the year the Matterhorn was first ascended by the Englishman Edward Whymper and his unfortunate companions. Mountaineering in Canada had not even begun by this time. The first climbers to visit Canada could hardly believe their good fortune; more mountains awaited first ascents than lay in the whole of the European Alps. But these were mountains with a difference. Getting there was more than half the problem. The building of the Canadian Pacific Railway broke down the first hurdle. But the bush remained. Many of the earliest accounts of Canadian climbing read much like general travel literature, with a heavy emphasis on bush and mosquitoes; the writers were charting the mountain regions of an exotic land whose geography was still only vaguely understood.

The pioneer mountaineers were a different breed than today's middle-class climber. A surprising number of clergymen led the way. Others tended to be professionals—professors, scientists, lawyers, engineers—with incomes considerably above average. Time and money were essential. Even the peaks close to the railroad were tough to get at; the remoter heights required an organization and tenacity akin to a military campaign. But the pioneers were also humanists. One rarely senses a frustration at the lengthy travel they were forced to undergo to claim a handful of peaks in a summer season. The rail journey, the packing, the river crossings, the camping, the horses and the summit were all of a piece. It was the full experience which counted for them, not just the numbers.

First the British, then the Americans led the way. Canadians were not prominent among the earliest climbers in Canada; they were too busy establishing a country.

~ Bruce Fairley

AMONG THE SELKIRK GLACIERS

Among the Selkirk Glaciers was the first book published on the Canadian mountains, and it remains one of the most delightful. The book resulted from a six-week visit to the Selkirks in 1888, during which the Reverend William Spotswood Green mapped the area surrounding Glacier House with admirable precision and made the first really celebrated mountain ascent recorded in Canada: Mt. Bonney via the northwest ridge.

Green was inspired to visit the Selkirks by his cousin, Henry Swanzy, who rode the CPR through the range in 1887 and reported to Green on the magnificent mountain scenery he had experienced. Swanzy accompanied his reverend cousin on the 1888 expedition.

Green expressed surprise at how little mountain exploration had been done in the Selkirks up to that time. He did not expect to have so clear a field three years after the official opening of the CPR line through Rogers Pass. After fighting the dense, unyielding bush barriers of the Selkirk forest in quest of measurements and data, perhaps he understood the problems better.

Despite being the first book-length account of mountaineering in Canada, and despite being written in a time when a somewhat ponderous style prevailed in climbing literature, *Among the Selkirk Glaciers* remains one of the most readable of all the narratives of mountain exploration ever published. Its charm is largely due to Green's ability to select incidents and detail from his days in the hills and relate them with humour and sympathy. He seems to have been a liberal churchman—certainly not above putting in a good rugged day in the mountains, Sunday or no Sunday!

Many passages in his writings testify to Green's humanistic outlook. He wrote with intelligence and surprising insight of the condition of the native Indians on the newly settled prairie. He also resisted the Victorian impulse to legitimize his mountaineering activities by cloaking himself in the mantle of science. *Among the Selkirk Glaciers* succeeds because its author was more interested in telling his story than he was in delivering learned geological and botanical observations. His account of one of the most important campaigns of mountain exploration undertaken in the Selkirks still rings with freshness, vitality and humour.

~ Bruce Fairley

Glacier House

William Spotswood Green

Glacier House, built on exactly the same plan as the little inns at Field in the Rockies, and at North Bend on the Frazer, is somewhat in the Swiss chalet style and possesses, besides the large *salle à manger* where dinner is served to the passengers of the Atlantic and Pacific express trains which meet here every day, six or seven small but snug bedrooms. One of these we took for ourselves. Another was soon afterwards occupied by Mr. Bell-Smith, a well-known Canadian artist, and the other rooms were occasionally, during our time, filled by guests who stopped off the train for the night and resumed their journey next day. Sometimes they stayed longer, and some most interesting people were amongst those we met. Some weeks no one came, and then again the little inn was overflowing. On one occasion when we returned from an absence of several days in the mountains, we found that besides our room being occupied, our two spare tents had also been pitched to give sufficient accommodation. After that a sleeping-car was brought up and left permanently on a siding, to accommodate the occasional overflow from the house.

The hospital manager, Mr. Perley, his wife, and their little niece, Alice, about nine years of age; Mr. Hume, the secretary, the French cook and his assistant Chinaman, three capital waitresses and the "boy" made up the staff. Another man, "Charlie," belonged specially to the railway, his chief business being to watch the white stones around the fountains which played in front of the verandah.

These white stones were nothing more than pieces of common vein quartz, broken up to rim the edges of the little ponds; but so impressed were the numerous emigrants who went westward, with the idea that quartz meant gold, that whenever the trains stopped men, women, and children, pounced on these white stones, and would have left not one but for the vigilance of "Charlie." It was a perfect farce sometimes to watch a man sneaking round with his eye on the custodian, trying to steal one small piece, and the very fact of their being so guarded served to enhance their value. The live stock on the premises consisted of a black bear cub, which at first made night horrible by squealing for its mother, but nevertheless was a most intelligent, playful and amusing little animal. Little Alice and the bear were great friends, and until it got too heavy she used to carry it about in her arms. Then there was her cat, some fowl and "Jeff," a most friendly dog, always ready to join in any expedition. Among the various traits and vestiges of ancestry which he exhibited that of Gordon setter predominated. So much for Glacier House. 🐾

A Surveying Escapade

William Spotswood Green

In undertaking any topographical survey, the first thing to decide is: On what scale shall we make our map? For many reasons we came to the conclusion that four inches to the mile would be sufficiently large on which to put down all the details of importance. The next step is to measure a line which shall form a base for our first triangle. If a baseline of one mile is measured, the picture of that on the map is a line of four inches, and thus the scale of the map is fixed, all other distances being in equal proportion.

In great trigonometrical surveys, such as that of Great Britain and Ireland, the measurement of the baseline is of such importance that it is done with microscopic accuracy. In our case such minute accuracy would have been impossible, so we were content with a measurement made with our steel wire one-eighth of a mile long.

One engineer said to me, "But surely with such a measurement you must allow for the expansion and contraction of the wire with varying temperature." All I can say is that I made no such allowance. The temperature of the day when I measured the wire and of those on which I used it, did not differ much over 10°, certainly not 20°, and if there is no greater inaccuracy in our location of peaks than the error arising from the expansion and contraction of our wire I am satisfied. A much more fruitful source of error arises from the difficulty of always being certain that you are observing the same particular knob, on a mountain summit, when seen from different points of view. This is particularly the case when the peak occupies a place much above the point of observation. In a mountain survey therefore the points fixed from the highest elevations are the most reliable.

When breakfast was disposed of on July 18th, we packed the plane table on our shoulders and set off for the opposite side of the valley, the top of the snow sheds there being the only level place where it seemed possible to measure a straight line of over a hundred yards in length. There was even here a slight gradient (which was unfortunate), but as no better spot could be found, we measured 660 yards and set up a pole, with flags at either end. The flag at No. 2 station was a piece of newspaper, and as it fluttered from its staff for over a week, some idea may be formed of the great calmness which prevails in these mountain valleys. From points at either end of our baseline we fixed a third station, at the opposite side of the loop made by the railway, and took, on the plane table, bearings of all the peaks in view, made profile sketches and photographed them, assigning them numbers for future identification. To accomplish all this took the greater part of the day, and as the sun was shining with intense heat and mosquitoes were biting like fury, we were not sorry when it was completed.

The cascade which forms such a feature in the view from Glacier House is no small source of difficulty to the railway people, as it objects to be controlled in any way. A bridge has been built for it to go under, but with the true spirit of freedom it uses the bridge only occasionally, and just then was with much hilarity dashing right down on the railway and knocking away all foundation from the track. By balancing ourselves carefully on the rails we crossed it without much difficulty; and Swanzy lay down with his chest on the rail to regale himself with a drink. Suddenly, to my horror, a freight train, coming down the gradient, swept round the curve. Men stood on the roof of every car screwing down the brakes. The whistle was evidently blowing, but the cascade drowned all other sound. I shouted to Henry "Here's the train." He took no notice! There was no time to speak twice; but at the very last instant he perceived the danger and rolled himself aside just as the train roared past. After this we were careful not to lie down with our heads on the main track again. ❧

The First Ascent of Mt. Bonney

William Spotswood Green

It seemed now quite evident to us that Mount Bonney was not to be conquered without a really big effort, so to prepare ourselves for that, we determined to make the 8th an off day. It was also necessary to fetch up more provisions from our cache down at the mouth of the valley. Henry volunteered to do this, and I remained at camp to work up notes and sketches. To be alone in this wilderness of forest and cliff, glaciers and mountain torrents, bright wild flowers, bright sunshine, and the weird cry of the marmots, and with leisure to let the mind dwell on it undisturbed, was an experience well worth a day, even if no other reason for pause existed. After breakfast Henry started down the valley, and returned in the evening with some meal and meal-tins and his half-plate camera. While he was away I was able to shoot a marmot and a little chief hare, and had them stewing for supper when he arrived. A spring of clear water, in the midst of sweet-scented, large red-flowered mimulus, oozed from the rocks near our tent, and fetching water thence we made the kettle boil on the cedar logs.

After supper we took a last anxious glance at Mount Bonney, rising from its bed of glaciers in dark cliffs to a height of 6,500 feet above our camp. Gold, grey wreaths of fleecy clouds wound in and out through its gullies, illumined here and there by shafts of lurid sunset light. The weather and its promise for the morrow filled our minds with many forebodings. I felt certain we were in for wind and rain, so I did not change the plates in my camera. If it should turn out fine Henry had six plates all ready in his. With what hopes we could conjure up we soothed our minds to sleep, and soon the roar of the torrent and all other sounds were as though they were not.

At 3.30 it was time to get up. Anxiously we stepped out of our warm bags into the chill morning air. Stars were twinkling brightly. Mount Bonney looked dark and sullen, but its arête was clear cut against the sky; lower down, grey mists lay like a blanket on the glacier. The flowers and trees were dripping with dew. All this looked promising, so shivering in the cold we lit the fire, made a cup of tea, and shouldered our swags which we had prepared the night before, closed the tent doors, and shortly after four o'clock started on our way. Henry carried his half-plate camera and the rope; I took the provisions and the plane table.

On former expeditions we had found that in making elaborate plans to avoid difficulties, we had involved ourselves in worse ones which were unforeseen; so now, as we intended to make our attack by the glacier descending from the col to the northwestward of our peak, we determined to take a "bee line" for its lower termination, and let difficulties come when they might.

After a small strip of forest, our way lay across an open area of large angular boulders; then came a very tangled piece of forest, which we had to follow down into a ravine and then work up a steep ascent beyond. Our aim was to strike the stream from the glacier as soon as possible. Leaving the tall forest, a desperate struggle ensued with alder scrub through which we scrambled for an hour. There was evidently a bear in it, for we saw the branches swaying to and fro as he pushed his way along a little below us. At last we entered the hollow worn by the glacier stream; it was all choked with compacted snow, which gave us good travelling towards the glaciers. Immediately on our left, above a slope of debris, rose steep cliffs, forest-clad above, and in their lower portions pierced by several dark caves. Through the grass and wild flowers on the shingle slope well-marked paths converged to the entrance of these caves; they were evidently the home of bears. We had no rifle, so we gave them a wide berth, for to meet a female grizzly with cubs was an adventure we felt disinclined to tackle with nothing but ice-axes. Louder and louder rose the roar of a waterfall, and turning a bend, we came on the open torrent making a fine leap of a hundred feet, from the flowery slopes above into a tunnel it had bored for itself beneath the snow.

We had now to begin a climb through tangled forest once more, but reaching the level, about 200 feet higher up, found a fine opening, clothed in a perfect meadow of *Veratrum viride* as high as our waists. Here again a bear was making tracks ahead of us. The broad leaves were so filled with dew that walking through was as wetting as if we were in the river, we therefore gladly followed the path he made; the stems being crushed down and the dew shaken from the leaves in his wake. For several hundred yards he had gone just in the direction desired, but when he turned off to the slopes on our left we had to say good-bye to him, and take the shortest line to the shingle beds near the stream, which stretched to the foot of the glacier. The cliffs on our left continued to rise higher and higher. Now the forest cap above had given place to one of glacier ice, from which seven fine waterfalls leaped down amongst the vegetation below, and made their way by countless channels to the larger stream. The whole air trembled with the roar and splash of torrents and cascades. And yet there was enough forest in the scene to give richness to it, so we found ourselves in a perfect Alpine paradise, which no being higher than a bear had ever entered before.

On reaching the recent moraine near the foot of the glacier, and noticing how much the glacier had shrunk in recent years, we halted for some refreshment. It was now four hours since we had left the camp, and we had risen just 1,600 feet. Following the side of the glacier as far as possible, we were soon forced by the closing-in of the cliffs to take to the ice. This we found so steep that without endless step-cutting we could not ascend by it; we therefore crossed it to the northward, and followed the moraine under the cliffs of the Ross Peak Range.

Once more the terminating of the moraine compelled us to take to the glacier, now covered with snow, and at 9.30 we found ourselves cutting steps at the foot of the couloir leading to the pass. The steep slope being scored by tracks of falling stones from the cliffs on either hand, we commenced our ascent in the centre.

After cutting a few steps and zigzagging upward, we looked up at the cornice overhanging the top; it seemed a long way off, and our hearts, I fear, failed us a little. I had hoped we might have got grips for our feet. To cut steps all the way up was, for us, next to impossible. Then I found we could get a little grip by kicking, and soon the snow became softer and our toes went well in. Holding good grips with our axes we now ascended at a fair pace. A bergschrund near the top forced us once more on to the rocks; we thus avoided the cornice, and at 10.30 just two hours from the foot of the glacier, we stood on the col. Before us the mountain fell away in precipitous slopes to a glacier-filled valley whence streams flowed into the Illecillewaet; and we could detect the railway track as a fine line, far below in the latter valley.

The two sides of the col presented a marvellous contrast; on the north a heavy cornice overhung a snow-filled couloir leading down to a glacier. On the south a perfect garden of Alpine flowers was in full bloom. There was the familiar *Dryas octapetala* and gay yellow *Haplopapus Brandigeii* all low-growing plants. Deep down however beneath the flowery slopes the valley was filled by a small glacier. The arête on our left leading towards Mount Bonney was broad and free from snow, and without any delay we resumed our ascent along it. The slope was gentle, and for half an hour nothing in the world could be easier. We could not see very far ahead owing to a series of knobs, one of which always rose a short distance ahead. I knew it was not all going to be easy like this, so we hurried anxiously upward, hoping soon to come in sight of the little curved peak visible from the railway, and which we feared would prove a serious obstacle to our progress.

Scrambling up some angular sharp-edged blocks of quartzite into which the arête had now contracted, the curved peak[1] came into view, and the look of it was by no means reassuring. From where we stood, to its foot, the arête was very sharp, flanked on the southward by steep snow slopes leading down for about 2,000 feet to the glacier on our right, while a heavy

---

1. This peak is now known as Mt. Green.

cornice overhung the almost vertical precipice to the northward. From this arête the peak sprang upwards in nearly perpendicular crags, snow-seamed, for over 200 feet. Two possible routes were all that were offered: one was to scale the apparently vertical face in front; the other was to skirt round the peak on the steep snow slope to the right, and so turn its flank.

The slope was so very steep and the snow so likely to slide, that we decided the latter route would be too risky, we therefore put on the rope and pulled ourselves together for a stiff climb. Having rested for a few minutes and deposited our spare food under a boulder, we started along the cornice with much caution, and then began to climb upwards. There was just enough loose powdery snow on the crags to make it most difficult to find a firm grip for either hands, feet, or axe.

The projecting shales, set vertically, were also so rotten that at every step we had to dislodge quantities of rock ere we could find any solid foothold. Every move needed the greatest possible caution, for we could not avoid being in a direct line one over the other. The ridge about half way up divided into two parallel ridges, the right hand one composed of bare crags, completely overhanging the snow slopes below, while the other was more or less a continuous snow arête to the summit.

After much scraping away of snow with my axe I succeeded in reaching these crags while Henry continued his way up the snow arête. We kept the rope tight between us and ascended abreast, he holding on while I sought out fresh grips, and when he moved I made myself as secure as I could. The crags on my ridge soon became more trustworthy, and at ten minutes to one o'clock the top of this first peak was beneath my feet. A snow cornice overhung the arête Henry was on, and as he sung out from below that he had no grip whatever in the loose snow, I gave him a good pull, and up he came making a fine gap in the cornice. We were up now, so much was certain, but the glance which passed from one to the other expressed the foremost thought in our minds, "What about the getting down!"

The view from the curved peak was superb. A perfect ocean of peaks and glaciers all cleft by valleys, and the main peak of Mount Bonney still rising in a dome of snow to the eastward. The weather looked threatening. Most of the landscape was bathed in sunshine, but there were heavy clouds hanging about the peaks, and one drifting towards us looked so lowering that we feared a thunderstorm. Our first thought was to hurry up with the camera, but ere we could get it fixed the clouds broke in a furious shower of hail accompanied by strong wind, and the photograph taken under such circumstances was decidedly of a shaky appearance. The gap in the cornice through which Henry had ascended was distinct enough, but the distant view was all doubled and confused.

As quickly as it came the storm passed away, and descending an easy slope of snow for a few hundred yards we commenced the ascent of the final peak. It was now nothing more than a tiresome trudge up steep domes of snow. When one was reached which we hoped was the final one another loomed up ahead. At last the highest crest was in sight, with a huge cornice overhanging the cliffs. Inside the cornice a narrow ridge of crags made themselves visible through the snow, and at ten minutes past three we were on the summit.

We placed the thermometer in a suitable position and took the reading of the barometer; it showed us to be about 10,600 feet above the sea,[2] probably a little more than this, and over 6,000 feet above our camp. It was too late in the day to admit of unnecessary delay, so I set up the plane table, took a series of observations, and then we turned our attention to photography. As much of our view, in the direction of what was most familiar in the panorama, was shut out by the cornice projecting from the summit, Henry ventured out on it, while I, taking a round turn of the rope on a crag held him firm. With his axe he pushed down some of the cornice, and fixing the camera took a photograph of the peaks of Mount Sir Donald and the névé of the great Illecillewaet Glacier.

At 4 p.m. we commenced the descent, and going as fast as possible, between glissading and running we were soon down to the col, beyond which the curved peak rose to the westward. As the evening sun was now shining on the side of the peak by which we had ascended, we felt that, soft as the snow had been in the morning, now it would be all slush, and the bad bit consequently much worse than before. We thought anything would be better than to attempt such a descent, so we determined to try and turn the peak in flank and cross the steep slopes of snow, plastered on to its face, which we had carefully considered during our ascent.

Accordingly, we bore away to the left, descending to a shoulder of the ridge below the peak. On reaching it we found ourselves on the brink of the precipice overlooking the glacier-filled valley to the westward, and it too was topped by a cornice. Farther to the right the névé we were on curved downwards, and though nearly vertical in its face, there was no actual cornice. It looked an exceedingly uncomfortable bit of work, but our only choice lay between it and what seemed the worse descent over the summit of the peak. The question was, could we reach the snow slope below the brink of the precipice? and having reached it, would it bear our weight?

Henry buried himself as deeply as possible in the snow, and when he considered himself quite firm I turned my face to the slope, and holding on to the rope kicked my toes in and went over the brink. I took the precaution,

---

2. The currently accepted height of Mt. Bonney is 10,194 feet (3,102 metres).

too, of burying my axe up to its head at every step. Just below the brink there was a projecting crag. This I thought would give a firm footing before testing the snow slope. I got one foot on to it, and was taking it as gently as possible when the rock gave way, a large piece of snow went with it, and fell on the slope twenty feet below. I stuck my knees into the snow, but felt my whole weight was on the rope. Then I heard a swishing noise in the air, and glancing downwards saw that the whole snow slope had cracked across, and was starting away down towards the valley in one huge avalanche. Henry hauled cautiously but firmly on the rope, and getting what grip I could with toes, knees, and ice-axe I was quickly in a safe position, and the two of us standing side by side, watched the clouds of snow filling the abyss below, and the huge masses bounding outwards. We listened to the sullen roar which gradually subsided, and all again seemed quiet except that a few blocks of consolidated snow went careering along, down the glacier, for some time, after the great mass of the avalanche had come to rest. This route was manifestly impracticable.

There was now no choice. We must retrace our steps to the summit of the curved peak, and go down by the same road that we had come up. We had eaten nothing since a few mouthfuls at 11 a.m., so between anxiety as to what lay before us and hunger, we felt far from happy. Never did anything feel more weary than that plod up the snow slopes to the peak. There we sat down to rest; I searched my pockets and found a small packet of tea and one cigarette. Henry ate the tea, and I enjoyed the cigarette, and feeling our nerves in a more reliable condition we commenced the descent.

As far as it was practicable we went down by the crags avoiding the snow, and made each step as secure as possible by shoving tons of loose slates and shales over the precipice. Then we had to quit the rocky ridge and cross the little snow-filled couloir to the other ridge. The snow on this was the chief danger, for it would not bear the slightest weight and it covered up the sharp loose slates. The axes were no use to us, so taking off the rope we tied them together and lowered them down, then making a bowline hitch on the other end of the rope we hung it on to a crag, and with its help scrambled down fifty feet to another firm foothold. A smart chuck brought the end of the rope free, and hitching it on again, we reached with its help the more secure portion of the ridge, and felt once more happy for all danger was past.

It took us some minutes to reach the place where we had deposited a few biscuits and a little beef in a tin, and then hurrying on we regained the summit of the col at 6.30 p.m. As we crept down the rocks towards the snow-filled couloir, we could not resist pausing to admire the marvelously beautiful sunset glow, which had flushed the whole range of the Rockies with bright carmine; while the nearer peaks and glaciers glowed with deep crimson. Never before or since have I seen such intense evening tints. Night, however, was close at hand, so on reaching the snow we glissaded, and ran downwards. Crevasses then forced us on to the moraine. Instead of following our course of the morning we determined to keep to the left side of the glacier and torrent, and take chance for the difficulties, but it was obviously shorter. Running and leaping from boulder to boulder, wading streams, taking a straight line through everything, and making many a stumble amongst falling stones, we found ourselves at last, with much-bruised shins, but fortunately without a sprained ankle or broken limb, at the margin of the forest.

It was now twilight, and this side of the valley was unknown to us, so as closely as possible we followed the course of the stream. When it plunged down in a waterfall, we slung ourselves downwards through fern and alder bushes by its side.

Ere we reached the ravine where the river was arched over with snow, night was upon us; but we had fixed a pole in the snow at the point where we left the forest, as a guide for us where to enter it on our return. The sky was overcast, and so dark was it now, that only by groping along did we find the pole; and, leaving the river bed, we entered the alder scrub in pitchy darkness. It had been bad enough in the light, but now in the dark it was simply heartbreaking. Never could one be sure of a footing on the slippery stems, and a fall every now and then nearly shook the life out of us. We hoped that we might not tread, by accident, on the tail of a grizzly, but took comfort at the thought of their deficiency in such appendages. We steered our course by the sound of the torrent, and by looking backwards at a certain peak which showed clear against a patch of sky. Then we were in the high pine forest, feeling with our axes for fallen logs, and fending off branches from our eyes.

Once or twice we almost despaired of getting through, and thought of sitting on a log until morning. We could see nothing whatever, in fact I kept my eyes shut most of the time, and only now and then glanced over my shoulder to see was the sky visible and the peak we were steering by. In the high woods there was soon no use in looking out for the latter, so we steered solely by the sound of the torrent. At last a white line was recognizable in the valley ahead, which we knew was a heap of boulders near our camp, and

> "Be the day weary
> Or be the day long,
> At length it ringeth to evensong."

11 p.m. found us round a blazing fire, sipping chocolate and picking the bones of a marmot. And so our long and successful day came to its close. ❧

APPALACHIAN MOUNTAINEERS,
PIONEERS OF THE ELDER DAY

Although the first climbers in Canada were mainly British, it did not take the Americans long to catch on. The American thrust was dominated by the Appalachian Mountain Club, founded in 1876 "for the advancement of the interests of those who visit the mountains of New England and adjacent regions, whether for the purpose of scientific research or summer recreation." By 1885 the adjacent regions were beginning to receive more attention. Come the mid-1890s the pages of *Appalachia*, the club's official journal, included many accounts of climbs and explorations in the Rockies and Selkirks.

The leading light among the Appalachian mountaineers was Charles Fay. In 1891 he travelled to Canada with a 20-member party (the majority were women) of the Appalachian Club to climb in the Rockies and Selkirks. Philip Abbot, later to become famous as the first fatality in Canadian mountaineering, and C.S. Thompson were among the men, and with Fay made the first ascent of Mt. Hector, a massive peak located north of Lake Louise just a few minutes drive from the present-day turnoff to Jasper. The trio also made a reconnaissance of Mt. Lefroy. Abbot read "The First Ascent of Mount Hector" before the Appalachian Mountain Club on December 27, 1895.

In 1930 Professor Fay, then in his 85th year, made his 25th visit to the Canadian mountains, attending the Alpine Club of Canada camp at Maligne Lake. In "Old Times in the Canadian Alps," written for the 1921-22 *Canadian Alpine Journal* Fay concluded that "the old times furnished grand opportunities for first-class ascents at short range from the hotels, and, so far as the peaks themselves are concerned, what ones of the remoter giants have afforded richer sport to their victors than Lefroy and Victoria, Deltaform and Hungabee, Goodsir and The Chancellor, Rogers and Dawson, to the pioneers of the elder day?"

 ∼ Moira Irvine

The First Ascent of Mt. Hector, Canadian Rockies

Philip S. Abbot

Our party that climbed Mt. Hector cannot, I am afraid, lay claim to much glory therefrom. We had no hair-breadth escapes; we did not even encounter great hardships, except such as are familiar to every bricklayer's apprentice. We did not need to exercise great generalship: the mountain was in plain sight, we walked to its base,—some distance, I admit, and not exactly over a paved road,—and then walked on till we reached the summit.

Furthermore, it cannot fairly be said that the expedition was one of unusual beauty. Grandeur of one sort there certainly was. In the single element of savage desolation—unrelieved, monotonous, boundless, and complete—I have never seen anything which equalled the view from the summit of Mt. Hector, and I do not expect to see anything which will excel it. But impressiveness and picturesqueness of detail, beauty of color, and, of course, human interest—except the imaginative interest which came from the mere immensity of the solitude—were, on the whole, lacking.

These are large deductions; but on the other side there are to be said two things. So far as the Club is concerned, Mt. Hector is the first alpine peak (and it can fairly be called alpine) which has been conquered for the first time by an Appalachian party, as such, climbing without guides. We do not claim to have achieved greatness, but we do expect to have greatness thrust upon us, as being the first parents of a very long and illustrious line to come. Secondly, the expedition was an interesting one to ourselves, because it was so fair and even a tussle with Nature—and with Nature in no accommodating mood. We did our own work, and fairly earned for ourselves what measure of success we had. There is a fascination in this which outweighs all aesthetic considerations whatever.

To tell the truth, aesthetic considerations were far from our minds when we left our train at Banff on the morning of Sunday, the 28th of July last year [1895]. We were fresh from our office desks, and the sight of the gray mountains encircling us on every side made our hearts leap like grasshoppers. How daft we became, the sequel will show. Our first step was to get hold of Wilson, the best guide and outfitter for that region, and to hold a council of war. Many plans were proposed, but none hit our fancy. Finally, for about the tenth time since he joined us, Thompson brought forward his fixed idea. Mt. Hector was reasonably near to Laggan,[1] the next stopping-place of the main party, but not too near; it had never been climbed; better still, it had been attempted without success; and it was high, because the

---

1. The present-day Lake Louise.

Canadian surveyors, when they turned back (so Baedeker said), had already reached 10,400 feet. It further appeared that Wilson himself had been with that party; and he said that he believed the peak could be climbed. He also told us of an enormous snow-field, lying to the west of Hector on the main watershed, and stretching away to the north for fifty miles, which was absolutely unexplored, and which might perhaps be crossed so as to bring us down into the valley of the Wapta by a new col over the backbone of the continent itself; and not only this, but there was a great snow-peak by the foot of which such a col would have to pass. What more could one ask? We brushed aside the reflection that this was a four or five days' trip; that no horses could be obtained; that we must carry our bedding and food on our backs, and that we had not begun to get into condition; in short, that the plan was absurd. We voted to start forthwith, and separated to make ready for the west-bound train which theoretically left Banff at six the next morning.

The train falsified our calculations in that instance by arriving nearly on time, and in consequence we had an agonizing five minutes. By a miracle, however, when it moved off, we were all there,—Professor Fay, Thompson, and myself, Wilson as guide, and a taciturn and admirably patient individual named Hiland, who was hired as a porter, and carried an enormous and shapeless pack composed of the tin things and all the other articles which the rest of us refused to touch. The other four of us had rucksacks—blessed be the man who invented them! With ordinary knapsacks we are all confident that we could not have made the trip. Each man carried his own blankets, Thompson the hand camera,—basely ungrateful after all our tender care,—and the provisions were equitably divided. We had four ice-axes, and for abundant precaution three lengths of alpine rope. I had also an aneroid barometer, an excellent instrument, with a proclivity which rivalled Mark Tapley's for taking a favorable view of things. It would have been more useful to us if I had not forgotten to compare its initial reading with the known altitude of Banff. For the rest—with all deference to my companions—we were a queer-looking lot. We none of us had coats; Thompson's sweater had been his companion since his Freshman year in college; as for Professor Fay's—*de mortuis nil nisi bonum*. He purposely left it after dark on the upper slopes of Mt. Stephen.

From Banff to Laggan—thirty-four miles—the railroad follows the broad glacial valley of the Bow, running in a northwesterly direction toward the heart of the range. A mile beyond Laggan the two separate: the railroad bends sharply a little to the south of west, and climbs the Kicking Horse Pass over the continental watershed, and the river turns to the north. On the left or western side of the Upper Bow valley, as you look north from Laggan, is a line of cliffs two or three thousand feet high, their evergreen-clad talus slopes rising abruptly from the level floor of the valley. These cliffs are out-posts of the Continental Divide; behind and above them, on the summit of the divide, but wholly concealed from below, lies the great snow-plateau I have spoken of. The eastern wall of the valley begins from Laggan much more tamely, in a broad low ridge, covered with burnt timber, which looks for all the world like a bit of New Hampshire. This lifts itself gradually to the altitude where a narrow belt of green forest still holds its own, and keeps on rising until the shale slopes of its crest begin to be mottled with snow; but it never becomes bold or mountainous. Eight or ten miles above Laggan the ridge is cut by a great gorge many hundred feet deep. Immediately beyond this gorge rises a single great peak, finely proportioned, massive rather than spire-like, with a coronal of black cliffs below its summit which are unrelieved by a spot of white. This is Mt. Hector.

Its tremendous southern precipices shoot up so suddenly, and its iso-lation is so complete, that even from Laggan Mt. Hector is the one feature of the view. We watched it eagerly from the station platform as we walked to and fro, giving our packs an occasional twist, waiting for breakfast to be ready in the section-house. As a matter of shape and outline, the mountain is finer from this side than from any other, but from a climbing point of view it is fortunate that it is double-faced. One does not risk much in prophesying that neither the southern nor the western wall of its final peak will ever be scaled.[2]

As for the valley—our more immediate concern—we saw in front of us the relics of an enormous terminal moraine choking it from side to side; and the bristly growth that covered this was gray instead of green. Wilson had warned us that we should encounter burnt timber, and he was certainly right. It cannot be less than twelve miles from Laggan to the foot of Hector, and I suppose it is not so much as fifteen. Of the total distance, one mile is along the railroad track. Of the rest, a little more than half had been swept by fire, and the remainder was swamp.

It was half-past nine when we finally started up the track with a swing-ing gait that was much too good to last. It took us three or four hours to work off our boyishness. The sun was hot, and beat down on the gravelly soil as freely as though the charred skeletons of the forest had never existed.

Multitudes of these had fallen, and lay across each other at all sorts of angles. We climbed over them or walked along them. To do this we had to take hold of them. The perspiration was streaming down our faces; we put up our hands and left finger-prints, which were well marked at first, but gradually became suffused and blended. We found that no form of pack is of

---

2. Abbot's prediction was proved wrong seven years later when E.W.D. Holway and J. Muller climbed Mt. Hector's south face.

assistance in balancing along a narrow log, but that our ice-axes, there as elsewhere, were invaluable. We used them as claws and as balancing-poles; we made blazes with them, and chopped away underbrush; the heads were convenient to sit on for a moment's halt; later we used the handle for a fishing-pole; and I think I have seen one of our party use the head of his axe to pass sardines at a picnic lunch. Not even the tail of a South American monkey is more variously adaptable. Every half-hour we sat down, fanned away the mosquitoes, and told one another what remarkable progress we were making; and finally, when the humps and log-backs of the moraine were passed, and we came out by the river, we thought ourselves in Paradise. We lay down in the hot sunlight upon the grass of the bank, and dabbled with our hands in the green water, and watched the sweep and swiftness of its tumultuous and yet strangely silent flow. In these glacial rivers, except when their current is checked, there is none of the brawling of our own mountain streams—only a half-sibilant hushing murmur. It more nearly hypnotizes one than any other sound I know in Nature.

By this time we had rounded the southern end of the low ridge to the east, and our course, instead of bearing a little to the west, turned due north. The valley broadened, and became almost as level as a billiard-table. The trees stood more sparsely, and here and there were not all burned. They were poor specimens, though,—spindling, starved-looking pines, that would neither blend into a forest nor look masculine as individuals. Now and then came little interludes of meadow, rather moist, but cool and soothing to the feet. Simultaneously we began to notice that the mosquitoes were making themselves too prominent. We had had them before in decent numbers, but now, when we stood still, it became a penance to stop flapping long enough to light a pipe. This began perceptibly to dampen our flow of spirits.

We lunched at three, principally on boiled tea, bread and jam, and fried pork eaten with the fingers. By this time we had uncovered enough of the west, or valley, side of Hector to be able to begin to consider our next day's route. As we saw it now, the mountain could not honestly be called graceful. It consisted of a high ridge or wall, with its crest about four thousand feet above the valley and perhaps a mile in length, sagging slightly at the middle, rising slightly at the northern end in a comical little protuberance which we nicknamed "Astyanax,"[3] and shooting up very suddenly at the southern end to form the summit proper. Somehow the final peak also did not impress us as dignified; it was too small for the bulky foundation from which it sprung. The whole mountain reminded me, from this point, of a canal-boat, with its prow ("Astyanax") rather high, and a pepper-box of

---

3. Astyanax was a young Trojan thrown by the Greeks from the walls of Troy so he would not grow up and take revenge.

a deck-house (the final peak) on its stern. We had occasion later to change our minds concerning the size of the pepper-box.

One thing was clear from the first glance. A direct attack from immediately below the summit was impossible. Our only chance was to win the crest of the main ridge some distance north of the final peak, and pass around to its unseen northeastern side, in the hope of finding there some line of ascent. So far as reaching the crest was concerned, a number of parallel ribs or buttresses, descending to the valley, offered a simple and very easy line of approach up to a certain point, where two or three horizontal limestone strata, apparently sheer, cut across the face of the entire wall, and at all points except one interposed an insuperable barrier. This point, where the strata appeared to be broken down and reduced to a slope of shale, was above the largest and most southerly of the buttresses, the one which is separated by a great amphitheatre from the abortive southwestern arête running down from the summit. By this buttress, therefore, we must ascend. It seemed as though we might reach its foot in an hour, push up through the timber, camp at the tree line, and so be in readiness to begin the next day's real climbing as soon as it was light.

It took more than two weary hours of swamp and mosquitoes before we reached the point where it seemed to me that we ought to turn off; and then Wilson objected to doing so, saying that he had camped the time before at the shore of Bow Lake, only a little way ahead. Our packs, too, were silent monitors urging us to keep on level ground; so we yielded, and tramped on. There were very few small jokes now. Six o'clock came, then seven, then eight, and no sign of the lake. The sun had set, and the mosquitoes were so thick that we could hardly see one another. About half-past eight Wilson said that the lake was still nearly half a mile away, and admitted that his camp was on a sandy spit between the water and the swamp. That settled it. There was no question now of reaching timber line, or even of returning to the foot of our buttress. We simply plunged into the pines of the lower slopes, not knowing where we were, and not caring much, if only we could get firm ground, a place to build a smudge for the mosquitoes, and a chance to throw down our packs. A hundred feet or so above the valley we found an opening in the woods, with a stream near by, coming down from the snow above. It was not a convenient place, for our fire had to be kept very small for fear of kindling a forest fire. But we would not have moved on for a palace.

It was half-past ten before we had finished supper, untwisted and stretched our rope, got things together for the morning's start, and were ready to turn in. Our plan was to be up by three. This became doubly necessary when we learned that Wilson must return to Laggan the next day, and could not give us the benefit of his knowledge of the ground during the first part of the ascent. Moreover, we had to leave time, after descending, to cross the Bow River, walk around the lake, and camp at its head so near the glacier coming down from the snow-field that we could be on the snow by sunrise the morning after.

Sleep was not easy that night. To lie with our heads exposed, at the mercy of the hordes of mosquitoes, was not to be thought of. We curled up in Indian fashion, with only the tips of our noses out. The night was warm, and we sweltered; but at least we imagined we could defy the multitudinous hosts of hell outside. Far from it. They could not bite us, it is true; but whole orchestras, shrill with rage, hovered above us and all around. Some even crept into the folds of the blanket underneath my ear, so as to make more noise. I stood this for an hour, twitching with nervousness; then gave it up, and crawled out into the smoke of the fire. Thompson was really asleep, being protected from the tumult of the mosquitoes by clamors of his own not wholly dissimilar. The others were only feigning. I stumbled out into the darkness, and replenished the embers of the fire with a few dead branches, and then lay down where the smoke blew over me, and lit my pipe. The night air was moving through the branches of the pines above us, which waved and creaked drowsily, now hiding and now revealing the stars. At rare intervals some small animal rustled over the dry twigs. Otherwise the night was absolutely still; even the brook had become silent under the influence of the evening frost higher up. The pine needles were soft, and it was almost as good as sleeping to puff away at one's pipe and watch the flickering of the firelight on the tree-trunks, and reflect that the nearest town was forty miles away, and that the wilderness in whose heart we lay stretched on without a break to the shores of the Arctic Ocean. By and by Hiland, the porter, threw off his blanket and came and smoked his pipe also by the fire, and told me endless yarns about grizzly bears. Finally I crawled back into my blanket, and the next thing I knew was the hateful sound of Professor Fay's voice announcing that it was three o'clock.

Then followed the usual accompaniments of an early start,—the search for water in the darkness; the depressing chill of the dying night; the half-warmed and wholly unappetizing breakfast; the silence, not to say crustiness, of the other members of the party; the unconfessed half-wish for some decent excuse for not starting at all; and the interminable delays. Before we got off, it was twenty minutes before five, and the twilight had almost brightened into day.

In a general way, we knew that we had gone too far up the valley the day before, and must bear to the south; we hoped, however, that we had not passed the northern end of the slopes which led up to our buttress. Fortunately we were right, but by a very narrow margin. If we had started up the north bank of the brook by which we had camped, it would have cost us at least an additional hour, and might not impossibly have landed us finally in a cul de sac. As it was, we bore to the right through pleasant open woods, each member of the party taking the lead in turn; and when the trees thinned out, about six o'clock, we were relieved to see above us what we knew from our observations of the day before to be the beginning of the buttress proper—a great rounded shoulder, almost a mountain in itself, which we had picked out from the valley as a landmark.

This part of the climb was encouraging. The footing was good, we kept to our work steadily, and every step told. Soon the steep grass began to give place to gentler shale slopes, and these in their turn became steeper and more fatiguing. The sun had risen long ago on the cliffs across the valley, and the golden line was creeping across the floor, which lay in clear day far below us, with the windings of the Bow and the alternation of open swamp and woods shown as though on a map. But we ourselves were in shadow; and the keenness of the air was not tempered by the early morning wind, which came down intermittently in gusts and made our hats flap viciously about our ears,—oftentimes so suddenly and so straight down that it gave a sort of shock like a douche from an icy shower-bath. The pace began to tell a little. Out of a sense of duty, we stopped at half past seven for a brief and rather shivery second breakfast, but the inclination was wanting to eat what we really needed.

The passage of the limestone strata—elsewhere, as we now saw, a per-fect barrier—proved even easier on our buttress than we expected. The cliffs were broken down so completely that we scarcely needed the help of our hands. Above the strata we were glad to exchange the wearisome shale, which now was very steep, for two or three long patches of winter snow, up which we zigzagged, kicking our steps and keeping guard with our ice-axes against slips, with an excess of caution rather ridiculous to look back on. None of us had our alpine legs as yet. The snow grew thin and petered out, and we were forced back on the slopes of shale, steeper than ever, and appar-ently endless. Our enthusiasm of the first two hours had been a little too much for us; we paid the penalty now in a lassitude which was only half justified by the despicable footing. Fortunately, however, our slopes were not really eternal. By and by the distance began manifestly to decrease between us and the edge of the cliffs, and by nine o'clock we were almost there—still in the shadow, with nothing in sight more alpine than the steep rock slopes and precipices up and between which we had come, and with the real difficulties and problems of the ascent as unknown as when we started.

The same step which brought us over the edge of the plateau created a new world. In front, almost blinding from the reflected rays of the morning sun, there stretched a broad and almost level expanse of dazzling white; sinking very gradually to the northeast, rising as gradually to the southeast, and toward the south first rising slowly, and then suddenly lifting itself up in a splendid snow-peak, nobly proportioned and very steep. Except for two or three dark lines which indicated crevasses, and except for a few rocks outcropping along the two arêtes and just below the summit, it was as pure and perfect an alpine picture as can be found anywhere. I do not know any other mountain so completely deceptive. From Laggan and from the Bow valley, one does not get a suggestion of the real character of the final climb.

Our first impulse was one of pure admiration; our second, after a careful scrutiny of the details, was to say to one another that if we were careful and took our time, the game ought to be in our own hands, but that it was no mere holiday excursion—to us, at least, for one member of the party had never climbed with the other two, and one had never had occasion to use axe and rope. There was little to fear from crevasses in themselves; but on the upper part of the peak the snow lay at as high an angle as snow ever lies except in couloirs, and there was enough of a bergschrund below to make a slip very undesirable. The climb was worth coming for, at all events. The fatigue of the last two hours had vanished; we felt as fresh and eager again as we had felt the day before at Laggan when we first saw our goal. We ate another light lunch, disburdened ourselves of one rucksack, put on the rope,—I ahead, then Thompson, and then Professor Fay,—and were off again at 9.30.

So far as choosing our way was concerned, there could not be a simpler problem in mountaineering than the one before us. To the south, along the edge of the valley cliffs, the plateau was level for a distance, and then for a while rose gently; but about a third of a mile away, where it merged into the northern arête of the peak, it sprung up in a succession of perpendicular steps which effectually barred all progress in that direction. The other arête, the eastern, was similarly broken at more than one point, and was too far away. The face between, on the other hand, was virtually uncrevassed except by a single good-sized bergschrund, and this was well bridged a little to the right of its middle point. Our cure, therefore, after following the edge of the valley wall to the foot of the first great step, was to cut drift from the arête, strike off to the left, and zigzag to and fro up the snow-slope.

Up to the foot of the step, and for a short way beyond, we went along merrily, for the snow was in perfect condition. Then, as the angle increased, we planted our feet with greater deliberation. Then I had to kick footholds,—first mere notches, then full-sized steps,—and finally we brought into play the holding powers of our ice-axes, not only for balance while kicking, but for actual support and distribution of weight. From the member of the party who had never used an ice-axe before, there became audible a steady paean of thanksgiving to the inventor of that admirable implement, which beguiled the monotony of our way until the speaker's breath was required for other purposes as the slope grew steeper.

By the time we had passed the bergschrund, the angle was one of at least 40°. There had been little choice of way hitherto. Like most snow-faces, this one was not flat, but consisted of broad rounded swells and hollows; and we had merely tried to avoid the latter because of the relative steepness of the concave slopes above them. Above the schrund, however, certain natural stopping-places developed themselves. The first was a sort of level platform, far to the right and above, on the edge of the northern arête. This enabled us to rest a moment and to signal to Wilson, who was waiting below to start for Laggan. Some distance above this platform, the arête was notched more deeply than usual, and a sort of funnel-shaped gully ran back a little way into the face of the mountain. Above this gully the arête seemed to turn a little to the right, so that it formed a sort of promontory projecting farther toward the valley than it had done below. From here up there was an uninterrupted slope to the summit; short—perhaps only one hundred and fifty feet—but as steep as snow can lie on in an unsheltered place. It was not all snow, however; the edge of the arête was of rock, and for the upper hundred feet, this broadened out so as to form a narrow face, offering—so it seemed from below—an easier passage than the snow.

We could reach these rocks by a long zigzag to the left and then back; and I calculated that we could profitably keep on as far as the eastern edge of the snow-face, and perhaps get a view there. We were so near the top now that the two arêtes had converged greatly. As we approached the eastern arête, however, it looked deceitful. Nothing could be fairer to the eye,—the smooth snow easing off a trifle in its steepness a few feet this side of the edge, as though to tempt us to find a pathway there. Personally, however, I preferred not to try experiments; investigation by one of the party—still on the rope, of course—confirmed my suspicions that it was a cornice.

When we began our long zigzag back, we knew that we were on the home stretch. We were monstrously cautious! I can testify personally that the steps I kicked were as large as coal-scuttles, and I inferred from what I heard behind me that Thompson was kicking them larger still. We had a good excuse, however, after we had got far enough back toward the northern arête to be above the gully I spoke of. If we had slipped within reach of its funnel-shaped mouth, there would have been no question of rolling down a comfortable slope of snow; we should have gone down a brief chute, and then been shot out over the edge of an abyss offering an uninterrupted descent of not less than a thousand feet. Therefore we took our time. At one spot we found the snow getting thinner; and our bootnails, when we kicked, rebounded from hard ice. This, of course, meant cutting steps. Very quickly, however, the snow grew deep again, and in ten steps more we put our hands on the first of the final rocks. We scrambled up the last hundred feet in pretty good time, for we knew the mountain was won, and at precisely 12.30 stepped on the summit. This was itself a little ridge of broken rocks; the snow on the northeast came up to within a foot of it, and then stopped.

One feels great reluctance in attempting the description of a mountain view; and yet two things should be said in regard to this one from Hector. There are few summits to which the approach is so spectacular. We had been climbing for three hours with our horizon limited by the edges of a narrow field of snow. We came to the end,—and it was as though we were suspended in mid-air. For three fourths of our circumference there was nothing below us for the eye to rest upon except so far below that it did not seem part of the same world. Professor Fay said afterward that no view he had ever seen gave him so astonishing an impression of being lifted up; and I can sympathize with him. Secondly, in its broader aspects, the view is one which in its own kind can scarcely be matched by any known peak in the Rocky Mountains of Canada, and that demonstrably cannot be matched in any other mountain system in the world except in Asia. There is no region of snow mountains in our own country, in South America, or in Australia which can equal the Alps in extent and height combined; and in the Alps I think there is no summit where the distant view is wholly mountainous which is not closely shut in, or else from which either the plains of Italy, of Germany, of France, or of middle Switzerland are not visible. But from Hector, though the eastward view was much the least imposing, yet the line of peaks of cold gray rock which finally hid the plains of the Saskatchewan were not less than thirty miles away, and the intervening space was crowded with range upon range of other mountains; on the west, over the great snow-field and the mountains around the north branch of the Wapta, our vision was bounded by the Selkirks, fully eighty miles distant as the crow flies; and on the north and south there was no limit. As far as our eyes could reach in those two directions—and that was about as far as the human eye can ever reach, for the day was brilliant, with no hint, from horizon to horizon, of either cloud or haze—there was nothing visible but the one unbroken wilderness of ice and snow and crag, an ocean without shores whose waves were mountain ranges.

Something like this, it is true, can be seen from many neighboring peaks; but it cannot be seen so well from any other summit as yet attained, because no other combines so perfectly both height and isolation. There is nothing around Hector to interrupt the view in any direction, not even a cluster of secondary peaks; it stands peculiarly alone. I do not mean, of course, that a panorama of this kind, without foreground and without relief, is so fine as views of many other kinds, for it is not. But I do say that, within its kind, I know of no other view, and outside of the great ranges of Central

Asia I believe there is no other anywhere, that is so overwhelming as this from Hector. As to height, we can speak from inference only. Our aneroid reading was worthless. We knew, however, that the previous party had turned back at an altitude of 10,400 feet, and from Wilson's account we believed we could identify their highest point. From this point to the top, our aneroid showed a rise of 800 feet. Allowing for an error of 200 feet,—an extraordinary proportion when one is going steadily,—we should give the summit an altitude of at least 11,000 feet[4]. If this is so—I speak here subject to correction—Hector is the second highest mountain in Canada whose ascent has been recorded.

It might be well for our reputations if I were to stop here altogether. Our senior, indeed, conducted himself rationally while on top, spending his time in photography and other good works. Thompson can plead in extenuation that he built the cairn underneath which Macaulay's New Zealander will find a jam bottle, partly but not wholly clean within, containing our names. But for my part,—regardless of the proprieties, and of the further fact that the summit rocks were angular and that the wind was cold,—as soon as the first congratulations were over, I deposited myself in the nearest approach I could find to a sunny corner, and went to sleep. It has been reported to me that Thompson soon after did the same, but I am not competent to testify on this point. I only know that I never relished a nap more thoroughly. After half an hour I tried to retrieve my reputation by studying our intended next day's route, and particularly Mt. Balfour, through the field-glass. Two or three great schrunds seem almost wholly to encircle it, and it is doubtful if the arêtes are practicable; but I am confident that a somewhat circuitous route can be devised which will successfully avoid all obstacles.

We stayed on top for over an hour, till we were shivering with the wind. I don't think we quite enjoyed the idea of descending the first two hundred feet, chilled as we were; but two reflections helped us,—we had little choice in the matter, and the worst part came at the beginning. We roped in reverse order this time,—Professor Fay first, then Thompson, I last. Professor Fay says the rocks were simple, but that he did not wholly enjoy the traverse above the gully, and Thompson agrees with him. I maintain that the rocks were not all they should have been. They needed sweeping badly; they were steep; they offered very few good handholds; and, most objectionable of all, they tended to slope out. The latter point, especially, is appreciated by the last man on the rope. However, we took all the orthodox precautions. We moved only one at a time, the others holding the rope taut, or standing ready to help, as the case might be. We made use of all our surfaces of adhe-

---

4. The currently accepted height of Mt. Hector is 11,135 feet (3,394 metres).

sion, our rate of speed and manner of progressing reminding one at times of the motions of the garden slug. When we left the rocks, we crept across the bit above the gully like the villains in a melodrama about to commit a crime. But when we had left the gully behind, our minds relaxed, our attitudes became normal, and our spirits gradually rose. The pace quickened correspondingly, until, after passing the bergschrund, we broke into a trot, and let ourselves tumble occasionally in pure wantonness. By three o'clock we reached our impediments at the edge of the valley wall, rather breathless, hungry, thirsty, very hot, but triumphant.

The next two hours and a half have nothing to recommend them in the memory, except a few moments spent in descending the same long and narrow patches of snow up which we had crawled in the morning. The sun had now melted the surface layer so that it was as slippery as grease. It was sufficient to fling ourselves down, and dig in our ice-axes behind us; Nature did the rest. This was good fun but for the rest I have only an impression that my knees ached with the incessant pounding, and that the shale in which we slid filled my boots with sharp pieces of rock, and that the air of the valley into which we were plunging was hot, and heavy, and dead, and full of mosquitoes. We did not aim for our old camp, for we had told Hiland to move the packs down to the Bow River. There we found him, and, to our surprise, Wilson also, who had never seen our signals at noon, and had waited in growing fear lest we might have broken our necks. It was 5.30 when we reached the rocks, almost thirteen hours from the time of our morning's start; a needlessly long time, of course, for a party in good training who were confident of their own powers and knew one another.

As we were eating (with our fingers, I regret to say) some freshly caught trout that Hiland had ready for us, Wilson gave us a few final directions for the evening's work still before us—the approach to the snow-field—and hurried away. We had not much heart for starting off again with thirty pounds apiece on our shoulders. On the other hand, no place could be worse than where we were. So we girded ourselves up, and moved on up the river, a little stiffly perhaps, in search of the place where Wilson said it could be crossed.

We could have hung somebody with pleasure two hours later. We had plunged through thickets of various kinds, and splashed through swamps; we had balanced ourselves across creeks on slippery logs; we had been to the lake and half-way back, and had examined every foot of the river for nearly a mile, and the upshot was this: it was possible to try the experiment of tying the rope around our waists and fording (or attempting to ford) a river of snow water, one hundred feet broad, running at least shoulder high in the centre and very swiftly; and then we could dry ourselves as best we might in the gray of the evening, tramp three miles and a half around the opposite shore to the head of the lake, and rise before daylight the next morning to attack an unknown glacier, and unknown snow-fields of great extent. On the other hand, we could admit that we were beaten, camp where we stood, between river and swamp, letting the mosquitoes do their worst, and return to Laggan the next day by the way we came.

We chose the latter, and joined our party at Lake Louise the following evening; but I know at least one member of our trio who means sometime to find himself once more at the foot of Bow Lake, at an earlier hour of the day, and sufficiently equipped to raft across if necessary. The memory of the great snow-field as we saw it from Hector, and of Mt. Balfour above all, is an abiding and haunting one. ✿

EXTRACTS FROM W.D. WILCOX

In "Earliest Visits to Lake Louise"—chapter 2 of *The Rockies of Canada*—Walter Dwight Wilcox (1869–1949) wrote,

> Some time before 1890, a rustic inn was placed on the swamp shore of the lake, and a waggon road was made to open communication with the railroad at the little station of Laggan.... But one day in 1893 this log building caught fire, and burned to the ground, so that there were no accommodations and very few visitors that summer. However, with a friend I spent two weeks of that season, camping out in a tent among the tall trees near the shore, and in a small way we commenced our earliest explorations of the neighbourhood, which was at that time comparatively new.

The companion was E.S. Allen. Both men were Yale students. "Our two weeks' work resulted in capturing two mountains on either side of the lake, and being defeated by Mount Victoria...and by Mount Temple." So began Wilcox's explorations.

Wilcox returned to Lake Louise in 1894 with a party of five. In the 1933 *Canadian Alpine Journal* Yandell Henderson recalled: "In that summer, now nearly forty years ago, I was a member of the party that discovered Paradise valley and the valley of the Ten Peaks, surveyed and mapped the lake [Lake Louise] and the surrounding mountains, and gave many of them names, and without guides crossed passes, ascended peaks, and hunted the wild goat." Of Allen, Henderson wrote: "He utilized every opportunity to learn words from the Stoney Indians of this region and from these words he developed some of the names that we gave to the peaks, particularly that of Mount Hungabee, the 'savage peak.'" Wilcox led Allen and Frissell on the first ascents of Mts. Temple and Aberdeen that year; Mt. Temple was the first peak over 3,400 metres (11,000 feet) to be climbed in the Rockies.

Mt. Temple was climbed twice more that year, with a Swiss guide carrying Big Bertha—Wilcox's camera. Wilcox was a meticulous photographer, ever ready to wait until conditions were right. Dr. J.W.A. Hickson, a Wilcox contemporary who climbed extensively in the Rockies and the Alps, judged Wilcox to be "well known beyond the mountaineering world for his writings and beautiful photography, in which he was an expert."

Wilcox was attracted by the mystery of Mts. Hooker and Brown (see chapter 6). In 1893 Stuart and Coleman established the elevation of Mt. Brown at about 2,750 metres (9,000 feet). Wilcox was one who thought the matter "worthy of further investigation, and in July, 1896, [he] started with Mr. R.L. Barrett with the purpose of visiting and measuring [those] mountains."

They crossed Bow Pass and were the first white men to ascend the North Fork of the Saskatchewan River, whence they came via Wilcox Pass to Fortress Lake, thus finding a route from the Saskatchewan to the Athabasca.

In 1901 Wilcox and Henry G. Bryant "had perfected plans for a double purpose, first to make an attempt to climb Mt. Assiniboine and secondly, to penetrate as far as possible into the great white area on Dawson's map, south of Kananaskis Lakes, marked with the magic word 'Unexplored,' that most fascinating and suggestive of all names to any lover of the wilderness." The Assiniboine attempt, with guides Edouard Feuz and Fritz Michel, ended about 300 metres (1,000 feet) short of the summit. Hickson wrote that Wilcox "really deserved the peak," but Outram came just after and took the first.

Wilcox was widely respected in his day for his photographs of the Rockies depicting the earliest days of "tourism," for his writings and for his amateur surveying. Many believe his accounts constitute the finest record of what camp life and the initial exploration by tourist-mountaineers was like in the early days in the Canadian Rockies.

The extracts that follow from *The Rockies of Canada* describe the discovery of Paradise Valley and speak of camp life on the trail.

$\sim$ Moira Irvine

The Discovery of Paradise Valley

W.D. Wilcox

We as yet knew nothing of the mountains east and south of Lake Louise. Certain glimpses of a valley beyond Mt. Aberdeen and Mt. Lefroy had been caught in our various climbs, but they gave only imperfect ideas of the geography of all that region. To push our exploration into this new and doubtless attractive place seemed a most desirable thing. Our plan was to explore the Lefroy Glacier and force a passage, if possible, over a snow pass eastwards, where, no doubt, all this unknown region would lie before us. Accordingly one day near the first of August our party of four might have been seen traversing in Alpine fashion the ice-fields near Mt. Lefroy. This entire valley, which is more than seven thousand feet above sea-level, is filled with glacier ice and perpetual snow. From the entire absence of trees or vegetation of any kind it is impossible to judge distance and heights of mountains in this place. It is a veritable canyon, of magnificent though desolate grandeur, with the bare limestone slopes of Mt. Aberdeen on the north, and on the other side the north face of Mt. Lefroy, which has a total height of nearly four thousand feet from the glacier. At the valley end there stands a curious pointed mountain, shaped like a bishop's mitre, and on either side of this there is a col, or snow pass, one of which we hoped to ascend.

As we were marching over the glacier, which was covered with snow and therefore somewhat dangerous, Warrington, who was third on the rope, suddenly broke through the frail bridge of a crevasse. "I could hear," he afterwards told us, "the noise of snow falling under my feet and the gurgling of water at the bottom of the depths over which I was suspended." We pulled him out of this dangerous place without anyone else getting in, and reached the foot of the snow passes without further accident. The one on our left seemed easier of slope than the other. It was very soon apparent that we had a considerable amount of work before us. Allen led the way cutting steps in the snow, for the slope was very steep and we had no desire to slide into one of the great crevasses which made the place formidable. We crossed some of these treacherous caverns by means of snow bridges, but others we were compelled to pass around, and in such places had inspiring views of blue grottos hung with dripping icicles. From the darkness of these yawning death-traps came the sound of sub-glacial streams.

After three hours of slow and tiring work we had climbed only one thousand feet. It was a cloudy day with a damp and cheerless atmosphere, and at this altitude of eight thousand feet there were occasional showers of hail and snow. Chilled by the long exposure and the necessary slowness of our progress, every member of the party became silent and depressed. It seems to me that the circulation of the blood has much to do with the mental state and that courage depends in a large measure on the pulse. The panting soldier will face a cannon's mouth, but dreads unseen danger when chilled by night watching.

To judge by our surroundings alone, we might have been exploring some lonely polar land, for our entire view was limited by high mountains covered with glaciers and snow and altogether barren of vegetation. At such times you wonder why you came. Why not stay at home and be comfortable? Every climber feels such temporary repulses, when the game is not worth the candle and he decides once and for all to give up mountain climbing. Like the ancients vowing sacrifices and temples to the gods in the thick of battle or on the point of shipwreck, which vows they forgot very speedily when they arrived at safety, the mountaineer forgets his resolves under the genial influence of hot Scotch and a comfortable camp. These Rockies have many surprises for the explorer, and there was one in store for us.

We sought temporary rest on an outcropping ledge and tried to regain some strength by eating lunch. The summit of our pass now seemed only a short distance above, but we had been deceived so many times on this interminable slope that we put no faith in our eyes. Recommencing our climb at a quicker pace, for the slope was easier and we were most anxious to see the view eastwards, we were soon near the summit. The last few steps to a mountain pass are attended by a pleasurable excitement equalled only by the conquest of a new mountain. The curtain is about to be raised, as it were, on a new scene and the reward of many hours of climbing comes at one magical revelation.

Arrived on the summit of our pass, 8500 feet above sea-level, we saw a new group of mountains in the distance, while a most beautiful valley lay far below us. Throughout a broad expanse of meadows and open country many streams were to be seen winding through this valley, clearly traceable to their various sources in glaciers, springs, and melting snowdrifts. With all its diversity of features spread like a map before our eyes, this attractive place was seen to be closely invested on the south by a semicircle of high and rugged mountains, rising steeply from a crescent-shaped glacier at their united bases. The encircling mountains extending then to the left, hemmed in the far side of the valley in an irregular line of peaks, to terminate, so far as we could see, in a double-pointed mountain with two summits about one mile apart. The strata of this mountain had been fashioned by ages of exposure into innumerable forms of beauty, like imitations of minarets, pinnacles, and graceful spires. The mountain itself resembled a splendid building, with nature as architect, the frost and rain for sculptors. Its outlines showed a combination of gentle slopes and vertical ledges like the alternating roofs and walls of a cathedral. On one side of this mountain, where nature had evidently striven to surpass all other efforts, there rose from the middle slopes a number of slender stone columns, apparently several hundred feet high. They were strange monuments of the past which had survived earthquake shocks and outlived the warring elements while nature continued her work. Compared with these columns, the pyramids of Egypt, the palaces of Yucatan, and the temples of India are young, even in their antiquity.

At the time of our arrival on the summit, a sudden change took place in the weather. The wind came from another quarter, and the monotonous covering of grey clouds began to disclose blue sky in many places. The afternoon sun poured shafts of light through the moving clouds, and awakened bright colours over forests, meadows, and streams.

This beautiful scene opened before us so suddenly that for a time the cliffs echoed to our exclamations of pleasure, while those who had recently been most depressed in spirit were now most vehement in expressions of delight. A short time before no one could be found to assume the responsibility of such a foolhardy trip, but now each member of our party had been the proposer of this glorious excursion. We spent a half-hour on the pass, and divided our work so that while one took photographs of the scene, another took angles of prominent points for our map, and the rest built a cairn to celebrate our ascent of the pass.

It was decided, by each one no doubt to himself, but at any rate by the party unanimously, to explore this new valley whatever should be the result. Though it was late in the afternoon and there was small chance of reaching the chalet that night, the desolate valley behind repelled, while the new one seemed to bid us enter.

Fortunately, a long snow slope led far into the valley from the pass. This we prepared to descend by glissading, all roped together, because one or two of our party were undergoing their first Alpine experiences. The slope was pretty steep, and we were just well under way in our descent, when someone lost his footing and commenced to slide at such speed that the end man was jerked violently by the rope, and lost his ice-axe as he fell headlong. With consternation very evident on their faces, our two comrades came rolling and sliding downwards, head first, foot first, sometimes one leading, and sometimes the other. Their momentum was too much for the rest of us and, even with our ice-axes well set in the soft snow, we all slid some distance in a bunch. Owing to the complicated figures executed in our descent, it required several minutes to unwind the tangled ropes in which we were caught. Then a committee of one was appointed to go back and gather the scattered hats, ice-axes, and such other personal effects as could be found.

In a short time we had descended fifteen hundred feet to the valley bottom. By our rapid change of altitude we had passed through all gradations of climate from polar to temperate, and now found ourselves surrounded by meadows of rich grass, gay with the wild flowers of midsummer, and open groves where squirrels were chattering, and the wild conies and other rodents were staring at us as we passed along. There were not a few mosquitoes in evidence also.

We followed a small stream and saw it finally grow into a river. Pursuing our way with rapid steps, like adventurers in nature's fairyland, where every moment reveals new wonders, we came at length to an opening in the forest, where the falling stream dashed among great stones strewn in wild disorder. They were colossal fragments of sandstone hewn by nature into angular blocks and poised one upon another as though they were ready to fall from their insecure positions. After several hours of walking, the stream became a large, muddy torrent which swung from right to left every hundred yards or so, and was now too wide and deep to cross.

The tremendous cliffs of Mt. Temple, one of the highest of the Canadian Rockies, guard the east side of this valley. For the space of three miles its precipices present an uninterrupted wall of rock, four thousand feet from base to top and a total height of five thousand feet from the valley. Henderson and I led the way, and at length lost sight of the others, who preferred a slower pace after such unusual exertions. In the early evening we came to a swampy place, beyond which we recognised the broad opening of the Bow Valley. Here we waited some time for our friends, who were a long way behind, and then at length wrote a note and fastened it to a pole in a conspicuous place. It read: "We are going to climb the ridge to the north and try to make the chalet to-night. Advise you to follow us." On the top of the pole we cut a slit and pointed a splinter of wood in the exact direction we were to take.

Having accomplished these duties in the best manner possible and in spite of innumerable swarms of mosquitoes from the swamp, we walked at our best speed, not relishing the prospect of a cheerless bivouac overnight after our long fast. Encountering the usual obstacles of fallen timber, we reached Lake Louise, by good fortune, at eight o'clock. After shouting in vain for someone to send over a boat, we forded the stream and entered the chalet, where a sumptuous repast was prepared forthwith and to which we did justice after our walk of twelve hours' duration.

Our friends did not appear till morning. It seems that they discovered our note, but decided not to take our route as they thought it safer to follow the stream to the Bow. This, however, proved much farther than it appeared, and they had not proceeded far before they became entangled in a large area of fallen timber, where they were soon overtaken by night and compelled to give up all hope of reaching Lake Louise till morning. In the dark forest they lit a small fire, and were at first tormented by mosquitoes, and later by the chill of advancing night, so that sleep was impossible. The utter weariness of exhaustion, embittered by hunger and sleeplessness, amid clouds of voracious mosquitoes, was only offset by the contents of a flask, with which they endeavoured to revive their drooping spirits and nourish the feeble spark of life till dawn. Fortunately the nights in this latitude are short, and at four o'clock they continued their way to the Bow River, which they then followed to Laggan. 🌺

Camp Life

W.D. Wilcox

Camp life in every part of the world is affected by environment. In the Rockies of Canada the only animal suitable to convey the explorer and his outfit through the mountain forests and over the swelling rivers that oppose his progress is the Indian pony. Mules cannot be used in these mountains as they are farther south because they lack courage in water, and their small feet allow them to sink deeply in those swamps that the larger hoofed horse can barely pass over.

Many customs of camp life in the North-west are derived from the fur traders. The earliest explorers and railroad builders have handed them down to the sportsmen and mountain climbers of to-day. But a new element is being introduced with the rapid increase of camping parties in the Rockies of Canada. While bacon and beans continue to be the mainstay of camp fare, as of right they should, campers are getting into the habit of carrying preserved fruits and vegetables, and such other luxuries as make the old-timers wonder at the change of customs. The rugged simplicity and semi-starvation of old days are passing. A guide once told me that upon a certain occasion he called at a wayside house for a meal. Seeing no pepper and salt to season the coarse fare, he ventured the polite suggestion that they would be appreciated, but was considerably startled when the old woman held up her hands in surprise. "What—luxuries!" she cried; "pepper and salt—luxuries, and all for two bits?" An instance of a similar nature concerns a hungry traveller who was invited to share a simple meal with a lone prospector. Nothing appeared on the festive board but a generous supply of bacon and mustard. The unfortunate guest, being unused to the ways of the country, declared that he did not eat bacon. "Ah, well," said his host, "I am very sorry. Help yourself to the mustard."

The number of camping parties that travel among the Canadian Rockies every year is rapidly increasing. About one-half the number of campers are sportsmen, and the rest are either mountain climbers or explorers. Many, of course, wander among these wilds for the mere love of nature, and for the simple and healthful life in the evergreen woods, surrounded by mountains, running streams, or placid lakes.

Imagine, then, that you intend to make a trip into the mountains. You must first engage your packer and cook, and procure saddle-horses and a full outfit of blankets, tents, and general camp necessaries. There are agents at Banff, the general starting-place for all expeditions in the eastern range, who will furnish you with horses, men, and everything needed for trips of whatever length or nature, and thus relieve you of all responsibility. One of the most experienced outfitters is Tom Wilson, who packed for the railroad surveyors many years ago. During the summer season "Wilson's" is frequently the scene of no little excitement when some party is getting ready to leave. Then you may see ten or fifteen wicked-eyed ponies, some in a corral and the rest tied to trees ready for packing. If the horses are making their first trip for the season there will be considerable bucking and kicking before all is ready. Several men are seen bustling about, assorting and weighing the packs, and making order out of the pile of blankets, tents, and bags of flour or bacon. The cayuses are saddled and cinched up one by one, with many a protesting bite and kick. The celebrated "diamond hitch" is used in fastening the packs, and the struggling men look picturesque in their old clothes and sombreros as they tighten the ropes, bravely on the gentle horses, but rather gingerly when it comes to a bucking bronco.

A crowd of the business men of Banff, who usually take about 365 holidays every year, stands around to offer advice and watch the sport. Then the picturesque train of horses with their wild-looking drivers files out through the village streets under a fusillade of snap-shot cameras and the wondering gaze of new arrivals from the east. But these evidences of civilisation are soon left behind and after a few miles the primitive wilderness is entered. Every year the packers who go on such trips gain knowledge of the passes and trails, so that the day is not distant when there will be efficient guides for many of the most interesting excursions. However, the necessity for self-reliance and the use of one's own judgment in picking a way through the countless obstacles of these mountains are great sources of pleasure.

The camper inexperienced in the methods of the North-west, has much to learn. It is quite possible that until the first camp is made he is quite ignorant of what all those mysterious bags and boxes contain which have been transported at great expenditure of horse-flesh and bad language a day's journey into the woods. The pitching of the first camp is a revelation to the inexperienced. After a suitable site has been chosen, with fire-wood and water conveniently near, and a meadow not far away where the horses may find pasture, the men cut tent-poles and the cook spreads his pots and pails round a crackling fire. The pack-saddles and blankets are usually piled beneath some large tree and covered with a canvas sheet,—while another sheet covers the bags of provisions. The cook soon has several pots on the fire, stewing apples or apricots, making hot water for tea or cocoa, or perhaps cooking the omnipresent bean. Two boxes, called cook boxes, stand near at hand, and they contain cans of condensed milk, all the spices and condiments, the small tins of preserves and pickles that have been opened or are in constant use, as well as the table dishes, plates, knives, forks, and spoons, which are no less necessary. It may be a week or more before the numerous small bags tucked away in larger ones have been sampled.

The best idea of Rocky Mountain camp life might be had by following in imagination the events of an ordinary day. The first sound that usually awakens you is the tramping of horses, the approaching shouts and curses of the packer, and the tinkle of the bell mare's bell as the ponies are driven to camp. The packer's first duty is to get up at dawn and go after the horses. They may be miles away or they may have crossed a deep stream. After one of the tamest animals has been caught, the packer rides bareback and drives the others in at a gallop.

By this time the imperturbable early riser has begun to make life miserable for his companions, though it may be an hour before breakfast. There is often found in camping parties one of those cranks with an old saw—as false as was ever written—about, "Early to bed," etc., to back him in his evil ways. He is up at the crack of dawn, even in these northern mountains where the sun shines eighteen hours a day. The evening camp-fire, the hot punch, and the good stories of adventure are all lost on him that he may prowl around alone in the darkness and frost of early morning, to the worriment of his friends.

At length, however, the cook shouts—"Breakfast is ready"—an announcement that was heralded by the sound of the axe, the crackling of firewood and the sizzling of bacon. A cold wash in a neighbouring stream or lake is a good awakener. Presently everyone gathers around the "table," a piece of canvas spread on the frosty grass and flowers. Porridge and milk, bacon and beans, hot coffee and bannock or camp bread, with possibly some kind of stewed fruit, compose the ordinary fare. The hour immediately after is busy for all. While the packer is "saddling up" the cook washes the dishes and packs the small articles in his cook boxes. Open tins are provided with rough-and-ready covers and placed so their contents will not spill while on the horse's back. The large bags are tied up and everything gradually becomes ready for packing. Meanwhile, you roll up your personal effects, toilet articles, changes of clothes, and make ready your camera and such scientific instruments as you carry. The tents, which have been standing so that the morning sun and wind may dry the dew or rain, come down last of all, and are rolled up as side packs. Then commences the real work of packing, which after the first day or so becomes easier. The particular pack for each horse is known, and everything is systematised. However, the constant change in the weight of bags, as provisions are used, requires some little attention on the part of the packer, because one of the most important essentials of good packing is to have the two side packs of equal weight.

The monotony of riding an Indian pony during the slow march of five or six hours as the poor beast struggles over logs and through swampy places, fighting bull-dog flies and grey gnats, is broken by that endless variety and change of surroundings, that are a source of delight in every part of these mountains. Sometimes the trail leads for a time through deep forests where the mountains are lost to view. In the cool depths of forest shade the rhododendron grows, and the moist and mossy ground is often dotted with the wax-like blossoms of the one-flowered pyrola; or the pretty violet-like butterwort, with its cluster of root leaves smeared with a viscid secretion. Some stupid fool-hen, a species of grouse, is more than likely to be seen in a tree near the trail, and proves that her name is deserved, when the bullets fly. She merely cranes her neck in stupid wonderment, till at last her head goes off, and then there is a great flapping of wings, but it is too late. The bird will, however, make a fine dinner to-night.

From silent forest depths the trail no doubt leads alongside a noisy stream, boulder-strewn, and hemmed by willows and birch, or across some meadow, gay with scarlet painted-cups, tiger lilies, or forget-me-nots. Here the horses take hasty mouthfuls of the rich grass, as they are hurried along to the other side. Perhaps the border of a lake is traversed, and while the splashing horses move willingly, there is time for glimpses of new beauty in water colouring and reflected mountains and trees. Stretches of burnt timber break the monotony of the unending panorama at more or less frequent intervals. Burnt forests, where the trees still remain standing, are easy to travel, but usually the fallen trunks are crossed three or four deep, and every year adds to the number. The procession comes to a halt after a few yards of progress in such places, and you often wonder what is going forward, but hear only the sound of the axe for answer.

The excitement of fording deep streams or noisy torrents of the lower valleys is in greatest contrast to quiet travel through some mountain pass where an eternal silence reigns. Here, perhaps, there are bare limestone cliffs, guarding a turf-lined pass, far above the limits of trees. Scattered pools are collected in the inequalities of rocks. No sound of bird or insect, of running water or woodland breezes, breaks the oppressive quiet. The tinkling of the bell and the tramp of horses give the only sign of our passing through these desolate high valleys.

A day's march is often attended by incidents that give zest to the work of making progress. Bucking ponies try to rid themselves of their packs or riders. Packs come loose and must be adjusted, and sometimes a panic is caused among the horses when a hornet's nest is disturbed. Horses sometimes get beyond their depth in crossing rivers, fall into muskegs up to their ears, or break a leg in fallen timber. Familiarity breeds no contempt for these agile Indian ponies, and new difficulties only cause renewed admiration of their wonderful skill, in jumping logs with heavy packs on their backs, threading the obscure trails and pitfalls of burnt timber, or fording the icy rapids of mountain streams.

The length of the march necessarily depends on various circumstances, though "camp rules" say that six hours of trail work is all that should be done in one day. There must be a swamp or meadow not far distant, where the horses may pasture, with fire-wood and water near the camp site. Happily the two latter requisites are almost invariably present in the Rockies of Canada. First the horses are tied to trees, quickly unpacked, and sent off to their well-earned liberty. While they are rolling on the grass, joyful that another day's work is ended, the cook builds a fire, and soon has hot water for tea and other refreshments, of which the details are unimportant, if things are served quickly, and many times. What is the use of putting a man in a glass cage, and taking his temperature and weight to find the heat- and energy-value of various foods? Let him come to the mountains, walking and climbing ten or twelve hours a day, and observe for himself. After a hearty breakfast of oatmeal (a splendid food for the sedentary) he will be ravenously hungry in two hours; of cornmeal, after three hours, of bacon and bread, in four or five hours, while pork and beans will sustain him from six to ten hours and give the utmost physical buoyancy and strength. Tea has the greatest stimulating effect on utterly weary muscles and nerves. Coffee, however, is better in cold weather, and cocoa for an evening drink around the camp-fire. In my opinion alcoholic stimulants should be used in camp life only for their reviving effect after exposure to cold and exertion, and never before or during any physical undertaking.

No one can travel far on a camping expedition without feeling an interest in the Indian pony, upon which so much depends. The Indian pony, or cayuse, probably owes its origin to a cross between the mustang and the horses introduced by the Spaniards in the conquest of Mexico. They are small horses with very great endurance and ability, combined with sufficient strength for all needful purposes. Some of them have "glass eyes," or a colourless condition of the retina, supposed to be the result of too much inbreeding. They are raised on the plains chiefly by the Indians, and their only food throughout their days is grass. In winter, most of the horses are driven from the mountains and pastured among the foothills, where they paw away the snow and find abundant nourishment in the "bunch grass." The hardest time comes at the end of winter, when the snow melts and freezes alternately. Then the ponies must starve unless they are driven in and fed by their owners.

There is as much diversity of temperament among horses as among men. Some are nervous and intelligent, while others are stupid and obstinate. Horses do not seem to do as much independent thinking as mules, and are slower in many feats of intellect. A mule may be taught to travel miles alone over a beaten route, but a horse will stop and eat grass at the first meadow. They say a mule will walk over a trestle bridge like a dog, while a horse will invariably fall through before he has gone ten yards. But in swamps and deep water, the horse is far superior. Almost all cayuses are liable to buck and kick after a long period of rest. These bad habits may have descended from their primitive ancestors, in efforts to throw off wolves or panthers, but are now used with effect on riders and packs. I have seen a horse stand up and fight with his forefeet, and an old bronco-buster once told me that he had had horses rush upon him and try to kill him by biting and striking.

Two of the most interesting pack-horses that I have ever known are the "Pinto" and the "Bay." The Pinto is a well-formed, graceful pony, with a light chestnut coat and irregular white patches on his flanks and chest. He has a long, beautiful tail and well-formed head, but he is so quick and nervous that I have never yet succeeded in getting a good photograph of him. This Pinto is tame and affectionate, but afraid of any sudden movement, because, no doubt, some former owner had abused him. The Pinto is wonderfully intelligent, and as Bill Peyto says, "knows more than anyone else about the trails." Sometimes we placed Pinto ahead and let him lead the procession for hours. Anyone seeing such a feat for the first time would find it quite incomprehensible. Once Pinto, when thus leading, took a small branch trail and left the well-defined open path. "You are wrong for once, Pinto, and have been caught napping at last," said I to myself. While the procession moved on, I followed the main trail, and soon came to a tree that had fallen across the trail and had caught about four feet from the ground. While I was examining this Pinto was about a quarter of a mile ahead, once more on the main trail, having gone round this unseen obstacle, unknown to any of us, but probably remembered by him from some previous year. The Bay is Pinto's inseparable companion and friend. The two horses are always at the head of the line, and rarely allow any others to precede. The Bay defers only to Pinto's unusual intelligence and gives first place to him. Each of these horses carries two hundred and fifty or three hundred pounds on his back, while the smaller animals struggle with less by an hundredweight. I once saw the Bay clear a log three feet and ten inches from the ground, of his own will, under a heavy pack. These intelligent animals know all the obstacles of the trail, what two trees their pack will go between, what low branches they cannot pass under, and at a gentle word they hurry along, where an ordinary cayuse will stop to feed, or when shouted at, will run off into the bush. The Bay is the tamest animal I have ever known, and often loiters about the camp and pokes his head over one's shoulder as a gentle hint for a taste of salt or sugar. His feet are never insulted with hobbles, nor his head with a rope, for you may walk up to him any time in the pasture and place your arm round his great neck.

Old Denny is a horse of another colour, a shaggy, thick-set cayuse, with a long coat and trailing fetlocks. No ambition ever stirs him to be in front, but on the contrary, Denny never allows any animal to be behind him, except the saddle-horse of some swearing packer who is hunting him along. Denny was born with an unconquerable tendency to be slow, and though you shout till you are hoarse, old Denny pursues his dignified way regardless. The result is that this singular animal always gets behind the procession, which he follows at his own sweet will. I have seen old Denny come strolling into camp half an hour after the other horses were unpacked. However, he is a conscientious old fellow, and never kicks or bucks or crushes his pack against trees. So he was selected to carry the most perishable packs, and has safely transported my valuable cameras hundreds of miles through the mountains. Peyto told me that Denny once had a brute for a master, who used to beat him terribly with a stick, till the poor animal would fall to the ground. After that he was taken to the coal mines at Anthracite, near Banff. In the perpetual darkness, however, Denny refused to work, in spite of the beatings and horrible cruelty that the miners practice on their horses. He next appeared as a pack-horse, and under the influence of kind treatment, became one of the tamest of the horses. Besides salt and sugar, which nearly all horses like after a few tastes, he would eat bread, flour, and even cornmeal, which, strange to say, these Western ponies do not consider proper food for horses.

No matter how wild your horses may be at the commencement of the journey, they will become gentle and tame with kind treatment. A little salt every morning for a week will gain their confidence, and will save, in many ways, far more than the outlay.

The afternoon after a day's march may be occupied in short excursions to adjacent valleys or points of interest in the neighbourhood, so that the period after dinner, when the long day ends and the camp-fire lights up the forest, is the best time for stories of adventure and for sociability. The best camp-fire is, in my opinion, a big one, with great dry logs that crack and blaze brightly and make but little smoke. The Indians laugh at us and say, "White man make big fire,—sit far off. Indian make little fire—sit close"—right over it, in fact, with a few sticks, like a pile of jack-straws—for a fire. The advantages are that there is but little smoke and not much of a wood-pile to cut. Of course there is a limit to size, and I have seen fires where you had to make toast or broil a grouse on a twenty-foot pole. A camp-fire on a dark night always seems most cheerful in a deep forest, when the cheery sparks soar away to meet the stars and a ruddy glow illuminates the sombre trees and picturesque figures grouped before the tents. 🔊

II EXPLORATION

The first wave of Canadian exploration will forever be associated with the fur trade; the second wave was also commercial in impulse, as the railroad surveyors and others sought to discover and map transportation routes across the continent. Mountaineers played a large role in the third wave: the delineation of the topography that lay more than a day's travel away from the major rivers and the charting of the natural beauties and recreational potential of the stunning mountain regions of the country. It was mountaineers who first reported on the glories of the many spectacular lakes, passes and peaks in what was to become Banff and Jasper National Parks; they were often the first to see the perfect mountain lakes, test the hot springs, map the glaciers and ascend the heights.

Although all of Canada is now mapped at some scale or other, this period of exploration continues today, as mountaineers like John Clarke in the Coast Mountains, or those travelling to Baffin Island to climb, fill the gaps in our knowledge of Canada's mountain regions with their more intimate explorations of the smaller features, the tarns, cols and glacier systems of the Canadian landscape. The extracts printed below describe the adventures of two of the most distinguished and important of these groups of explorer-mountaineers, whose names are each associated with the discovery of major icefields: Stutfield and Collie, remembered as discoverers of the Columbia Icefield, and Don and Phyl Munday, the great explorers of the Waddington Range.

~ Bruce Fairley

STUTFIELD AND COLLIE: THE FREEDOM OF THE WILDS

In 1903 *Climbs and Explorations in the Canadian Rockies* was published in London. The authors were Hugh E.M. Stutfield, author of *El Maghreb: 1200 Miles' Ride Through Morocco*, and J. Norman Collie, FRS, author of *Climbing on the Himalaya and Other Mountain Ranges*.

As a young man Hugh Stutfield (1858–1929) had visited Spain and Morocco, writing about his Moroccan travels. His holidays from 1881 to 1897 were spent mostly climbing in the Alps.

In 1898 Stutfield joined Collie and Herman Woolley up the north fork of the Saskatchewan, ending his holiday with some time at Glacier House, in the Selkirks. On his way home, Stutfield stopped at Donald, a station on the Columbia River about 20 kilometres north of the present town of Golden, to inquire about lines of access into the Rockies from the Columbia River Valley. Obviously something he heard tweaked his interest, for, returning in 1900, Collie, Stutfield and Sidney Spencer tried to gain the Columbia Icefield area via the horrific Bush River approach from the west, but met with complete defeat. Joined by G.M. Weed and Hans Kaufmann, the trio returned in 1902 for a trip over Bow Pass, making a number of first ascents. After 1902 Stutfield did no more climbing.

J. Norman Collie (1859–1942) was a man of many accomplishments: connoisseur and collector of Japanese and Chinese art; widely read, particularly in medieval science and English literature; authority on cigars and wine; excellent judge of food and cooking; photographer and pioneer of colour processes; and organic chemist of repute, who wished to be remembered for the discovery of neon and for taking the first X-ray photographs.[1] Geoffrey Winthrop Young wrote in the 1943 *Canadian Alpine Journal*, "He was an originator, in every one of his interests living only to explore…and mountaineering, with its many appeals to his abnormally acute senses, best satisfied this passion."

Collie began his climbing career on Skye in 1886. By the time of his first visit to the Alps in 1892 he had climbed widely in the British Isles. In 1895 came the expedition to Nanga Parbat with Geoffrey Hastings and Alfred Mummery, on which Mummery and two Gurkha porters disappeared high on the mountain. This was the first major British Himalayan expedition which had as its foremost object the attaining of a Himalayan summit.

Collie was a man who always had his eye fixed on the farther summit. In 1897, after making first ascents of Mts. Victoria and Lefroy in the company of Charles Fay

---

1. With a curriculum vitae like this it is small wonder that Collie served as a model for Conan Doyle's Sherlock Holmes, and was in fact once mobbed in Norway by Holmes fans who thought they were seeing their hero in the flesh.

and other members of the Appalachian Mountaineers, he set off up the Bow Valley, keen to try Mt. Balfour, seen from the south. He climbed instead Mt. Gordon, and looking north spotted a high rock peak. A further trip that year in search of this new challenge yielded the ascent of Mt. Sarbach; not until his return to England did Collie determine, from reading Palliser's journals, that his big peak was Mt. Forbes.

On another venture, this time from the slopes of Mt. Freshfield, Collie spied country to the north that caught his attention. A.P. Coleman had already climbed Mt. Brown and established its modest elevation, but Collie was not quite ready to give up the possibility that mountains of fantastic height might exist still further north. In 1898 he returned with Stutfield and Hermann Woolley and travelled up the north fork of the Saskatchewan River. Climbing Mt. Athabasca, Snow Dome and Diadem, Collie and his party became the first white men to see the great Columbia Icefield spread before them.

In 1902 Collie was back in the Rockies, this time chalking up ascents of Mts. Murchison and Freshfield. The climb of Mt. Murchison is described in one of the selections below. Although Collie's private correspondence shows that he was not enamoured of Sir James Outram, another famous pioneer climber of the time, he and Outram teamed up that year to finally capture the first ascent of Mt. Forbes, the big rock peak that had caught Collie's eye five years earlier.

The extract "To Bear Creek" shows that some aspects of travel never do change. Collie was part of a generation for whom "mountaineering" meant many things other than climbing. Much of the finest writing in these early accounts of life in the Canadian Rockies focuses on the experiences of just getting to the peaks. Collie and his contemporaries were wanderers in a new land when they came to Canada; for them mountaineering was the opportunity to experience the intensity of companionship and the wildness of nature as well as the exhilaration of treading new summits. Mountaineering was an activity that took them into a realm where everything—from cooking breakfast over the fire to tramping along the trail—was imbued with a sense of total adventure. They called it "the freedom of the wilds."

Reading his account of his 1911 trip, "North of Yellowhead Pass," before the Alpine Club in London in December 1911 Collie concluded:

> As one sits in one's armchair on the winter evenings the dreams of the camp life return once more, of the tepee with a roaring fire and the door snugly closed; of Fred's stories, of John's leisurely methods of playing plier, of Moritz's fears that we were lost in a strange land and that the 'grub pile' was very low; all these small happenings, as they come back to one, stir the remembrances of the life in the wilds; it mattered little to one that the snow was racing round the tent and the fir trees singing in the wind outside; inside all was well with us both in

mind and body; on the morrow the sky would have cleared, the great mountains would glisten in their new robe of snow, the sun would shine over the fair valleys and the trail that led through the mighty pine woods, the glades by the side of fair lakes and the open uplands of the passes would call us ever onward. Yes! a wanderer's dreams are good dreams, and fortunate are those who have stored up in their memory dreams of such a land, it is one of the most beautiful of mountain countries, and still has the mystery of the unknown clinging about it. There is plenty of room at present for everyone who cares to wander through its fastness; it is land of great mountains and great woods, of lakes and glaciers and running rivers, of rain and snow and blue skies, and it is still a land of mystery—a 'Land of the Far West.'

Although probably the greatest mountaineer among the early climbers of the Rockies, Collie has never become a well-known figure in this country. His fame is eclipsed in the Rockies today by the packers and outfitters who guided him up the river valleys to the great peaks. In 1939 he left London to live permanently in Skye, where he died quietly in 1942.

⌇ Moira Irvine and Bruce Fairley

To Bear Creek

Hugh E.M. Stutfield &
J. Norman Collie FRS

At Banff we made the pleasing discovery that three pieces of luggage, containing a large proportion of our camp outfit, were missing: one turned up in two days, but we could obtain no clue whatever as to the whereabouts of the others.

As the lost trunks obstinately refused to turn up, we got together such things as were procurable in the village to replace the missing outfit, and prepared to start. Mr. Mathews most obligingly lent us several useful articles; among others, a most magnificent bedroom mattress, which on the journey proved as great a solace to its temporary owner as it was an annoyance to the packers; and on Wednesday the 23rd we left for Laggan, where Fred was awaiting us with the horses and men. "Number One" was less punctual even than usual, and we reached Laggan too late to make a start that day. On the platform we found Fred with his friend Jack Robson, who was engaged to take charge of the culinary department in our somewhat extensive outfit. Fred, expecting us to arrive earlier, had sent the other two men, with the tents and most of the horses, ahead along the Bow trail; so we spent our first night *à la belle étoile* outside the station.

The evening was spent in sorting the baggage, which, owing to our fixed determination to make ourselves comfortable, was somewhat bulkier than usual. One depraved person, for instance, had brought a camp-bedstead. This luxury was viewed with the strongest disapproval, as out West, for some occult reason, it is considered unmanly to sleep otherwise than on the ground. Weed, a hardy man, had neither cork mattress nor bedstead; but, like a true son of America, lay in his blanket and ground-sheet. Worse even than the camp-bedstead, however, lurked behind; and presently Fred's all-seeing eye fell on the bedroom mattress.

"What's this blamed truck?" he inquired, and his good-humoured face assumed an expression of unwonted severity.

"Truck," it should be explained, is one of those delightfully comprehensive western words, like "outfit," which can be applied to anything or everything; to creation at large or a water-bucket; to a rifle or a kitchen utensil; a maiden aunt or a mother-in-law. We explained that the "truck" was nothing more or less than what it appeared to be, a mattress, and that we meant to sleep on it; whereat Robson, with quite unnecessary politeness, inquired if we should wait for the wardrobe and the rest of the bedroom suite, which he supposed was to follow later; and Fred was certain that a decent pack could not possibly be made of such a monstrosity, that no self-respecting cayoose would submit to carry it, etc., etc. So the talk went on till night fell; the bedding (including the mattress) was spread on the ground, and further argument was quenched in slumber.

It froze hard during the night, though thunder could be heard rumbling at intervals, and our blankets next morning were white with rime. We waited till noon, in the faint but delusive hope of finding our baggage on "Number One" when it arrived, and then started up the Bow Valley.

Our journey to Bear Creek was an uneventful one, and we were far from regretting the absence of incident. Things seemed so entirely different in this charming valley from that miserable region of the Bush. The weather was fine on most days; we had a well-stocked larder, and an excellent tent that kept out the rain; the mosquitoes were not too bad, though the bulldogs were terribly numerous and worried the cayooses a good deal; while the latter seemed to have a smaller allowance of original sin than most packhorses, and, on the whole, behaved extremely well. Now and again one of them might be seen wildly careering through the woods, shedding pots and pans and kettles as he went; while Moses, a sprightly old sorrel that carried the obnoxious mattress, showed his disgust at his burden by depositing it on the trail at every convenient opportunity—but they never tried to drown themselves in the lakes or swam about in rivers merely for the fun of wetting our baggage. Everything, in short, seemed to combine to make our pilgrimage the pleasant picnic we had intended it to be; as though Fate, repenting of the trials wherewith she had formerly afflicted us, were now bent on making all possible amends.

[At] the Bear Creek camping-ground, ...our examination of the river over, Collie's first care was to search for two bottles, one of whiskey, the other of brandy, which he had buried at the foot of a tree in 1898, with elaborate instructions as to how they were to be found. You stood, compass in hand, at the foot of a certain tree; then walked twenty-two paces northwest to another tree with a blaze on it; then twenty-five paces due north to a tree with a white stone at its base, under which the bottles were buried. The secret had been confided to Fred and Peyto, and many and diligent had been the searches made by them and other thirsty trappers and prospectors, but all in vain. The ground looked as though bears or wild boars had been rooting around; but the men had dug at the foot of every tree but the right one, across which another trunk had fallen, covering the white stone and the burial-place of the bottles. We, however, had no difficulty finding them, and copious libations from their well-matured contents were drunk round the camp-fire that evening. ❧

Mount Murchison

Hugh E.M. Stutfield &
J. Norman Collie FRS

Fred Stephens was by no means inclined to risk his newly-purchased outfit by the passage of Bear Creek in its present swollen condition; and the river was, if anything, rather higher next morning. Moreover, an examination of the bacon which had been stored in the shack showed that it had got slightly mouldy, and a thorough drying in the sun was considered desirable. The customary day's halt, without which few outfits leave Bear Creek, was therefore decided on; and by way of spending the time we arranged to attempt the ascent of the rocky pinnacle of Mount Murchison which faces and, as it were, overhangs the valley where the tents were pitched. It was thought that the highest summit, or what we had always deemed to be such, lay too far to the east for us to climb it, at any rate in one day, from our present camping-ground.

Next morning, therefore, Collie, Stutfield, Weed, and Hans Kaufmann sallied forth for what we imagined would prove quite a moderate expedition. Leaving the trail about half-an-hour from the camp, we ascended the dry bed of a torrent that comes straight down the mountain side…and we soon found ourselves at timberline, ready to tackle Mount Murchison with legs untired by log-jumping or fighting our way through brushwood. As we were all more or less out of training this was a matter of no slight importance. Straight above us was a series of shale slopes leading up to a narrow snow couloir, which, though very steep and possibly somewhat risky owing to falling stones, looked quite feasible; and, as it obviously offered much the most direct way up the mountain, we determined to try it.

In a grassy basin at the foot of the rocks we disturbed a young he-goat who, after the manner of bachelors of his class, was having a quiet lunch by himself on the succulent herbage that abounds at tree-line. On seeing the intruders he cantered off in leisurely fashion, traversing some tiny ledges along the face of the most gruesome precipices in a fashion that made us wonder why the epithet "giddy" should, of all others, ever be applied to a goat, and disappeared slowly round the shoulder of the mountain. There was a good deal of ice at the bottom of the couloir, which in dry seasons is almost bare of snow, and to avoid the risk of falling stones we took to the rocks on our right. These were distinctly difficult in one or two places, and we soon had to put on the rope. Above the rocks we got on to the snow which, though at a very steep angle, was in excellent condition. At the head of the couloir we crossed over to its northern side, enjoying on the way a striking glimpse, through the opposing walls of rock, of Bear Creek Valley and the mountains rising beyond.

From the top of a rocky promontory, where we halted for our second meal, it was perceived for the first time that our objective rock peak was cut off from us by a mighty cleft, or notch, in the mountain, with perpendicular cliffs on either side some hundreds of feet in height. We were more than consoled, however, by the discovery that a snow-clad summit, invisible from Bear Creek, which rose straight in front of us and immediately to the right of the rock peak, was much higher; and we had no doubt of our being able to climb it. A long, but easy, scramble up alternate rock and shale-slopes took us on to the final snow arête, which, as usual in these mountains, was very heavily corniced; and we had to traverse along the slope, which was excessively steep, a considerable distance from the edge.

At four in the afternoon, more than seven hours from the start, we stood on the maiden crest of Mount Murchison—or rather, a few feet below it, the actual top consisting of a tremendous cornice of snow that projected some distance over an abyss several thousands of feet deep. To our surprise, and great delight, we found we were on one of two peaks of about equal height—the clinometer made ours slightly the higher—which easily overtopped all the other numerous pinnacles of the Murchison group.

A very brief examination of our barometers showed that Mount Murchison would have to suffer the degradation which, sooner or later, is the lot of most mountains in this region; and to be classed henceforth among the fraudulent, or semi-fabulous, mountain monsters which have so long imposed upon the makers of maps. So far from its being 15,781 feet, or 13,500 as Hector imagined, Collie's Watkin barometer, lent him by the Royal Geographical Society, only made it 11,300 feet above sea-level: possibly some future mountain explorer will bring it down further still[1] until, as some American geographer predicted would one day be the fate of these mountains, it becomes a hole in the ground.

We managed to strike the trail before dark, and reached camp at 9.30, where we rejoiced to find that Bear Creek was considerably lower; the bacon was thoroughly dried, and all promised well for a start on the morrow. ❧

---

1. The currently accepted elevation of the NW peak is 10,936 feet (3,333 metres).

THE MUNDAYS AND THE APEX OF THE COAST RANGE

It has become an apocryphal story that Don and Phyllis Munday, a famous husband and wife climbing team from Vancouver, "discovered" Mt. Waddington by viewing it from the summit of Mt. Arrowsmith during a spring climbing trip. Actually, they were not the first to see Mt. Waddington, and, as Don Munday himself once observed, it is not possible to see Mt. Waddington from Mt. Arrowsmith. What the Mundays did see was a range of snow-capped summits, and one in particular, which seemed to approach metres 3000 metres (10,000 feet) in height, and which most certainly dwarfed the low, forested summits of the Vancouver area. Over the next 20 years of their lives, Don and Phyl Munday devoted themselves to exploring this unknown mountain area, becoming in the process the most important explorers to ever visit the Coast Mountains.

The quest demanded perseverance and dedication to an extraordinary degree. Their claim to have reached the base of a mountain hidden in the depths of the range which out-topped Mt. Robson was politely disbelieved. Even when Mt. Waddington had been officially surveyed, A.O. Wheeler, president of the Alpine Club of Canada and the country's greatest mountain surveyor, insisted on checking the calculations himself, before he could be persuaded that the peak was higher than Mt. Robson. The Mundays even had to fight for their name; the government early favoured naming the peak Mt. Dawson, after an eminent geologist and surveyor associated with the Geological Survey of Canada. But Alfred Waddington, who initiated the doomed project of building a road up the Homathko River, was the figure most closely associated with the area, and the Mundays eventually got their way.

Previous exploration in the Coast Mountains was confined to the river valleys. Gathering two friends, Agur Athol and T.H. Ingram, Don and Phyl headed in 1925 for Bute Inlet, having been convinced from their observations on Mt. Arrowsmith that the large peaks they had seen could be reached from this direction.

At the head of the inlet they ascended Mt. Rodney. Climbing slightly ahead of the rest, Don Munday suddenly emerged from the bush onto a shoulder, and for the first time saw the range of peaks that would come to dominate his life:

> Pathfinding ahead of our party, at about 2,500 feet above
> Bute Inlet I broke through the brush to the edge of a windy preci-
> pice. Before me lay the broad fiord mightily walled, with remains
> of winter avalanches still in gullies within a few hundred feet of
> tidewater. Beyond the head of the inlet extended the 8,000 foot
> trench of the Homathko, nearly straight for about 20 miles. Be-
> yond this great corridor was a vast expanse of glacier out of
> which rose a range of splendid rock peaks. Above their imposing
> summits lay a thin roof of level, wintry cloud, and piercing this in

lone majesty towered the pinnacled monarch of the Coast Range. It was one of those supreme moments sometimes vouchsafed to mountaineers, and one has little quarrel with fate if he has been granted such a sight.[1]

The Mundays knew that Alfred Waddington had tried to approach the interior of the province via the Homathko River, which runs into Bute Inlet. His road project ended in disaster when his crew was murdered by Chilcotin Indians one dark night at a spot on the river now called "Murderer's Bar." However, had the Mundays considered Waddington's accounts of the ferocity of the Homathko approach, they might have thought twice before taking it on; it is a jungle of dense bush, savage streams, log jams and precipitous cliffs. Sixty years after Waddington had pushed a roadway 30 miles up the river, not a trace of his efforts remained.

The party started on May 31, 1926. Travel was grim; "difficulties grew worse at every mile." Particularly troublesome were the creek crossings which had to be made each time one of the tributaries fed from the many glaciers to the north entered the main channel. Finally, after 13 days of torturous relay-packing with 30 kilogram packs, the party reached Coola Creek, fed by the Waddington Glacier. Turning west up the Coola valley, they pushed ahead, and then, in one strenuous 32-hour round trip, reached the base of Spearman Peak, Mt. Waddington's southern neighbour. Out of food and supplies, they retreated, but they had seen at close range one of the last great "unknown" mountains of the world.

In the spring of 1927 the Mundays headed north from Vancouver again, this time to explore the approaches from Knight Inlet. From a high ridge, they viewed the Franklin Glacier, and chose it as the best approach. After cutting trail 10 kilometres to the glacier snout, they returned to Vancouver, gathered their supplies and Mrs. Munday's sister and returned to the attack.

The 1927 Waddington expedition was the greatest of the Mundays' many campaigns. On this trip they first ascended the Franklin Glacier, explored all the western approaches to the peak, making attempts on the summit via the Dais and Corridor glaciers; ascended the largest of the Franklin's northern tributary glaciers, the Confederation; and came within a few hundred feet of scaling the Northwest Peak of Mt. Waddington itself. The knowledge gained in this expedition allowed them to return the following year and climb the Northwest Peak, the highest point they ever attained on Mt. Waddington.

One cannot help feeling a little sad that the Mundays failed to capture the first ascent of the greatest prize in the Coast Mountains after investing so many years in

---

1. "Exploration in the Coast Range," W.A. Don Munday, *Canadian Alpine Journal*, Vol XVI, p. 122.

laying the groundwork. Ultimately it was two exceptional American climbers, Fritz Weissner and William House, who first reached the summit of the main tower in 1936. But as Don Munday said, there was a kind of exhilaration in knowing the mountain had proved so great.

The account which follows is taken from the *Canadian Alpine Journal* of 1926/ 1927. Readers may find Don Munday's style a little abrupt at first. Although he made his chief living from freelance journalism, he never developed a smooth journalistic style, and his writing is full of sudden changes in direction. This choppiness is emphasized by the mixing of ideas within one paragraph and by abrupt shifts in topic. Few connectives are employed, so that one can almost feel oneself bumping along the trail over the glaciers, step by step, with Don and Phyl ahead in the lead. The style takes some getting used to, but is unmistakable in the literature.

Don Munday focused his accounts on event and on geological and glaciological observation. Missing, however, is anything much in the way of personal comment about the companions who shared his adventures. One receives an impression of Don Munday as a competent, resolute figure, but probably to all but his wife somewhat distant; one who commanded respect rather than love. There is a certain lack of emotional colour in the writing, and a certain woodenness. The overwhelming vitality which it must have taken to have seen these expeditions through does not come across very strongly in the telling.

Nonetheless, the achievements of the Mundays deserve to be more celebrated. They were among the most important of the third wave of explorers of this country who sought to discover more about the nature of its geography not for commercial gain, but because they were driven by sheer curiosity and a deep sense of adventure. Between the two of them, Don and Phyl covered thousands of kilometres of unmapped territory, climbing some of the highest peaks in the Western Cordillera. Their exploits rank with the grandest mountain adventures of all time.

~ Bruce Fairley

The Apex of the Coast Range

W.A. Don Munday

Phyl and I took the steamer *Venture* to Knight Inlet Cannery on July 18, 1927 with her sister, Mrs. E.M. McCallum. Because a spare part could not be got in less than two weeks from Vancouver for the engine to our small boat, we rowed [up the inlet] to Kwalate. From there Mr. W. Perkus towed us about eight miles more to Grave Point where we spent the night in an old Indian smoke house. In the morning we rowed the remaining 20 miles against the tide and the current produced by the two big glacial rivers [flowing into Knight Inlet].

Bulldog flies plagued us on the water, and became almost unendurable at the mouth of the Franklin. Caching boat and engine and unpacking supplies used most of the following forenoon, we broke camp on the 23rd and moved up-river opposite the first tributary from the east. The river was rising rapidly and by forcing us on the higher rougher ground increased greatly the task of relaying supplies, and also necessitated some heavy trail cutting through devil's club, salmonberry, etc. The glacier appears to be discharging more debris than the river can carry, so the level of much of the valley floor is rising. Old moraines are still subsiding towards the river, thus opening root-bridged fissures in the woods.

Ice blocks were seen plowing up the boulders in the river bed. At times they were sufficient in quantity to choke channels and divert the river. A rock weighing approximately 30 tons, and on which we had cached supplies, was moved later about 50 yards down a new channel cut through green timber.

The glacier has retreated about a mile in the past 100 years. The cavern of exquisite violet and blue from which the river emerged in July and August was about 150 feet in width; in June the cave did not exist; in September it was breaking down.

The Mystery Glacier [now known as the Franklin Glacier] proved disappointing as a highway. It has a complex flow and descends in a series of steps, ice-fall conditions being hardly smoothed out before another break occurs; each promontory constricts it sufficiently to produce high pressure ridges. Intense thawing at low altitudes steepens southern faces of ice, and the strong cold wind down the glacier serves to accentuate the differential thawing. Fortunately we had crampons, for, although the gradient of the glacier is generally gradual, much of the footing was so steep that step-cutting would otherwise have been a necessity with heavy packs.

The lateral moraines average about 250 feet in height, and the steep mountain sides above them present surprising difficulties in the matter of finding a site on which to pitch even a small tent. Some of the surface streams cut such deep gorges in the ice that they were obstacles to be reckoned with.

Lit by the setting sun, the twin summits of Mystery Mountain [now known, of course, as Mount Waddington] came into view on July 29 from an elevation of 1,500 feet on the glacier.

The evening of August 1st found us with heavy packs almost baffled by a maze of great chasms in our attempts to get "ashore" to the foot of a pretty water-fall on the east side. A flowery but rough morainal bench looked delightful, but obviously was only a fair weather camp.

This turned out to be our base camp. The elevation was 4,200 feet. Having brought all our supplies up the glacier and indulged in a day's rest, we climbed 3,200 feet behind camp to a crest we named Marvel Ridge. Visibility was perfect, and the summit revealed the immensity of Mystery Glacier as well as the unchallenged supremacy of Mystery Mountain whose 10,000 and 11,000 foot guardians were dwarfed by the monarch's mass and height. It became apparent that the glacier covered fully 100 square miles and was 25 miles in length. The day was one of unforgettable memories.

We left base camp next day with four days' grub and no certain destination as we did not know how close to the Mystery Mountain we could find firewood. The place we had in mind was Icefall Point on the west side of the glacier.

Shortly after descending the troublesome moraine at base camp, we had to tackle an imposing mass of seracs. I put my pack down while cutting steps around a huge pinnacle, whereupon a muddy torrent burst through within a yard of my pack. Later we found that this was the suddenly released water of a marginal lake formed by one of the streams from Yataghan Glacier. Sometimes the lake did not exist, but sometimes it was 40 feet deep. Longitudinal crevasses proved vexations on this trip.

At Icefall Point we found an exposed campsite at 5,500 feet near a little morainal lake. There was enough wood for a small party for a short time.

For a mile above this main icefall Mystery Glacier was badly crevassed, so next day we climbed over Icefall Point carrying with us a supply of cooked food and a limited amount of firewood. By way of the first of the large southerly tributary glaciers we descended to the main glacier and ascended its westerly fork. Crevasses were troublesome to a degree, and about 4 p.m. we became involved in a series crossing each other at right angles and almost completely masked though highly unsafe. For an hour we travelled away from our objective more than toward it. Shortly before the sun went down we found a ledge of 7,000 feet on a cliff cluttered with loose debris by recently retreating ice. Here we bivouacked. Many meteors were noted this night.

Starting at 4:15 a.m., we had an anxious climb of 900 feet up glaciated slabs heaped with loose boulders. We then descended 600 feet to Dais Glacier, crossed it to Regal Glacier, and ascended the latter. Regal Glacier offered enough problems to be exhilarating to the leader at least, and its snow formations were splendid even in a region where glacial features are on a colossal scale. A bergschrund guarded the base of the cliffs everywhere. Two attempts failed to force the upper lip, and finally we had to cross a slender bridge and traverse a steep ice slope to steep rocks, where a shower of fragments greeted us as we took off crampons with one hand while hanging on with the other.

The rocks were shattered, the ledges sloping. We went straight up to the apex of a small peak about 11,000 feet high. Much of the south face of this ridge actually overhangs. Advance along it was not perhaps impossible but certainly impracticable, calling for the traverse of difficult towers that almost attained the dignity of individual peaks.

But we were now only level with the top of Dais Glacier, above which rises the immense south wall of the Mystery Mountain, crowned at the nearer end with the impending blue cliffs of Epaulette Glacier. Forest fires dimmed distant views.

The worst part of the descent was the glaciated slabs above our bivouac, which we reached at 7:10 p.m. The tedious tramp back to Icefall Point next day was by way of a cliff-foot capped by a lively hanging glacier on the side of Mt. Cavalier.

From Icefall Point we went on the 9th to base camp and brought up more grub. Then the weather broke and we found our camp site very bleak. Snow fell on all the peaks.

On the 13th we set out for Corridor Glacier, the east branch of Mystery Glacier, by the same route over Icefall Point. Finding the ice much shattered at the angle of Jester Mountain, we climbed the cliffs 350 feet to a small grass patch which made a fine bed, although a little rain would have made it untenable. The elevation was 7,000 feet. A handful of juniper sticks helped out the scanty supply of wood we brought in our packs.

By brilliant moonlight we left at 12:40 a.m., descending to the broken marginal ice of Corridor Glacier and working out to the middle where the longitudinal crevasses were completely masked by thin, brittle snow. At dawn we sat down for second breakfast on an ice mound at the foot of the great trough plowed for 2,500 feet down the icefall on Buckler Glacier by avalanches from two hanging glaciers high up on the face of Mystery Mountain. Richly violet, the shadow of the earth hung in the southwesterly sky under a band of glowing rose so vivid it might well have been the sun's vanguard instead of night's rearguard.

The massive ruins of the icefall were a delight to the eye, but serious obstacles. More than once a single bridge was the only possible route in the whole width of the icefall. To avoid passing immediately under the hanging glaciers we were forced to find a way up a succession of toppling 100-foot walls, and we crossed the glacier three times among their immense fragments before we found a causeway to the basin above. Tawny smoke-clouds were now pouring over Spearmen Peak [now known as Spearman Peak] and Mt. Munday from the north.

The sunlight had struck the upper face of Mystery Mountain and the great precipices reverberated with loosened rocks and ice and snow. Most of the southerly face is so swept by avalanches that the edges of ledges are distinctly rounded off.

We hoped to gain the crest of the eastern ridge by way of a belt of cliffs under the snow slope on the western face of Spearmen Peak which guards the end of this easy-looking ridge. The ladies described the rocks of Spearmen Peak as "looking like marble cake, only more so." The rocks are intricately mottled with several colours from white to nearly black; the effect is a most baffling camouflage giving the misleading impression of easy climbing where it is wholly impossible. The nearly vertical slabs of granite schist break with numerous small overhangs.

We tried three easy looking ways, the last one being nerve-racking in the extreme as the heat of the day was bringing down snow and rocks along the wall. Both women were bruised repeatedly; Mrs. Munday's hair was matted with blood, and her arm severely bruised by interposing it toward a rock from her sister's head. Finally a place was reached where to have advanced would have violated the rudimentary principles of good climbing.

Therefore we started down, reaching the bergschrund at dusk. Frost had not yet strengthened the snow bridges, walls were dripping, pinnacles collapsing. When we had groped an anxious way through the worst of the icefall, the moon topped Spearmen Peak. Steep slopes by this time had become especially trying as the frosty crust broke away from the sodden layer below. Four hours were required to descend 2,000 feet of the icefall. We reached the bivouac at 3:45 a.m.

Shortly past noon we were packing up, and we reached Icefall camp at 6:55 p.m., having decided to start on the morrow for the base of the formidable west ridge which Mrs. Munday thought held the secret of the route to the summit.

We spent the next night about 200 feet above our first bivouac, but the inviting little grass patch was mostly afloat in a pool, and it proved a cold, uncomfortable camp. Continuing the following morning, we again climbed over the spur of Mt. Cavalier to avoid the icefall at its westerly base, and descended into the immense basin into which empty Dais, Regal and Fury glaciers. Travelling was tedious owing to the snow being deeply pitted. Fury Glacier descends from Fury Gap in a thousand-foot icefall. Near the top of this we got off on to the rocks and bivouacked just below the glacial crest of the Gap, at 8,700 feet.

Fury Gap is not a true pass, the descent on the north to Scimitar Glacier being impracticable. Dead insects and small migratory birds littered the snow. The Coast Mountains here have a well-defined crest and Fury Gap is the only real break in it for many miles east and west.

We overslept, not getting away until 5 a.m. At 7:10 we reached the summit of Fireworks Peak, 10,500 feet. Beyond this we met the summit icecap which extends the full length of the mountain although scarcely hinted at in views from the southern side. Quite extensive sections of the crests of the peaks of the west ridge actually overhang the southern wall. Alternating with equally narrow ribs of ice, these peaks form the splendid skyline route. We had no crampons, the changes from rock to ice being too frequent to use them to advantage.

We met the first big gap in the ridge at 11,500 feet. The enforced descent of 300 feet was by way of the badly shattered end of the rock wall which was like a narrow buttress leaning sideways appreciably. We then approached what we had referred to as the Bulge, as in some lights its ponderous icecap appeared to swell out over the edge of the southern cliffs. After failing to outflank it on the north, we cut steps directly up it for about 100 feet.

While lunching on the summit, about 11,500 feet, the rocks beneath our feet seemed to quiver with the thunderous descent of thousands of tons of rocks from one of the peaks of the southwest ridge, and we watched the tremendous mass crash down upon the tiny line of foot-prints still marking the route of our first attempt.

The descent of the Bulge for about 300 feet was as curious a situation as a climber is likely to meet. A lip of broken rock averaging 18 inches in width dipped diagonally steeply along the base of the precipitous icecap, and between the rocks of the ledge the rashly inquisitive glance might note that the whole ledge overhung like a cornice.

Negotiating a bergschrund, we descended into a deep and steep glacial trough, mounted a huge snow dome and faced the amazing knife-edge of the west arête where it runs into Epaulette Glacier. The northern face of the arête was largely a smooth slope of bare, blue ice down which small rocks slid almost silently. Descending eastward into another glacial trough, we stood at last at the foot of the 1,500-foot incline leading into cloud toward the peak.

Part of our route was strewn with ice blocks from impending masses above. The surface of the deep powdery snow was wind-packed to a condition resembling "wind-board" and tended to avalanche. The crevasses here were of stupendous size and wonderful beauty.

To the dense smoke was now added the murk of gathering storm. We plodded laboriously upward, Mrs. Munday now breaking the trail most of the way. At about 6 p.m. we stopped and ate on a flattened slope nearly level with the base of the north peak which was again clear of cloud.

As we were changing places on the rope at 6:40 p.m., preparatory to cutting steps up the final 400 feet of nearly bare ice, a snowcloud swirled redly between us and the low sun. We caught a brief glimpse down Tiedemann Glacier's 15 miles of ice, and looked down on top of Mt. Munday's 11,000-foot crest, then cloud hid all.

With all haste we retraced our blurring footsteps through the deepening shadows, but a little light remained as we climbed the "cornice" ledge; it failed as I re-cut steps down the west side of the Bulge. Groping our way slowly up the other two cliffs in the dark was a nightmare experience as the blast shrilled across the ridge. Had we not got back before these cliffs iced up, our situation would have been grave indeed. Mrs. Munday led with a carbide lamp. In spite of darkness and a frozen rope, the last man was not endangered by falling rocks. Part of our carbide supply had been mislaid, and the lamp gave out before we crossed the last treacherous stretch of the icecap to Fireworks Peak at 11:30 p.m.

On this exposed rock face the full fury of the storm smote us, the wind nearly pinning us to the rocks; lightning and thunder now came simultaneously, flash following flash so closely that the alternate brilliance and blackness left us almost blinded; rain, hail and snow lashed us in turn. Our ice axes buzzed with blue fans of flame up to three inches in length for three hours; a dancing fringe of flame around the brim of my hat made a beacon of me when the storm was not too thick, the flame of my ice axe being of less guidance to the others because jutting rocks around us glowed with similar weird lights. The snow on our clothing shone with ghostly light.

Seracs fell frequently, and from the heights the avalanches swelled the echoing thunder. We sheltered briefly under a projecting rock, but the only footing was rocks shakily wedged in a wide, deep crack below. The storm showed no sign of abating, snow was rapidly making the rocks more difficult, so we went on down, dropping from rock to rock in a way we would not have dared in broad daylight.

We came unerringly through the storm to our bivouac at 2:30 a.m., only to find water pouring across the ledge; wood, spare clothes, grub, bedding, all alike were soaked. A pot caught four inches of water this night! The tent intended for high camps had been ground under the heel of a huge shifting rock while cached on the lower glacier. We shivered under the tarpaulin until daylight, then made our way down the icefall. Storm still raged on the mountain, but a little feeble sunshine greeted us before we reached Icefall Camp at noon. Here we cooked a scanty meal, then broke camp in renewed storm which lashed us down the glacier to base camp, reached at 8 p.m., 39 hours after starting the climb.

Unfortunately for our chances of resting after these two attempts on the mountain, Mrs. McCallum had to leave for home the next day. Unsettled weather continued. We put her on board the *Venture* at Glendale Cove on the evening of August 23. Six days later my wife and I were back in base camp an hour ahead of a storm that lasted six days and seven nights with only three hours' intermission. One night the harmless-looking little waterfall behind camp swelled in a few minutes to a width of 100 feet and swept through camp. By desperate efforts we saved everything but a little grub and a pair of snowglasses.

Bright cold weather followed, but it failed to restore even minor peaks to climbable condition. We were able to dry our belongings, and also made a pleasant exploratory trip up Confederation Glacier, a big western branch of Mystery Glacier. After caching various things that might be useful for our 1928 expedition, we started down the glacier on September 9, and boarded the boat at Glendale Cove on the 13th, wind and tide not having proved more than ordinarily troublesome. Quicksand along Franklin River had been a real danger.

Despite the necessity of "man-packing" from sea-level, Mystery Glacier is the logical route. The region possesses considerable geological interest, but the time spent unravelling the intricate defenses of the big mountain prevented trips in other directions. ✒

III ACCIDENTS

Accidents and fatalities are not to be wished, but there is no doubt that their occurrence has spawned some of the finest and most gripping mountaineering prose. Many of the most famous stories in the literature of mountaineering concern tragedies, from the ghastly accident on the first ascent of the Matterhorn, when four of the climbing party fell to their deaths high on the peak, to the account by Doug Scott of his ordeal in descending the Ogre, a peak in the Himalayas, on two broken ankles, magnificently told in his story "A Crawl Down the Ogre."

While all mountaineers dread accidents, it must be admitted that they are today surprisingly frequent; in the Himalayas in particular the toll among the stronger climbers represents a significant percentage. Canadian mountaineering, however, has an excellent safety record. In an average year, more climbers will die on one of the major peaks of the European Alps than in the whole of the mountains of Canada, and the climbing fraternity is small enough that fatal accidents are keenly felt by mountaineers across the country.

The three extracts which follow point up some of the differences in situation and attitude between climbers of today and their early counterparts. When Philip Abbot became the first fatality in Canadian mountaineering, he was a member of a large party, but today the tendency is for smaller parties, often consisting of just two climbers, to attack the bigger routes. These small parties move quickly, and give each climber a bigger stake in the climb; but as the article "Shattered Dreams" shows, when disaster strikes, the smaller party is much more exposed to the grim realities of evil fortune.

The social historian, as well as the historian of climbing, will find considerable meat in a comparison of the first piece in the chapter, "The Accident on Mt. Lefroy," with the two other pieces, which were written almost a hundred years later. After reading C.S. Thompson's account of the accident on Mt. Lefroy the modern reader is left baffled at how little affected Thompson appears to have been at the death of a man who was presumably a friend; writing of it as if it were of no more importance in his memories of the day than the view over the continental divide. Compare this to the profound sense of loss that pervades Steve DeMaio's "Jimmy and the Kid," and the change wrought by the passing century is striking.

Can the cultural remove of a hundred years be that great? Or would our great-great-grandfathers, reading Thompson's story in 1897, have found it moving in a way that we can't? Would they have been able to read something between the lines that the passing of a century has obscured, or was the suppresion of emotion so complete in the Victorian gentlemen who were Canada's early climbers that even the death of a friend could not be acknowledged as a loss?

∿ Bruce Fairley & David Harris

THE ACCIDENT ON MOUNT LEFROY

James Outram, an early climber in the Canadian Rockies and the first to climb Mt. Assiniboine, "in perusing the records of earlier climbers [was] struck by the very special providence that has watched over their initial efforts." Many of the pioneers were quite inexperienced in the techniques of mountaineering. Outram thought "the rope and ice-axe were...novelties to almost all."

Philip Stanley Abbot was one of the experienced few, although, ironically, he is best remembered today as the first fatality in Canadian mountaineering. His early climbs, though ranging from Popocatapetl, the Sierra, Alaska, Yellowstone, to the Lake District and Norway, were really vacation outings. By 1892, however, when he climbed in the Alps with guide Peter Sarbach, the commitment to mountaineering was dominant, and Abbot was fortunate to find in the Appalachian Mountain Club others who shared his enthusiasm and were equal to his skill. He had already probed Mt. Lefroy on one occasion before making the attempt which claimed his life.

It is interesting to note how little space in Thompson's article is devoted to the accident; he does not get around to it until almost the final paragraph. A modern writer would have very likely opened with the fall, and made it the focus of the piece. Nonetheless, of the various versions of this famous fatality, we feel this one, taken from *Appalachia*, Vol II, No. 1 (January 1897) to be the most readable.

~ Moira Irvine

Mt. Lefroy, August 3, 1896.

Charles Sproull Thompson

Shortly after dawn, on Monday, August 3, 1896, four men gathered, in eager preparation, upon the platform which surrounds the Canadian Pacific chalet at Lake Louise. A year before—to the very day, as it chanced,—Prof. Charles E. Fay, Mr. Philip S. Abbot, and the writer had endeavored to reach the as yet untrodden summit of Mt. Lefroy by a couloir which offers the only feasible passage through the cliffs of its northern face. The failure of that endeavor, a failure fraught with possibilities of ultimate success, increased our desire. All winter we had planned and plotted to overcome the difficulties of that mountain. Now, with a less rigid itinerary, with an added comrade, Prof. George T. Little, we made ready for a second, and, as we believed, conclusive, struggle.

The surpassing beauty of the view westward from the platform that morning remains with me. In the foreground, completely filling the lower end of the valley, lay the dark-green waters of Lake Louise, as yet unruffled by the inevitable noonday wind. Four miles away, seemingly but two, beyond rock avalanche, terminal moraine, and low-lying glacier, the summit range of the Continental Divide swept across the valley, a wall of gray precipice and hanging ice, the snowy battlements of a Canadian Asgard. Before its face, now rising, now falling, now dissolving, strangely stratified clouds floated in curious undulations. The abruptly rising sides of the valley fittingly framed the picture, the quiet waters of the lake doubled and intensified it.

Our route lay up this valley. To the left of the mountain wall, known to us as Mt. Green,[1] thrusting its imposing mass between the Green and the Mitre Glaciers,[2] stood the goal of our anticipated effort, Mt. Lefroy. Up its eastern face, fronting us,—a snow-corniced precipice, falling four thousand feet to the Mitre Glacier,—it is safe to say that man will never go. The northern face, on the other hand, offered, as we knew, one possible line of ascent. From where we stood, its profile showed a varying slope, inclined at an angle of about thirty-five degrees, steepest in its middle part, ending below in a line of cliffs eight hundred feet high, which overlook the Green Glacier. In this line of cliffs a re-entrant angle held an unseen but well-remembered tongue of snow, rising with ever-increasing gradient to within a compara-

---

1. Mt. Green is now known as Mt. Victoria.
2. The Green and Mitre Glaciers are now known as the Victoria and Lefroy Glaciers respectively.

tively short distance of their summit. Above, two rock chimneys offered a passage, possible but at the time of our former visit quite impracticable, to this upper slope. But the rising sun warned us to hasten. Already its rays touched and glorified the snowy apex of Mt. Green,—a Pythian oracle, read by us as a prophecy of success.

It was a quarter past six as our boat pushed out from the floating wharf; it was a quarter of seven as its keel grounded in the sand of the delta at the head of the lake. Thence our way held through a last line of forest trees, over rock-strewn and stream-swept flats, over lingering patches of winter snow, up, slowly, steadily up, across lateral moraine and debris-covered glacier, to the uncertainly defined line where snow began to hide the hitherto open crevasses. Here, 7450 feet above sea-level, 1500 feet above the chalet, we paused to put on the rope. We were at the open end of a gigantic amphitheater, walled from left to right by the perpendicular cliffs of Mt. Lefroy and Mt. Green and the hardly less precipitous slopes of Mts. Nichols and Despine. Its floor was the Green Glacier upon which we stood. Not far from us, open to plain view, rose the couloir on Mt. Lefroy of which I have already written. In addition to the difficulties previously encountered, a transverse schrund now completely divided the tongue of snow into approximately equal parts. To pass the schrund, by a difficult traverse across the face of a prominent buttress on the right, was doubtless possible, but to me the thought of such an ascent was far from pleasing. Uninviting as it was, we might ultimately be forced to go that way. On this day, however, our hopes centered in an ascent through the Death Trap.

Quite unseen from the chalet, quite unseen even from where we stood, a curious side passage, hitherto unexplored, led from the amphitheater to the summit of the divide. Hidden in the angle between Lefroy and Green, its major axis parallel with and between the major axes of those mountains, the passage splits the summit range as a wedge splits an oaken log—with the grain. In the early spring the entrance is swept by avalanches from both mountains; in July and August the only danger lies in occasional ice-falls from the hanging glaciers on Mt. Green, a danger easily avoided by keeping under the bare walls of Mt. Lefroy. Doubly impressed by the thunder of these ice-falls, and by the ferocity of the cliffs at the narrow entrance, an earlier traveler, Mr. S.E.S. Allen, has given to the lower portion of this passage the name by which we knew it, the "Death Trap." Thither we turned our steps.

A magnificent sight opened southward as we swung rapidly around the corner of the farther buttress of Mt. Lefroy. It came suddenly, almost in the twinkling of an eye—a glacier-filled gorge a mile and a half long, at its widest perhaps three hundred yards, rising in rounded terraces to the summit of the pass, over two thousand feet above. The lower slope, deeply cut between Lefroy and Green, lay in heavy shadow; the higher névé glistened a dazzling white under the undimmed rays of an Alpine Sun. Far above, a curved line separated sky from snow, azure quartered upon argent. For the next three hours—from ten minutes of nine until ten minutes of twelve—four tiny specks moved up this glittering causeway. The ascent was neither difficult nor toilsome. Once, below the debris of an avalanche which had swept far down the narrowing slope, we paused to photograph and lunch. As we ate, a block of ice broke from the overhanging glacier on a cliff near us and fell, pounding into dusty fragments, almost at our feet. Two cameras caught its first down-rushing. Thus fifteen minutes passed; then upward through the avalanche debris and over or around crevasses, one, the last, crossed "on all fours" by means of a snow bridge. Ahead the sharp white line upon the blue sky grew sharper, nearer, then dropped away altogether. The snow broke upon an edge of scree. We looked across the summit of the continental watershed.

Wonderful, tremendous; not beautiful, save as the sublime always contains elements of beauty; almost overpowering. Three times that day this scene was burned upon my visual memory,—three times,—never to be forgotten. Here Mt. Green ended. Below, a great pit, funnel-shaped, holding in its depths a sea-green lake, Oesa, glacier-fed, glacier-hemmed; beyond, a flamelike peak—Mt. Biddle—and the crescent line of the Ottertails, ended at either horn by the fierce Goodsir and the snowy Vaux; in the far distance, the Selkirks, soft, unreal, cloud-tipped. This at a glance. Then, thrusting themselves upon us by their nearness, the truncated summit of Ringrose, the ragged shoulder of Hungabee, and the white curves of Glacier Dome. At hand, overshadowing us, Lefroy. Never before was such a combination of the far and the near. It was surely true:— "They have not seen the snowy hills of God who have yet to look upon the Rocky Mountains, absolute, stupendous, sublimely grave." (Gilbert Parker, *Pierre and His People.*)

In this first view, the conquest of Mt. Lefroy seemed assured. That portion of its western slope which lay directly above us was covered by three icestreams, or, rather, by one ice-stream, broken, more or less continuously, into three parts. Above this ice-covered slope, crowning the mountain, was an almost level palisade of yellowish limestone cliffs, weathered into rude turrets and bastions. The ice reached to the foot of these cliffs, curved to the north, and, sweeping by their right flank, separated it from an inconspicuous mound of gray rock, the probable summit of the mountain. Hidden beneath a thin layer of fresh snow, the surface of this ice inclined at a very considerable, but not prohibitive, angle. Should that surface prove soft and rotten, as from the condition of the ice-slope in the pass there was every reason to hope, we should be on the summit within two hours. Satisfied with the prospect, we turned up a bowlder slide, and near its head (barometric altitude, 10,000 feet), immediately above the pass, we ate a second lunch. I noted curiously that Abbot and Fay were in British Columbia, while Little and I remained in the District of Alberta, Northwest Territory. It was half-past twelve.

The first blow of the axe upon the ice, heavy, dull, resistant, altered our plans, dashed our hopes of easy success, and, little suspected, turned the fortune of the day. No longer an easy, rapid ascent along footholds carelessly taken, kicked in the snow; instead, a long, arduous scramble over intermittent ledges, changing to ice, and toilsome step-cutting only as a last resort. Abbot, as ever, went first; passed to the right over a whitened scree slope, and up a low escarpment (barometric altitude, 10,300 feet) on the southern edge of the largest and most northerly of the three ice-streams, the one, in fact, which led directly to the summit. We had cause to remember that escarpment later in the day. Beyond, moving one at a time, carefully, cautiously, with no thought of things temporal save the glasslike surface beneath our feet, with no knowledge save that the slope opened into the Oesa pit, we cut a way up and over the second ice-stream, dug tooth-and-nail up the treacherous friable limestone of a second ledge, passed across the third ice-stream, climbed another ledge more degraded, more abominable than its predecessor, then moved out upon the ice-dome beneath the crowning cliffs.

Nothing can surpass the supreme exultation of such a moment, the clear, exhilarating atmosphere, the great silence, the virgin peak almost won, the icy dome on which we stood falling into air. The eye, too, swept a broadening horizon. Over the tremendous southern precipice of Green came the snowy top of Huber, prism-pointed; to the northwest, beyond Nichols, lay the unmapped, untraversed ice-field of the Waputtehk Mountains, holding in their midst the white cone of Balfour, promising two days hence an easy victory; to the north, rose the massive bulk of Hector, sulking, as usual, behind a cloud. All the visible mountains were even now beneath us—all save five. Perchance the coming conquest, perchance the quickened heartbeat, enhanced the beauty of this second view. Its memory gives added glory to the first.

Across the pleasure fell a deepening shadow. The day was passing; already it was half-past five. At such an hour our position on the slope became indeed critical. Pushed more and more by the general configuration of the ledges toward that end of the cliffs farthest from the summit, we were now driven either to scale their face or to cut a traverse below them to the main ice-stream; to turn their left flank, a line of perpendicular rock conveniently near us, was manifestly impossible. Apparently, chance favored us. As Abbot touched the base of the cliffs, his face brightened, and with a ring of certainty in his voice, he exclaimed: "There is a good crack here." A minute later we had gathered together upon a tiny bed of scree, perhaps eight feet long, and at greatest six feet wide, the floor of a re-entrant angle. (We were, I should judge, 200 feet below and 300 feet south of the summit at the time of the accident. Abbot was, of course, considerably higher.) Jutting into this bed of scree, a narrow knee of rock, some four feet high, offered a first up-ward step. Above the knee, one to the right, the other to the left of a broad stone face that filled the inner corner of the angle, were two crevices through which a man might press. A plan was quickly formed. In rapid succession Abbot bade us put off the rope. Thus released, dragging both our two ropes tied together behind him, he passed up on the knee, and immediately thence to the right-hand crevice. Little followed. Both, entering the crevice, disap-peared behind the rock-face. Fay and I remained upon the scree awaiting the time when, with the aid of the rope firmly fastened, we might easily and safely join our comrades on the top of the cliffs. To the men above two ways opened; one, along a narrow ledge about a foot and a half wide, skirting the face of the cliff, summitwards; the other, at right angles to it, up a shallow groove, hopper-shaped, leading directly to the arête. Abbot chose the groove, and, entering it, vanished from Little's view, the rope, dragging be-hind, followed foot by foot.

Success or failure hung in the balance of the flying moments. Idly leaning against the protruding knee, I watched the mists whirl and eddy around the inaccessible pinnacle of Huber. Fay stood about three paces from me, under the safe protection of an imposing buttress. By leaning a little outward, we both could distinguish the separate bowlders of the summit mound. Five, ten, fifteen minutes passed. In the impressive silence came the dull thud of a falling body, faint and rattling at first, heavy and crashing as it came bounding nearer. Crying to Fay that a great stone was coming, I made two steps toward him, turned, saw Abbot pitch through the left-hand crev-ice, strike upon the top of the knee, turn completely over, and, clearing the scree, plunge headlong down the ice-slope. Some seconds thereafter we saw him lying at the edge of the escarpment, the ropes wound about his body. (We shall never know how Mr. Abbot chanced to fall. From the nature of the death-wound, a V-shaped fracture of the left parietal and the occipital bones, it is probable that his hand-hold gave way, and that he fell backward, receiving the fatal injury in the initial fall.)

Three hours later we stood beside him. Looking up, I saw again in the gathering twilight those most wonderful peaks of the known Canadian Rockies; above them were the slowly drifting clouds of a coming storm and the depths of an infinite sky. A cool north wind drew gently through the pass—Abbot Pass, in remembrance of him who lay there motionless upon the snow! ❧

SHATTERED DREAMS

When I climbed Mt. Robson in 1979 we used the Kain Face route, one of the great historic lines in the Canadian Rockies. We were in good shape, the day was brilliant, and by 3:30 p.m. we stood at the top of the Kain Face, ready to begin our descent. But in the six hours since we had first started up the snow and ice of the face, conditions had changed drastically. The firm ice had degenerated under the pulverizing sun and the face was laced with a layer of rotten ice crystals. We chose to spend an uncomfortable night hunched together in our jackets, rather than risk the descent under those conditions, and descended at four o'clock the next morning.

On our way out from the climb, descending the Robson Glacier, we met two parties. One, a party of four from Alaska, was heading for the Kain Face. They carried packs so large that each needed the help of another to lift the pack onto his back. The other party, a man and woman, seemed lightly equipped; they were dressed in shorts and carried what seemed to be no more than large day packs. They were headed for what at that time was considered the most serious of the routes on Robson—the north face.

As the classic routes in the Rockies have become better known, and as climbing equipment and knowledge improves, mountaineers have developed new attitudes to challenge. The commonest party size on the big routes of the Rockies today is probably two persons. Yet the factors that make a route difficult are still the same as they have always been. Weather, snow and ice conditions, avalanche and ice-fall danger are all unpredictable. "Shattered Dreams" is a story of a party who found themselves a little over their heads, in the wrong place, at the wrong time, when conditions were simply too much for the skills and equipment at hand. Their experience is a reminder that equipment and technique are sometimes little defence in the face of unpredictable phenomena.

Despite his terrible ordeal following the avalanche on Mt. Robson, readers will be interested to know that Richard Howse has today fully recovered and in 1988 summited on Pumori, a satellite peak of Mt. Everest in the Nepalese Himalayas. His account is taken from the 1987 edition of the *Varsity Outdoor Club Journal* published annually by the Varsity Outdoor Club at the University of British Columbia. We believe that readers will find the straight-from-the-heart telling of this astonishing tale gripping and unforgettable.

~ Bruce Fairley

Shattered Dreams

Richard Howse

July 25–August 3, 1987

It is Friday night in late July and a laughing, talking crowd of people are gathered outside around two charcoal barbecues and a table laden with food. Everyone is gaily trying everybody else's offerings, enjoying themselves at this coming together of friends. Somewhere is Enrico, and the two of us are not giving too much thought to the long drive we have ahead of us tomorrow, to Mt. Robson Provincial Park. We are here to say farewell to Geoff, who leaves to return to Australia soon, and as the party eventually dissolves in the fondness of parting words, no one can realize that they are also saying good-bye to Enrico for the last time.

Our main goal is a route of imposing beauty, the icy sweep of the north face of Mt. Robson (3,954 m./12,972 ft.). "With its purity of line and directness of purpose, this elegant face may fairly claim to offer one of the finest ice-routes in the Canadian Rockies" (*The Rocky Mountains of Canada, North*, Kruszyna and Putnam). We have dreamt of this climb for some time, yet also feel its seriousness and will not commit ourselves if conditions are not favourable.

Late on Saturday night we pull into the campground with gentle rain falling, yet by morning the sun is beaming down from a clear sky and we are packing, in our shorts, by the car. We have taken the precaution of telephoning a weather forecaster at Environment Canada in Jasper, and the outlook for the next few days is good.

The 20 km. hike into Berg Lake beneath the north face is a grunt, but towards the end we are rewarded as, little by little, both the Emperor and north faces edge into view. Our intended route is an ethereal white silk sheet suspended in the sky, turning to red as the sun favours it with the last of its light.

The recommended routes to the base of the north face look unpleasant, so we opt, on Monday, for an approach up the gentle Robson Glacier to sidle under Mt. Waffl. The intense sunshine has rendered the surface of the lower glacier nice and crunchy, giving an excellent grip for Vibram soles. The glacier at this elevation is old and has no secrets, all of the crevasses being in plain view. Crampons and rope are thus much more of a hindrance than a help, yet we pass two parties who have religiously put them on. I have long ago learned that the only rule to follow when in the mountains is that "there are no rules." This is to say that there is no substitute for an intelligent and continuing appraisal of conditions and behaviour in order to find the safest options.

At one point we hike up beside a perfect half catenary arch of ice; a free-standing curve which balances all tensions and allows the pillar of ice to be self-supporting. As we go up, Enrico and I are continually marvelling at all that is around us, for this is a special place.

We closely examine the way by which we will be descending: the Kain Face route. The normal line through ice-falls below the face looks unusually difficult and dangerous, and our discussion with one of the other climbers who has done the Kain route before confirms that this is so. Fortunately, we see that an easier, safer way has become feasible, and we plan to come down this alternative route after our descent of the Kain Face.

We step off the Robson Glacier onto the grassy benches below Waffl Peak, and discover an enchanting place. A waterfall tumbles into a beautiful tarn, and picas or marmots pop in and out of burrows in the rock outcrops. I discover a trilobite in a piece of the scree lying about, and realize that this scene is a patina of the very recent over the incredibly old. In our scratchings on the surfaces of mountains we are very small, very transient, indeed. Perhaps for that very reason we are always seeking to enrich our experiences in this way.

Enrico and I stop for the night here after going up to where we could get our first close-up view of the north face. As far as we can tell, conditions on the face are good, and the access looks all right. We are once again impressed by its beauty and scale. One is always measuring current experiences by the yardstick of those which have come before, and I cannot help thinking of the steeper ice climbing on a higher face which I did in the dark cold of a winter in New Zealand. Then, my partner and I took a day and a half to go up and down. The very view of the north face of Robson, however, ensures that in no way will I take this route lightly.

As we cook dinner, a thunderstorm darkens the sky and soon passes over us. We know that the forecast has predicted the possibility of weak disturbances moving through the area, and we go to sleep expecting to find that these are worse than predicted and we will have to leave the route for another time. The next morning is instead gloriously fine, and some time after starting we are putting suncream on as we find our way, roped, through the glacier below the face. At last, a tricky pull up in soft snow over the bergschrund gets us onto the north face! The snow becomes firmer and at first we move together, always keeping a couple of ice screws between us. Soon, however, harder ice forces us onto our front points and we begin fixed belaying. As we gain height, the ice becomes more and more difficult: an unstable, rotten layer over hard ice. We are now high enough to be committed though, and must continue on.

Every ice screw placement is hard work, for a great hole must be excavated to get down to solid ice, and several swings of our ice tools must be made before they bite. We cannot safely do without this protection, for the surface crud makes a secure footing impossible. Our climbing becomes nerve-wracking. It is difficult to believe to what extent these bad conditions are slowing us down. To compensate, a rich and spectacular view is unfolding below us. We are hanging up amongst the blue of the sky, looking down on Berg Lake and the elegant, intricate lines of the lateral moraines left by the last ice advances.

Finally, the unthinkable happens. Sixteen pitches of rotten ice is a lot to climb in one day; we are not yet up the face, and so we must bivouac on it! We had planned to spend one night on the mountain, and had a stove and a little extra food, but to have to stop on the inhospitable steepness of the face is daunting.

I reach a spot where there is deeper snow, and we work for a while to cut out a ledge with our axes. As we sit in our nylon bivouac bags and brew up, we are treated to the most magical sight that either Enrico or I have seen. On the very edge of the horizon, over the Prairies, a line of cumulonimbus clouds flashes orange with the energy of lightning. Above us, the stars are partly veiled by the eerie, writhing tendrils of the Aurora Borealis. This is my first view of the Northern Lights. We discuss the sky, the climb, and other things, until the need for sleep quietens us.

The next morning we continue up a seemingly endless succession of pitches and at last reach our much hoped-for goal, the summit ridge. We have dreamed of climbing relatively quickly along this to the summit, before going down at least part way today, but as I climb up through soft snow to the crest I am cruelly disappointed. The ridge is made up of barely balanced, wildly contorted rooster combs of double cornices built of the softest snow imaginable. All this fresh, weak snow must be the consequence of a storm a week before. I can poke my hand through the ridge beside me to a drop on the other side just as steep as the way we have come. I barely notice the great view.

Continuing along these pinnacles is out of the question, so with a heavy heart I gingerly climb back down to Enrico with the bad news that we must traverse the entire north face to the left of us.

The ice conditions are worse than ever, but we set off nonetheless, and instead of descending from the summit, night finds us half way along the traverse. Another ledge is excavated, and we settle wearily down.

The next morning we are shrouded in cloud. There is little wind, but we cannot even see each other after half the rope has been led out. The climbing is grim. I experience the helplessness of wanting very much to be off this face, off the mountain, yet we are locked in our prison and must go on enduring the pain in order to free ourselves. Enrico and I say little to each other as we meet at each belay, for all of our energies are going to the climbing. I want to whimper, to give up, as I start leading out on each pitch, but do not because I cannot. We are drawing on those deep wells of determination we never knew were there. Our calves are screaming from pitch after pitch of traversing, and we waste time getting lost amongst the ice-cliffs at the top left-hand side of the face: I go up a couloir of ice and, misjudging the steepness in the murk, find myself suddenly doing some of the most desperate ice-climbing of my life, a long way out from my last screw, only to find that the gully does not lead to the summit but terminates in a massive ice-cliff face. I lower off an ice screw, and after another traversing pitch we at last gain a rib of soft snow and need only pigeon-hole our way up—off our front points after more than 25 pitches.

Being on the flat snow of the summit plateau is such a relief! In the mist the scale is all wrong, and the actual summit pyramid seems to be a hundred metres high. As Enrico comes up, the cloud clears and we see that it is actually just a bump 10 metres up.

We take turns to climb this and photograph each other, and are treated to a view of the land 2.5 kilometres below. Enrico is happy and proud; I am glad we are off the face at last, but we are still not down.

It is windy now, and we quickly head part way along the southeast ridge to scout out a way down. It is only an hour from darkness and we do not wish to begin the descent now and be compelled to make a windswept open bivouac. There is a crevasse just below the summit, and we instead rappel down into this icy cavern to spend the night. With the last of our food we make a thin soup and settle down to a cold but sheltered night.

The next day we emerge to a blustery, snowy white-out. A storm has set in; the stable weather has come to an end.

We retrace our exploratory steps of yesterday and descend until we must rappel through the summit ice-bulges. Below this we continue to make a descending rightwards traverse, aiming to reach the southeast ridge. We can see little, but when we finally begin down the ridge, we get glimpses of the col from which the Kain Face drops. We are both very tired, and when we reach the level snow of the col we have a brief rest.

It is critically important that we choose the right spot from which to begin our descent of the Kain Face, in order to avoid the ice-cliffs which abound on one side of the face. Our enemy in all our efforts at route finding is the white-out. It slows our progress and makes our climbing hesitant.

Snow is falling thickly as I fearfully reverse down over the ever-steepening curve of the face. I am afraid that this part of the slope might avalanche, so until I have run out the full length of the rope, Enrico sits on the col and belays me. I stop once to excavate an anchor, and we continue down. Further down we gain the firm, safe snow in the base of an avalanche runnel, and so can dispense with placing runners. Small sluffs periodically pour down the gully over our legs and hands as the slope rids itself of the new snow, and as long as these remain frequent and regular we are in the safest place.

Each of us is in his own world. We are connected by the rope, but we each have to deal on our own with the never-ending grind of the descent. At one point the runnel goes over steep, bare ice and I moan inwardly but place an ice screw there for Enrico. Each step has been requiring two or three kicks to get to firm ice, and this must be repeated hundreds of times.

By now we are in a real corridor of snow and the volume of the sluffs has increased, so I exit into a smaller runnel. Eventually we are perched above the bergschrund, pounding in our last snow stake to leave as a rappel anchor, and after sliding down the rope into the whiteness we are free of the Kain Face and steep ground!

We now must race to reach that sanctuary below Waffl Peak, where we have cached some extra food and clothing, before darkness catches us. We are exhausted and weak from lack of food, but we have made it this far and have done all the correct things to stay on the right side of safety. Roped up for glacier travel, we stumble away from the steep slopes of the mountain and search our memories to fit the line of the descent route, which we picked out days earlier, with our map and compass and the little of the terrain that we can see now. How trivial this would be in clear weather!

Occasionally we come up against obstacles: a drop-off below us or crevasses which must be avoided. In the lead, I steer us around these obstacles and we are rewarded with more gentle terrain and the realization that our route is working. We put on our headlamps and soon come to an area littered with ice-blocks. Enrico's energy and headlamp both begin to fade, but we must hurry through this spot, and I gently cajole him back to his feet after each rest. Stumbling like drunks we weave our way through the uneven ground, but soon we are free of it. We draw strength from each other and we will come away from this ordeal with a special bond which permits no pretenses or facades, for we have had to rely on each other in the worst possible circumstances.

The last obstacle, a steeper broken-up section of the glacier, swallows us up and requires us to meander around crevasses and sheer drop-offs, left and right, and even backtracking, in order to make any progress. The wind is picking up, snow is falling more heavily and eventually we just cannot see where to go. Damn this white-out, damn this weather, and curse the darkness which has come to compound their impenetrability and seeming hostility when we are so close to easy ground!

We are sparks of warmth and life in a cold world which beats at us without rest. For the moment we are defeated: long past mere exhaustion, we must wait for tomorrow before we search for the right route. We hope to find a sheltered spot where we can seek solace in our bivy bags, but our search of nearby partly filled crevasses yields nothing useable and we must enlarge a wrinkle in the slope in which to huddle from the wind.

Our little hole rapidly fills with snow, and the night goes by in unsatisfactory efforts to keep warm. There are times when I have come back from a trip in the mountains thinking how desperate it would have been to spend a night, or another night, out. This is such a night.

In the morning the wind has reached storm force. It roars down the slope at us, bringing a constant blast of snow and ice crystals, and rising in strength at intervals to batter us so that we must crouch on the ice with our ice-tools and crampon front-points dug in to avoid being picked up and blown away. It is futile to even try to look up-slope, and the only way out is to rig a rappel down the steep ice-wall which bars our way.

With the rope doubled through the eye of an ice screw anchor I clip in and walk down to the edge to find that the rope hangs free of the overhanging ice. I cannot see the end, only 25 metres below, but the rope is swinging around in a way which suggests that it may not reach the bottom. I might not have the energy to prusik back up, so we must remove the anchor and move our way to the right where the slope promises to be shorter. We crab our way across the ice above the drop off, flattening ourselves for really strong gusts. Enrico is just to my right in the screaming maelstrom.

Of what happened in the next seconds, I have absolutely no recollection.

I am confused. I do not know where I am, and my limbs are being held awkwardly by something. I feel the emotions of being brutalized, a sense of great violence having just passed, but there are no images. An urge to panic comes, and I struggle to free myself, although for some reason I do not have the capacity to form thoughts about what may be holding me. I search my mind for something I can hold onto, and my name comes slowly. At first everything is dark. I have no sense of identity to retreat into, nothing.

Perhaps I pass out again. After another frantic struggle my limbs are free, and I begin to see. I have been held by a shallow layer of snow. Down the slope there is the suggestion of a dark shape. Out of all my confusion there comes an insistent message: "that is important!" My mind is slowly coming together, and I know that Enrico must be down there, although at first I cannot remember what we had been doing. There is an overwhelming sense of finality to everything, and dazed, I stagger down to Enrico who is also partly buried.

Enrico has already gone and all that I try is of no help. Enrico was right beside me on the ice above, and later I am able to become certain that he must have lost consciousness with no realization of what was happening, much as I just have. With Enrico, however, there is to be no awakening. One of the greatest events of his life has ended tragically. We have safely gone through so much where others might have succumbed, and have, so close to easy ground, been overwhelmed.

Now I cannot even stand up. My mind is dulled, and the will to survive which burns deep within me does not allow me to let go of my emotions. For days we have had to steel ourselves to endure the unendurable and, still on the mountain, I stay clenched tight like a fist.

The amount of snow which buried us is small, and it was the fall which did the damage. We must have been knocked off the ice by the last part of an avalanche from the steep slopes of the mountain far away, and it would have been a very large avalanche to have travelled so far. The very strong winds and heavy snowfall of the previous day would have caused these unusually dangerous conditions, although the place where we are is a fairly "safe" area, a long way from dangerous slopes. I do not yet know that the unstable weather conditions have given rise to another destructive agent out on the prairies at Edmonton, where a tornado has just left a trail of destruction.

I slide the thin nylon of my bivouac bag over myself to shelter from the storm, and spend three more days without food, lying on my pack not far from Enrico. To avoid the worst effects of dehydration, I eat snow whenever I feel I can spare the warmth, but mostly I succumb to the strong pull of sleep.

We are covered in snow during the first day and night, but after this the storm eases a little and I begin to hope for the rescue which I know will be instigated now that we are overdue. I have always thought in terms of self-rescue, but now I cannot even walk. I blow a series of three shrill blasts on my whistle whenever I think of it, in case a foot party is out there in the gloom.

On the second day the fog breaks up a little and for a short time I hear a helicopter coming and going in the distance, high above me where the clouds must be absent. The clouds return and the next day the weather is uncertain. I begin to realize that if the bad weather sets in again I may be here forever. I can accept this, with great sadness, but I am almost overwhelmed by the thought of my wife, Catherine, my family, and the others whom I will leave behind.

Later on, the clouds swirl, coming and going, but at last I can see the snow-covered terrain about me. For a time I am even able to let the sun warm my weak body. Finally there is the thud-thudding of a helicopter, still unseen, somewhere below me. It works its way in my general direction, when, too far away for the occupants to see me, it suddenly starts towards me. I find out later that the crew have seen a wolverine making its way up the flat Robson Glacier towards us, something has clicked in their minds, and they are now following it up. It is only after this that they see me sitting up, waving my jacket. Perhaps the wolverine has mistaken the sound of my whistle for the distress calls of an animal.

On the second visit of the helicopter the rescue mountaineers come in on a strap under the aircraft and I am soon being loaded onto a stretcher for the flight out. Swinging slowly beneath the helicopter with my face covered, I am aware of little of our passage until the sound of the rotors changes and I am set down with a thud on firm ground, before being loaded into the helicopter itself. On this and many other occasions during the rescue I am at last able to let myself go. I am overcome with grief, and I weep for my dear friend Enrico. His incredible enthusiasm, his laughing face, have gone. Soon his family will know.

After being transferred to an ambulance at the roadhead I am in MacBride hospital. On my left side, the cartilage of my rib cage has been broken in numerous places, three ribs at the back have also been broken and my lung has been punctured (a pneumothorax). My pelvis is broken on my right side, and my lower back is very painful. I am emaciated, and soon my mind is clouded by the morphine which is the first of a series of drugs which I must take for my pain. In spite of this I begin a period of reflection. I am deeply affected by the concern and support of friends who talk to me from Vancouver and who help me so much later on.

During the days when I was waiting on the glacier, when the noise of the storm eased, I was able to hear the waterfall by our first, very pleasant bivouac. Enrico had been really touched by that place, and it may mean something to those who loved and knew him that he passed away so near to there. &

JIMMY AND THE KID

"Jimmy and the Kid" is the shortest of the three pieces included in this chapter on accidents, and yet it is by far the most emotionally complete. Partly that is because economy with words will almost always concentrate the emotional impact of a story, but mainly it is because Steve DeMaio has recognized the need to put the event—the death of a close friend—into a context wider than the climb on which it occurred. By doing so he forces us to confront both our own motives for climbing and our own mortality.

An interesting sidelight to the intrinsic merit of this story is its place as the final exhibit in "The Great Profanity Debate."

One of the great dilemmas facing the editor of a magazine or journal is the disposition of articles by new writers who show promise, but who, literarily speaking, aren't quite there yet. In the case of the *Canadian Alpine Journal* the choice is complicated by the fact that literary merit is not the only, or even neccessarily the prime concern. Consider 1988, when Steve DeMaio sent in a short story describing his solo first ascent of a new route on Mt. Yamnuska.

The writing was not good—on literary grounds the piece had "Reject Me" stamped all over it—but the climb seemed important. Yam had long been the launching pad for new trends and new faces in Rockies climbing, and here was a relative newcomer who had not only done the first ascent of a difficult route, but had done it solo. Furthermore, there was an enthusiasm and intensity which no lack of writing skill could hide, and I felt that to ask for a rewrite would send the wrong message. It had obviously been almost as much of a struggle to write the article as to do the climb and it seemed unlikely that revision would produce any great improvement, so I tidied up the spelling and imposed what grammatical order I could without altering the essential voice of the writer, and published it.

And in came the letters of protest. For at that time Steve DeMaio's "essential voice" was a fairly profane one. He was a young man, full of the fire to climb, full of himself, full of the desire to be seen as a rebel thumbing his nose at the world and its conventions—including the conventions of polite language—and this did not sit comfortably with some long-time readers of the *Canadian Alpine Journal*.

The next winter brought two more submissions from DeMaio. The writing was better—not great, but definitely better—and the profanity level was up. What to do? In the end I decided that profane or not, the writing conveyed the intensity of the climbing experience and that however much I might offend some readers by publishing it, I would be doing an unforgivable disservice to Canadian climbing history by not publishing it.

The volume of unhappy letters and phone calls increased, the club's publications committee scratched its collective head and debated the difference between neccessary profanity and gratuitous profanity, and in the end, to their everlasting credit, decided that honest representation of the climbing experience was more important than worrying about how many times any particular word appeared.

Vindication of this approach arrived with the submission in the following year of "Jimmy and the Kid," surely one of the most sensitive and haunting climbing articles ever published in this country and one that would probably never have been written if DeMaio had had his knuckles rapped for the 'bad language' of his first literary efforts.

~ David Harris

Jimmy and the Kid

Steve DeMaio

Feeling, again, the first in a series of small holds, the limestone cut into the fleshy pads on my fingers. I was aware of the sun on my neck, the rack sling on my shoulder, my presence on the cliff. Too aware, but not of the rock around me, rather of my presence in another place, removed from the cliff, somehow above and away as though I was watching myself pounding in a piton and dipping into my chalk bag. Observing, almost as one might observe a gladiator, from the rows of stone in the Coliseum walls above, sitting quietly in the heat, watching his struggle for survival within the arena. I was preoccupied with the clatter of chariots on cobbles in the streets behind rather than with the clash of iron on iron below, but still aware that my reality lay in the arena, down there in the dust and not here at this vista, nor in the clamor from the streets behind where horses' hooves clicked on the hard stone...the hard stone...

My eyes focused again on my white knuckles wrapped firmly around the shaft of my hammer. Almost shocked, I heard only the echo of its last blow. In this state, I knew the arena would show no mercy. I had grown to recognize this feeling and learned to act on it—unlike the gladiator, I had a choice.

Could this be true enthusiasm; failing without frustration? Pumped already, I was still fifteen feet below the crux moves. Uncharacteristically, the idea of backing off the pitch did not disappoint me.

On every move, on every pitch, I strive to measure the difficulty and danger of the climbing against my mental and physical capability as well as my ability to focus on the task at hand. I continuously make the decision, 'To climb, or not to climb'. Here I concluded '...not to climb'.

By no means was I shocked. I knew I wasn't fit. The idea had been to go out with the Kid and have a good time.

In an earlier time I'd have been flushed with frustration; hard climbing was the good time. Partners were relevant only in that they made a more difficult route possible. Today, just being out with the Kid, even though I was about to lower off, defeated by a difficult section, I was having a good time.

I rapped back down to the belay. "Sorry, old man. I'm just not tough enough for it right now; must have had the devil up my ass when I led it last time."

In four years I had not backed off a limestone lead. I had been proud of the fact, perhaps even quietly arrogant. But now I was content to let the

Kid take over the lead. Both of us knew it was okay to climb hard, scary pitches; but we had learned that they had to be done safely and in control. There was no anger or frustration in the fact that I was now unable to climb a pitch I had led just over a year ago.

Bringing tension onto the belay slings, I strained above to see if Jeff had reached the high point, and hollered, "Don't be shy to drill a bolt up there if you have to!"

The pitch had been led without it, so technically it would be unethical to drill one. But we were here to climb and have fun, not break a femur.

In these last years we had learned the fragility of our egglike bodies and the Kid did not hesitate. He put a bolt in.

Rather than second the pitch, I clipped on the jumars and lowered out of the belay in a complex system of tension, leaving a minimum of gear behind. A favorite motto of mine in my formative years had been "I make up with enthusiasm what I lack in experience." It seemed now that I made up with experience what I lacked in fitness!

Enthusiasm? I believe it was still there, but in a different form than it once was. I'd had what I still consider to be the best day's climbing of my life on this cliff. What made it my best effort was that I was on fire, a rebel (but with a cause); with a desire to test myself, a desire to climb at the cutting edge of my ability, to howl in the face of protectionless pitches, to roar on new terrain. I was lean, real lean. A set of sixty pull-ups was no problem. The 'healthy dissatisfaction' that I lived with daily spurred me on to do bigger, better and increasingly more improbable projects.

"Wildboys always get their way!" we said.

Since then we had learned that there are things that we have no power or control over, things that you can't change no matter how fit, strong or lean you are.

When a fellow climber falls, reality overwhelms the power and joy in the struggle of difficult climbing. Naive, passionate enthusiasm becomes pain; fervor, folly, valor become vain. All become futile.

. . . .

Shrouded in cloud, we cried out into the mist. On the north face of Lougheed, Brian Wallace had fallen. Gone, hopefully to another place where he could continue to be the wildboy he truly was, getting his way.

The rain first appeared sympathetic, comforting almost, to our mourning spirits. Even the first chill in our damp bodies seemed to help deaden the guilt of our own survival, though soon it would threaten it.

With vengeance, we pounded piton after piton into the rain-drenched rock, questing continuously for the crack or seam into which we could bury our iron. There were no thoughts of our friend, or his death. Only the task: to get away, away from this place, this storm, this North Face…an arena turned savage.

The wall went dark earlier than it should have. Mist clung to us and to the dripping limestone. Soaked wet through, our fevered minds heavy with the day's events, we cleared rubble from a small ledge to form our perch for the night. Snow collected in our collars, chilling already chilled bodies.

At first it seemed right, honorable almost, to endure this for our friend—with our friend. We were alone, but not so alone; cold but not so cold. Brian was with us, pushing us.

"No one sleeps tonight."

Jeff's voice cut the silence. I made no reply. He didn't expect one. Both of us continued in our preparations for the night.

To make room for my numb feet I pulled my rock shoes and chalk bag out of my pack. I knew I probably wouldn't be able to find them in the morning. I didn't care.

Somehow in the gloom, Jeff could see the top pocket of my pack folded over onto my lap. "James, can you get that other chocolate bar out?"

I heard the question but didn't comprehend it. Drifting away, soon I believed that he had not said anything. Vaguely I became aware of half a chocolate bar being stuffed into my mouth…

Why weren't "they" coming with hot chocolate or blankets? I wondered. Gazing into the snow-filled blackness… "There's that cliff below us…and that shale slope. They'll never get up them…in the dark…in the snow…"

I stood up on the ledge. More snow fell into my collar, my body rattled harder. "Jeffrey, you're going to have to take care of me."

There was no reply; I didn't expect one. We both knew that in the next eight hundred feet of steep, snow-covered shale there would be no anchors. Together we would be alone, like Gladiators at the mercy of the arena. We had no choice.

. . . .

That was almost a year ago, on the steep, rotten North Face of Lougheed just across the valley. The enthusiasm we shared now was far different from that of our naive howls of '86 and '87. Somehow, now, I felt old.

On the last pitch, my limbs felt heavy and I moved slowly. Topping out I looked left toward the summit, thinking that there I might find an answer. Wind lifted the hair under my helmet. I crouched and pounded in a belay station. Looking back down the route I tried to muster a howl, but it was flat and empty. I didn't try again. Why had I come? There was no answer. I didn't expect one.

I didn't climb again that summer. 🔊

IV A.O. WHEELER AND
THE ALPINE CLUB OF CANADA

A.O. Wheeler was, for almost 40 years, the most influential mountaineer in Canada. Surveyor, mapmaker, writer and climber, he was the first president of the Alpine Club of Canada (ACC), serving from 1906–1910, editor of the *Canadian Alpine Journal* for 22 years, and author of *The Selkirk Range*, the most important and impressive work ever written about Canada's interior ranges. Elected an honorary member of the Alpine Club of England in 1908 (his sponsor was Edward Whymper), he was a pioneer in glaciological studies in Canada, fought in the Riel Rebellion, surveyed the Selkirks along the line of the Canadian Pacific Railway, ran camps and climbs for the ACC, inspired the first ascents of Mts. Robson and Logan, and culminated his amazing career by surveying the 1,000-kilometre long divide of the Rocky Mountains. He was in every way a busy and important man.

Fortunately, Wheeler was a good writer. He enlivened his writing with personal anecdotes which betray a keen sense of observation and a shrewd understanding of human personality. It is fair to say that he was pre-eminent among Canadian mountain authors active in the first third of this century and in many ways was the most significant of the ones who were born in Canada.

The influence of Wheeler on the development of climbing in Canada makes an interesting subject. Clearly he had strong views, and he ran the camps of the ACC with a stern hand. Women were expected to wear skirts out of camp and for a suitable distance thereafter, before changing into more practical knickers.

Certainly his principle in running the ACC was safety first. He was overly committed to the view of guided climbing, which had been largely discarded by better British climbers since the 1880s. Yet Wheeler never abandoned the notion that guides were essential to safety in the mountains, and straightforward climbs which an average mountaineer could easily manage continued to be led by guides at

ACC camps long after such climbing had passed from the scene in Europe and the United States. Thus, while the ACC had an excellent safety record, its record in pioneering bold new ascents was much less impressive.

Wheeler's chief mountain interest was exploration. The idea of the new, technical route on an already climbed summit does not seem to have provided him with inspiration. Alpine Club members do not seem to have been driven under his leadership to attempt more and more challenging ascents. Conrad Kain is somewhat unique in this period in his personal search for technical challenge in the mountains. But his activities did not always meet with Wheeler's approval. Finding himself bored at the Mt. Robson reconnaissance camp of 1912 (Wheeler insisted that no one attempt Robson, as he wanted it left for the official Robson camp in the following year) Kain went off and made a solo first ascent of Whitehorn, a 3,400-metre (11,000-foot) peak northwest of Robson. When he returned, Wheeler told him the ascent would never be recognized. (He was wrong.)

As for the ACC, which Wheeler co-founded with Elizabeth Parker in 1906, it has had a distinguished history which is considerably less dull than many would suppose. It broke ground by admitting women from the day of its inception, and in the early years women made up a third of the membership. Its achievements in publishing the *Canadian Alpine Journal* alone should earn it the commendation of all climbers; fully 40 percent of the material presented in this volume would never have been published without this support, and the *Canadian Alpine Journal* has remained unchallenged as the journal of record for mountaineering and mountain exploration in Canada since 1907.

Critics, of course, have always looked at the club's patchy climbing record, but the reality is that great ascents do not come from club outings, they are made by individual climbers struck by inspiration. In the early years the ACC played a more significant role in opening up new mountain opportunities by sponsoring expeditions (the Logan Expedition, for example) and scheduling their annual camps in remote areas. But mountaineering has changed, and better alpinists today have the mobility and motivation to make their own way into the mountains. Nonetheless, nominally or otherwise, most of the better climbers in Canada today do belong to the ACC.

The ACC of the 1990s is a business-like organization which runs a chain of 15 mountain huts, sponsors ten regional sections across the country, publishes a quarterly newsletter, operates a clubhouse and an office in Canmore and continues to run camps and courses. As recent articles from regional newsletters attest, its operation continues to generate controversy, particularly in light of the rigorous environmentalism of some of its members, who view huts operations and large gatherings in the backcountry as destructive of wilderness values. The ACC has also become involved in the recent phenomena of sport climbing, sponsoring indoor climbing competitions, which have been described graphically as an "atrocity against alpinism." While this trend was solemnly criticized by *Explore* magazine among others, the ACC's harshest critics have always come from within, and the club will no doubt roll happily into the next century with members hotly contesting and debating the policies of Canada's national mountaineering club, just as they have always done.

~ Bruce Fairley

ROGERS PASS: THE SELKIRK SUMMIT

Rogers Pass, located in the Selkirk Mountains between the towns of Golden and Revelstoke, is the most famous mountain pass in Canada, not only because its discovery gave the Canadian Pacific Railway the great breakthrough it needed to punch the railway line through the Selkirk Mountains, but also because it was the first great centre of alpinism in North America. Today the climber approaching the peaks of this region may well begin his journey from a mountain hut run by the Alpine Club of Canada and named the Wheeler Hut in honour of one of the first great exponents of the climbing to be found in this magnificent range. Many of the climbs Wheeler knew remain popular today, for the powerful scenery of the pass, combined with the great variety of rock ramparts and glacial features, present irresistible challenges.

One who knows something of Wheeler and his attitudes cannot resist a smile at the way he opens the article reprinted below: "Word has gone forth…" It is almost like a Biblical invocation, summoning the faithful to the sacred shrine. But the piece is a good example of Wheeler at his best, carefully selecting amusing anecdotes and lively stories to paint a human face on the canvas of the wilderness of the soaring Selkirks. And certainly Wheeler could claim to be the greatest authority alive on the climbing and exploration of Rogers Pass, for he knew most of those involved personally.

Mountaineering literature takes a different strain these days from the almost naive gusto of this piece. But 65 years later it is still refreshing to turn to the patriarch of the grandest centre of mountaineering in a young and emerging nation. For whatever else one may say of Wheeler, his enthusiasm and love of the mountains were beyond question.

∽ Bruce Fairley

Rogers Pass at the Summit of the Selkirks

Arthur O. Wheeler

Word has gone forth that the 1929 camp of the Alpine Club of Canada will be held at Rogers Pass during the latter half of July. It is on the route of the Canadian Pacific Railway across the Selkirk Range. Only one other camp of the Club has been held there—in 1908—and the decision to repeat it after a lapse of twenty years calls up many recollections of the early days.

Rogers Pass is at the climax of Selkirk scenery. From it the water flows east and west through the range. East by way of the deep, dark gorge of Bear Creek, a tributary of Beaver River; west by the valley of the Illecillewaet River, a valley filled with semi-tropical, primeval forest, tangle-foot and devil's club, alder-grown avalanche slides, giant rockfalls, box canyons and swirling torrents.

First among explorers came Walter Moberly in 1865, who penetrated to the forks of the Illecillewaet River at Albert Canyon. He continued his exploration up the north fork, but it was late in the season and his Indians refused to go up the east fork, fearing they would be caught by the winter snows and never get out of the mountains.

Following in his footsteps came Major A.B. Rogers, the "Railway Pathfinder," who, in 1881, explored up the east fork to the summit of the pass—subsequently named after him—and then discovered the route adopted by the railway. At that time he named Mt. Sir Donald, whose towering heights dominated the pass, "Syndicate Peak" after the recently formed syndicate to complete the construction of the gigantic railway enterprise. The object in view was to discover the shortest feasible route through the range, for Moberly had already established the possibility of a low-level route by following the Columbia River around the Big Bend. Had the main object been to find the best possible scenic route, no more magnificent one could have been found than that through Rogers Pass.

The decision was made and construction forthwith begun and pushed through as rapidly as possible. In 1883, Sir Sandford Fleming, Chief Government Engineer, accompanied by the Revd. Dr. George Grant, Principal of Queen's University, made his famous trip over the road through the mountains, so vividly portrayed in his charmingly written book *England and Canada, A Summer Tour Between Old and New Westminster.*

It was on this occasion, while resting on a grassy knoll at the summit of Rogers Pass, that Sir Sandford, inspired by the towering heights on all sides, conceived the idea in a leisure moment of organizing a Canadian Alpine Club. In his own words: "The horses are still feeding and we have some time at our command. As we view the landscape, we feel as if some memorial should be preserved of our visit here, and we organize a Canadian Alpine Club. The writer, as a grandfather, is appointed interim president; Dr. Grant, secretary; and my son, S. Hall Fleming, treasurer. A meeting was held and we turn to one of the springs rippling down to the Illecillewaet and drink success to the organization. Unanimously we carry resolutions of acknowledgement to Major Rogers, the discoverer of the pass, and to his nephew for assisting him." Although a whimsical conception, due to the superb mountain influences all around, it was a prophetic inspiration; for when, twenty-three years later, the club was organized, Sir Sandford Fleming was elected its first honorary president, a position he filled until his death in 1915, and his keen interest and support were strong factors of success during the early years of its growth.

Completion of the railway through the Selkirks in 1885 led to the coming of mountaineers, explorers and lovers of Nature. The following year, 1886, Glacier House, a pretty little chalet nestling in the forest at the base of Mt. Abbott, and facing a fine cascade falling 1,100 ft. from the slopes of Eagle Peak directly opposite, was built by the Railway Company. It was right beside the track and was built with the object of "feeding the trains," for the palatial dining car had not then been introduced. It soon became apparent that this beautiful spot, apart from the train service, would be a favourite with mountain climbers and votaries of the great out-of-doors. A manager was installed and a register book opened. It has been computed by Prof. Chas. E. Fay that during the first year thereafter, 1887, independently of the daily stopping of the trains for meals, some 708 guests registered at the chalet.

A log book also was opened and was a joy to read. The unbiased sentiments of those who braved the terrors of the surrounding peaks with the Swiss guides stationed at the chalet were most confiding. One entry in particular appealed to me. It had reference to the climatic conditions at the Selkirks' summit during the latter part of the summer, which, to put it mildly, are somewhat variable. The entry was by a disappointed climber who had waited a long time to make the ascent of Mt. Sir Donald. It read as follows:

> "First it rained, and then it snew, and then it friz, and
> then it thew, and then it fogged, and then it blew,
> And very shortly after then, it rained and snew and
> friz and thew and fogged and blew, again."

In 1888 came the Revd. William Spotswood Green, the author of *Among the Selkirk Glaciers,* one of the most delightful books of the mountains that has been written. The story of Mr. Green's experiences in his survey and mapping of the Selkirks in the vicinity of Rogers Pass is a classic of the region, and his wit and humour as he tells the tale will be enjoyed by all who have had the good fortune to read his book, which alas! I fear, is out of print. The sharp peak on the ridge north from Mt. Bonney was named Mt. Green in his honour.

Mt. Sir Donald is the highest peak of the Sir Donald Range, 10,808 ft. above sea level. It is situated at the southern extremity, directly above the Illecillewaet Névé. A delightful path through the primeval forest leads beside a rushing, leaping torrent from Glacier House to the foot of the massif and to the ice tongue of the Illecillewaet Glacier. It is very beautiful along the shady pathway. The huge boles of giant fir, cedar and hemlock are all around; long beards of moss depend from the limbs. The undergrowth is thick with shin-tangle, honeysuckles, white-flowered rhododendrons and the ever-present devil's club, fascinating in its bright-green tropical foliage and scarlet berries, but always ready to repel the intruder with its sharp, poisonous spines. Luscious huckleberries of several varieties are plentiful and furnish acceptable refreshment to the traveller. Many feet have trod this path by lantern light on their way to make the ascent of the mountain.

Thirty years ago the icefall of the Illecillewaet Glacier was a magnificently spectacular spectacle from the station platform at Glacier House, falling 5,000 feet from skyline until lost to view amid the forest tree-tops. As each daylight train rushed in, the crowds on board assembled on the platform and filled the air with cries of wonder and delight. One of the most frequent questions was: "How deep is the ice?" to be answered by those who knew, "Thousands of feet." Alas! for the inaccuracy of human knowledge! To-day the immense cascade of broken, glittering ice has so greatly melted that the ground floor rock shows even above the treetops. In those days a great cave was annually carved out from the ice tongue by the sub-surface torrent. It was possible to penetrate into it for a considerable distance, and it was a huge delight to visitors. The C.P. Railway Company was supposed to be responsible for this spectacular feature, as evidenced by the lady from Seattle who, having gazed at it in awe and wonder, wanted to know if it was a real glacier or one put there by the C.P.R. for an advertisement. This impression of the creation of spectacular effect was not confined alone to the Railway Company. I was once camped at Albert Canyon, close beside the station. My men were busy loading a pack-train to go farther afield. Suddenly an express train crowded with passengers from the Orient rushed in and stopped directly opposite my camp. In a moment all was wildest confusion. The horses became unmanageable, reared on their hind legs and careered around with men swearing frantically and trying to hold them. One horse broke away, dashed into the brush, leaped a log four feet high, burst its cinches and scattered its pack to the four winds. The people on the train, who had been thoroughly enjoying the miserable spectacle, clapped their hands, waved their handkerchiefs and shouted "encore."

Mt. Sir Donald was first ascended in 1890 by Carl Sulzer and Emil Huber, of the Swiss Alpine Club. The same year they also ascended to Uto Peak, 9,610 ft., the next peak north.

The first ascent by a lady was made by Mrs. E.E. Berens, of Kent, England, on her honeymoon. The important question then was what should she wear for the occasion. A council of war was held by the ladies at the hotel, and it was decided that a pair of her husband's knickerbockers was the proper thing. She naturally chose his best pair, and was surprised several times during the day to find herself holding them up by a finger and thumb as though it had been a skirt. Such a thing would not occur now-a-days. Her remarks in the log-book were indicative of wisdom: "Be wise, friends, and do not despise a mountain; it always gets the better of you in the end... In climbing, look for the next hand and foothold and nothing more, for if you look down it is apt to frighten you and if you look up you get discouraged."

In 1899 the Railway Company brought to Glacier House the two Swiss guides, Eduard Feuz and Christian Hasler, of Interlaken. They were fine fellows who have passed, insofar as the Canadian Rockies are concerned, although old Eduard still climbs in Switzerland. We have their sons and nephew now with us, and prime favourites they are: Eduard Jr., Ernst and Walter Feuz, Christian Hasler, and in addition we have Rudolph Aemmer and Conrad Kain. For endless patience, indomitable courage, steadfast perseverance and unsurpassed good temper they have no superiors. They take the veriest embryos on any and every climb; they haul them up cliffs, lower them down precipices, place their hands and feet where they should go, soothe their ruffled feelings, carry their paraphernalia and cheerfully assume the responsibilities of life and death; then, just before reaching the summit, they stand to one side, take off their hats and say, "After you, sair"; you step on the summit, and, according to mountaineering etiquette, have made a first ascent or otherwise, that is blazoned forth far and wide.

The coming of the Swiss guides created a new era. Climbing became more general, and not confined only to mountaineers of repute in alpine circles and mountain clubs.

In 1890 came members of the Appalachian Club of Boston, represented by the "Grand Old Man" so well-known at our camps and in mountaineering circles the world over, our distinguished honorary member, Prof. Chas. E. Fay, of Tufts College, Massachusetts. He was much impressed, and his coming was soon followed by other ardent members whose names are well-known to us through the annals of the Club: Abbot, Thompson, Wilcox, Allen, Parker, Noyes, Little and others. They made many first ascents in the Asulkan Valley and in the vicinity of Rogers Pass, noticeably Mts. Castor and Pollux, the Dome, the Rampart, Mt. Cheops, Eagle Peak, and Mt. Rogers.

I first met Prof. Fay at Glacier House in 1901. We then discussed the formation of an American Alpine Club, organized in 1902, of which he was the first president. I was one of its original members and have been since organization. This year the great and much appreciated honour of life membership has been conferred upon me. We also discussed the formation of a Canadian Alpine Club, but the time was not yet ripe, and it was not until 1906 that our Club was organized.

In 1897 the Alpine Club (England) was represented in the Selkirks and the Main range by Prof. J. Norman Collie, also one of our distinguished honorary members, Prof. H.B. Dixon and G.P. Baker, who brought with them the first Swiss guide in the Canadian Rockies, the veteran Peter Sarbach, of Zermatt.

These keen mountaineers have made history in the Main and Selkirk ranges, and the stories of their doings are found in the issues of *Appalachia* and the *Alpine Journal*; also in the pages of Wheeler's *Selkirk Range*.

Glacier House resort soon became famous and additions were necessary to supply the demand for accommodation. A very charming and efficient lady, Mrs. J.J. Young, was made manager. Two distinct qualities stood out: a keen sense of humour and a sympathetic interest in all with whom she came in contact. She was lovingly known to those around her as "Mother Young," and all, from the highest plutocrat among her guests to the lowliest section man of the railway service, brought their needs and woes to her, to be met with ready sympathy and a humorous smile, and many of the needs were supplied from her own resources. Her particularly keen sense of humour furnished an endless supply of anecdotes culled chiefly from the idiosyncrasies of her guests. Two instances will suffice: A fine-looking old gentleman registered at the hotel and was given a room. Shortly after he appeared at the office in a state of great excitement. "Madam! I cannot sleep in that room." "Why?" asked Mrs. Young, "it is one of our best." "My dear Madam, the bed is not in the magnetic meridian." "Well!" replied Mrs. Young, "can you not put it there?" "Oh, may I?" "Certainly; you can put it outside the window, if you like." And he went off quite happy, with his little pocket compass, to put his bed in the magnetic meridian.

Then there was the young midshipman who was on his way to Hong Kong. Mrs. Young was wakened in the middle of the night by the violent ringing of his room bell. Thinking some one was sick, she went to see. On opening the door, she discovered a wild-eyed youth in pyjamas who could only exclaim: "My tickets! My tickets!" Having calmed him down and extracted an explanation, she found that his railway and steamboat tickets, supplied him by the British Admiralty, were in one of the pockets of his tennis flannels sent that day to the laundry. Mrs. Young forthwith went to the laundry and retrieved the tennis flannels, and, sure enough, the tickets, reduced to a ball of pulp in the washing, were in one of the trouser pockets. Thanks to Mrs. Young's good offices and those of Mr. Tom Kilpatrick, Superintendent of the Mountain Division of the Railway, matters were promptly straightened out and the youth sent on his way rejoicing.

From the very beginning the hotel was a favourite. It has a most charming location in a little cultivated clearing cut from the primeval forest. Towering heights surround it on all sides. The mighty peak of Mt. Sir Donald seems to hang over it; and the wildly broken icefall of the Illecillewaet Glacier, glistening in the sun's rays, is in full view. Directly opposite, a strikingly picturesque cascade, with a little summerhouse at its crest, leaps down 1,100 feet amidst the trees. North, a glorious view of Rogers Pass with the snowy spires of the Swiss Peaks beyond; west, a far-reaching vista of the Illecillewaet Valley bounded by snow-crowned monarchs, capped by billows of white cumulus cloud. The deeply cut, densely forested valleys are filled with violet haze, creating an atmosphere of mystery and imagination that belongs to the Selkirks alone.

Nightly around the blazing log fire in the assembly room the crowd gathered and swapped yarns, told of their day's experiences and planned for the morrow. There were all kinds and nationalities, from the finished mountaineer to the passing tourist, and hair-breadth escapes were well in order. I remember one occasion of great excitement: A party had gone to climb Mt. Sir Donald. They had been seen through the big telescope on the summit during the afternoon and were expected back for dinner. Dinner was over and darkness had begun to fall. A search party was suggested, and it seemed that action should shortly be taken. Just then they hove in sight and a chorus went up, "Where have you been?" "Why are you so late?" A German gentleman of the party acted as spokesman: "Oh! Ve have had such an experience. Ven coming down, ve vere captured by an avalanche, vhich took us down ze mountain side, and my only vonder vos vhy ve did stop."

The chief charm of the hotel was its home-like atmosphere and the informal hospitality that led to a fine feeling of comradery and good-fellowship. It is deeply to be regretted that for the time being the hotel is not in operation, and that climatic conditions have caused the present building to be condemned. There is little doubt, however, that when circumstances permit a new hotel will be built, and that Glacier House will again come into its own. The location is too splendidly beautiful and the scenic attractions far too unique to be allowed to remain as an unvisited part of the mountain wilderness. ❦

CLIMBING CAMPS

Climbing camps were once the backbone of Canadian climbing. They were established to simplify arrangements for individuals to climb in particularly attractive and sometimes remote areas. They also provided opportunities for the inexperienced to meet and climb with more seasoned climbers. Because of the companionable setting, the challenge of the activity pursued, and the absence of other distractions, friendships and memories formed that often lasted a lifetime. Phyllis Munday, one of Canada's greatest pioneer climbers, still attended Alpine Club of Canada camps well into her 80s.

Early club camps, particularly in the Rockies, were grandiose in purpose and execution, involving sometimes up to two hundred people, including European guides and climbers from all over the world. Participants did not just climb. They listened to informational lectures presented by climbers occasionally of world-famous stature (Edward Whymper among them), sketched and made notes on natural history, sang at campfires, presented impromptu skits and attended Sunday services. While today most climbs made from these camps appear modest, the 1913 gathering of the Alpine Club of Canada at Mt. Robson produced some very fine climbing, including several attempts on different routes on Robson and the famous ascent of the peak by Kain, MacCarthy and Foster.

Admittedly camps today are not as popular; the mountains are more accessible to everyone. Also, environmental considerations loom larger today; pictures of the jolly campers in the Lake O'Hara meadows in the early days are now used by the Park Service as an example of modern forces of erosion at work! However, the capacity to create friendships remains a lure which continues to attract climbers to today's more modest camps, and given the special closeness that often develops at such gatherings it seems odd that they are not more popular. As usual, the irrepressible Conrad Kain had some sly observations to make on the conduct of Alpine Club of Canada general mountaineering camps. The extracts on the 1909 club camp at Lake O'Hara printed below were taken from his diaries and stitched together by his friend and biographer, J. Monroe Thorington. Kate McQueen's story is from a camp in the summer of 1914.

↝ John Manual

Our Summer Camp at Lake O'Hara

Conrad Kain

Throughout an entire week we were busy at putting up 50–60 tents, a difficult task. It was necessary to collect poles for doing this, and to fit them up with brush for beds, and prepare everything for the arrival of club-members and guests. We had assistance during the last few days (six young club-members), and with hard work things were ready by August 1st. Every evening we were almost dead from fatigue, and suffered martyrdom from mosquitoes. We were cursing in five or six different languages! Our necks swollen, we ourselves somewhat feverish—there was nothing to do but get out. Mr. Fynn fled several times to timber-line, since when one ascends and emerges from the woods the mosquitoes cease.

Sunday was a day of rest. I proposed to ascend Mt. Victoria. Past Lake O'Hara and the lovely waterfalls, I followed the little brook coming from Lake Oesa; it is renowned as being a frozen lake, open during only four to six weeks of the year. From it there is a magnificent outlook: two glaciers go directly into the lake, in which blocks of ice float. I took a short rest. Suddenly the thunder of avalanche! An avalanche fell right into the lake. That was something to see! I continued over scree to Abbot Pass, between Mts. Lefroy and Victoria.

This pass is well known in Canadian climbing circles; there, on August 3rd, 1896, occurred the first accident in the Rockies: a Mr. Abbot fell on the slopes of Mt. Lefroy and was killed. I ascended Mt. Victoria in a short time, as I discovered old tracks. It is one of the finest tours in the Rockies and may be compared with Swiss climbs. The view of the famous Lake Louise and the Chalet is exceptionally beautiful.

During descent I met on the pass the Swiss guide Aemmer with another man, who also was in the mountains for the first time. They descended the "Death Trap," so called on account of avalanche danger. I returned to camp by my same route and went on to the two little lakes near Lake O'Hara that I had seen from Victoria's summit. Oh, that was a lovely picture, unforgettable and indescribable! A bit of forest separates the two lakes. One is deep blue, the other light green, hemmed in by candle-stick firs. Countless moss flowers grew on the bank. I thought at the moment of my old mountain friends at home, those who love flowers so much. It was like a dream, and I am not yet sure but that I dreamed it all.

That evening the first guests arrived, about fifty people, and we had our first big camp-fire! On the following day we made the first tour on Mt. Huber (named for a Swiss, one of the first explorers of the Rocky

Mountains); Mr. Fynn, three men from Calgary and I. Where the climbing begins we fixed a rope for the parties following, for Mt. Huber is selected as the "climbing mountain" for graduating members who wish to become "active."

First we attempted to reach the summit from the right, but the bergschrund forced us back. So we went to the left, over a rather steep ice-slope, cut big steps, after which it went easily to the top. About six o'clock in the evening we were back in camp and were received with congratulations. The place was full of tourists (mostly women). There were also three Swiss guides there, which the C.P.R. had loaned for several weeks to make excursions in the vicinity of the camp.

Next day quite a number went on Mt. Huber, led by the Swiss and some amateur guides of the Club. I went with twenty people to Lake McArthur, a fine lake in which a glacier terminates, so that little icebergs float about, most interesting to see. In the background is Mt. Biddle, with Mt. Schaeffer to the left, named for a lady well known in the Rockies who has carried out many explorations. On the way back we saw numerous mountain goats.

That evening all the registered guests were present; more than two hundred people! Not in vain have so many pleasant stories been written about the camp-fires in the Rockies! It makes a unique picture to see so many people grouped about such a huge fire, lying, sitting, standing. There are songs, laughing and joking. Recitations are given; in short, everything in the best humor.

When I went into the tent I saw a familiar face sticking out of a sleeping-bag—I could not recall whose it was. Next morning, at table, I recognized him: it was Moritz Inderbinen, whom I had met on the Sudlenzspitze in Switzerland. A gentleman as guide! He had already travelled for twenty-three summers with his employer and had been to all parts of the earth.

Again I had a party for Mt. Huber and by evening was very tired; so I sneaked off to the two beautiful lakes in the forest and stayed there until dusk. I fell asleep, for the mosquitoes were not so bad. Later that evening, by the camp-fire, I became acquainted with the famous trapper, Jim Simpson. ❧

Hip-Hip-Hurrah!

Conrad Kain

Again a group for Mt. Huber. Fifty-five people all told. It was a frosty morning, and when we, climbing through a gully from Lake O'Hara, reached the pass between Wiwaxy Peaks and Mt. Huber, it began to storm and to snow. Everyone turned back. Only Mr. Fynn, who also led a party, and I with three women and a man, waited in the shelter of the rocks for better weather.

I promised sunshine, and told amusing little stories of climbing and from experiences as a guide, so that the people would not lose their courage and desire for the ascent. We waited in the cold, and at last, at last, a blue patch appeared in the sky! For a few minutes the sun even appeared through the fog. Right above the pass some easy climbing begins. But the rocks were very cold and progress was slow. Mr. Fynn had to turn back with his party, as one of the ladies had almost frozen her fingers. I would have had to do the same thing if I had not fortunately brought several extra pairs of gloves for my women. Now we came to the glacier, which we ascended diagonally, then over a short ice-ridge to a wall of rock, a step which interrupts the glacier. Then over the glacier again to the col between Mt. Victoria and our peak.

The weather changed in the meantime, but as the ladies knew that we were the only ones out of fifty-five people who had not given up the tour they were full of joy and desire to reach the summit, despite the obstacle presented by the unfavorable weather. I promised to bring them safely back to camp, and told them they should not be dismayed by the fog, and that if only a wind did not arise we would attain the peak without trouble. In this fashion I kept up their confidence and courage.

The man had nothing much to say (as is usual when ladies are in the majority) and without difficulty we reached the ice-slope, now covered with fresh snow, where there are the only really dangerous places of the whole excursion. I was obliged to improve the old steps, which Mr. Fynn and I had made several days before, as they had melted out considerably, but without especial incident we reached the summit of Mt. Huber. For the few minutes of our halt we had a good view down to camp.

While descending the risky spots on the ice-slope a wind sprang up, and away went our good steps in the snow. That was not pleasant for me, for, as guide, I could not go first in descending and my tourists were all beginners. I put the strongest woman in front. Slowly and with great care we went down step by step. A single mis-step would have been fatal, for I could not anchor myself. I breathed easier when the last woman descended over the little bergschrund.

As we approached camp I announced our approach by a loud yell. Everyone came toward us, more than a hundred people with the Club President at their head. Mr. Wheeler offered me his hand and said: "I thank you, Conrad. Now you have your witnesses, and I see that it is just as Dr. P. wrote to me about you, that Conrad never stops until he has completed his task." As he finished his speech, the young men lifted me on their shoulders and carried me to the camp-fire, with a fearful shouting of "Hip-Hip-Hurrah," and singing "He is a jolly good fellow!" Naturally the ladies were also given a thunderous Hurrah.

The Swiss guides present in camp did not join in the felicitations. When I entered the sleeping-tent, one said to me rather scornfully in his dialect: "Well, they thought quite a lot of you today!" [*"No, heit ham's Di aber verehrt!"*] and began to grumble that such a trip was a stupidity and that in his home no one went out in such weather. I replied: "If I had not met with even bigger storms in Switzerland I would not be able to say very much about the dangers of the mountains!" He: "O, what do you know about Switzerland?" And I: "I know Switzerland, your home, better than you do, and certainly have made more ascents there than you!"

And when he still looked unconvinced I became angry, hunted up my guide's book and threw it to him. He read it and discovered the truth of my assertions. He approached me pleasantly: "Don't be angry! You look much too young, and one can hardly believe that you have travelled so much." We shook hands and were friends. ⋟

Trials of the Campfire

Kate McQueen

Now was it there, or at one of the other camps where Colonel [W. W.] Foster showed his presence of mind. Attending this camp was quite an eminent English painter [C. J. Collings]. I think he was staying in Salmon Arm. He had joined the camp because he was to do some painting. Well, he was on the camp fire program and I think Colonel Foster was perhaps chairman. This artist was simply carried away by his own description of the lovely colourings in nature up here. Well, he was just having a lovely time. But it was getting on, and the camp fire dismisses early because some of the members are getting up very early for a climb. So something had to be done. Something tactful. Well, Colonel Foster had it. Very quietly he approached the speaker with a drink. The painter gladly accepted the drink, and while he drank the next speaker was called. ❦

A LIGHTER VIEW

Very little serious climbing took place in Canada during the years of the Second World War. Nonetheless, the Alpine Club of Canada continued to hold its annual camps. The military/climbing connection was much stronger in the 1940s than today, yet strangely there had never been any attempt to establish a mountain division in the Canadian forces. The absence of mountain training for the troops was remarked on by Major Rex Gibson, a president of the Alpine Club of Canada, who noted the contrast with the German army, able to boast a full 14 mountain divisions!

To fill the gap, the Alpine Club of Canada agreed to convert their annual mountaineering camp in 1943 into a troop training program. The decision followed upon the 1942 camp, where a group of officers had been instructed in mountain techniques. The 1943 camp was held in the Yoho Valley in the Rockies, and by all accounts was very successful; a number of senior officers in the army hierarchy attended for a day or longer, and all had great praise for the work of the club. The program was continued into 1944, when winter training for the Lovat Scouts was provided in the Jasper vicinity.

Despite the apparent success of the program, little concrete seems to have resulted; Canada never developed a specialized unit trained in mountain warfare. A number of articles were published about the program, the most amusing of which is this one by Don Munday.

⁓ Bruce Fairley

Mountain Troops: A Lighter View

W.A. Don Munday

No actual attack of stage-fright occurred among the most representative group of North American mountaineers ever gathered at one time in the Stanley Mitchell Hut in Little Yoho Valley. They were the twenty-five volunteer civilian instructors at the Canadian Army Mountaineering School, and they realized they had to teach themselves and each other how to teach mountaineering at high speed to soldiers not picked for this special training.

Also, many of the instructors were past middle age—the troops were fresh from rigorous training at battle-school. Could these instructors stand up physically?

Surely it would have been amusing, and doubtless instructive, to have listened-in on the troops when they returned from the first day's training. But our own evenings in the hut were instructive always, and often amusing. As squads of trainees were passed on from groups of instructors more or less specializing on some part of the training, each man's aptness or ineptness came in for some comment, and effective training tricks were passed along.

We often used rougher methods than common among climbers. "I couldn't convince my gang they were safer standing upright when traversing a snow slope," one instructor told us. "The leader peeled off and brought them all down one by one without anybody making any effort to stop himself or anybody else."

A U.S. Army officer sent from Camp Hale as an observer told us our percentage of "duds"—made up of the incompetent and malingerers—was no higher than among the picked men at Camp Hale. On the training ground these duds gave us the most anxiety, but gave us the most smiles in the pre-bedtime sessions in the hut.

"Sergt. M—— slipped while carrying a stretcher up an ice-worn slab below President Glacier," said an instructor who is a sober scientist in ordinary life. "He spread himself all over half an acre like a pound of butter. I fielded his ice-axe and then his pith helmet. His feet twitched feebly, so I stuck the point of my ice-axe against his boot although I could think of other places to put it to discourage him from slipping down."

"I never heard so much 'Basic English' in my life," dryly observed a climber renowned for his work in connection with Basic English.

The soldier who rated foremost in camp for his command of foul and profane language became an assistant instructor due to his aptitude for climbing. An instructor lent him a spare pair of boots—there not being enough of the army issue. When the boots were returned to their owner a fellow-instructor advised him earnestly, "The only safe thing to do before you take those boots home will be to cut their tongues out."

We made a mass ascent of the President. "Imagine asking a man to fight for a country like this!" scoffed one soldier when he reached the top and got his first wide mountain view of the Rockies and Selkirks. "I'd give it all to the Japs!" We never quite forgave that fellow.

It must have been a brother at heart who was sent scouting during one of the battle exercises during advanced training. When he came back he reported, "It's no different to here sir; just more mountains ahead."

When dealing with large groups we found the simple and effective way to keep them off dangerous cornices was to mark off the area with a line in the snow and write "Out of Bounds."

Glissading seemed the most sensible part of training because it was fun. The men who had skied usually could be singled out by their glissading skill. The rush to glissade down snow slopes when coming back to camp often kept the instructors busy. A good many trainees could be counted on to throw away their axes the moment they lost their feet. On one particular slope when undirected bodies came hurtling down in bunches towards the boulders where the snow ended, I have vivid memories of a high ranking officer of the Club stretching to catch a soldier with each hand at the same time. He got a stranglehold on one's throat and spun him round so his feet instead of his head met a rock.

"You know I always get dizzy and fall off high places," confided a soldier to me as I led my group along the trail toward the glacier below the Vice President. Apparently he had hoped I would say, "Under those circumstances you'd better waddle back to camp, because we're going places today where there'll be lots of chance to fall a long way before you bump."

I had not dealt with him before, and he had no way of knowing that I "had his number" in more ways than one. "Well, don't fall too far," I advised him as though having men fall off a mountain merely bored me. "We won't have a single stretcher on this side of the mountain today."

He walked along in worried silence for a while. "Has an instructor really got the right to push a man off a cliff if he will not climb down?" he demanded. This threat reputedly had been used effectively on him the previous day. "Captain G. says he pushed a man off a ledge," I answered with apparent approval, not telling the man the incident was supposed to have occurred on a private climbing trip when rough measures seemed the best way to make a temporarily unnerved climber "snap out of it."

It did not seem to occur to my "problem-child" that he was quite big enough to push me off if it came to that. He said nothing more. We got on the glacier and set each man to cutting his own way, unroped, up a steep bulge of the ice. A man for whom I was not responsible did "peel off." But when I got round to my particular problem I located him nearly at the top of the steepest ice and going up steadily in steps so small that I would have cut their like only if accompanied by some such trusted companion as my wife. He gave me no trouble throughout the day and I only declined to give him an "A" rating on his day's performance because of his unwillingness.

Although all officers up to the rank of major-general told the troops that we were not getting $10 a day for our services, as the rumor ran, the story was easier for most of them to believe than that of having given our services free. (Actually, we paid camp fees to the Club.) The army did not succeed in getting any climbing ropes from the U.S. army. We used our own ropes and those belonging to the Club. Mine was worn out at the end, and I imagine most others were too.

"He'll be coming round the mountain—if he comes," the troops chanted in derisive disbelief when told that Major-General G.R. Pearkes, V.C., G.O. in C. Pacific Command, would actually visit them while training on the glacier and cliffs below President. The troops reminded us that he was over sixty years of age—we forbore telling them that a number of instructors were creeping up on the sixty mark. Also, one instructor told us the doctor had told him not to climb above 4,000 feet. From other credible sources the version was "Don't climb. Period."

We got some amusement from pointing out in due course Eric Brooks guiding the General and his party up the long spine of the lofty western moraine, and thence to the "Yellow Slab," a wettish, ice-worn limestone cliff. It formed a fine place to illustrate how easy a descent of such difficult rock can be by roping-down.

Gen. Pearkes watched for a few minutes, then came down in creditable style. We thought that closed the day's activities, but discovered him climbing the cliff across the glacier stream. This cliff overhung so that one swung wholly clear of the rocks for nearly seventy feet. The General insisted on coming down, although on this and later occasions some of the trainees always flatly refused to rope-down even with a safety rope added. We called it Pearkes' Cliff. The purplish and yellowish strata make a closed fold.

"Aw, he's lived his life," they countered sullenly when taunted with having less "guts" than the General.

Of course it is about the most spectacular of climbing tricks, and beginners find trouble in believing it calls for no real display of strength, and only the skill almost anyone can win by obeying instructions. Mastering it is excellent for the morale of a beginner because he looks such a bold fellow to the uninitiated, and it is harmless showing-off.

No instructor won more respect from the troops than the late Andy Sibbald. In spite of his lifelong handicap, which would have kept most men out of the mountains, he climbed day after day with no signs of tiring.

The only serious accidents during the whole camp were a broken ankle as a result of jumping a stream, and a shoulder broken by a rock dislodged by a man ignoring orders to stay still until his companions got clear below.

The instructors mystified many of the troops by the way so many of them used their off-days to make ascents far more strenuous than the routine of troop-training. But in fairness it must be mentioned that some of the trainees showed themselves mountaineers at heart and in deed. The official account in the *Canadian Alpine Journal*, 1943, shows that all trainees improved their ability to travel in alpine regions to a degree gratifying to the Club and to army authorities.

The soldiers who received the army climbing boots invited the stock quip of having plenty of "understanding." Marked size were about two larger than in ordinary boots, so many were worn with all the socks a man owned plus insoles. The bigger sizes were useless. Possibly the U.S. Quartermaster-General's department visualized Canadians as all being the "big silent men of the North" of the movies. Certainly many pairs of boots could have been worn without pinching by the she-grizzly that had mauled the park superintendent just before camp opened.

The troops laughed when they heard of a porcupine which, relying on the sanctity of wild life in the park, made a midnight meal on most of a suitcase belonging to the camp commandant. We surmised porky was appropriately "dissuaded" from getting into the bad habit.

Instructors who had served in World War I or II understood how army humor trends toward the slapstick variety. Once while a horde of soldiers lunched on the rocks of Barometer Col a prankster on the glacier below the cliffs deftly tipped the pith helmet off the head of the man in front of him on the rope. A whole series of ragged crevasses split the glacier below. The helmet somehow balanced on its brim as it rolled and bounced down as though under animate guidance so that at the precise moment an extra leap saved it from a chasm, or a sudden twirl turned it aside on a new course. The troops cheered with delight until its unpredictable career ended by a sudden flop to rest in a pocket on the brink of a black abyss. Only the army knows the number of lost helmets.

One of the more advanced bits of training was an overnight bivouac at Summit Lake, followed by a traverse from that side of the Vice President. The troops carried rifles and equipment.

At the most difficult place on the rocks an instructor encouraged the harassed troops with the suggestion: "This is like hitting yourself on the head with a hammer—it feels so good when you stop!"

"Float up and ooze down," one tall rock expert reiterated to the men he taught, but even a few of the instructors could approach his fluidity of progress up or down. He left camp one day at six p.m.—after a day's training—climbed Mt. McArthur, traversed Pollinger, then Kiwetinok and the north peak of Kerr to the main summit. Darkness approaching, he came back to camp at eleven p.m. On one occasion he furnished amusement in the hut by squirming on the floor in what was supposed to be an effort to solve the tying of a butterfly knot as a formula. But very often he could be found "relaxing" over some abstruse mathematical problem dealing with the structure of paper and its significance in the war effort.

The nearest approach to friction between officers and instructors occurred in the course of a trip up Yoho Glacier and back to camp by way of des Poilus Glacier. In some manner a platoon commander reached the edge of the latter glacier well ahead of the leading instructors. He led boldly out on the snowfield. "Rope up!" the instructors continued to shout after him. The snow stretched away flat, unbroken, innocent. He carried the rope and at last stopped sulkily to put it on. He drove his axe viciously into the snow in front of him and nearly lost it, for he knocked a good-sized hole through the roof of a big crevasse. He accepted more expert leadership after that.

Of course experienced mountaineers have been known to err badly in judgment as to when to rope. But John Wheeler and I were a bit scandalized the day we were sent out with ninety-six men to climb Vice President. This was near the end of the second training period and the number of instructors had dwindled to about half a dozen. However, John and I were allotted about half a dozen assistant-instructors picked from the more skilful soldiers in the first training group.

A foot or more of snow had fallen with a high wind. Most crevasses were hidden with flimsy bridges resulting from drifting snow sticking against the lip of the crevasse and building into the wind till the gap closed. A climber who has seen it taking place generally has more respect for snowfields.

John had the difficult task of bringing up the rear where he had to display the wisdom of Solomon in dealing with would-be deserters allegedly afflicted with anything from ingrowing freckles to impending appendicitis. John must have achieved nobly, for I counted ninety red noses on the windy ridge leading to the summit cairn.

But I discovered here that not one of the assistant-instructors had shown enough respect for the glacier to attach himself to any rope-party. When we got below the bergschrund the party turned into an undisciplined mob plunging down in the fatuous self-delusion that if they reached camp not too long after the lunch hour the sergeant-cook might forget and give them an extra meal. Most rope-parties closed up within arm's length of each other and took their own untested courses. I had two of my own party partly into crevasses at the same time, and for the next five minutes their handling of the rope was quite good. After that I was sorry the crevasses had not been bigger.

But during most of the training, snow conditions on the available glaciers did not co-operate with our efforts to manoeuvre trainees into planned breakthroughs. In fact, on one occasion the instructor, who happened to be the heavyweight on the rope, dropped through to his armpits when travelling second on the rope.

Instructors generally worked in pairs more or less, partly for mere safety, but as our numbers lessened while the number of trainees remained the same, the strain became pronounced.

Once while I stood unroped on a foot-wide shelf halfway down a crevasse to direct the practice of rescue work, I became aware of sudden enthusiasm in the use of an ice-axe on the surface of the glacier. Directly over my head a soldier was blithely trying to detach a big block of ice. He had not troubled to look down. I robbed the soldiers of a real rescue.

When the "victim" of a practice rescue was raised till his hands reached the surface, the men on the rope almost always joined in a mighty tug which shot him clear like a leaping fish before he landed with his chin ploughing through the snow.

Quite possibly Edward Whymper had camped across the creek from the site of the Stanley Mitchell Hut. Waggish instructors soon littered the mantelpiece with souvenirs—Whymper's wine bottle, twigs he had slept on, a remnant of his galoshes, and so on, culminating in the bringing down from a glacier of a stocking clasp on the strength of which it was gravely asserted Whymper must have had a feminine companion.

Yes, we had a lot of fun in the Little Yoho. It was remarkable how a group so strongly individualistic in character co-operated so smoothly to make the Club's plan of training a success. Doubtless a fairly general sense of humor helped a lot.

The last day of the training period for each group called for crossing Emerald Pass to Emerald Lake. Rifles and equipment were carried. Emerald Lake Chalet spelled women to some of the soldiers till they learned it was closed for duration of the war.

But the soldiers never quite realized that the park was not closed to tourists. As a result there were roadside incidents when men were not arrayed for civilian gaze. Most notable of these occasions resulted when the first contingent reached Emerald Lake on a hot afternoon. Those who have driven to the lake will recall the sharp bend by which the road dramatically reveals the lakeshore. This day it revealed a hundred or more naked soldiers on the shore, and not all the occupants of the auto were males.

It was there on the lakeshore that we instructors waved goodbye to the mountain troops, men with whom we had shared food on the heights, men whom we had cursed, coaxed, coerced, ridiculed, encouraged towards worthiness as mountaineers and increased fitness to help win the war. But perhaps more lasting worth lay in the assurance that among their number were a few, a goodly few, in whom had been aroused a love of the high places of the earth.

V CLASSIC ASCENTS

No adjective in the mountaineering vocabulary is more overused than the word "classic," which can mean anything from a short pleasant rock climb to a huge multi-day climb only achieved after repeated attempts and persistent sieging. In this section, however, we have selected the stories of four climbs which seem to us to be indisputably important to Canadian mountaineering; classic in the sense that they made history and have proved to be climbs of enduring worth.

~ Bruce Fairley

CONRAD KAIN AND THE ASCENT OF MOUNT ROBSON

"No doubt he will run away again and most likely get mixed up with the Socialists and end on the gallows."—Austrian Burgomaster's comments on Conrad Kain, following a youthful escapade in Kain's home town in Raxalpe.

Conrad Kain was born and raised in a small Austrian village. The society he grew up in was rigidly stratified. His most likely fate, following a youthful stint as a poacher, was to have ended his days as a worker in a local quarry. That Kain was able to escape from such a poverty-stricken life was due to personal qualities of determination and vision, and a love for the mountains.

Kain naturally began his mountain travels by exploring local peaks. He became a licensed mountain guide and was encouraged by his clients to go further, as they found him not only a skilled guide, but one who delighted in sharing his enjoyment of the mountains with them.

As his skills and reputation grew, Kain expanded his horizons, climbing in Switzerland, France and Italy, before travelling to Canada to guide in 1909. In this new land he was particularly struck by the fact that his employers would work alongside of him, and that they would eat at the same table. How different this was from Austria, where he was not permitted to eat in hotels because of his class.

It took Kain some years to establish roots in his new homeland. Work available to a mountain guide was not sufficient to live on, and so he tried trapping, went on a natural history expedition to Siberia, and guided for three alpine seasons in New Zealand. Following his third New Zealand season, he returned to Canada, married and settled down to a life of farming and trapping in the Columbia Valley, never to leave Canada again. He continued to climb extensively, often solo.

Kain had many notable ascents to his credit on three continents. Outstanding among his achievements in Canada are the first ascents of Mt. Louis, Mt. Robson (in 1913) and Bugaboo Spire. He also made the first ascents of many of the highest peaks in the Purcells, including Jumbo, Farnham, Karnak and the Howser Spires. It is obvious, however, from reading the accounts of those who climbed with him, that Kain's accomplishments as a climber impressed them less than his warmth and humanity as a person. He died in 1934, at the age of 51.

"But he was so much more than just a guide—he was your friend, playing a part in the inspiring moments of many lives and giving more to life than he asked of it. He had no routine moments on a mountain, and, if you had not employed him, he would have been climbing by himself for the pure joy and beauty of it all."— J. Monroe Thorington.

~ John Manual

The First Ascent of Mt. Robson

Conrad Kain

Translated by P.A.W. Wallace

On reaching the Robson Glacier after the ascent of Mt. Resplendent, I went down to the timber at 6700 ft. Here I met my Herren for Mt. Robson. Both were busy about the fire, Mr. Foster (Deputy Minister for Public Works for British Columbia) with cooking, Mr. MacCarthy with gathering wood. After a good supper, we went up, laden with firewood, to the foot of the Extinguisher. The rock bears this name on account of its form (candle extinguisher). On the moraine we made our shelter beside a wall of stones, over which we stretched a piece of canvas and crept under it like marmots into their hole.

I awoke early next morning and felt pain in my eyes, and for a long time I could not open them. It felt as if my eyes were filled with sand. My snow glasses were no good. I saw a starry sky, which was more than we had expected. I applied cold poultices for half an hour and the pain in my eyes began to abate. I lit the fire and wakened my Herren. Both were delighted at the sight of a cloudless sky.

At 4.30 a.m., after an early but good breakfast, we left our bivouac. We followed the route of the previous day (ascent of Mt. Resplendent), over the glacier. Before we came to the Pass, we swerved to the right. From this point began the real climb of Mt. Robson. We climbed up an avalanche trough, then under some dangerous ice bridges to the right. The snow was in bad condition. We proceeded without any difficulties towards the steep snow-slope that descends from the Dome (10,000 ft.) and reached it at 7 a.m. We took a rest and deliberated over the route ahead.

Two years ago I spent hours studying this route, and did not take the bergschrund very seriously. From the Dome, one had a nearer survey of the bergschrund. We approached it over the glacier, which is here not very steep. A rib of rock comes down almost to the schrund. Over this rock I planned to ascend, but after every possible attempt we were forced to give it up, for at this place the glacier breaks off sheer. For about two hundred feet we followed along the bergschrund to the right. Here was the only possibility at hand of overcoming it. After long chopping at the ice, I stood on its 65-degree slope. Across the schrund I made more steps. Then I let both Herren follow.

A thin layer of snow lay on the ice, and, owing to the melting of the snow, the ice was in very bad condition for step-cutting. I made the steps in a zigzag. Mr. Foster counted 105 steps to a ledge of rock. The rock, when seen from below, promised good climbing and a rapid advance. But it turned out otherwise. We climbed up an icy wall, and then to our disappointment had an ice-slope before us, fifty or sixty meters high. I kept as well as I could to the rocks that protruded here and there, which saved me a few steps. At the top of the slope we had another wall of rock, and above that an almost hopeless ice-slope. One could see the tracks of falling stones and avalanches. On this slope I made 110 steps. It was a relief to climb on rocks again, though they were glazed with ice. But unfortunately the satisfaction was short, and for several hundred meters we had to climb again upon a slope of ice and snow. The snow here was in danger of avalanching. For safety, I lengthened the rope on the dangerous slope.

At last we reached the shoulder at twelve o'clock noon. I do not know whether my Herren contemplated with a keen Alpine eye the dangers to which we were exposed from the bergschrund. In the year 1909 this route was attempted by Mr. Mumm and Mr. Amery with the guide Inderbinen from Zermatt. The party were in danger of their lives from an avalanche. I spoke with Inderbinen: he said, "I never before saw death so near."

On the shoulder we took a mid-day rest. There came a snowy wind that wet us to the bone. We pulled out all the clothing stowed away in our rucksacks. We found the shoulder less broad than we expected. It was a snow ridge, on the northeast side of which were overhanging cornices fringed with long icicles glittering in the sun, a glorious picture.

For a few hundred meters we had to keep to the southeast side. The snow on this side was in good condition, so that we made rapid progress. There was on each side a splendid view into the depths below. The more beautiful view was that of the Robson Glacier, Smoky Valley and Mt. Resplendent and the Lynx Range opposite.

From the shoulder to the peak, the route was no longer so dangerous, but complicated by the loose, powdery snow. It was as if we were on an entirely different climb on the southeast side. The complications arose from walls of snow. Never before on all my climbs have I seen such snow formations. The snow walls were terraced. The ledges between the walls were of different widths, and all were covered with loose snow. I often sank in to my hips. There were forms on the walls like ostrich feathers, a truly strange and beautiful winter scene. Unfortunately we had no camera with us. Some of the walls were fifteen to twenty meters high. It was difficult to find a way up from one terrace to another. At one place I worked for over half an hour without effect. We had to go back. A very narrow and steep couloir offered the only possibility. I warned my Herren that the piece would take considerable time to negotiate. Both had a good stand and kept moving as much as possible in order to keep warm. The wind was so bad here that I often had to stop. The steepness alone, apart from wind, made step-cutting very hard work. For a number of steps I had first to make a handhold in the ice, and swing the axe with one hand. I do not think I need to describe this method any more fully, for everyone who has ever been on the ice, knows that cutting steps with one hand is a frightfully slow process. I know that in such places it is not pleasant either for those behind. As soon as I was convinced that I could make it, I called to my Herren: "Just be patient, the bad place will soon be conquered, and the peak is ours." Mr. MacCarthy answered: "We are all right here, we are only sorry for you. I don't understand how you can still keep on cutting steps."

When we had the difficult place behind us, the reward was a fairly steep snow-slope, with the snow in good condition so that we could all three go abreast. At the top of the snow-slope was another wall, which, however, could be outflanked without difficulty.

The last stretch to the summit was a snow-ridge. I turned to my Herren with the words: "Gentlemen, that's as far as I can take you."

In a few seconds both stood beside me on the peak. We shook hands with one another. I added my usual Alpine greeting in German, "Bergheil." Of course, I had to explain the word Bergheil, because both knew no German. There is no word in the English language which has the same meaning as Bergheil.

On the crest of the king of the Rockies, there was not much room to stand. We descended a few meters and stamped down a good space. It was half-past five o'clock. Our barometer showed exactly 13,000 ft.

The view was glorious in all directions. One could compare the sea of glaciers and mountains with a stormy ocean. Mt. Robson is about 2000 ft. higher than all the other mountains in the neighborhood. Indescribably beautiful was the vertical view towards Berg Lake and the camp below. Unfortunately only fifteen minutes were allowed us on the summit, ten of pure pleasure and five of teeth chattering. The rope and our damp clothes were frozen as hard as bone. And so we had to think of the long descent—5.45 o'clock.

As far as the steep couloir, all went well. The descent over this piece was difficult. All the steps were covered with snow. Except for this, we had no difficulties till the shoulder. As it was late, I proposed to descend by the glacier on the south side, for greater safety. Besides the question of time, it seemed to me too dangerous to make our descent over the route of ascent. As a guide with two Herren, one has to take such dangers more into account than do amateurs, for upon one's shoulders rests the responsibility for men's lives. Also as a guide one must consider his calling and the sharp tongues that set going on all sides like clockwork when a guide with his party gets into a dangerous situation. It was clear to me that we must spend a night on the mountain. The descent was not quite clear to me. I was convinced that on this side we could get farther down than by the way we came up. My bivouac motto is: "A night out is hardly ever agreeable, and above 3000 meters always a lottery."

After the shoulder, we had a steep snow-slope to the glacier. I made about 120 steps. Once on the glacier, we went down rapidly for a few hundred meters until a sheer precipice barred the way. So far and no farther. Vain was my search for a way down. We had to go back uphill, which was naturally no pleasure. Between rocks and glacier was a very steep icy trench which offered us the only descent. I examined the icy trench for a few minutes, and the ice cliffs overhanging us. I saw the opportunity and, of course, the dangers too. Mr. Foster asked me what my opinion was, whether we could go on or not. I answered, quite truly: "We can; it is practicable but dangerous." Captain MacCarthy said: "Conrad, if it is not too dangerous for you, cutting steps, then don't worry about us. We'll trust to you and fortune."

That made matters easier for me, as I could see that both Herren had no fear. I lengthened the rope and left the Herren in a sheltered spot. I made the steps just as carefully and quickly as I could. When I had reached a good place I let both Herren follow. Mr. MacCarthy went last, and I was astonished at his surefootedness. This dangerous trench took a whole hour to negotiate. The rock was frozen, but the consciousness that we had such terrible danger behind us, helped us over the rocks. In greater safety we rested beneath the rocks.

Below us was the glacier, which, seen from above, promised a good descent almost to timber-line. I remembered that the glacier had still another break-off and knew that we must camp out. However, I said nothing of this to my Herren, but the opposite. I pointed with my axe to the woods with the words: "It will be a fine night down there in the woods beside a big fire." Both chimed in, for the word "fire" makes a very different impression when one is standing in soaking clothes upon ice and snow; from the word "fire" when one is aroused by it from a sound sleep.

We did not find the glacier as good as we expected. We searched our way through ice debris in an avalanche bed. Here on the glacier the sun bade us good night. The sunset was beautiful. It would have been more beautiful to us if the sun had been delayed an hour. It was a melancholy moment when the last glow of evening faded in the west. We rested and spoke on this theme. Mr. MacCarthy said: "It is as well that the law of nature cannot be changed by men. What a panic it would raise if we succeeded in delaying the sun for an hour! It is possible that somewhere some alpinists will tomorrow morning be in the same situation as we are, and will be waiting eagerly for the friendly sun."

Despite the approach of darkness we went on. About ten o'clock in the evening we reached the rocks. It was out of the question to go any further. Our feet felt the effects of the last seventeen hours on ice and rock, and so we were easily satisfied with a resting place. A ledge of rock two meters wide offered us a good place to bivouac. We made it as comfortable as we could. We built a little sheltering wall about us. Our provision bag still had plenty of sandwiches, and Mr. MacCarthy, to our surprise, brought a large packet of chocolate from his rucksack. We took our boots off. I gave Mr. Foster my dry pair of extra mitts for socks, so we all had dry feet, which is the important thing in camping out. The Herren had only one rucksack between them, into which they put their feet. Both Herren were roped up to a rock.

I gave a few hints on bivouacking, for there are some tricks in sleeping out on cold rocks that one can only learn by experience. Fortunately the night was a warm one, threatening rain. Clouds were hanging in the sky, which, however, the west wind swept away to the east. In the valley we saw flickering the campfire of the Alpine Club and of the construction camp of the Canadian Northern and Grand Trunk Railways. I was very tired and went to sleep without any trouble. A thundering avalanche woke me from a sound sleep. I heard Mr. Foster's teeth chatter as he lay beside me. I uttered no word of sympathy, but went to sleep again.

Later I was awakened by a dream. I dreamed that we were quite close to a forest. I saw wood close at hand, and dry branches ready for kindling. In the dream I reproached myself what the Herren would think of me, sleeping here in the forest with firewood, but without a fire and almost freezing. With these reproaches I awoke and sat up to convince myself whether the forest and firewood were really so near. But I saw only a few stars and in the east a few gray clouds lit up with the dawn. I could not get to sleep again, but lay quietly and listened to the thunder of the avalanches which broke the almost ghostly silence of Nature. At daybreak it became considerably warmer, so my Herren, who had spent a cold and sleepless night, now fell sound asleep.

At six o'clock the friendly beams of the sun reached us. I wakened my Herren. Both sat up and described the pain in their eyes, which they could not open. The eyes of both were greatly swollen. It was not a pleasant sight. I thought both were snow-blind. Snow-blind, at a height of 9000 ft., and in such a situation—that might have an unpleasant ending. After some cold poultices, the pain abated and both were able to keep their eyes open.

I told my dream. Both Herren had dreams of a similar nature, which had reference to the cold night. Mr. Foster dreamed that a number of friends came with blankets and commiserated the barren camping ground, and no one covered him. Mr. MacCarthy, in his dream, implored his wife for more blankets, and his wife stopped him with the curt reply: "O no, dear, you can't have any blankets. Sleeping without any is good training if we want to go to the North Pole."

I searched for a descent over the rocks. After a quarter of an hour I came back.

"Yes, we can make it without further difficulty."

At 6.45 a.m. we left the bivouac, which will certainly remain in our memory. We did not get down so easily after all. We had to get around sheer walls. The climbing was difficult, and at some places the rock was very rotten. This was very unpleasant for my Herren. They could only see a few steps through their glasses and swollen eyes.

At last we had the most difficult part behind us, but not the most dangerous. We had to traverse a hanging glacier. For ten minutes we were exposed to the greatest danger. I certainly breathed freely when we lay down to rest under some overhanging rock. Our barometer showed 8200 ft., time 10.15 a.m. That eight hundred feet had taken three hours to negotiate. I said to my Herren: "I am happy to be able to inform you that we have all dangers behind us. We shall reach the green grass in the valley safe and sound even to our swollen eyes."

We crossed loose stones to the southwest ridge. This ridge should be the easiest way up to the peak. From here we had a beautiful view of Lake Kinney below. Without further difficulty we descended through old snow. At eleven o'clock we took a long rest and devoured everything eatable we could find left in our provision bag. Then we followed the newly-built trail to camp.

About five o'clock in the afternoon we came, hungry and tired, into camp, where we were hospitably received by our fellow campers with food and drink and congratulations.

From what Donald Phillips himself said, our ascent was really the first ascent of Mt. Robson. Phillips' words are as follows: "We reached, on our ascent (in mist and storm), an ice-dome fifty or sixty feet high, which we took for the peak. The danger was too great to ascend the dome."

Phillips and Kinney made the ascent over the west ridge. The west side is, as far as I could see, the most dangerous side that one can choose. Kinney undertook the journey from Edmonton alone with five horses. On the way he met Donald Phillips who was on a prospecting tour. Mr. Kinney persuaded Phillips to accompany him. Phillips had never before made this kind of a mountain trip and says himself that he had no suspicion of its dangers. They had between them one ice-axe and a bit of ordinary rope. They deserve more credit than we, even though they did not reach the highest point, for in 1909 they had many more obstacles to overcome than we; for at that time the railway, which brought us almost to the foot of the mountain, was then no less than 200 miles from their goal, and their way had to be made over rocks and brush, and we must not forget the dangerous river crossings.

Mt. Robson is one of the most beautiful mountains in the Rockies and certainly the most difficult one. In all my mountaineering in various countries, I have climbed only a few mountains that were hemmed in with more difficulties. Mt. Robson is one of the most dangerous expeditions I have made. The dangers consist in snow and ice, stone avalanches, and treacherous weather.

Ever since I came to Canada and the Rockies, it was my constant wish to climb the highest peak. My wish was fulfilled. For this ascent I could have wished for no better companions. Both Herren were good climbers and Nature lovers, and made me no difficulties on the way. Each had a friendly word of thanks for my guiding. In this country people are much more democratic than with us in Europe, and have less regard for titles and high officials; but still it was a great satisfaction to me to have the pleasure of climbing with a Canadian statesman. ❧

THE FIRST ASCENT OF MOUNT LOGAN

No one had even set foot within 100 kilometres of Mt. Logan when Albert MacCarthy, Andy Taylor and Miles Atkinson set off up the Chitina River one day in 1924 on a reconnaissance expedition to determine if it would be feasible to assault the mountain from that direction. At 5,960 metres (19,550 feet), Mt. Logan is Canada's highest peak, and the second highest summit in North America. Located in the Yukon Territory adjacent to the Alaska boundary, surveyors determined only in 1913 that the peak lay entirely within Canada. The story of how a small and meticulously organized team succeeded in climbing it in 1925 on the first attempt is one of the greatest chapters in the history of North American mountaineering.

As impressive as the actual climb is the story of how MacCarthy and his team of five companions made a journey with dog sleds and horses up the Chitina River and the glaciers beyond in the dead of winter to establish the supply camp that would make an assault possible in the following year. This was one case where success came not so much because of the technical performance of the climbers, but through impeccable organization and control of logistics—the sort of military-style fastidiousness which is quite out of fashion in Western mountaineering circles today.

MacCarthy's official account of this climb, published in the 1925 *Canadian Alpine Journal*, makes for a slow read. The account reprinted below, from Paddy Sherman's *Cloudwalkers*, is a much livelier telling, benefitting from the selectivity and sense of drama that a trained journalist brought to the task of recreating the essence of the expedition's accomplishments.

Sherman occupies a position in Canadian mountaineering writing comparable to that of James Ramsey Ullman in the United States. He was a popularizer of mountain tales. I suspect that *Cloudwalkers* was the first introduction many Canadian climbers had to the literature of their sport. I recall that in my high school library it occupied a prominent place in the almost non-existent mountaineering section.

In writing *Cloudwalkers,* Sherman said it was part of his purpose to make known to Canadians a slice of their history that had been overlooked and to demonstrate to them that the feats of their countrymen in the mountains were comparable to the more famous exploits of American and European climbers. His book was the real forerunner to this volume.

Ullman has endured criticism in the United States by some who feel that the original accounts of mountaineers are the only true mountaineering literature. The tendency among those writing for a popular market is to sensationalize climbing and to emphasize the dangerous and dramatic. All good storytellers, of course, use exaggeration, and mountaineers are no exception. But it is just for the very qualities of drama and a "sense of the desperate" that Sherman's account has been selected. No one should minimize the hazards of the final ascent to the summit of Mt. Logan made on June 23, 1925. It seems fairly certain that if the violent storm that struck the party on the summit plateau had continued another day, MacCarthy, Allen Carpé and William Foster would have died. Theirs was a dramatic and dangerous situation, and Sherman, the professional writer, has done it justice. The official account, on the other hand, is stiff upper lip. We feel most readers—all but the purists—will prefer Sherman's more vigorous and no less truthful account.

Although Sherman's account of the Mt. Logan expedition is sympathetic, other commentators have questioned the leadership shown. Chris Jones, for example, has written in *Climbing in North America,* "Official accounts played down or omitted obvious questions about reasons for the hardships." Certainly there is room for a more searching analysis of this historic climb.

One final aspect which deserves a passing word is the team composition. There has been recent discussion as to the extent of Canada's participation in the venture. An article published in the British periodical *Mountain* in 1986 referred, rather shockingly, to the *American* first ascent of Mt. Logan.

The facts are these. The project was conceived of by the Alpine Club of Canada and promoted by its founder and first president, A.O. Wheeler, following the ascent of Mt. Robson in 1913, in which MacCarthy and Foster took part. The Toronto professor and explorer A.P. Coleman, during his term as president of the Club, took the occasion of an annual club camp, held in the Larch Valley, to strike a directing committee, which consisted of MacCarthy, H. Bell, Wheeler, Foster and Lambart. Of these only MacCarthy was an American, and at the time he was living on his ranch in British Columbia. There was also an advisory committee formed, consisting of some of the bigger names in the English-speaking climbing world. Although the American Alpine Club contributed heavily to the expedition, other major contributors included the Canadian government and the CPR.

Climbing personnel were both American and Canadian. Foster was a well-known public figure in British Columbia: deputy minister of Public Works. Lambart was Canadian; Carpé was sent as the representative of the American Alpine Club. Read, Hall and Morgan were Americans who paid their way to come on the expedition. Andy Taylor lived in Alaska, but was a Canadian citizen. Thus, of the summit team, three were Canadian and three American—making the Mt. Logan climb one of the more successful joint expeditions ever undertaken.

~ Bruce Fairley

The Mightiest Hump of Nature:
Mount Logan

Paddy Sherman

Mount Logan, some two hundred miles west of Whitehorse in the Yukon Territory, is Canada's highest peak; it soars to 19,550 feet. Twelve years after the first ascent of McKinley, the apex of North America, in 1913, Logan was the highest unclimbed peak on the North American continent.

Many of the world's great peaks are taller than Logan. But it is a coastal mountain, rising almost from the sea, not from a Tibetan plateau 15,000 feet above sea-level. Glaciers from its base flow right to the Pacific Ocean. If Logan's uplift above its base were to be super-imposed on a Tibetan interior plateau, it would rank with Everest. And seldom is there found a single mountain massif with Logan's monumental bulk. It measures 100 miles around at the base, a snow-white fang protruding from 25,000 square miles of ice that constitute the biggest glacial area in the world apart from the Antarctic and Greenland.

If the mountain could be sliced off at the 16,000-foot level, which is higher than Europe's loftiest peak, the resulting plateau would cover thirty square miles. Its many-toothed summit ridges, twenty miles long and 3,000 miles farther north than Everest, are a cosmic comb, raking the moisture from countless year-round storms spawned in the far Pacific. The result is astonishing.

On the cold north side of Everest, eternal snow and ice stretch down to the 16,500-foot level, giving a vertical snow-and-ice region of 12,500 feet. The comparable zone on Logan covers 16,000 feet, and the summit broods, remote and frightening, a clear 14,000 feet above the general level of the surrounding glaciers. At the time of the first attempt on Logan, the nearest habitation was 150 miles away, and the approach included almost eighty miles of glaciers on which no man had ever set foot.

The first recorded sighting of the giant mountain was by Israel C. Russell of the United States Geological Survey. In 1890, he was trying to make the first ascent of Mount St. Elias (18,008 feet), then believed to be the highest peak in Alaska. He didn't reach the peak but he did spot Mount Logan, twenty-six miles away. He reported his find this way: "The clouds parted towards the northeast, revealing several giant peaks not before seen, some of which seemed to rival St. Elias itself. One stranger rising in three white domes far above the clouds was especially magnificent. As this was probably the first time its summit was ever seen, we took the liberty of giving it a name. It will appear on our maps as Mt. Logan, in honour of Sir William E. Logan, founder and for long director of the Geological Survey of Canada."

In 1913, H.F. Lambart of the Canadian Geological Survey decided from his triangulations that Logan, almost astride the Yukon-Alaska border, was in fact not an Alaskan giant but Canada's highest mountain.

In 1913, Albert H. MacCarthy and William Wasbrough Foster were also making a big contribution to Canadian mountaineering history: they made the first ascent of Mount Robson[1] (12,972 feet), then believed to be the highest peak in Canada outside the Yukon. As they celebrated the event around an Alpine Club of Canada camp-fire, the club's director, A.O. Wheeler, proposed that Mount Logan should be climbed. Plans were started at once, but had to be abandoned when the war came.

In 1923, Albert MacCarthy, now a captain in the United States Navy, was appointed leader of the expedition, and he soon realized just what he was in for. The mountain's "stupendous bulk," he said, after a lot of research, made it "the mightiest hump of nature in the western hemisphere if not the largest in the world."

There were three possible approaches: from Yakutat Bay on the coast; from Kluane Lake on the north-east; or from McCarthy, Alaska, which was to the north-west. Yakutat Bay was ruled out almost at once. Although the Duke of the Abruzzi had used it for St. Elias, the area was notoriously stormy and dangerous. There was no satisfactory base there then, and the approach wound up the wrong side of the mountain. The Kluane Lake route, which is today crossed by the Alaska Highway, then involved a stretch of sixty miles that was completely unexplored. It was obvious to MacCarthy that whichever way he tried to reach the mountain he was in for many problems. So, instead of attempting to climb it in 1924, he decided to spend a season on reconnaissance, concentrating on the route from the village of McCarthy.

This meant an eighty-six-mile trek alongside the Chitina River, an unpredictable glacier-fed stream—one moment peacefully murmuring among the rocks, the next hurling giant boulders about like peas, and fighting to burst from its low, confining banks. Apart from winter, the only time a climbing party could use it safely would be in the slack spell between the early run-off from melting snow and the main run-off caused by melting of the billions of tons of glacier ice.

With Andrew M. Taylor and Miles (Scotty) Atkinson, two McCarthy guides, Captain MacCarthy made a thirty-seven-day trip up the Chitina and over the fifty-two miles of ice beyond it to Cascade, the logical site for base

---

1.   The third member of the party was the Austrian guide, Conrad Kain.

camp. Despite a tremendous amount of work, they were frustrated by bad weather, and the farthest point they reached was eighteen miles from the peak and only 10,200 feet in altitude. But he made the decision: tough as it was, this was at least a possible way to get onto the mountain. From there, the mountaineers would have to make their own way.

It was obvious to him that if they were to have a chance of reaching the summit the climbers must arrive on the mountain in good condition, not exhausted by carrying in tons of supplies. So it was proposed, almost casually, in the way of men of forceful action, that the supplies should be taken in and cached during the coming winter.

This feat in itself was worthy of comparison with Antarctic sledging epics, and it is still considered one of the greatest winter freighting jobs ever tackled in that wild and inhospitable border country.

It began in February 1925, at the height of an exceptionally cold winter in the valley, with everything buried deep under an unusually heavy snow-fall. Almost three and a half tons of supplies had to be taken in for the climbers to allow them to make an extended siege of Logan. A ton of hay and oats had to be transported for the climbing party's pack-horses, as no grass would be growing when the assault got under way in May. On top of all this, the freighting party itself needed more than five tons of supplies for its three-month task. To move this total of ten tons a distance of some 150 miles over frozen river-beds and tumbling glaciers, a party of six men was chosen, with six horses and three teams of seven sled dogs.

From February 4 to February 13, Andy Taylor and Austin Trim, with six horses, broke trail up the first forty-five miles of the Chitina Valley. Often the temperature went down to -45° F.; once it dropped to a paralyzing -52°. Despite this, the two big bobsleds pulled by six horses left McCarthy at 9 a.m. on February 17. Two hours later, the wildly excited dogs hauled their sledges along McCarthy's main street and down to the frozen river at a run. The fight was formally on.

The route along the river-beds was longer than the land trail, but had the great benefit for the heavily loaded horses that it was generally at an easy gradient.

MacCarthy's party had no serious trouble on the first day's march of sixteen miles, which took them to the junction of the Chitina and Nizina rivers. But the snow-storm that began next morning was just the start of weather problems that plagued them from there on. Nature seemed to have got everything backwards, MacCarthy complained. Because of the bitterly cold winter, the river level was low and the sleds often had to be hauled over boulder-strewn gravel bars. Despite the cold, stretches of open water often appeared, forcing them to make difficult detours. And, when they reached stretches that they knew should be good, insurmountable ice jams, piled high by the tremendous pressure of the river, confronted them.

The dogs somehow seemed to thrive on the difficult conditions. They always had enough energy to start a furious fight at the least little chance. On the second day of the trip, Driver, leading one team, set too fast a pace for a team-mate known as Scotty Dog. Scotty attacked Driver from behind and with a sudden slash bit out his left eye. There was nothing the men could do for the poor dog, but as it seemed reluctant to lie down and die they left it in the harness. Time and again Driver licked his paw and then rubbed the wound. Within a week, it had healed completely. MacCarthy marvelled: "What would have happened to one of us had we sustained such an injury and received such scant treatment? Dumb animals are possessed of much that men must envy."

But there was not much to envy about the horses. For thirteen days it was impossible to take off their harness. It was frozen solid. And in the mornings, it was not hard to be sorry for both horses and dogs. To make the most of the daylight, early starts were important. Yet day after day they had to wait until 10 a.m. because the early air was so cold that the deep breathing needed for the hard work of hauling would have frozen the lungs of all the animals. The carefully planned schedule fell apart. But by February 27 they reached Hubrick's Camp, the ramshackle home of a former prospector at the head of Chitina Valley. Barely two miles away was the bush-covered snout of the Chitina Glacier.

Right in front of them was a major worry. They had to get to the west side of Baldwin Glacier to know they were sure of reaching base camp on Ogilvie Glacier. There were two conceivable ways to get there—along the south side of Chitina and Logan Glaciers, or along the north side of Chitina and across it and another glacier to the Logan. The second was obviously impossible for heavy loads, and the first had been abandoned as impossible by Lambart's party when it was surveying the border in 1913.

MacCarthy decided to try the route that the earlier party had abandoned. On February 28, he and Atkinson set out on snow-shoes for the south side of Chitina Glacier, and headed with considerable trepidation up the canyon formed by the steep edge of the ice and the mountain side. MacCarthy went as far as a narrow, impressive cleft between vertical granite cliffs 150 feet high. He called it "The Portal." The summer river boils through here in an angry spate.

Atkinson pushed on and late that night reported that the route was feasible right onto Baldwin Glacier. He cautiously refused to guess at how long it would stay feasible. But before he knew this MacCarthy was working back from The Portal, marking an ice route into the valley. He was not a demonstrative man by nature, but even as he worked he found himself calling the route, in his own mind, "The Gorge of Fate." Some subconscious instinct, with its roots in frequent association with danger, must have been warning him of trouble to come. But even this did not tell him how near the whole party would come to catastrophe.

By March 5, the entire load of supplies was cached four miles beyond The Portal. This was the limit at which the heavy horses could work. Already there had been problems with their weight on the sometimes flimsy ice-bridges. Next day the horses went back to McCarthy, and the rest of the party headed another two and a half miles up-stream to find a final, safe camp where everything could be stored.

The final part of the gorge was by far the most dangerous. Here the tumbling cataract raced along, and many patches of open water leered up at them, inviting the misstep that would promptly bury them under the solid ice a few yards down-stream. Often the only way to go was on a fringe of ice still sticking to the steep rock-wall. A few feet to the side, the torrent gradually undermined their road. One piece especially bothered them—the last apparent danger on the route. This was a ten-foot slit in granite cliffs "…which because of its narrowness, its latent dangers and the satanic appearance of an ice pinnacle that seemed to stand guard over it, we called the Devil's Door."

On March 6, they set up Gorge Camp beyond these dangers. Next day, while MacCarthy stayed to wash the dishes, the others left with the dogs to start the dangerous business of hauling heavy sledges of supplies through on the inadequate bridges. Already the ice was showing signs of deterioration. Would it last long enough for them to finish the job?

MacCarthy went quickly through the camp chores that morning. Then he hurried on down to help at the bottle-neck wooden bridge. Here, each sledge-load had to be unpacked, carried across item by item, and then loaded again on the other side. Within a few minutes, the worries he wouldn't admit fully even to himself came true.

The dog-teams were coming back—the sledges empty and defeat scrawled dully in the haggard, bearded faces of the men.

Andy Taylor told him, "The Devil's Door is shut. The ice we crossed on yesterday is ten feet under water. The trail for 200 yards up-stream is now twenty feet down at the bottom of a lake."

Almost everything they had was stored in the cache below the blockage. There was no food in camp for the dogs, and practically none for the men.

The dogs were immediately taken back to camp and tied up, and by 10.30 a.m. MacCarthy, Taylor, and Atkinson set off on snow-shoes to try to find a way down to the supplies. They crossed the river up-stream, struggled onto the glacier, and then, in five hours of desperately hard work, outflanked the Door. They felt it would have been impossible to get the loaded dogs through by this route. Inching slowly back into the gorge below the Devil's Door, they soon found the cause of the trouble.

It was simple but spectacular: thousands of tons of ice had broken from the towering glacier-wall and filled the bottom of the gorge. The speeding river was stopped, and it rapidly backed up into a lake. But the current was fortunately still at work. Already the surging water had cut a small channel through the ice-jam. By the time the tired men were ready to pack their loads of food back, the gorge was passable again.

The warning was obvious, and they took note of it. Next morning they were out at dawn. Taylor and MacCarthy hacked at the ice-jam with axes and shovels, clearing a narrow, reasonably smooth route for the dogs. Atkinson and Henry Olsen started rushing supplies up to the wooden bridge, using twenty-one dogs on the two sledges. As they made repeated trips to the bridge, there was ever-increasing need for haste: the slabs of ice on which the logs were resting were being noticeably eaten away by the rushing water.

They worked until dark. As Taylor brought the loads from the bridge, he found things rapidly nearing the impossible stage at the door. Their original trail had followed a fringe of ice along the southern wall. But this had now broken off, and its northern side was under water. It was still possible to cross it, though it lay on its side, but the angle was steepening as the water worried away at the edges.

Even the dogs were frightened by its obvious threat. They cringed, tails down, as they approached, and slid along it on their bellies. Some of the dogs refused to cross it at all, and had to be dragged by their drivers. With every trip, the tension increased; there was much to be done yet, but if the bridge went out, so would their plans.

It went at 6.30 that night. A quiet crack as if it was weary of holding out so long, and the slab sank slowly into the hurrying waters. But the last load was through—less than five minutes before. The tension cracked too, and the men found themselves laughing, almost involuntarily—cheering and pounding each other on the back.

This was no time for rest and relaxation, however. They were far behind schedule and still had several glaciers to negotiate. MacCarthy wrote: "No matter how long and how hard we worked, the task seemed to be unending. But we had had the temerity to undertake the job and there was no help for us. We must carry on and see it through to some sort of finish."

From here the going became progressively rougher. On some steep stretches the dogs could barely pull even a light load. Slowly, exhausted by hard work and monotony, they crossed the Baldwin Glacier and started towards the open, easy-looking flat stretches of Logan Glacier.

Before they could reach it, though, they had to cross three miles of moraine—a jumbled, senseless tangle of boulders gouged from the cliffs by the irresistible ice and piled in millions of tons across their path. It was March 31 before they finally set up camp in the middle of the smooth white face of Logan Glacier, pitching the tents three feet deep in a bank of snow. The slow-motion rush went on, step by step, up the Logan Glacier and onto the Ogilvie. On April 13, two and a half tons of equipment, comprising the whole advance base camp the climbers would use, was stored nine miles up the Ogilvie. All the meat and other uncanned foods likely to attract bears, wolves, or wolverines were carefully stowed in the centre of a huge mound. The whole thing was covered with heavy tarpaulins, and weighted down with rocks and cases of gasoline for their stoves.

They took photographs of the cache in relation to prominent landmarks so that the climbers would be able to find it, and on April 14 the party ran for home. They reached McCarthy on April 26, having been forced to take a different route to get around the Devil's Door. Even travelling light, they took five days to negotiate twenty miles there, proving to their satisfaction that the job would have been impossible with heavy loads.

Under Arctic conditions and in dangerous country, the winter party had travelled over 950 miles in ten weeks, and cached in various key places the four and a half tons of food and equipment without which the ambitious assault on Mount Logan could not even begin. Their exploit is still without equal as a mountaineering preliminary, despite the great exploration that has been done in some of the world's highest and most remote ranges. It fittingly prepared the way for one of the world's great feats of mountaineering, which today is almost unknown though it qualifies as perhaps the most outstanding epic of endurance in Canada's rich and vibrant frontier history.

MacCarthy was waiting on the dock at Cordova when the steamer arrived on May 7, 1925, bringing the climbing party from a trip along a thousand miles of some of the world's most spectacular coast. The official party consisted of MacCarthy himself as leader, Foster, Fred Lambart (deputy leader), and Allen Carpé, who represented the American Alpine Club. It was an unusual group. Lambart was the man who first measured the mountain. MacCarthy, of Annapolis, Maryland, and Wilmer, British Columbia, was forty-nine. So was Lieutenant-Colonel Foster, a former deputy-minister of public works for British Columbia, holder of the Distinguished Service Order and two bars. Allen Carpé, thirty-one, was a research scientist in radio and telegraph, and one of America's best exploratory mountaineers.

Many United States mountaineers had volunteered to pay their own expenses and help in any way requested if only they could be taken on the trip. On this basis, three outstanding United States climbers now arrived on the steamer. They were Henry S. Hall, Jr., of Boston, R.M. Morgan of Dartmouth College in New Hampshire, and Norman H. Read of Manchester, Massachusetts. Hall, later president of the American Alpine Club, became one of the best and most experienced climbers in the United States and made many difficult expeditions in British Columbia's wild and difficult Coast Range. These men brought the climbing party to seven. To them were added Andy Taylor as transport officer, and H.M. Laing, a naturalist who stayed at Hubrick's throughout the expedition and surveyed the wildlife and plants of the Chitina Valley.

They left McCarthy on May 12. On May 26, they reached the final, main cache at 6,050 feet on the Ogilvie. Cascade, the site of their advanced base camp, was clearly visible eight miles away over the ice, and they immediately started to relay the stores there from the tarpaulin-covered mound.

By May 31 they were established in their advanced base camp. It was 7,800 feet above sea-level and took the name of Cascade Camp from the cataract of a splendid ice-fall that tumbled from a branch of King Glacier to the Ogilvie.

If a glacier is likened to a river, then the ice-fall is the counterpart of the rapids. A sudden drop in elevation speeds and disrupts the smooth flow, and the tortured ice fractures and splinters in all directions. Blocks as big as skyscrapers fall often, dwarfed in the giant perspective of the peaks. Each looses a roar to match its majesty, and rarely is there peace in the ever-moving ice-fall. Even then it is at best a patchwork truce, shattered by the sporadic crack and rattle of dissension as more blocks settle, preparing to leap to their own spectacular ends.

It was an incomparable spot, epic in its scale and beauty, and a perfect psychological stimulant for the mighty task that had now fairly begun.

The stimulant did its job well. During the next two days the eight men carried three-quarters of a ton of supplies to the top of Quartz Ridge, a rib of rock that soared a thousand feet above camp on the west side of the ice-cascade. Beyond was the world of eternal snow and ice where man has a different set of problems, and sometimes has a hard job holding on to his sense of values. Once here in the vast deep-freeze, the body and the mind begin to get rough treatment.

As they walked, for instance, their feet would get numb from the cold of the snow beneath. Yet their faces, not six feet away, would be blistering in a temperature perhaps fifty degrees higher. Snow and ice act as a magnifying reflector, doubling and tripling the burning power of the sun. The thin air never really warms up, but anything directly exposed to the sun's rays will almost bake. At all times, from now on, the climbers' faces were smeared with thick layers of protective cream. Their eyes, too, were guarded, with various types of dark glasses. MacCarthy's eyes, never very strong, were shielded by two pairs, but the glare was so strong that even then he had frequent pains and headaches. The climbers now embarked on a stay of forty-four days on snow and ice. The snow route up to the top of the ridge was steep enough for all of them. For considerable stretches, the slope measured forty-five degrees, and they quickly decided to put in a fixed rope handrail for safety as they hauled up the loads.

Early on the morning of June 3, they abandoned Cascade and with heavy loads began the leap-frog march up King Glacier. Along the west side of the glacier, mountain ramparts soared to 12,000 feet. Bulging along them were heavy loads of hanging ice, which frequently broke off and fell towards the party. But along the base of the ridge was a huge crevasse, which swallowed up the avalanches and kept the climbers safe. It took them three more days to move the loads to Observation Camp at 10,200 feet.

This was the highest point MacCarthy had reached during his summer reconnaissance the year before. From here on, they were heading where no one had been before. Yet, by the standards of most of the world's mountain ranges, they were not even at the foot of their peak. They still had eighteen miles and almost 10,000 vertical feet to go.

The weather maliciously emphasized their isolation. They pitched the tents in a strong wind that lashed stinging sheets of snow in their faces. That night, it rose to a pitch of extreme violence and several times the climbers struggled to hold up the tent-poles, frightened that their three tiny shelters would be torn away.

Then, suddenly, in the freakish, unpredictable way of big mountains that brew their own weather, the storm ceased. Instead, there was a dead calm and dense fog. The fog swathed and muffled them as they left camp at 9 a.m. next day. This was to be an easy day. Packs weighed only thirty-one pounds, and fastened to each one was a thick bundle of willow wands. This was Andy Taylor's idea, and like all great ideas a very simple one. On big areas of featureless snow and ice, which are common on Alaska's giant glaciers, there is nothing to guide the traveller when the clouds come down. Perspective vanishes; the frowning cliff that towers ahead may turn out to be a foot high. As skiers know to their cost, it is sometimes impossible to tell even whether the ground ahead slopes up or down.

But when a slim willow switch is planted in the snow, without even a break in the planter's stride, the picture changes. The eye has something of recognized stature to focus on. The willows are placed about a hundred feet apart. This way, even in the worst of weather, the last man on the rope can stay with one wand until the leader, casting about in the blizzard, can find the next. Step by hundred-foot step this continues, making safe travel relatively simple in weather that would otherwise be impossible. The thin wands stand up well to storms.

By 1 p.m. they were four miles above camp, at the base of an ice-fall a thousand feet high. It was a gentle gradient, however, and the hundreds of crevasses were well bridged with firm snow.

But if the gradient was gentle, the weather was not. It became worse as they pushed upwards, and when they went over the top of the ice-fall the blasts became so strong that several of the men were almost skittered into crevasses. They struggled on for another mile in what they called a "mild blizzard, with temperature about zero." At 13,200 feet by their small pocket altimeters they stopped and dumped most of the contents of their packs into the snow. This was about two miles short of the saddle, which they had hoped to reach. As they returned, visibility became even poorer and the wind had wiped out their track, but the wands were easy to follow.

Their success at following the wands gave them the resolve to push ahead the next day, June 7, no matter what the weather, and relay more loads to the col. Almost seven hundred pounds of food and fuel were loaded onto the sled, and with all eight either hauling on the lines or pushing on the handles they made four miles to the foot of the ice-fall in four hours. Then they carried the loads to a spot a mile beyond their earlier cache and a mile short of the saddle itself. Terrible winds can howl through high saddles in the mountains, and the site they chose would be sheltered from at least some of them. It was at 14,500 feet. They could hardly wait to dump their loads there and hurry along to the saddle. This was the key: did it lead easily to the base of Mount Logan? Or was it impossible? Nobody had ever seen it.

They stumbled and ran the last few feet to the crest. Then their hope, like their footsteps, staggered at the view. The smooth slopes of the saddle did not connect gently with the upper slopes of their mountain. There was a gap of at least a thousand feet, filled with a chaotic mass of steep and broken ice-blocks. And, just beyond where these finished, the slope curled away out of sight, with no view of the problems beyond.

At the other end of the saddle, however, gentle slopes led to 15,000 feet on King Peak, giving the possibility of a better view of the route. So, while Lambart took his rope of climbers back to camp to get more loads ready, MacCarthy's rope climbed the shoulder of King Peak. The going was fine when they strapped crampons to their boots and set off. Soon they were on top of the shoulder, within 2,000 feet of King Peak's summit—yet it would not be climbed until 1952!

From their eagle's eyrie, almost as high as the greatest peak in the Alps, they could see the route, at least to 17,000 feet and it was possible.

Several of the climbers had now begun to suffer badly from the effects of high altitude. This depression can hit at any height above roughly 10,000 feet. It is a feeling for which there is no valid single basis of comparison at sea-level. The air is thin; it contains less oxygen and is under far less atmospheric pressure than our bodies are normally accustomed to. The lack of oxygen is enervating, quickly bringing on the symptoms of exhaustion; but the lack of accustomed nitrogen pressure affects the responses of the brain. One experienced Himalayan mountaineer, describing his feeling of altitude sickness, said he felt like "a sick man climbing in a dream."

Men of strong will find their drive evaporating. Men of gargantuan appetites often want to do nothing more than nibble. And men of great physical strength and perfect condition puff and pant from merely turning over in their sleeping-bags. The brain doesn't work very well, but often, as with drinkers, this seems to bring a feeling that the judgment is better than it is. Usually nobody else in the party notices, as the critical faculties of all are likely to be impaired, even though different people react at varying heights.

At this height of 15,000 feet, however, these men of long experience on big mountains were able to shake off the effects of the altitude for a while. They hurried back down to Observation Camp at 10,200 feet and immediately felt better. On June 8, once more they wearily carried more loads up to Col Camp. Foster, Read, and MacCarthy stayed there, digging several feet down into the snow to provide some sort of wind-break for the tents. Lambart took the others down to continue the exhausting, uninspiring, yet all-important job of bringing up the food.

This night was one of torture for MacCarthy. He tossed and turned for hours in the agony caused by the intense glare in his weakened eyes. Foster, getting into practice for grimmer things to come, treated him as best he could, and they set off at 8 a.m. to see if they could find a way through the worrying ice-fall.

In seven hours they reached 16,500 feet, after five miles of turning and twisting through an incoherent jumble of ice-blocks, many of which were given names like Tent City or the Stage (each in case a rendezvous should ever be needed in this wilderness of ice). They chose a camp-site at 17,000 feet, to be known prophetically as Windy Camp.

They were within 3,000 feet of the summit now and were beginning to feel a vague optimism when the weather cleared. But the mountain was simply playing another mean and cunning trick on them: it gave them a clear view of the double peak that topped the ice-mass ahead. This looked suspiciously like the summit and built their hopes too high.

Close as they seemed to be, however, they were once again a little like an advancing army that has to stop its triumphant march to let the supply train catch up. At every camp they had to be prepared to wait out a siege of blizzards that might pin them down for a week or more at a time. So all day on June 10 the back-breaking work went on as they hauled supplies to

Col Camp, making it a fortress. If they were routed anywhere else on the giant peak, here at 14,200 feet at least was warmth, comparative comfort, and safety.

Early next day it began to snow, which was common for June 11 at this height and so far north. But this was the start of a chain of developments fraught with implications of disaster.

It was almost noon before MacCarthy, Lambart, Foster, and Hall set off with heavy packs towards Windy Camp. The carefully placed footsteps in the snow they had made before, so big a psychological stimulus when men are weary and long for rhythmic guidance to their feet, had vanished under the heavy fall of new snow. They planted willow wands as they navigated the route now established through the clouds, and the careful observation that had gone into the naming of the ice-blocks served them well. Tent City still looked like a city of tents, even if more opulent with its rich re-roofing. Hog Back was still a hog's back, though the hog was sleeker, fat with its surfeit of snow. A little higher, at 15,400 feet, the wallowing became too tough; so they dumped their packs and turned back.

The snow continued to fall monotonously throughout the next two days. They could do little but lie in the tents, joking constantly to hide the fact that although they were vexed and anxious at the delay they were rather glad of the chance to rest.

When all eight set out again at 6.30 a.m. on June 14, the snow had an exasperating crust of ice that was not quite strong enough to support them on snow-shoes. And there was a new danger around them now, the threat that the fresh top layer of snow would peel off with a sibilant hiss and sweep the whole party to destruction. In five and a half hours they climbed 900 feet to the Hog Back—a pleasant half-hour saunter at sea-level. To their forty-five pound packs they now added the loads dumped here earlier, and moved on, almost imperceptibly. Five trying hours later, they had gained a mere 400 feet, and as they were trying to decide what to do the weather solved their problem: a blizzard hit them with frightening speed. It roared to new heights as they pitched their wildly flapping tents and struggled to crawl through the circular sleeve entrances.

It blew throughout the next day, and the clouds were so thick that it was hard to see the adjoining tents. Early on the sixteenth the wind dropped; so they set out at 6.30 a.m. Twelve battling hours later they reached Windy Camp at almost 17,000 feet, beneath the great south-west wall of Logan. It was a strenuous day, one with which any climbing party could be well satisfied. Instead, Foster, Lambart, and MacCarthy left Hall to set up camp and climbed on to prospect the route ahead.

When they came back, just before 8 p.m., the temperature was 27° below zero. That night it went down to 33° below.

Before he settled down for the night, so close to the summit, MacCarthy took a realistic look at the men around him. He was as optimistic as he could reasonably be, but the best entry he could make in his diary was: "Party all in fair shape, but not strong for the work to be done." The night did not improve things. All slept badly, despite the insulation of their sixteen-pound Arctic bedrolls.

When men reach a tired and worn-out state like this, the start of each new day brings a difficult conflict of feeling. The part of the mind that has the body's welfare to worry about puts up a protest. It half prays for fog, snow, a blizzard—anything to give a valid reason for resting longer. The other part, focused by conscience on the job to be done, prods dully but usually irresistibly at the will, striving to convince it that a fine day is most welcome so that they can get on with the hard work.

June 17 started out to be a fine day and, the sleeping-bag skirmish with conscience having been won, they all turned out and began to prepare. MacCarthy summed up their situation with a piece of priceless understatement that would have made any good English stiff upper lip quiver with admiration: "There appearing some need for relaxation from drudgery," he wrote, "all hands went on a reconnaissance in order to determine our exact location on the massif." Many people would have abandoned the whole project right there, for what MacCarthy's statement meant in simple English was: We were too tired to pack camps any farther, and we didn't know where we were anyway.

What the weary troops needed to renew their vigour, MacCarthy decided, was…some mountain-climbing. But without heavy packs. In five hours the team had circled to the north side of the mountain and reached a saddle at 18,800 feet that separated two high peaks. Thick fog blocked out the view as they waited in the bitter cold, straining their eyes to see ahead and pick out a route. Where should they turn next? Was one of these double peaks the summit? Which? Or was the highest point even farther away?

Next day, Foster, Read, and MacCarthy climbed back to the saddle again while the others went down for more food. This time, a gale was sweeping the saddle. Lying down in the snow, peering through ice-rimmed eyes over the edge of the saddle, they had a brief glimpse of another double peak about three miles away. As they lay in the snow to avoid being bowled over the edge by the gale, they started to argue. Was that the top? Or was there yet another in this damnable, never-ending ridge?

Only one thing was sure: even a camp at 17,000 feet, where sleep was difficult and the thought of hard work revolting, was not high enough. Windy Camp was too remote from the top for weak and exhausted men to make a safe "dash" to the still invisible summit.

As they turned in that night, the temperature was 32° below zero. At 7 a.m. next day, it was still 25° below, and snowing heavily, but all eight went down for supplies. For an hour in the afternoon, the sun poked holes through the layers of cloud and the temperature began to climb rapidly. At last, it seemed, the weather might help them. An hour later a gale whipped away the last vestige of summer and replaced it in minutes with Arctic winter. This was the worst weather so far, and almost trapped the party between camps. All took it in weary turn to punch foot-holes in the snow, and it was after 9 p.m. when they reached Windy Camp again.

Several fingers were frost-bitten from uncovering them for even the few seconds needed to tighten bootlaces or pack straps. But far more serious was the fact that Morgan's feet, which had been frozen some years before, were now quite badly frost-bitten. This proved to MacCarthy that they had reached the limit of usefulness of the rubber shoe-packs they were wearing. These are rubber shoe-pieces with leather boot-uppers attached to them. In the ever-wet going of the lower glaciers, they were a great success. Here, where the snow never melts and the temperature rarely gets as high as freezing-point, the rubber wasn't necessary—and they were far from warm enough. They were big enough for only two pairs of socks. So the party switched to a type of Indian moccasins, dry-tanned and with room enough for up to five pairs of thick socks.

Keeping warm had now become the all-absorbing problem, and the tents were at once the focus and the shield of life. To keep out the crippling cold, each man was now wearing two sets of the heaviest woollen underwear, with long legs and sleeves; windproof canvas trousers; up to three woollen shirts; at least one sweater; and hooded, knee-length parkas of windproof drill cloth. Everybody wore a woollen balaclava helmet and two pairs of wool gloves with windproof over-gauntlets. The tents in which they lived were eight feet square at the base, seven feet high at the one pole, tapering to eighteen inches at the other end. Each weighed ten pounds and slept four men.

Each one had a sewn-in waterproof groundsheet, and on top of this were individual air-mattresses of heavy-gauge rubber. Each of these weighed eight pounds, and a bicycle pump was used to inflate them. Finally came an eiderdown sleeping-bag weighing sixteen pounds. Two of these could be fastened together to make one bag about six feet wide. For twelve days, four of the climbers slept together in one of these. It kept them fairly warm, but they were so cramped that they all slept badly.

Another important aspect of keeping warm at these heights is food. At high altitudes the heartiest eater often becomes finicky. Mountaineers are generally marked individualists, and many acquire an almost fanatical belief in the value of one food or another. One climber, for instance, almost refused to join this party because he understood no cocoa was being taken. Without it in the diet, he said, the assault would not succeed. Another insisted that jam was the key to success on the mountain. He didn't mind what else was taken provided there was enough jam to permit huge amounts at every meal.

Two of the party fell out on how to cook the bacon. One said vehemently that to be useful it must be burned to a crisp. The other swore it provided most benefit when not cooked but just warmed through.

MacCarthy, who drew up the menu, solved the problem as best he could. He provided far more than he thought the climbers could eat of a variety of meats, butter, cheese, dried eggs and vegetables, powdered milk, and brown sugar. Then for those who wanted to convince themselves they were eating something else, he provided liberal amounts of black pepper, cinnamon, nutmeg, curry, horseradish, and sauces. It seemed to work. Nobody made any real complaints.

But despite the care that had gone into the planning, now at 17,000 feet they were faced with the serious fact that Morgan's feet were badly frostbitten. He must go down. Henry Hall, so close to one of the finest prizes of his long climbing career, casually did something that showed why he was one of the best known and most respected of United States climbers. He gave up his chance at the peak and offered to take Morgan down to safety. But first, he insisted, he must take the biggest and heaviest pack up to the next camp-site. It didn't matter too much if he wore himself out, he said—he was going downhill from then on. But it would at least lessen by a fraction the odds against the others making it.

He did his last big carry on June 20, when all except Morgan moved up in a storm to a tiny saddle at 18,500 feet. This held for many years the record as the highest regular camp established in North America.

At 10 a.m. the wind eased off long enough for Hall and Morgan to set off down from Windy Camp. They shook hands quickly with the remaining six climbers, and wished them well; then, looking frail and puny, they vanished within a rope's length into the swirling clouds of snow. No sooner had they gone than the gale swept back. By 3 p.m. all six had crept into their sleeping-bags, morose and a little anxious about both the prospects above and the pair going down. But there was nothing they could do about either, and they had time to reflect on the futility of man's boast that he "conquers" peaks. When impersonal nature makes a personal issue of it, the strongest climber hasn't a hope of winning. All the great feats of mountaineering have been achieved by skilful men who were ready and waiting for the momentary relaxation of nature's guard that would let them slip in.

So it was now. As suddenly as if somebody had flicked a switch, the wind dropped a few minutes after they crawled into their sleeping-bags. The clouds vanished, and sunshine flooded the slopes. They scurried around packing, and by 10 p.m. were settled in for the night at 18,500 feet. Their two small brownie tents, smaller and a little lighter than the ones they had used so far, made a brave show of pretending to be safe and comfortable at this near-limit of man's ability.

They found that night and the next morning that the effects of altitude were really beginning to hit everybody. Everything they did was slow and clumsy. Several just lay in their bags and looked with half-glazed eyes at jobs that must be done, thinking dully of ways to avoid them. Even the exertion of getting into the bags, or turning over inside them, set the heart pounding. That night, the temperature was seven degrees below zero—thirty-nine degrees below freezing-point, Fahrenheit. In fact from June 16 to June 26 the thermometer went above zero only once. So befuddled were they next morning, June 22, that it was 11 a.m. before they could start. Thick-gloved hands fumbled drunkenly with packstraps and snow-shoe bindings, and the main thing that got them going was the collective, not individual, feeling that it just had to be done. All pleasure had long since vanished from the undertaking. This feeling of collective responsibility is one of the major benefits of team psychology. It is nothing unusual for all the members of a climbing rope to feel inside that this is the limit; each feels too tired and dispirited to go on. But nobody will admit it, so they do go on. And what each man thought to himself to be impossible is once again accomplished.

So it was now as they moved away. Their route at first took them down from the saddle, skirting the double peak so they would not have to fight for valuable height, only to lose it again on the other side. Yet though they were going down, they made only one and a half miles before deep, soft snow halted them on a plateau at 17,800 feet. This they decided to call Plateau Camp, and with faltering, half-desperate movements they pitched their tents near what was later to be grimly known as Hurricane Hill.

It was fortunate they stopped. As the last man crawled panting through the entrance sleeve, a violent gust of wind raced over the hill, bringing a blizzard that shrieked all night. Hardly anybody could even doze as the night crept slowly on. The splendid peace and tranquility of the heights that the poets praise was nowhere evident. The wind made so much noise that they rather fancied they were spending the night inside a busy railway tunnel. Much of the time they clutched the vibrating bamboo tent-poles, expecting any moment to see the fabric split and tear apart.

But once again came the seeming surrender of nature that lures men on to try impossible deeds. By 10 a.m. the storm had blown out and the clouds of snow whipped up by its passing had settled down again.

The sun came out—and came nearer to immobilizing the party than even the blizzards. The fearful glare from new white snow was almost intolerable, and the severe pains of approaching snow-blindness shot through MacCarthy's eyes, though he wore two pairs of the darkest snow-goggles made. He was leading the first rope, followed by Carpé, with Foster bringing up the rear. So the rope switched around, to put Foster in front— Foster, whom MacCarthy called "our sheet anchor no matter what the difficulty." Foster seemed to take all types of problems in his stride, and versatility was his forte. He had already been a member of the Legislative Assembly of British Columbia, and, at thirty-five, had been Deputy-Minister of Public Works for the province. He was to become chief of police in Vancouver, and a major-general in the Second World War. In addition to the D.S.O. and two bars he won in the First World War, he also won the Croix de Guerre from France and Belgium—and many years later in England, another colonel was to state that Foster had turned down a nomination for the Victoria Cross, the Commonwealth's highest award for bravery.

Billy Foster led them on the wandering route among crevasses, over a shoulder of ice, and to the base of a steep slope supporting the saddle between two peaks. The Double Peak was clearly visible now, but it was impossible to say which of the summits was the higher.

A brief rest here, and MacCarthy tenaciously took back the lead. During the 1924 reconnaissance he had tried vainly to decide which of these giant twin peaks was the summit. At various times he and his binoculars had awarded the title to each. Now he set off up the nearest one, with the feeling that this was probably not the summit, but that the only way to find out was to go up it.

The slope was now steeper than anything they had met so far on the mountain. Two weak men would find it almost impossible to hold a third who slipped. But their eight-pointed crampons bit firmly into the icy crust. All they had to do was keep placing each foot in turn in front of, and a little above, the other.

At 4.20 p.m., with the sun glaring from an unclouded sky, all six reached the top. As they tramped slowly onto the summit the first place everybody looked was to the south-east. There the companion dome glittered wickedly two miles away. There was a painful silence as they looked, for what they felt was far too deep for mere curses. The distant mound was obviously higher than the one on which they stood.

MacCarthy, Foster, and Carpé set off directly towards the exasperating summit. Lambart, Read, and Taylor, gambling that this peak was their goal, had left most of their equipment at the base of it. They would have gone back for it anyway, but they particularly wanted the last few willow-wands that were tied to their packs. Half an hour later, they were all together once more in a saddle beneath what they hoped was their final trial, the ultimate apex of Canada.

The pitiful pace slowed even more. In this region of almost perpetual wind, the powdered snow could not stay for long. Brittle, shining ice gleamed in the open, and as they maneuvered around these patches they had to cut almost two hundred steps in the crusted snow. The slope was frighteningly steep to tackle at this height—in several places it was about sixty degrees. Every movement had to be safeguarded carefully, by ramming the ice-axe as far down into the snow as possible and then paying the rope out slowly around it. Carpé was exhausted, and had to be helped to move on the final stretch. But finally, while MacCarthy was cutting steps like an automaton, with no conscious thought to guide his axe, his head came level with the top of the ridge. A hundred yards away, at the top of a gentle rise, stood the summit.

It was here, so close to victory, that MacCarthy thought for a moment he had gone mad. For days the altitude and hard work had made them all light-headed, with delusions that they were hopping through time and space, like giants in seven-league boots performing prodigious feats. Now into MacCarthy's tired and disbelieving brain flashed the picture of a giant's head, framed in a vivid, circular rainbow.

"Now I was possibly seeing the unreal," he wrote, "perhaps one of nature's brilliant hoops through which I must jump when legs and feet felt like lead after their long ordeal." It was a relief to his brain when Carpé, the scientist, said matter-of-factly that it was a "Brocken spectre with a halo." When the sun's rays coincide with the direction in which the climber is looking, the shadow of his head is sometimes projected onto the outside edge of a cloud to form the spectre. The rainbow halo comes from light hitting the liquid droplets in the air which stay unfrozen even at the temperature of near zero. MacCarthy had never seen either before.

A few more minutes took them to the top, crampons crunching with a squeak into the hard snow of the knife-edged summit ridge. It was 8 p.m. The summit was a thirty-foot pinnacle of ice, just big enough for the six of them to stand on. The sides dropped thousands of feet to remote untrodden glaciers below.

But even as they revelled in the view—and the faculty of observation, curiously, remains virtually undulled as altitude saps the other senses— clouds began bubbling and boiling up in the direction of Mount St. Elias, a cauldron filled with storm and trouble. As they stood numbly on the summit, burying in the snow a brass tube with their names and the date, and munching cheese, chocolate, and dried fruits, they shook hands all round.

"We were foolishly happy in the success of our venture," said Captain MacCarthy, "and we thought that our troubles were at an end."

Lambart was the first to leave the summit, with Taylor and Read on his rope. It was almost 8.30 p.m., and as Carpé, Foster, and MacCarthy left a few seconds later it was obvious that they were in for a dangerous race with the weather. In a few short minutes, it was equally obvious that they had lost it. Thick cloud enveloped them, and they had trouble following even the big steps they had hacked out on the way up the final steep slopes. Where the going flattened out between this and the other Double Peak, there were no steps to follow. The sharp crampons had left no trail in the hard crust—and the last of the willow-wands was a mile away where the supply had run out.

The wind rose, and began to punch the reeling party in shattering gusts that all but knocked them flat. Flying snow in the air blended with the snow on the surface to produce that phenomenon so much feared by Arctic travellers: the *white-out*. In this condition it is impossible to tell direction, or even which way the ground slopes. Now they were wandering aimlessly. Five hours after they left the summit, at 1.30 a.m., they were still at the 19,000-foot level, and hopelessly lost. They had no choice but the one that many experienced climbers would have considered near-certain death—to spend the night huddled in holes in the snow.

Moving like sick, apathetic shadows of the men they had been two weeks before, they began pecking out holes with the narrow points and adzes of their ice-axes. Snow-shoes served, though not too well, as shovels, but the energy that is the primary tool for digging reasonable shelters just was not there. They had reached the penultimate plateau of exhaustion, a plateau sloping gently down towards oblivion, where the body's strength has gone and only the spur of the mind is left.

This in itself, though usually on a less epic scale, is part of the fascination of mountaineering: the realization that each difficult climb can take you far beyond the physical limits of ordinary life, and that each worth-while success may bring a new boundary of self-realization to cross. It is the dogged crossing of this boundary that gives rise to all the great feats of adventure.

There was little thought of adventure in their minds as they chipped away at their task. There was little, if any, conscious thought that they must do this to survive. The holes they made were so poor and inadequate that if they had been forced to put sled-dogs in them, the climbers would have felt sorry for the dogs. "They were pitiful evidences of the weakened state of our party," wrote the leader. Carpé still had the will-power to check the temperature: it was -12° F., and dropping quickly. But when the thermometer fell into the snow, he didn't have the energy to scramble for it, and it soon vanished in a soft drift. Exhaustion fought with the fear of freezing to death, and won in fitful snatches. But wild attacks of shivering and frightening nightmares woke them time and time again. Much to their surprise, all lived to see the dawn, which was indicated merely by an infinitesimal lightening of the dark shades of gloomy grey. Still they could see nothing in the whirling snow.

Writing of this grim situation, MacCarthy once more outdid himself in understatement. He wrote: "A further period under such trying conditions might have reduced some of our members to a helpless state. So at noon I called all hands and ordered a start with Andy leading."

Andy Taylor, who lived in the north and was accustomed to the bitter cold of Arctic winter, was probably less affected by the long exposure than any of the others. He was ready to go at once. But the leader and Foster, who was hero-worshipped by the men he had led into dangerous battles, found it was one thing to order—even in a weak and faltering shout—and quite another to get people to obey, even when the order was meant to save their lives. It was another two hours before the rest of the party could be pried from the near-death stupor they had sunk into in the holes that so nearly became their tombs.

The great need now was action—exercise to start the frigid blood pumping through their stiff, sore bodies. But almost as great was the need for caution. One false move in the deceptive, dangerous, flat light could put them over the brink of an ice-cliff. MacCarthy was barely able to see the others on the rope, and he marvelled in a detached sort of way, at the exaggerated drunken swaying of his companions. Suddenly, the caution drummed into him by years of imminent danger in the mountains snapped his mind back into focus. A faint black streak, hardly visible, appeared through the mist a few feet to his right. Cautiously he edged nearer to investigate it, and found to his horror a cliff dropping off into the bottomless shroud of space.

"I hastened forward to give Andy warning, but it was too late," he wrote. "In a moment he disappeared from sight, with the rope left taut in Read's hands." MacCarthy hurried up to help Read take the strain on the rope, and moved carefully to the edge of the precipice, afraid of what he might see when he looked down. Thirty feet below, motionless and half buried in the snow, was Taylor. MacCarthy called urgently to him, but he did not move. MacCarthy called again, his voice pitched higher now in desperation. And this time Taylor answered. He was unhurt, but temporarily paralyzed by having his breath knocked out as he landed.

A few feet farther along, the cliff curved down to a low point close to the level where Taylor had landed. The five climbers moved along to this, and after Taylor had a few minutes to get his breath back they were able to haul him back to safety.

MacCarthy was so relieved to have escaped disaster that he found the energy to pull Taylor's leg about it. It was frightfully bad form, he said, for Taylor to have left the other members of his rope without giving them proper warning. It raised a laugh, but as a joke it backfired.

A few minutes later MacCarthy tumbled over an unseen ice-cliff and dropped fifteen feet before Carpé and Foster held him with a rib-crushing check on the rope.

Despite an ordeal that would have destroyed lesser parties, they still pushed slowly on. And finally they had a stroke of luck—the kind that comes only to top-flight men of long experience. Nobody really knew where they were going, but Taylor, with nothing but instinct to guide him in the white-out, kept heading obstinately to where he insisted they would find the last willow-wand. They found it, with Read's sharp eyes spotting it first. Just the sight of a slender stick they had cut from a wilderness bush was enough to send new strength into their legs, proof enough of the mind's control of the body's limits.

MacCarthy summed it up this way: "The reaction was the same as I once felt when struggling in a hopeless surf that rapidly carried me seaward, with combers strangling every effort I made to catch breath. I finally gave up, let go—and my feet touched the bottom. In an instant I had the strength of a giant, and incautiously jumped to my feet, only to have them swept from under me again. But deliverance was there, and I did not say good-bye to this world that day."

He didn't say good-bye to the world on this day of trial by ice on the mountain either—in fact he lived to be eighty, and died in Annapolis, Maryland, in 1956. But neither did he say good-bye to the terrors of being lost high on Mount Logan.

Taylor, Read, and Lambart followed the wands to Plateau Camp, the two flimsy tents at 17,800 feet. Taylor would hold onto one wand while Read, at the other end of the rope, would pass by him and look for the next wand, a hundred feet away in the driving blizzard. Then Read would hold on to this one while Taylor passed him.

But MacCarthy, Foster, and Carpé, the most experienced climbers of them all, stopped for a moment to tighten a packstrap. They lost touch with the other rope in a few seconds, became confused by the storm, and headed on, hoping to pick up the willow-wand trail again. They tramped slowly for an hour, and as they went something niggled at the methodical mind of Carpé. At first his weary brain just sensed that something was wrong, although it was too tired to puzzle it out. Suddenly he realized: the rise of the slope was on their right now, instead of on their left as it had been before. They all realized instantly what had happened. In their brief pause the fury of the storm had made them turn completely around and they were now heading back towards the peak—away from safety. With spirits too drained for emotion, they turned around, and plodded back for another hour. By now, however, the grey of night was blending with the whirling clouds, and they were forced to stop until daylight.

It was a night of delirious rambling, of hallucinations and moments of cold sanity when they "knew" they would never escape a second time.

"High cliffs of ice would seem to rise up before us to block our way," MacCarthy wrote, "and yet we never encountered them. Barns and shelters would suddenly appear that we knew could not exist, for otherwise one's companions would surely suggest taking refuge in them."

It was so cold that they abandoned their idea of staying in one place until they could see properly. They trudged on automatically through the night, twice routinely scraping out feeble shelters for naps that never lasted long enough to overcome their shivering.

With dawn, however, came visibility. With it, the pressing problems vanished; they could see their way to Plateau Camp and by 5 a.m. they were wolfing chicken for breakfast after a harrowing thirty-four hours. By 6 a.m. they were asleep. They awoke at 4 p.m., and stayed awake just long enough for another meal; then went back to sleep to build up strength for the trip out. It was no downhill stroll, as they first had to climb to the Camp at 18,500, a difficult task in their present condition.

Now, with the lash of imminent death no longer curling around their shoulders, reaction to their terrible ordeal began to hit all the climbers. They were up by 6 a.m. on June 26, but even though "mares' tails" in the sky warned them that more storms were on the way, it took five hours to get ready to move off. Even then, they left the tents, mattresses, clothing, and spare food behind. Taylor's rope went first, snow-shoeing along the line of looming willow-wands. The going was good, rhythm began returning to the weary legs, and spirits improved.

Then they reached a steep, rounded snow dome where the winds had compressed the snow to a hard crust. It was impossible to get up it on cumbersome snow-shoes, so they began to change to their sole-fitting crampons.

As they did so, the weather launched its most vicious attack yet. A hurricane hit them, and the temperature plummeted. The normally simple task of tying the long tapes of the crampons became almost impossible. The strings rapidly became almost unmanageable bars of ice. Bare hands were needed to manipulate them in the freezing wind.

Everybody suffered frost-bite in the fingers as the painful but imperative task of tying the crampons went slowly on. Most of the party had touches of frost-bite in their feet too, and several were temporarily blind from the combination of glare and icy particles hurled horizontally into their faces. The agony of Hurricane Hill was unanimously voted the most terrifying experience so far, even by those who survived the two nights out near the summit.

Somehow they managed to finish the job and push on. By 3 p.m. they were at the site of the Camp of Eighteen-five, where a small granite rib split the fury of the storm and gave them some shelter. Now the way out was all downhill—and the retreat gave the first signs of turning into a rout. Already they had abandoned two tents at Plateau Camp, and had no safeguard in case of a high-level accident. They struggled on to Windy Camp (16,700 feet), where there was another tent and a cache of supplies. This too they abandoned, with only one thought in their cold-dimmed brains: "Get down before it is too late." The six strong men could hardly muster the strength to pull the shoepacks from a corner of the partly-collapsed tent; then on they went again.

Once more, they were back in thick fog and fast-flying snow; but this time the thin green wands stood out like oak trees. New avalanches of disintegrating ice had blotted out parts of their route through the ice-fall, but as they passed the last unstable pinnacles of ice they could see three tents half-buried in the snow at Col Camp (14,500 feet). Getting to them was still a major task, however. Avalanche danger was now extreme, with masses of newly-fallen snow poised to slide. The urge was strong to rush straight down to camp and the safe comfort it represented. Instead, they forced themselves to be slow and desperately careful. An accident here could turn triumph to disaster just as surely as one at the summit 5,000 feet above. And this was the likely place for an accident to happen: most mountaineering accidents happen not in the difficult places where mind and muscle are at top pitch, but on the way down, in the anti-climax after success.

It was 1.30 a.m. when they reached camp, and they stayed thirty-six hours, although the altitude was high for sick, bone-weary men. When the body has taken so much punishment, it is hard for even the most active mind to persuade it to leave any level of comfort, no matter how slight. Even the thought of a well-stocked camp at Cascade, at an elevation where a man would feel like a whole man again, was barely able to move them. When finally they did move, on June 28, they once more abandoned almost everything and pushed on down. Andy Taylor went first. He went unroped, despite the ever-present danger of vanishing into a crevasse, and dragged behind him his pack, wrapped in a canvas sheet. This gouged a deep, smooth trench in the soft snow and made it easier for the others to get down. It was a brave and dangerous performance by Taylor, and the fact that he volunteered to do it at all indicates how tired and sick his companions must have seemed to him.

By 9 p.m. they were back at Quartz Ridge, at the top of the last 1,000-foot snow slope above Cascade advanced base camp. On June 2, they had made this descent in fifteen minutes. Now it took them twelve times as long—three hours. They crawled through the tent-sleeves just after midnight, and MacCarthy noted in his diary: "Tents in bad shape, but I in worse condition."

For two days they rested here while Foster took ceaseless care of the sick. They set off again on July 1. The glaciers were fast losing their deep mantle of winter snow to the summer sun, and the travel was wet and slow. It was dangerous, too, as the constant melting rotted the firm layers of snow that had bridged the deep crevasses on the journey in. So they began to travel at night. At this elevation, the snow still froze at night, strengthening the crevasse bridges, and generally making the surface easier for pulling the two heavy sledges.

Now the worry of high, stormbound camps had gone, and was replaced by a restless drive to get home. Even the discovery that the first big food-cache had been destroyed by bears did not bother them. They rested a few hours near the ruins, and pushed on. On July 4, they stepped off the ice of Chitina Glacier onto vegetation that looked startlingly green and lush to eyes that had seen only ice and snow for forty-four days. Bears had demolished the food-cache here too, but on July 6 they reached the comfort of Hubrick's Camp.

It had taken tremendous endurance to walk so far on frost-bitten feet, but here Lambart, Carpé, and Read decided their feet were so bad they couldn't possibly walk any farther. Raw flesh was visible where the dead surface tissues had sloughed off. Yet the base at the village of McCarthy was still eighty miles away.

In desperation, they decided to try to float down the turbulent Chitina River system on home-made rafts. For several days they worked, building two small rafts that were solemnly christened Logan and Loganette. They looked frail, inadequate things to carry six lives through the rapid, twisting channels of the Chitina. Each was made of six small logs, lashed together, with a small platform on which the baggage could be carried high out of the water.

Early on the afternoon of July 11 they set off. Taylor, Read, and Lambart were riding on Logan, and MacCarthy, Carpé, and Foster on Loganette. After a hair-raising ride of more than fifty miles, Taylor's craft landed that night on a beach at the nearest point to the village of McCarthy. This still left them a thirty-mile walk across rough country to safety. Lambart's feet were far worse than anybody else's, yet he managed the trek next day without food and practically unaided.

The three men on Loganette, who had been forced to spend the second night out near the summit, ran out of luck here too. Only eighteen miles from their starting-point, they met disaster, and barely escaped alive. In one particularly rough stretch of river their raft turned completely over, pitching all three into the glacial water. They managed to grab the raft and paddle their way to shore, but all their camping and cooking equipment was lost. There were still seventy miles to walk, and all they had was a few scraps of emergency rations.

On their pain-wracked feet, the seventy miles took them four days. Just as they reached the village on July 15, they met a party led by Taylor that was setting out to search the bars of the Chitina for their bodies.

The details of their tremendous feat thrilled the mountaineering world—and obviously frightened it a little too. It was twenty-five years before anybody even attempted the mountain again. 🍂

GANGAPURNA STORIES

John Lauchlan died on February 5, 1982 while attempting a solo climb of *Polar Circus*, a waterfall ice climb in the Canadian Rockies. An avalanche swept him off the climb and over a cliff. It was a bad year for avalanches in the Canadian Rockies and climbers had been warned of the high hazards. But Lauchlan was used to walking the razor between risk and adventure. At the age of 27, he had already built a climbing résumé that would have made any mountaineer deeply envious. Intense, intelligent, driven, he was arguably Canada's most important climber when he died.

It was on the walls of Yamnuska, the limestone edifice just east of Canmore that was the training ground for so many of the great Calgary climbers of the '60s and '70s, that Lauchlan really came to life as a climber, but he was also at home on the waterfall of ice of the Rockies, establishing a number of classic winter lines. He was first up many of the steep waterfalls in the National Parks, including the thousand-foot frozen Takakaw Falls in Yoho Park and the elegant *Slipstream*, a bold and innovative ice climb on Snow Dome in the Columbia Icefield area. He completed a three-day ascent of the rotten east face of Mt. Kitchener in winter, a remarkably gritty climb where he and his partner Jim Elzinga were forced to bivouac two nights on a steep face in sub-zero temperatures without sleeping bags or shelter.

Lauchlan also demonstrated an interest in the great peaks of Canada's St. Elias Range early in his climbing career. In the 1970s he was a member of several strong Canadian expeditions, including one that climbed the difficult and technical Southwest Buttress of Mt. Logan, Canada's highest peak. But given his ambitious nature, it was inevitable that Lauchlan would want to test himself in the world's highest range. He was a natural candidate for the Canadian Everest expedition and a strong proponent of the complex South Pillar route. His death robbed the Canadian Everest climb of its most committed home-grown member.

As a writer, Lauchlan is more intimate with us than any previous Canadian mountain storyteller; willing to reveal more of himself. Whatever one may say of the craftsmanship of the earlier Canadian mountain writers, their prose suffers from a certain lack of frank human emotion. They describe with precision the quality of rock, the quality of snow, the turns in the weather, the force of the storm; on the quality of companionship they tend to be eulogistic and tactful. Norman Collie, a great explorer of the Rockies, wrote letters about his rival James Outram describing him as an interloper and opportunist, bent on self-serving first-ascent missions built on the work of the real explorers who had preceded him. But not a word of this appears in Collie's published writings. The tone is that of the gentleman at the club.

Lauchlan's style could not be more of a contrast; it boils over with intensity, reflecting a personality that was extravagant and enthusiastic. He gives the feeling of what it would have been like to have been there, as few others have done. The feeling of immediacy arises from the honesty of the telling. Yet Lauchlan is great enough as a writer to be honest without being mean-spirited.

The following account of the first ascent of the south face of Gangapurna describes a climb which was certainly the biggest achievement of Canadians in the Himalayas up to that time. The brash style of the ascent is mirrored in the rapid prose; there is a great and uplifting sense of exhilaration in the struggle. Yet the story illustrates well the chances Lauchlan was willing to take when prize achievements were at stake.

He was dead only a few months after this story was published.

～ Bruce Fairley

Gangapurna Stories

John Lauchlan

By the time I reached him James had dug the last three days' snow off the belay and was ready to go. "I'll lead this one," he said with determination. We both had been looking at this pitch—steep water ice leading to the serac—but this was James' opportunity to show that he would stick to our decision. We were carrying on alone…and we were determined to give the south face of Gangapurna our best shot before turning back. We'd been in Nepal a month and a half, spent countless hours of preparation time and every nickel we owned to get here. Now it was time to push. To ride that fine line between control and chaos, safety and recklessness. Here, at the base of the hardest climbing of the expedition and still four days from the summit, we knew that we were riding the line pretty close.

* * * * *

April 16, 18,000 ft. James and I carried two heavy loads up from the cache at the top of the first icefall while Dave and Dwayne explored the second. They reached the bottom of the route, the bergschrund on the right-hand side of the ice face and reported the ice to be easier angled than we expected—about 50 degrees. As this is the longer side and we may not have enough polyprop to fix it anyway we are talking about trying the face Alpine Style. James and I will go up to have a look to-morrow. Dwayne and Dave will bring up the rest of the cache and we'll decide to-morrow night.

April 17. Snowing fairly steadily. About four inches overnight. Our camp is in a very exposed place—avalanches from Glacier Dome/Gangapurna col could hit us…we may have to move camp.

* * * * *

James set off. The ice was steep right off the belay, about 80 degrees. Stopping to struggle in some protection he found himself winded after the first 20 ft. He bridged out to the little ice corner to catch his breath. We were at 22,000 ft. I leaned out on the belay and gazed around; 3 kms below in the Modi Khola valley the daily storm was beginning to rise. Soon we'd be in it. James readied himself and set off from the ice screw. The ice was thin and steepening but he picked his way slowly and delicately through. At the base of the serac he stopped again. "Looks like I can traverse around the next steep part!" he shouted down and soon disappeared from view. The snow had started to fall lightly as James hauled the packs. I looked out into the mist across the immense rock wall of Gangapurna towards Annapurna III. Should we come down that way? Traverse the peak and descend by A III col? A long way but certainly a lot easier than descending the face! I took out the belay and jumared up into the swirling snow.

April 19. Morning weather much clearer but extremely windy…you can hardly stand up outside. GLAD TO BE UNDERGROUND. *The snow cave is holding up really well; any snow that builds up in the doorway we shovel into the crevasse down the hall. The storm has pinned us down in the best of all positions; at maximum acclimatizing altitude and when we were a couple of days ahead of schedule. No problem yet…other than boredom. Got some good footage of McNab outside in the wind organizing gear. Looked horrendous! We plan on moving up to the base of the ice face to-morrow. Wind seems to be dying down finally. Have made the decision to go Alpine Style.*

* * * * *

"No clouds in the valley!" Hard to believe, but I could feel the warmth of the sun as its first rays crept over our tiny bivouac platform. It was as if the sun was blessing our boldness…our puny attempt at reaching beyond ourselves. We got up and set off. James belayed me out the door of our bivy tent…no point hurrying; from this point we'd lead out the whole 400 ft of our 9 mm rope. I traversed left across the snow covered slab to gain the main groove. Mixed climbing, not too difficult but enough to keep you honest. After about 180 ft I traversed back right and pulled into a narrow ice gully. Good ice, fine weather and "Look at that!" I pulled out of the gully at the end of the rope length to see Dhaulagiri poking over Glacier Dome col. What a day! Probing the unknown in the sunshine at 22,500 ft!

I rappelled back down to the tent after setting up an anchor and we soon had hauled the packs up. Stopped for a brew on the ledge, soaking up the sunshine and staring out at Annapurna III, Machapuchare, Annapurna South, the Fang, Glacier Dome, Dhaulagiri…what an incredible place. I marvel at James' decision to continue with me, after having decided to descend. The change in psyche that he had put himself through amazed me. It had been so hard for him, and yet beside me on this skimpy ledge sat a determined, enthusiastic James. I feel very fortunate to have such a friend. With one hand on the rope I spend the afternoon tilting my head into the sun and clicking photos as James picks his way up the 'Ramp.'

* * * * *

April 23. Bergschrund camp, 19,200 ft. Stopped snowing at a reasonable time last night so we'll go on the route today after all. Very clear day—best sunrise in ages. Spindrift all night half buried the tent though; had to get up and dig it out during the night and again for breakfast!

* * * * *

We got underway quickly. Dave and James left first, climbing the ropes they had left the day before. They would lead the whole day, taking turns stringing the ropes for us to follow. While leading they would climb without a pack, leaving it at an anchor point. Dwayne and I left a few minutes later.

We would pull the ropes up behind us to supply the leaders with another rope to fix. We would also take turns carrying the extra pack that was left at the bottom of each fixed line. It was an exhausting system but did allow us to move much faster than if we'd climbed in a more conventional style.

The day stretched on; so did the ice face. We were sweating, panting in the thin air, moving slower all the time. The loads bore down heavier and heavier. Ankles strained from constant twisting as crampon points bit into the ice. Arms ached from hanging and pulling on ascenders. Occasionally a crampon would slip out, flipping a heavily laden climber onto his face, hanging from a sling—panting.

At our backs, unnoticed at first, a thick bank of cloud rolled up the glacier. I had been glancing left to the Glacier Dome col to gauge our progress. Where the west ridge of Gangapurna meets the jumble of hanging glaciers and feathery snow fluting of our neighbour is the same elevation as the top of our ice face. Somewhere around noon the col disappeared. I lifted my sweating head and, through the steam on my glasses, saw that we were enveloped in cloud. It began to snow. We were well over half way up the face so retreat was inadvisable. There was no discussion of our dangerous position, just a slight increase in our rate of progress. We were running out of steam. I pulled through the mist to the anchor Dave was hanging from. Although he was frantically swinging his right foot in an effort to increase circulation to his toes, the sticky, wet snow clung to his clothing everywhere. We were all soaked from perspiration and the snow that had been falling steadily for several hours. It was 5 o'clock. Soon it would be dark. We weren't going to make it.

*　*　*　*　*

We got up early to jumar the Ramp in hopes of making it to the top of the rock band that day. Jugging the ropes it became obvious that we would have a hard time getting that far. We were both moving a lot slower than usual. The excitement and successes of the previous day had drained our strength, the sitting bivouacs and continuous week in the 'death zone' were conspiring to run us down. The weather looked as though it wanted to make up for yesterday's sun with today's storm. By the time we arrived at the top of yesterday's fixed rope we were being buffeted by driving winds and snow. I attempted to run out my 400 ft lead with the pack on but it proved too much. I left it at a piton and continued up the icy gully which dead ends in a rock wall about one pitch high. As James prepared to jumar up I stared ahead, looking for a line through. We were whited out before I could see one. James was shouting from below, too burned to carry his sac. We'd have to bivy. He left his pack behind and came up the rope. We were in real trouble. A gully, especially one directly below a snow face, is no place to bivy but the storm was too violent; we had no energy to fight our way up a steep rock pitch in its midst. We tensioned across to the rib left of the gully. A skiff of snow over a verglased slab—you take what you get.

After a hasty excavation we got the tent out. To secure it James put a piton above. Not very good placement so we just ran the rope through it, leaving the ice screws back in the couloir to the right as our main anchor. I had just undone my knot in preparation for climbing into the tent when James leaned back on the rope to pull his crampon off. The peg pulled. We both pendulumed, the rope untied but still through my harness. When we came to rest 30 ft to the right I was hanging upside down with my leg wrapped around the rope several times. I don't remember doing it; reflex actions of a drowning rat I guess. James, tied in just above, was splayed out on the ice too. Pulling himself together he looked down. "Whoops," we said in unison and left it at that.

*　*　*　*　*

James had soloed ahead to look for a place to cut a tent platform; he returned with bad news. The higher he got the thinner the snow covering the ice. We had neither strength nor time to cut platforms in solid ice; we had to bivouac where we were. "I can't sit still, my feet are freezing. You guys hack a platform and I'll go down to help Dwayne with the packs." David slid down the ropes into the mist and driving snow. I hung my pack from the ice screws and traversed across the ice face with James. Through the cloud we could just see the outline of a rock outcrop sticking through the ice far above. If we could position our tents directly beneath these rocks there was at least theoretical protection from the avalanches that were sure to come.

We began to hack frantically at the slope—hurrying to get the tent up and out of the wind and snow—hurrying to keep warm—hurrying out of desperation. A ledge began to take shape. On our knees—chopping— chunks of snow, ice chips flying everywhere. Too frantic, I caught my jacket with my ice axe. A cloud of down flew from my shoulder. Who cares. We hit ice. It soon became obvious that we would not have time to get two platforms chopped before too many of us were hypothermic. Less than two feet wide, the ledge would be the only resting place for all four of us that night. Dave arrived back at the anchor just as the tent went up. Twice the width of the ledge, its corners dangled wildly in the air. We secured the tent to some ice screws above, then Dave and James climbed in to warm Dave's feet. We had modified our tents so that we could tie in to the anchors from inside. At least we wouldn't fall off—unless an avalanche pushed us off. Somewhere in the cloud below Dwayne was slowly grinding his way up the rope. Arriving exhausted and hypothermic, he collapsed into the tent. After ferrying the last pack across I paused for a moment, staring with hollow eyes at the vague outlines of the rocks above. It was almost dark. I turned my back on the driving snow and struggled into the tent.

Tents can be wonderful places on a big mountain, a nylon wall between you and the grim reality outside. Things can suddenly seem calm, controlled again. The inside of a tent on a mountain face looks little different than it does when set up in the back yard. If you can't do anything about the horrors that loom outside, at least you don't have to look at them. The inside of this tent, on this ledge however, held its own little horrors. Four bodies were crammed, roughly in sitting position, across the tent. Steam filled the air with the smell of perspiration and sodden clothes. Dave writhed in agony as feeling gradually returned to his toes. James' feet were in Dave's sleeping bag—his bag had been left outside in the confusion. He seemed warm enough though; Dwayne had passed out on his lap. The 'pit,' the part of the tent that hung over the edge, was filled with boots, packs, food bags and other frozen items. A rope which we were all clipped to stretched in one door and out the other—in case the ledge gave way.

*   *   *   *   *

April 23. Last night goes in there with the collection of 'worst night of my life' stories. Got up at 5 am to start cooking. I led the pitch out of the rock band and onto the snow bowl to a pleasant surprise. It's smaller than I'd thought and has good hard snow. It's now 9.30 am. I am back in the tent with James. We have decided to go for the top today and rap the route as was plan 'A'; rather than go one more day to the top with loads, and down the A III col. This could be it!

6.15 pm, pulse 120, weather snowing. Today James and I reached 24,457 ft, only turned back by lack of mountain. WHAT A DAY. *The snow was firm and the sun shining. Instead of breaking left under the rockspur we cut straight for the summit. We found an easy traverse line through the short rock wall that guards this approach and broke onto the ridge no more than 200 ft from the summit. Around the time we crossed the rock barrier though the fair weather had given way to our usual afternoon storm. We could barely see the other side and only the rocky ridges descending to the east and north let us easily know we were on top. We paused to take photos of each other then reached for some food. Suddenly our cameras started buzzing. The wire in my Sun-Ice hood started humming and so did all the metal stuff in my pack. For the first few seconds it didn't dawn on us what was happening—electrical storm! I threw the pack on and James and I ran back along the ridge to the spot we'd marked with a prusik and 'biner. I dug my axe in and lowered James down the slope as fast as we could go. I was screaming for him to hurry because I was getting large shocks* into my lower back from the gear in the pack. We are now back in the 'Miserable Bivy' preparing for another shitty sitter night before we can go home. I'm very frozen in the tootsies but otherwise BUZZZZZZZED!!!!

* * * * *

April 24. We are all burned out and our gear is soaked. We are now in the process of moving up to a camp on a pronounced rib about 200 ft below the rock band (about 400 ft above last night's epic on the ice face).

4 pm. Dave is quite yucked out from the altitude. He has no energy and feels nauseous. Earlier it looked like he might be coughing blood but closer examination proved it to be coming from his gums—still pretty weird. I am now in the process of trying to cram fluids down his neck.

6 pm. McNab worse. Will be making water for most of the night I think.

April 25. Just had a big talk about what to do. Dave, essentially, wants to go down. Dwayne is bummed—would go on but slowly. James is very noncommittal. Will have a rest day while we go up and look at the route some more. Am on the verge of tears.

Noon. The die is cast. Dwayne and I will take six days food and go for the summit. James will go down with Dave.

April 26. I guess the die is never really cast. We woke up this morning to a sick Congdon, wanting to go down. I went up and talked with him and James. There ensued one of the longest, most emotional scenes I've ever been through. There are no words to adequately describe how I (and surely he) felt. Eventually we decided to descend with Dwayne and Dave so I went up to pull down the fixed ropes to go home. Suddenly James was behind me saying "let's go."

* * * * *

May 1. The end of the most intense mountaineering day of my life. Descended the entire rock band today, James very sick, puking. I am physically and mentally blown by the experience but know that I will gain great strength from today—I need so badly to be home. 🍂

THE THIRD PARTY

Sluice enough gravel and eventually you can expect some gold. Amongst the many thousands of pages of Canadian mountain writing we knew we would find enough nuggets to fill this anthology, so finding them, while pleasurable, was not really a surprise. But when you're mucking for gold and somebody walks by and drops a diamond into your hands...

When I wrote Barry Blanchard for permission to use his story "The Wild Thing" I got back more than I expected. Included with his permission was a short manuscript entitled "The Third Party" and the following note:

> "The Third Party" was written by John Lauchlan in 1978 after he
> and Jim Elzinga climbed the North face of Kitchener in winter. That as-
> cent changed the whole game around here. To the best of my and Jim's
> knowledge it has never been printed.... I don't think [your anthology]
> would be complete without it. What do you think?

Well, no, I didn't think so either.

John Lauchlan and Jim Elzinga were the leading climbers of the time and this was an ascent of major importance—a technical and psychological breakthrough in the tradition of the best of Brian Geenwood's climbs. Lauchlan's telling of the story is masterful. "The Third Party" is original, insightful, moving...so why was it never published? I can't imagine any editor drunk enough not to grab it with both hands the instant it crossed his or her desk, so I can only assume that Lauchlan never submitted it. Why not? We'll probably never know, and it really doesn't matter anyway. It's in print now and can take its rightful place as one of the gems of our mountain literature.

~ David Harris

The Third Party

John Lauchlan

The car skittered to a halt on the icy road, the driver somewhat surprised that we had thumbed a ride for such a short distance. Piling out in a flurry of enthusiasm, Jim Elzinga and I dropped over the moraine to where we had stashed our packs an hour before. We headed immediately for the ridge which, once crossed, would lead us to the base of the north face of Mt. Kitchener.

It was a boring slog through deep snow up the moraine ridge, and I was sweating despite the cold. The weather looked good though, and our spirits were high...we spent the time talking over our recent successes and failures; trying to figure out whether the pattern dictated a hit or a miss this time. It was good to be out on a big trip with Jimmy again, and talk of 'the good ol' days' was flowing hot and heavy.

After a couple of hours, we broke over the ridge and were confronted with our first view of the face.

"Looks incredible, are you sure we're up for it?" said a familiar voice.

I was startled. I had to resist the urge to turn and look at him. I should have known he would come along on this trip, I suppose it's only to be expected...but I wish he could be a less of a pest...or maybe it's been my fault for letting him get to me.

I resolved that I wouldn't let him destroy this trip though. I hadn't heard his voice in such a long time; but as the three of us trudged down the glacier all I could remember were the confrontations of the past, the old scars. This time would be different. This time I would ignore him. He's like a little kid you know—if you let him know he's getting to you it just gets worse.

The next morning was cloudy. Jim and I sat looking out of the big tent trying to figure out how thick it was. Snow lightly drifted onto the nylon, we were getting a little wet.

Sensing a decision to stay had already been made, he was (of course) especially keen to get started.

"What's a bit of new snow? You're just looking for excuses lightweight!"

As he became more and more forceful however, the clouds parted for a moment to reveal just how thin they really were. We quickly packed up and started off.

Things went well that first day. After lunch in the bergschrund, we moved together as Jimmy booted the steps up the couloir. Our third party wasn't even being too much trouble, or I was too absorbed to pay any attenion.

As the day drew to an end and we began chopping out a bivy platform, he began to get a little nervous.

"Jesus, we're a fair ways up! I wouldn't want to have to descend some of that stuff."

I could hear in his voice that he was beginning to get worried, but I could tell that he was holding back a bit, that he wasn't going to let loose yet.

A couple of things did get us going a bit that night though…first, the adze on my ice axe broke as we were hacking out the bivy shelf. This wasn't all that serious in itself, but it indicated the the metal in my axe was becoming brittle with the cold…and that the pick could break too. Naturally this was pointed out in an almost hysterical manner.

Then later, an avalanche swept off the ramp above and roared down the coulior beside us. Jim was relieved it had gone and the new snow was no longer hanging above us. The other opinion of course, was that we were all about to die.

I scolded myself for listening to him, and tightened my resolve not to listen to him, or even acknowledge his presence.

We actually managed a bit of sleep that first night, and first light saw us bashing our way towards the first rock pitches. They were further away than we had thought, and it was past noon before Jim set off.

It was harder than it looked, and took quite a while. We would need to hurry if we were going to make the ramp that day. I followed the pitch, and stopped to take a piss before leading on.

The next thing I knew, I was watching my mittens skitter down the ice below us.

"Oh God man, you'll lose fingers for sure now!"

'Shut up' I thought, and pulled out the spare mitts.

The next pitch was deceptive too. Snowed-over slabs led to a roof along which I had to tunnel precariously to round the corner. It took too long too, and once I got to the corner I realized I would have to cut the pitch short in order to haul the packs. Not much of a belay though, and it was getting late.

After hauling the packs 'round the corner, I left them hanging and continued across to what I thought would be the bottom of a snow gulley. I hoped to find enough snow and ice to cut a bivy platform.

"Oh no! That's not a gulley at all! It's an overhanging corner! We'll never climb that in the dark! There's nowhere to bivy!"

Jimmy assured me that bivouacking on his stance was out of the question, so he came up. It was nearly dark when he arrived. We checked out the iced-over slabs below us, but there were no ledges. I tried to lead the next pitch by headlamp...the belay was a joke...I backed off.

He was sobbing, screaming; Jim and I were concerned, trying to stay calm, in control. We rapped down to the slabs again and started hacking. By midnight we had cleared enough ice and 'almost rock' away to half sit, half hang from tied-off screws. The tent that we tried to pull over us only diverted half the spindrift down the mountain. The rest went into our pits. Not a pleasant evening.

...and all night long he sobbed:

"You're soaked...you can't sleep...You dropped the windscreen for the stove...Jim's dropped his Polarguard bootie...We're screwed. How are you going to lead that pitch in this condition?"

He was getting to me, he was really getting to me...but I still pretended to ignore him, to shut myself off from everything...to close my mind.

Several years later, when the sun finally came up, Jim remarked that it was a pleasant surprise to still be alive. Our third was still hysterical...screaming about how we couldn't get down but would never be able to get up the corner above.

I grabbed the rack and set off. Cold...sweat...snow...shit rock—the first bulge. Our friend wailing, Jimmy tense, me flailing. Eventually I just had to go for it...and made it. There was even a good placement above. The next bulge went more easily. I was gaining confidence. Jim was shouting encouragingly as I broke out of the corner into the gulley above.

We were ecstatic. Elzinga jumared in a flash and led onto the edge of the ramp. He yelled down that after a couple more hard pitches it was in the bag. We'd be off today if we hurried.

The next lead was hard alright, it took quite a while. More snowed-over rock, more bad pegs, more unstable snow ramps. But eventually it went and the way ahead became easy. We were on the snow ramp.

Pitch after pitch of easy snow and ice. Hurrying cautiously towards the seracs, the summit smells closer and closer. It's late, but we can pull over the cornice in the dark if we have to.

One more little rib to cross, then into the upper bowl and over the cornice. I pull across onto the shaley rib and look around the corner.

He is there. No longer behind me, no longer whining in my ear but now facing me...staring me right in the eyes. I have seen him only once before and I am horrified. Horrified by his awesome ordinariness, the overwhelming insignificance of my own life reflected in his hollow eyes.

Behind him are the ice cliffs. Between us and them stretches a rock band…invisible from below…plastered with snow, overhanging, ugly. The clouds suddenly close in all around us and it begins to snow. There is no possibility of finishing today. The rush for the top which we had gambled on has failed. We are soaking wet, have eaten nothing all day, and now must endure another storm-bound hanging bivouac.

Staring him once more in the eyes I feel no fear…I have no choices. Where there is no choice there can be no doubt, no hesitation…I will survive because I must survive. He vanishes.

I shout down for Jim to follow, and we silently prepare the bivouac.

Morning. Heavy sac. No illusions now, I lead off. Snow-covered slabs. Nailing. Roofs. Steep ice, bad belays, black fingertips… fucked. The world, time is frozen and only Jim and I remain.

I mantle over the cornice and roll into the frozen gale…laughing …crying…We stagger off down the ridge…two men, alive. 🙞

VI   CONTROVERSIES

Mountaineering is not without its disputes and controversies. In fact, at times it seems as if mountaineering periodicals exist for little purpose other than to incite scatological duelling between various schools of thought. Today's debates are often about the chipping of holds, the style of ascents and whether it is legitimate to use drilled anchors (bolts) to protect climbs that could be climbed safely otherwise.

The development of sport climbing and climbing competitions has sparked debates over the place of these activities in clubs that had previously been devoted to alpine expeditions, like the Alpine Club of Canada, as has another modern development—the use of profanity in mountain writing.

But controversy is nothing new to Canadian mountaineering, as the first selections in this chapter demonstrate. Controversy entered the Canadian scene with what is likely the first ever recorded ascent in Canada—the purported climb of Mt. Brown by the botanist David Douglas in 1827. The kettle has been boiling ever since.

~ Bruce Fairley

THE HEIGHTS OF MOUNTS BROWN AND HOOKER

It seems that every country has its mountaineering hoaxes and controversies. And with remarkable consistency they centre around the highest peaks. In the continental United States the question of who was first up the Grand Teton, the highest peak in Wyoming, has provoked extensive debate but has never been definitely settled. In Alaska, the first ascent of Mt. McKinley was once claimed by Frederic Cook, who wrote a bogus account of his climb called *To the Top of the Continent.* Later research showed that his "summit" photographs were in fact shot on one of the low foothills surrounding the mountain. In Canada, the first ascent of Mt. Robson, the highest peak of the Canadian Rockies, was once ascribed (and with some justification) to the Reverend George Kinney. Today his name is almost unknown and Conrad Kain, guiding Albert H. MacCarthy and Colonel W.W. Foster, is credited with the first ascent.

The most famous of all the Rockies controversies, however, was initiated astonishingly early. In 1827 the Scottish botanist David Douglas climbed into Athabasca Pass, the trading route through the Rockies to the Columbia River that had been discovered by David Thompson in 1811. Douglas was on a remarkable expedition sponsored by the Royal Horticultural Society, and he had spent several years tracking down and collecting plant specimens; becoming in the process one of the world's greatest expeditionary botanists (the Douglas Fir is named after him).

He had joined a Hudson's Bay trading party for the journey east from the Columbia River and made with them a cold, arduous trek up into the pass. Resting there a day, Douglas took the occasion to make the ascent of the peak that formed the western portal of the pass, a peak that he named Mt. Brown in honour of a famous British botanist.

It was the account of this climb, reported by Douglas back in England in a paper read to the Royal Horticultural Society, that set off the greatest controversy in Canadian Rocky Mountain history, and which, as the following articles will show, was still provoking argument and discussion one hundred years later. Douglas claimed that the Mt. Brown he ascended was 4,900 metres (16,000 feet) high, making it the highest in the range by a considerable amount.

Douglas's remark sparked a number of abortive expeditions to locate and climb this supposed monarch of the Rockies. In retrospect, one can view these eager mountaineers/explorers as almost comic in their devotion to the truth of Douglas's assertion. Visions come easily to mind—bearded figures in baggy tweeds squinting through the mist at peaks close to half the purported height, riddling how they could have so misconstrued Douglas's directions as to be unable to find the peak.

Yet despite the fact that no mountain near Athabasca Pass comes anywhere near the great heights Douglas ascribed to his Mts. Brown and Hooker, charitable writers for years have sought ways of explaining how the Scottish scientist could have innocently created his preposterous legend.

One man who seems to have had no difficulty reaching a conclusion, however, was A.P. Coleman, who made it a personal project to get to the bottom of the story, and to locate and climb these fabulous summits. Coleman was a professor of geology at the University of Toronto. In the summer of 1888, while the Reverend Green and Swanzy were exploring the Selkirks, Coleman and a companion were pushing north up the Columbia River from Beavermouth, hoping to approach Athabasca Pass and the fabled summits. Coleman only got as far as Kinbasket Lake on this excursion—some 40 kilometres up the Columbia and still a long way from his destination.

Coleman went back in 1892, this time approaching from the east. His trip was very productive indeed, for he located and mapped Fortress Lake, and the Sunwapta and Chaba Rivers, the two principal streams that feed the Athabasca River. He also made a number of first ascents around Fortress Lake, hoping always to see from the summit the long-sought 4,900-metre (16,000-foot) peaks. He seems not to have realized that he was only 20 kilometres due east of the pass itself.

In 1893, on a third trip, Coleman finally reached the Athabasca, descended it to the Whirlpool River, and then followed that stream into Athabasca Pass, putting to rest once and for all the legend of 4,900-metre (16,000-foot) peaks in the Canadian Rockies. The bitterness of disappointment is only evident in his writing.

While Coleman himself was thus convinced that Douglas had perpetrated a fraud, others were not so sure. Years later, hopeful explorers were still searching the Rockies for elusive summits higher than Mt. Robson and still hoping that every big new peak discovered might prove to be David Douglas's vindication. Norman Collie is a good example. He tried to make Mt. Columbia (the second highest peak in the Canadian Rockies) fit the description, even though it is many kilometres southeast of Athabasca Pass.

The definitive case for David Douglas, however, was made in the pages of the venerable *Canadian Alpine Journal*, in a debate conducted by the two most eminent authorities on the Rockies alive at the time: J. Munroe Thorington and Arthur O. Wheeler. Thorington's scholarly exposé seems fairly conclusive and one cannot suppress the thought that Wheeler simply could not conceive that so famous an explorer and scientist could simply have fabricated the details of his historic climb out of whole cloth.

Innocent or otherwise, however, Douglas's remarks certainly enlivened the history of the Canadian mountains and provided the spark for the many and varied expeditions which followed.

↷ Bruce Fairley

The Rediscovery of Athabaska Pass

A.P. Coleman

The real Whirlpool River fulfilled all our expectation. It was rapid, as one would expect of a river tumbling two thousand feet in thirty miles; it was turbid with glacial mud, and it came from between lofty mountains.

It was my turn to lead the procession as we turned towards the Whirlpool Valley; and in spite of clouds of those little winged tigers, the black flies, at first I enjoyed picking a way up this famous pass, once a thoroughfare—as mountain passes go—with thousands of dollars' worth of rare furs travelling eastwards. It was seven or eight miles before we reached the entrance to the actual valley, and we camped at its mouth.

Crossing the Whirlpool next morning, we were surprised to find the old fur traders' trail so well cut out and with such frequent blazes. It had, no doubt, been freshened up by the early CPR survey parties, though Indians must have used it later. Then came the usual alternations of green timber, with soft mossy pathways, in a green twilight; of burnt timber, with a confusion of fallen logs, through which one must twist and turn to avoid too much chopping; of muskeg and shallow, muddy lakes, which one must skirt cautiously lest some animal get mired.

Before the second camp on the Whirlpool a serious accident happened to me in the woods. A splintered sapling, long and sharp, drove through the broad, wooden stirrup beside my left foot and pierced my horse's side, the farther end of the stick catching against trees and pushing the point deeper into his flank. Andy was frantic and out of control, and dashed among the trees; then the axe which I carried in my hand to clear the trail jabbed his neck, and in a moment I was smashed against a tree and flung from the saddle. I was stunned for a minute, but managed to climb on my horse again after he had been caught and quieted and rode on to camp. Though I was badly bruised no bones were broken, and I hoped in a day or two to be ready for climbing when we reached Mount Brown.

After a bad night my left knee proved to have been so seriously wrenched that I could only get round with the help of two sticks; and it was clear that climbing was out of the question during this season—a bitter disappointment, with Mount Brown almost in sight. I rode Andy through thick and thin for the rest of the trip with only my right foot in the stirrup, and it was years before I could trust myself in the mountains again.

This was a bad handicap for the party, since the other three had all the work to do; and, to relieve them, the dish-washing fell to my lot, a task I always hated.

It is a curious sensation for an active, self-sufficient man suddenly to find himself a cripple, to be cared for by others.

We advanced steadily along the old trail, with its rotten log bridges over creeks and muskegs; sometimes the boiling river, with the eddies and whirlpools that its name suggested, had carved away the bank, trail and all. A fine snowy peak ahead must surely be Mount Brown; and the other three worked like heroes to quicken our speed, while I spent the time pulling Andy to the right of the trail so that my swollen knee should not be bruised against tree trunks.

The trail was lost for some time, and the others scattered to look for it, while I waited by the river among the slender pines and spruces. They were long away, and the river voices and the voices of wind in the trees made a doleful music, so that sometimes I thought there was a shout from Stewart or Lucius that the trail had been found, but it was only a louder surge of the rapid.

The Whirlpool was here spread out over a wide flat, after the manner of glacial rivers; and, as often happens under these circumstances, there was no defined trail, since the river channels were constantly shifting with the flooding due to hot sunshine. We had to pick the best way we could, fording branch after branch, and keeping along the openest gravel flats.

Our camp was not far from a glacier coming down to the valley, comparable in size to the Rhone Glacier in Switzerland, and furnishing probably half the water of the river, which henceforth was only a moderate creek, easily forded. We were near the headwaters, and therefore near our goal, but camped on the flats, where there was pasture, since up the valley only woods could be seen.

On August 19th, five days after leaving the Athabaska, we set out, expecting to find camp in the evening at the foot of Mount Brown. The horses had stuffed themselves, as Indian ponies do when the grass is good, and hated to be saddled; and as I crouched under a tree old Black, who had just been cinched up, was whimpering like a puppy left out of doors on a cold night. Presently all were saddled and packed, and I climbed on my own horse ready for the start, keen to see the giants Brown and Hooker, which should loom up just round the bend of the valley ahead.

The timber presently became more open, for we were above five thousand feet; and our horses' feet sank noiselessly in the moss, only here and there clattering over a small, open, gravel flat. There were flowers of autumn in the open places—red and yellow paint-brushes and lilac-coloured asters; and at first all was moist and cool and pleasant; then the sun grew hot toward midday, the river turned to a muddy, foaming torrent, and the bulldogs and buffalo flies drove the horses frantic.

At noon there was a good feed for the animals, for the sward was kept green by innumerable small rills of cool water; but they preferred to line up in the drifting smoke of the smudge built for their benefit, since sand-flies and black flies had not joined forces with the other tormentors.

Less than an hour's journey after lunch brought us to a pond sending a little stream down the valley, and we had reached the headwaters of the Whirlpool. From the other end of the pond a rill flowed southwards, doubtless to the Columbia; and we halted on the green shore of the Committee's Punch Bowl, which sends its waters to two oceans nearly two thousand miles apart. Some of the maps make the Punch Bowl a lake ten miles long, but here in real life it was only a small pool less than two hundred yards long. There could be no doubt that it was the Punch Bowl, for beyond it the water flowed in the opposite direction. We were on the Great Divide, the ridge pole of North America, but we felt no enthusiasm. Instead we felt disillusioned.

If this was the Punch Bowl, where were the giant mountains Brown and Hooker?

We looked in vain for magnificent summits rising ten thousand feet above the pass, one on each side. Instead, we saw commonplace mountains with nothing distinguished in their appearance, undoubtedly lower than half a dozen peaks we had climbed as incidents along the way for the fun of the thing, or as lookout points from which to choose our route. It was clear that our glacier rope and ice equipment would not be needed. We got the saddles off the ponies and pitched the tent beside the Punch Bowl silently. We had reached our point after six weeks of toil and anxiety, after three summers of effort, and we did not even raise a cheer. Mount Brown and Mount Hooker were frauds, and we were disgusted at having been humbugged by them. Personally, I found some solace for the disappointment, as I hobbled round camp, in the thought that if I could do no climbing it did not really matter much, for there was no glory to be got in climbing Mount Brown.

We had expected to row our canvas boat round the lake on the summit, an occupation that would have suited me, since it did not demand legs; but the Punch Bowl was too small a pool to make it worth while, and the boat remained in its pack cover of green canvas. 🍂

The Centenary of David Douglas' Ascent of Mount Brown

J. Monroe Thorington

Read in part before the Alpine Club of Canada, New York Section, 17th Annual Dinner, March 26th, 1927.

It is probable that more than a few mountaineers attending the 1926 Camp, in Tonquin Valley, were unaware that they were within a few miles of Athabaska Pass; that from the névé of the Fraser glacier, on the slopes of McDonell Peak, one may look past the western ridges of Erebus, and almost directly through the gap in the Continental Divide which, for so many years, was travelled by pioneers going to and fro between the Columbia and Athabaska valleys. And if anyone had inquired about David Douglas, the answer would no doubt have been a vague one: "Oh yes, a botanist. Years ago. Named Mount Brown and Mount Hooker. Climbed Mount Brown, and thought the mountains were the highest in North America. Got on the maps and fooled people for a long time before someone found out that he had made a mistake."

This year, 1927, is the Centenary of David Douglas' crossing of Athabaska Pass. He left us one of the most picturesque and entertaining stories concerning the Canadian mountains, the first recorded account of an ascent above their snow line. After a century it may not be out of place to re-state the fragmentary facts bearing on this occurrence.

Douglas was employed by the Royal Horticultural Society on a botanical expedition to the United States in 1823; and, again, in the year following, on a more extensive journey to California and the Northwest, lasting until 1827.

On the 20th of March, 1827, he left Fort Vancouver, homeward bound, with Ermatinger's York Factory brigade. Ascending the Columbia to Boat Encampment, they made camp, on May 1st, a little distance down on the western slope of Athabaska Pass.

Even at this date there was a tradition of height in the region. David Thompson, from an incorrect boiling point determination, was certain that the Athabaska Pass was 11,000 feet above the sea. Ross Cox and Thomas Drummond concurred in this opinion, and all thought that the mountains were between 16,000 and 18,000 feet in height.[1]

Douglas became desirous of ascending one of the peaks, and, accordingly, set out to climb that on the left or west side which seemed the highest.

---

1. Thorington: *The Glittering Mountains of Canada*, p. 151 ff.

The ascent took him five hours and the descent one hour and a quarter. He recorded the event in his field journal—a heavy ledger of some 130 pages, with entries covering the period 1824-27—but without mentioning any peak by name or elevation. He does not state that his mountain is the highest in North America—that does not happen until later—and he specifically states that there were many other mountains in the neighborhood higher than the one he was on.

After his return to England, probably late in 1828, Douglas transcribed his journal into a short sketch, presumably for reading before the Royal Horticultural Society.[2] In this he made some remarkable changes. He states that the mountain he climbed as "on the north or left hand side. The height from its apparent base exceeds 6000 feet, 17,000 feet above the level of the sea.... This peak, the highest yet known in the Northern Continent of America, I felt a sincere pleasure in naming Mount Brown in honor of R. Brown, Esq., the Illustrious Botanist.... A little to the south is one nearly of the same height rising more into a sharp point I named Mount Hooker in honor of my early patron the enlightened Professor of Botany in the University of Glasgow, to whose kindness I, in great measure, owe my success hitherto in life."

Here we have the mountains named for the first time, the height of Mount Brown given, and the information that they are the highest on the North American Continent. The names were doubtless given with the thought of pleasing his patrons, and the fiction of their great altitude may have been added for the same reason, although Douglas was probably influenced by the opinion of his predecessors on the Athabaska trail.

We know that Douglas did not name the mountains until after he returned to England; the dated watermarks in the paper of his journals are proof positive of this.[3] His statement that Mt. Brown was the highest in North America was prevarication pure and simple, as Douglas knew, having set down the truth in his field journal.

In the year following Douglas superintended a map (it is dated 1829) which Hooker published in the first volume of Flora Boreali Americana. One finds the name Mount Brown, 16,000 feet placed on the western side of Athabaska Pass, and Mount Hooker, 15,700 feet, on the eastern side, approximately southeast of Mount Brown. This is the first time that figures are given for the elevation of Mount Hooker, and Douglas adds to the complexity of the problem by lowering Mount Brown by a thousand feet. Perhaps he had overshot probability.

---

2. In 1914 the Royal Horticultural Society published a monograph in which the Douglas journals are printed in full.
3. *Alpine Journal* XXXVII, p. 327 ff.

All that we know definitely is that the names and heights were created in England, and that Douglas knowingly falsified in claiming the peaks as the loftiest on the continent.

We can bring forward little additional evidence to help Douglas. It is really questionable whether a man untrained in mountaineering could climb the present Mt. Brown on snowshoes in five hours from Ermatinger's camping place.[4] He may of course have reached the snow plateau on the southern shoulder, and it should not be forgotten that this was at a time in mountaineering history when many a man "climbed" a mountain without attaining the very summit. It was only necessary that one should reach a considerable height.

The Interprovincial Survey, visiting Athabaska Pass in 1920, has perpetuated the names Brown and Hooker.[5] Douglas probably did reach some point on the present Mt. Brown. The Survey decision and recommendation for Mt. Hooker is far-fetched, and is not helped by the fact that it was made at a time when the Commission was ignorant of the existence of Douglas' field journal.[6]

The Kane icefield intervenes between Athabaska Pass and the present Mt. Hooker, and the latter is quite invisible from the pass. In fact it cannot be seen at all until one climbs quite high on the slopes of Mt. Brown. One would believe, therefore, that if Douglas looked up from his camping place and tried to decide which of two peaks was the higher and the more laudable goal he must have compared the present Mt. Brown with McGillivray's Rock. These would have been the most conspicuous peaks from his viewpoint. It seems likely that McGillivray's Rock is Douglas' Mt. Hooker, a view brought forward by Professor Coleman on the occasion of his own visit to the Athabaska Pass in 1893.[7]

The most promising lead for further work on the Brown-Hooker problem is the knowledge that Joseph Sabine, then secretary of the R.H.S., received from Douglas several volumes containing field sketches, meteorological and geographical observations relating to the Columbia River and its tributaries. One conjures up a vision of a drawing of Athabaska Pass, with the mountains neatly labelled. But these volumes have become lost and cannot be traced. Perhaps some day they will come to light.

---

4. Collie: *Climbs and Exploration in the Canadian Rockies*, p. 153. C.A.J. VI, 90.
5. C.A.J. XII, p. 163 ff. *The Glittering Mountains of Canada*, p. 167.
6. Letter from A.O. Wheeler to the writer, dated November 23, 1922.
7. Coleman: *The Canadian Rockies*, 207. *The Glittering Mountains of Canada*, p. 294 ff. (App. G.)

This is the true story of Mount Brown and Mount Hooker. Fragmentary and uncertain it yet remains the outstanding legend of the Canadian mountains, adding no little to the allure of the heights of Athabaska. For this reason one may well pause to remember the man who created it a hundred years ago.

Supplemental Notes

In any consideration of Douglas' character as bearing on the Brown-Hooker problem, the following paragraphs, written by W.J. Hooker [*Companion to the Botanical Magazine*, vol. 2, p. 142] are of considerable weight:

Qualified, as Mr. Douglas undoubtedly was, for a traveller, and happy as he unquestionably found himself in surveying the wonders of nature in its grandest scale, in conciliating the friendship (a faculty he eminently possessed) of the untutored Indians, in collecting the productions of the new countries he explored; it was quite otherwise with him during his stay in his native land. It was, no doubt, gratifying to be welcomed by his former associates, after so perilous yet so successful a journey, and to be flattered and caressed by new ones; and this was perhaps the amount of his pleasures, which were succeeded by many, and, to his sensitive mind, grievous disappointments... His company was now courted, and unfortunately for his peace of mind he could not withstand the temptation (so natural to the human heart) of appearing as one of the Lions among the learned and scientific men in London; to many of whom he was introduced by his friend and patron, Mr. Sabine... As some further compensation for his meritorious services, the Council of the Horticultural Society agreed to grant him the profits which might accrue from the publication of the Journal of his travels, in the preparation of which for the press, he was offered the assistance of Mr. Sabine and Dr. Lindley: and Mr. Murray of Albermarle-street was consulted on the subject. But this proffered kindness was rejected by Mr. Douglas, and he had thoughts of preparing the Journal entirely himself. He was, however, but little suited for the undertaking, and accordingly, although he laboured at it during the time he remained in England, we regret to say, he never completed it. His temper became more sensitive than ever, and himself restless and dissatisfied; so that his best friends could not but wish, as he himself did, that he was again occupied in the honourable task of exploring North-west America.

This information would seem to explain the origin of the second manuscript—the "Shorter Journal"—written by Douglas after his return to England, and substantiates the thought that the changes made therein—the creation of Mt. Brown and Mt. Hooker and their altitudes—were introduced for purposes of personal publicity.

Some interest attaches to the attempt at discovering just who fixed the height of Athabaska Pass at 11,000 feet. Washington Irving [in an appendix to *Astoria*] preserves a conversation between David Thompson and James Renwick in which Thompson states that one of the mountains in the vicinity was twenty-five thousand feet high. As this occurred at a dinner in New York, it may have been that Thompson, departing from his custom, had partaken heavily of liquid refreshment; but as the incident took place about 1822 it antedates the crossing of Athabaska Pass by either Sir George Simpson or David Douglas.

Thomas Drummond mentions a Lieut. Simpson, R.N., who was surveying in the vicinity of Jasper House during the winter of 1825-26. This was Lieut. Aemilius Simpson, R.N., a half-brother of Thomas Simpson, the Arctic explorer of the Dease and Simpson Expedition. Thomas Simpson was a nephew of Sir George Simpson [*Dictionary of National Biography*]. Douglas, himself, at Fort Vancouver in November, 1826, became acquainted with Lieut. Simpson.

Drummond informs us that, "The height of one of the mountains taken from the commencement of the Portage, Lieut. Simpson reckons at 5,900 feet above its apparent base, and he thinks that the altitude of the Rocky Mountains may be stated at about 16,000 feet above the level of the sea." The wording of this sentence is closely paraphrased in Douglas' second journal [the "Shorter Journal"] and may have been the source of his information, especially as he returned to England with Drummond, sailing from York Factory on the Hudson's Bay Company's ship, Prince of Wales.

Lieut. Simpson died in 1831 [*Life and Letters of Thomas Simpson*, Alexander Simpson, 1845], and appears to have been one of the many Hudson's Bay men who, after the Franklin Expeditions, carried or had instruments of various kinds, although they may not have known how to use them.

There is no evidence in literature consulted that David Thompson and Sir George Simpson ever met. It is likely that Sir George Simpson made a boiling point determination of Athabaska Pass, although his name is bracketed with it by David Thompson. Thompson's manuscript, in which this occurs, as published by the Champlain Society, was written when he was seventy years old. It may well be that after so many years Thompson assumed that the Simpson concerned with the altitude determination was Sir George; but the facts of the case make it appear that the man responsible was really Drummond's Lieut. Simpson.

Thompson's original notes have recently been examined on this point [by J.B. Tyrrell] and there is nothing in them about the heights of the passes. 🔊

A Bibliography of the Athabaska Pass Region, arranged in Order of Publication:

1820 Gabriel Franchere. *Voyage à la Côte du Nord-Ouest de l'Amérique Septentrionale.* Montreal. Also English Translation, 1854: *Narrative of a Voyage to the Northwest Coast of America.* Redfield, New York.

1829 William Hooker. *Flora Boreali Americana*; Vol. 2.

1830 Thomas Drummond. "Sketch of a Journey to the Rocky Mountains and to the Columbia River in North America." In Hooker's Botanical Miscellany; Vol. 1.

1832 Ross Cox. *Adventures on the Columbia River.* J. & J. Harper, New York.

1836 William Hooker. "A Brief Memoir of the Life of David Douglas." *Companion to the Botanical Magazine*; Vol. 2.

1836 Washington Irving. *Astoria.* 2 vols. Philadelphia. Vol. 1, p. 276.

Mounts Brown and Hooker

Arthur O. Wheeler

In the 1926 and 1927 issue of the Canadian Alpine Journal appears an article entitled "The Centenary of David Douglas' ascent of Mount Brown" by Dr. J. Monroe Thorington. It is a collection and classification of the information available concerning Douglas' naming and giving of heights for Mts. Brown and Hooker, situated respectively on opposite sides of the Athabaska Pass, and deals with the records left by Douglas, Thompson and others of the early explorers. It has doubtless involved much study and tracing of old records by Dr. Thorington, and is in itself a valuable record of the information on the subject.

There are, however, several statements made that appear to be questionable and uncalled for,[1] and open to criticism. The statements referred to are as follows:

Page 187: "All that we know definitely is that the names and heights were created in England and that Douglas knowingly falsified in claiming the peaks as the loftiest on the continent."

With regard to the statement that Douglas "knowingly falsified" the heights: this seems to be a somewhat dogmatic one. Dr. Thorington refers to Douglas' transcription of his Journal, "probably late in 1828," and quotes his reference to Mt. Brown as follows: "This peak, the highest yet known in the Northern Continent of America, I felt a sincere pleasure in naming Mt. Brown . . . etc." Directly after, Dr. Thorington writes: "Here we have the mountains named for the first time, the height of Mt. Brown given, and the information that they are the highest on the North American Continent." In making this statement the fact that Douglas said "the highest yet known," not unlikely had reference to his own ascent and naming of the mountain.

With regard to the error in altitude, Dr. Thorington points out David Thompson's incorrect determination of 11,000 ft. for the altitude of the summit of Athabaska Pass, which very probably had to do with Douglas' error in altitude for Mts. Brown and Hooker. To say that he "knowingly

---

1. From communications which have reached the Editor, it would seem that others share this viewpoint. It must, however, be remarked that we live in a critical age, and the attempt to create the impression that any institute or historical character is above criticism tends to produce the feeling that it is unable to withstand impartial investigation. Not even the characters of the Pilgrim Fathers and of George Washington have been exempted from unfavourable remarks on the part of accredited American historians. A centenary celebration seems to be a highly appropriate occasion for making a balanced estimate of an individual's achievements from which his character cannot be dissociated.

falsified" the heights seems to be going it rather strong. Also, "that the names and heights were created in England" seems to convey the reflection that England had something to do with it. It is natural to suppose that Douglas' deductions would be compiled from his field-notes at the place of his residence.

Further on, Dr. Thorington casts doubt upon Douglas' statement that he made the ascent of Mt. Brown. This doubt must naturally be surmise, and would be no more credible than Douglas' statement that he did. The writer of this note has climbed Mt. Brown twice, and has located the Ermatinger camping place as nearly as is possible from the description given of it. He has no hesitation in saying that it would have been quite possible to ascend Mt. Brown from such camping ground in five hours, the time stated.

Page 188: "The Survey (Interprovincial Boundary) decision and rec-ommendation for Mt. Hooker is far-fetched, and is not helped by the fact that it was made at a time when the Commission was ignorant of the exist-ence of Douglas' field journal."

With reference to this statement by Dr. Thorington concerning the Interprovincial Boundary Commission's decision and recommendation for the location of Mt. Hooker, it may be said that the writer was the Commis-sioner in charge of the mapping of the mountain area along the portion of the Great Divide which constitutes the boundary between the Provinces of Alberta and British Columbia. With Douglas' description before him, from the summit of Mt. Brown, he made every possible endeavour to locate Douglas' Mt. Hooker, and the mountain most nearly coinciding with the description is the one so named officially, notwithstanding Dr. Thorington's statement that the recommendation was far-fetched.

He, Thorington, states that "it seems likely that McGillivray's Rock is Douglas' Mt. Hooker." McGillivray's Rock is a low hog-back ridge, directly northeast of the summit of the Athabaska Pass, that in no way conforms to Douglas' description of Mt. Hooker, which he writes of as "rising more into a sharp point than Mt. Brown." The altitude determined for Mt. Brown by the Boundary Commission is 9,156 ft. and for McGillivray's Ridge 8,800 ft. While the writer is not prepared to say that the ridge is not the Mt. Hooker of Douglas, there is no information to definitely locate it, and the actual po-sition is purely a matter of surmise.

Page 192: Referring to Washington Irving's preservation of a conversa-tion between David Thompson and James Renwick, in which it is said Thompson stated that one of the mountains in the vicinity was twenty-five thousand ft. high, Dr. Thorington writes: "As this occurred at a dinner in New York, it may have been that Thompson, departing from his custom, had partaken heavily of liquid refreshment." Since there were two parties to the conversation, the recorder and the recorded, it is presumable that the accusation would apply equally to one as to the other.

A number of Dr. Thorington's strictures seem to be his own personal views, and he does not appear to make allowance for the mid-winter aspects of unknown mountain solitudes for which there were absolutely no data available, or for the effect of these vast and ice-bound regions upon a solitary traveller. Travelling through them in mid-summer, with available data for position and height ready to hand in the form of reliable government topographical maps, is quite a different thing, furnishing as it does every opportunity for criticism at ease.

The writer, for one, prefers to make due allowance for the abnormal conditions under which the explorations by these first of all pioneers were made, all the more so because in the absence of definite knowledge much in the records is a matter of conjecture. There are certainly discrepancies that seem inexplicable in the light of latter-day knowledge, but discrepancies as to the magnitude and effect of many natural features and causes are frequently found among the writings of the early explorers, and are not unlikely due to a magnified impression of the dangers and terrors of mountain travel, especially in mid-winter, before such travel became an every day happening to summer tourists.[2] ❧

---

2. There is one aspect of this question to which sufficient attention has, it seems, not been paid. Douglas was an expert botanist. In accepting the height of Athabaska Pass as 11,000 ft., he must have noticed that the tree line in the Canadian rockies was still higher—over 13,000 ft.—an inexplicable corollary for a man of his knowledge! – Editor.

Mounts Brown and Hooker—A Reply

J. Monroe Thorington

It is gratifying to the writer that his paper on "The Centenary of David Douglas' Ascent of Mt. Brown" has elicited discussion, for the legendary heights adjacent to Athabaska Pass have attracted mountaineers to this magnificent playground for more than three decades. One feels sure that Douglas himself would have been more than pleased could he have foreseen such result.

My answers to Mr. Wheeler's friendly criticism may be summed up as follows, according to the paragraphs of his discussion:

Par. 3. I am quoted incompletely. In the Canadian Alpine Journal I stated that "Douglas knowingly falsified in claiming the peaks as the loftiest on the continent." In his field journal Douglas wrote of the view from his attained point: "Nothing, as far as the eye could perceive, but mountains such as I was on, and many higher..." If Douglas means that no one had previously climbed higher in North America than himself, he certainly does not say so.

Par. 4. In the Supplemental Notes to my paper I presented the summary of Douglas' character as given by Hooker in the *Companion to the Botanical Magazine*. It should show Mr. Wheeler exactly what Douglas' sojourn in England had to do with the production of the second journal. Douglas could not have made deductions about Mts. Brown and Hooker, and their heights, from his field journal. Hence my reassertion that "the names and heights were created in England."

Par. 5. As to doubting Douglas' ascent of Mt. Brown, it is probable that he reached some point on the mountain. He may have reached the summit. But when so great a mountaineer as A.L. Mumm expressed similar doubt (C.A.J., vi., p. 90), I shall ask the reader to decide whether this or Mr. Wheeler's opinion is preferable.

Pars. 7 and 8. If Mr. Wheeler had placed himself in Douglas' position in the Ermatinger camp, instead of trying to solve the problem from the summit of Mt. Brown, he would have seen that McGillivray Ridge, from the lower viewpoint, appears as a peak. It looks not unlike Mt. Brown and the similarity would be increased by snow. Furthermore, from this viewpoint, the peak selected by the Boundary Commission to bear the name of Mt. Hooker is practically invisible.

Douglas' field journal makes no mention of any peak at all that could be taken for Mt. Hooker. If credence is to be placed in the second journal we must take Douglas' own words: "A little to the south is one nearly of the

same height, rising more into a sharp point, which I named Mt. Hooker ..."
Is it conceivable that he was looking at the Boundary Commission's Mt.
Hooker, which rises 1,628 ft. higher than Mt. Brown? Douglas placed Mt.
Hooker, on his 1829 map, in the location of McGillivray Ridge, which is
more definite than Mr. Wheeler's attachment of the name to another peak.

In my book, *The Glittering Mountains of Canada* (Appendix G), I
pointed out that if Douglas' elevations are based upon the incorrect figure
(11,000 ft.) for Athabaska Pass then current, something might at least be
learned from the difference between his figures for Mts. Brown and Hooker.
The actual difference in elevation between Mt. Brown and McGillivray's
Rock is 376 ft. (9,156-8,870; Boundary Commission), while the difference between Mt. Brown and Mt. Hooker as given in Douglas' map of 1829 is 300 ft.
(16,000-15,700). It is quite evident that Douglas considered his Mt. Hooker
to be lower than Mt. Brown. The Boundary Commission's Mt. Hooker simply cannot be brought into line with these figures.

Par. 10. If Mr. Wheeler prefers the thought of David Thompson, a man
of precision, soberly making the assertion, or of Renwick, a gentleman of integrity, soberly receiving the statement that "he (Thompson) had discovered
the height of one of the mountains to be about twenty-five thousand feet
high...," I have no objection.[1]

Finally, while appreciating Mr. Wheeler's discussion, I may say that
the views expressed are by no means my personal ones. I have presented the
actual documents, making a trip to England for the express purpose of examining the Douglas journals at first hand. These and the other narratives
tell their own story, and the choice of interpretations is left to the reader
should he prefer a different one from that which I have advanced. ❧

---

1. Can one take as authoritative a statement that comes at second or third hand? And is it
not possible that Washington Irving may have fallen into error? – Editor.

SPORT CLIMBING

Mountaineering is a purely voluntary activity and climbers have complete freedom in their choice of companions, so one would expect the Alpine Club of Canada to be a paradigm of harmony. A cheerful meeting ground for a group of like-minded people, a place where they can escape the discord that lumbers their "real" lives. And so, for nearly a century, it mostly has been.

But its members are human and over the years they have managed to find a variety of alpine-related subjects over which to disagree. Much of that disagreement has been private—or at least kept within the family and soon forgotten—but occasionally someone's anger or frustration has boiled over into writing, and the club's publications preserve a rich tradition of spleen-venting.

The example we have chosen is an open letter to Peter Fuhrmann (then president of the Alpine Club of Canada) from a long-time member who saw the club's decision to sponsor indoor climbing competitions as a serious mistake. It was published in the newsletter of the club's Calgary section in 1988.

~ David Harris

Climbing Competitions

Orvel Miskiw

For a start, let me say that formal climbing competition is an atrocity against alpinism, and since the ACC is supposed to be an ALPINE club, we must not sponsor, must not support, must not endorse, and must not even CONSIDER any sort of climbing competition.

I was amazed and disgusted to hear that the UIAA,[1] another supposed "Alpine" organization, was so unprincipled and weak-kneed as to allow itself to be cowed into participation in this sport, and further, that the illness has been transmitted into the ACC, apparently through carriers with European roots and no higher aspiration for Canada than to stumble aimlessly along behind Europe in its every wandering, as if on a leash.

Whereas a few people claim to support Peter Fuhrmann's climbing competition scheme, of those I have heard, talked to, or whose 'reasoning' on the issue I have heard indirectly, the strongest support they seem to be able to give for the activity is "Why not?", if you can believe it. This must certainly be weaker than the obvious counter of "Why?", since formal competitions, though not a new idea, would be a new element in ACC activities after more than 80 years, and present members can not presume to know all the reasons for which competitions have never been acceptable in the ACC. If the known reasons don't supply the answer, then perhaps "Why not?" lies in the reasons they do NOT know; and yet "Why?" is only the WEAKEST argument against competitions.

In my case, I don't pretend to know all the reasons either, but the few I do know amply define why competitions have never been an ACC activity, are unacceptable for all time, and should be banned in the ACC constitution to avert future confusion of our purpose caused by members who drew straws as to decide which club to join.

Alpinism is a SOCIAL sport, as it entails the co-operation of a team of people in meeting a mutual challenge, so that all may share the satisfaction of its successful outcome. Mutual support, caring, safety, sharing and other human concerns are stressed in alpinism. Radically, competition climbing is an ANTI-SOCIAL activity, since it glorifies the INDIVIDUAL, and that for accomplishments which contravene safety considerations and sacrifice team co-operation and harmony. Next thing we know, Mr. Fuhrmann will be en-

---

1. Union Internationale des Associations D' Alpinisme, the international umbrella organization to which most of the world's alpine clubs belong, and which tests and sets standards for mountaineering equipment and safety practices, among other functions.

dorsing SOLO climbing by sponsoring solo climbing competitions. A falling climber accelerates just as fast now as in 1906, and THIS is not progress.

The ACC must have nothing to do with climbing competitions for this and also the following reasons:

The few quantities that can be measured or estimated in a competition have almost nothing to do with alpinism; yet by even ENDORSING formal competitions, the ACC would make sort of a public declaration that the winner is a superior ALPINIST. This is the inevitable appearance presented to the public, who know us as an organization of mountain CLIMBERS, and so when we hold a CLIMBING competition, we will be perceived as crowning a superior MOUNTAIN climber. The public are, naturally, quite naive about climbing and mountaineering, and the type of misinformation described above is certainly not what is meant by "the education of Canadians" in the ACC constitution.

The ACC still has the opportunity to remain a unique and dignified body by reaffirming its original social mountaineering purpose and determining to never tolerate the encroachment of petty sensationism and gaudy commercial 'progress.' Such things are not progress at all in our case, as there will always be a healthy group of alpinists and sport climbers in Canada who respect and demand the wholesome objectives for which the Club was conceived. These exclude competition climbing almost by definition.

Our club does not need a lot of crazy new schemes (even if that IS what they are doing in Europe?) to carry it into the future, just some good old-fashioned integrity and a realization of its meaningful objectives and available means. I hope you will work toward harnessing the enthusiasm of our president to this purpose. ❧

WHERE HEATHEN RAGE

Every time the editors of the *Canadian Alpine Journal* publish an article like "Where Heathen Rage" a few members write in threatening to cancel their memberships. Partly this is an objection to profanity, which did not make its appearance in the CAJ until the mid-70s, and which still upsets some members. One suspects, however, that traditional alpinists are offended more by the disclosure of vulgarity within their midst than they are by the language itself. Mountaineering, after all, was once known as an activity touching on the sublime. It was bad form to admit competitiveness, even though all the top climbers have always been competitive about beating other climbers to new routes and doing harder routes than the next guy. The men and women who founded mountaineering were really romantics; the mountains were a place of spiritual fulfillment; appreciating the flowers, the fauna and the vistas was what it was all about. Read the first selections in this volume and then dip into "Where Heathen Rage" and one bumps flat up against the gaping clash in perspective.

"The back of the lake," where the story that unfolds in this article takes place, is something like an outdoor arena for sport climbing. The routes are short, steep and challenging. Sport climbers feel at home there, and in fact most of the climbers referred to in this article have at one time or another had some involvement in competitive climbing, including David Dornian himself, who has been for a number of years the Chairman of the Sport Climbing Committee of the Alpine Club of Canada. While sport climbers may also be mountaineers, many of them are just as likely not to be, and yet the essence of what they do—moving in control up a rock face—seems at root to be the same activity that mountain climbers love.

But sport climbing has taken on something of a life of its own and comes with an ethos which does not enter into mountaineering much: overt competitiveness, technique for the sake of technique, training, vitamins, and even sex appeal. The new development is like a precocious and green kid, growing away from his parents, learning to strut his stuff, a bit cocky and making a few mistakes along the way, but evolving into a personality that is inevitably different from what his parents quite expected, or hoped. Such births and maturings are often fraught with controversy. Perhaps this is why an activity that really seems so innocent has been capable of producing such violent disapproval among some members of the mountaineering fraternity. And it is why an article like "Where Heathen Rage" can still provoke very mixed feelings among those who love mountains.

~ Bruce Fairley

Where Heathen Rage

David Dornian

At ten in the morning even the upper parking lot is teeming. You open the back of the vehicle and dump ropes, hardware, dirty towels, flip-flops, rock shoes, stained packs, beer cans, bananas, wadded serviettes, beach clothing, 7-11 bags, battered dairy crates, sunglasses, chalk wrappers, carpet squares, empty styrofoam cups with little drinking holes torn in their plastic lids, and water bottles wrapped in shredded duct tape out onto the asphalt. Blinking at the heap in the bright sunlight, you wonder briefly if it contains even one of the "ten essentials" ("twelve essentials"? "five essentials"?) you were once taught to carry on every climb.

Over at the urinals, while passing weak convenience-store coffee into a urinal, you meet a guy from Wisconsin. He is cheerfully tucking a checked shirt into creased khaki pants that he cinches dramatically with a tooled belt. He is wearing, uh, interesting looking footwear with real leather laces and genuine crepe soles. He describes himself as "...a Winnebago Warrior— not like you real mountain guys, heh, heh." You think about that a little bit as you fill your water bottle at the drinking fountain.

Back in the parking lot with your partner, there is some discussion regarding what equipment might be needed for the day's activities, and some further discussion regarding just what those activities should involve. Eventually, after even *more* discussion, because thinking hurts, and it being Sunday and all, *everything* goes into the packs, and you stagger off down the stairs to the church of your choice.

It's another weekend at the Lake.

Moving through the crowd along the pavement between the Chateau and the water is like filing into the infield at a rock concert. People are everywhere but going nowhere, wearing blank looks and bright clothes with large logos printed front and back. They turn in all directions and stand on benches and on the rocks beside the water and on the lawn and especially in your way. They all seem to be looking directly and expectantly at you as you pause for the foot traffic to clear. They say, "Excuse me, please."

"What?"

"Excuse me. Please." A hand wave like they're dusting lint from your chest.

"Oh. Sorry."

A mother and two children are wedged together in the middle distance, with hesitant smiles and tiny waves toward a camera. Your pack shifts as you weave drunkenly out of their line of sight, just another panel truck manoeuvring in the mall parking lot of life.

My favorite things in these sunny Sunday crowds: The first is the portable business that is set up on the walk every weekend with a little felt-penned cardboard sign mounted on a camera tripod. For two bucks passing pedestrians can pose for a picture and then have the polaroid put on a broad Shriner's-convention style button. They pin the button to their pack or hat, thinking that everyone they meet on the trail will then know what they look like. I guess.

My second favorite things are the video pilgrims. These are the guys (why are women never caught with these things stuck to their heads?) with the full-harness, directional microphone, news-at-six Hitachi and Sony and JVC rigs who stand out on the rocks over the water doing complete color and sound of Victoria Glacier as it lies still as death, snow white and Paleozoic black above the postcard grey of the moraine at the other end of the lake. As I pass, I always wonder why these people don't just buy souvenir place mats. And then, despite myself, I glance nervously up the valley where they point, nagged by the vague worry that they can see something that I can't.

Of course, never to be denied, the crowd has *its* favorite things, too. Right now, up there at the top of their list along with the above mentioned Mt. Victoria and the length of the line to get ice cream at the kiosk by the pool, are the black and red and blue and gold cartoon characters with French dialogue balloons that are printed all over my lycra tights. These supremely way-hot babies (made to my order at Spirit West in Calgary—tell Andy I sent you) cause definite photographic excitement among the Asian males as we go by. They even draw a few careful glances from some of their wives. I try to stand a little straighter under my pack and smile engagingly. But everyone pulls back in fear from Leo, my partner, who by this hour of the weekend looks like a heroin addict. I drop into his wake where the walking is easier. He turns his head so the Chateau is reflected in his mirrored ski glasses and speculates about bringing along skateboards next time to ease this street-style stage of the approach. Half an hour later, clear of the crowds and down the lake somewhere near *Splash Down*, we run into Marc. Leo remembers Marc from the year before, when we met him partnering the girlfriend of another friend of ours. A friend who was away working in Montreal at the time. Today Marc was with a different woman when we said hello on the path. Marc has thin strong features and oversize eyeglasses and a way of moving his head that makes him look like some kind of large raptor. If his daily calorie intake adds up to more than the equivalent of two soda crackers and a carrot, the difference looks like it might be made up in mice, rabbits, and amino acid tablets.

Leo and I talked about this, and about the other woman, and about our friend in Montreal, and about Marc's pioneering role at the Lake—especially about the pioneering role—later as I slicked around on wet, algae-covered rock thirty feet above some broken tree stumps. It had rained the night before and things were pretty slimy here in the shade and security was half a fixed pin rotting in a limed-up crack under a roof somewhere below and fingers in bits of greasy lawn somewhere above.

At the twisted ring piton that made the belay I rubbed the mud off my Megas in the long yellow grass on the ledge. Sure. Okay. Fine.

Oh. And would you look at that view, now. Maybe this one *will* be okay, after all.

Leo had come up to the stance and we were playing I'll-hold-yours-if-you'll-hold-mine and scoping the next pitch and starting to warm up in the sun and thinking we were having fun when Shep and Tuzo walked by on the path below.

Now, we should pause here for a moment. With Tuzo and Shep, if you haven't had the pleasure, a little background might be in order: Largely inseparable, the two of them share the same lifestyle, and perhaps even the same bath water, if and when. If it were dark, and you were up close, you would be hard pressed to tell which was who—they both have approximately equal body weights, identical subcutaneous fat ratios, and roughly equivalent amounts of hair. In this latter respect, Shep's is a little longer and more tangled, whereas Tuzo's is thicker and lighter colored. That's how you know. They seem to be nice folks. Shep likes to climb. Tuzo likes to hunt.

I waved at them. Shep called up, asking if we had seen Marc. I said that he was around the corner near a route called *Vital Transfiguration*. We exchanged a few pleasantries about the line I was on (something called *Just Jazzed*) as I was beginning the next lead. Then Shep conferred with Marc on the other side of the arete and soloed up to a ledge out to our left and danced into his harness in preparation for being dropped a rope. When I glanced over, he looked to be maybe thirty meters off the deck. Tuzo was still on the ground below.

Around this time, a wrangler and a string of trail riders paced out of the trees from the direction of the Chateau. The line was going slowly in the confined quarters, the novices in the back sneaking only the odd look at the scenery while they worked the horns on their saddles like the joysticks for some exotic video game. Each with a yellow slicker rolled and tied behind them, they appeared to be ready for the occasionally inclement mountain weather the brochures had warned about. Little did they know.

Semi-simultaneously with the appearance of this procession, a small group of pastel polo shirts wearing daypacks and Hi-tecs wandered around the corner from the direction of the Plain of Six, going the opposite way.

And so, with the people ahead, an alluvial fan on one side of the path, and a pond, deadfall, and steep rock on the other, the only thing missing for a full Mature rating was a row of feathered lances against the skyline. Tuzo looked at the riders and the hikers and then up at Shep, too far above to do any good, and then back again at the riders and the hikers. And then back up at Shep, who had stopped what he was doing and was watching the proceedings with some attention. Tuzo decided that this was a dream come true. This was ducks in a bucket. This was Big Meat Heaven.

Custer and his cavalry got off easy compared to what happened next. For a moment Tuzo just lay there panting in a puddle of drool, holding quiet while the riders committed themselves to the cul-de-sac. Leaning out on my holds, I could see Shep over on his ledge. Shep wasn't doing anything, but he looked more than a little apprehensive as he watched the tableau beneath us. I was just beginning to wonder what was going on when, exploding into insane barking, Tuzo struck at the line of horses from the rear, for all the world like the wolf from your junior high school textbook going for the last, and presumably the weakest, caribou in the string. Shep began screaming commands.

"TUZO! NO!"

"DOWN, TUZO!"

"DOWN!"

"NO TUZO! NO!"

There were horses in the creek. There were horses in the deadfall below the crag. There were yellow slickers on the ground. The wrangler's horse was rearing. A couple of the poor beasts were trying to break past the hikers, who were trapped between the trail and the water, and escape up the valley to the Teahouse. Some riders were trying to dismount. Others were more concerned with staying in the saddle. The barking and general mayhem went on and on and on. It was hard to see through the chainsaw smoke haze of obscenity from the wrangler, but it sounded as if Tuzo was casting back and forth across the gravel of the stream bed trying to herd everyone into one group—a single group that could then be held at bay and disposed of at leisure. There was panic.

Shep noticed a young couple who were trying to scramble to safety in the bracken directly below us.

"HEY, YOU! COULD YOU GUYS GRAB MY DOG?"

They weren't going anywhere near his dog. The couple gave Shep their best "Buddy, are you unclear on the concept here or what?" look and moved closer to the rock.

"YEAH, MY DOG? JUST GRAB THE COLLAR TIL THE HORSES GET BY, OKAY? NO, TUZO! DOWN, TUZO! DOWN! JUST HOLD ON FOR A MINUTE! NO! NO, TUZO!"

There was a splash and then the sound of cracking wood. The barking became more frantic.

I couldn't look any longer. I just didn't want to know. Besides, my fingers were fading on their holds and the crux of the route was supposedly still to come. Getting back to the business at hand, I put a TCU in my teeth and returned to changing 5.10b into a life or death proposition.

The sun was two hours further west when Leo and I toiled up from the trail and into the Amphitheater. By this stage of the game there was wood in my hair, chalk to my elbows, and bloodstained tape around a couple of fingers. (Both cruxes on *Just Jazzed*, including the one at the bottom of the last rappel on the descent, where you drop into the dead pine, had been real bitches.) I was a mess. Leo... Well, Leo still looked like a heroin addict—our adventures didn't seem to have affected him at all.

To that point the day had been rough, or at least I was feeling that way, but here in a kind of alcove, spread around on warm ledges, everything seemed pretty nice. The rock was all caramel and gold and toffee, tipping over us like a wave about to break, dappled with light. Branches sighed gently in the breeze and from down the hill there was the distant chunking of paddles against the aluminium gunwales of rented canoes. It was somehow all very peaceful and, like, Mediterranean, or something.

Scott and Simon, a couple of friends from Calgary, had established basecamp at the foot of *Distant Early Warning*, a savage looking arete that had been a bit of a focus for them in the past weeks. Lounging in a salad of ropes, sandwich bags, and steaming rock shoes, they were rummaging for food and discussing strategy for Simon's next attempt as Leo and I came up. Matt was visiting with them while he waiting on a partner, hanging beta in the air with his hands. Marc was with Shep up on the big boulder behind them, gazing at the wall above *Extra Dry*. And Tuzo was lying in the shade, tied to a massive fir with a piece of well-chewed perlon.

Scott looked me over and gave a little smile and asked about the mud on my tights. When I snarled at him, he shrugged and changed the subject, nodding toward the route and saying, "Simon's going to rest for a while longer. You want to have a try at this?"

As we dropped our packs, I craned my head back and gazed up at the runners dripping out into space. Hoo boy. Steep. Trying to look like I was thinking about it, I wondered if I really *needed* something like this, today.

But then I *was* thinking about it. What the hell—all those motivational/performance experts say that with the right attitude, anything is possible. If I could make a mess of 5.8d R and 5.10b++, I should have no problem putting together a total fiasco on some bit of mild 5.11 (I reasoned coherently). And it wasn't even my rope that would get stretched.

I sat down and started to root for my shoes. As I was fussing around, Shep lowered from a recon of the blonde sky up and to the left of our route. I squinted at it and then quietly asked Simon the name of the line Shep had been on.

"*Where Heathen Rage,*" Simon said.

I raised my eyebrows inquiringly. He pursed his lips.

"12c," he said.

Now Shep was changing places with Marc and Marc was making all those complaining noises that guys make when they get the loose end:

"I don't know, man. I feel pretty tired today."

"It's been three weeks since I've been climbing, with work and every-thing."

"I don't know about my hands, man. I'll try to scout it. You know—just get a pump. Train for it."

Then he kneaded his knuckles one more time, dusted up, and meticu-lously picked his way to the top of *Extra Dry* in two minutes flat, moving through to clip the first piece above before downclimbing to the stance to get ready for his attempt. I sighed. He looked pretty good to me.

"You look pretty good from here," Shep shouted up. "How's it going?"

Marc was already well into the route, hanging sideways from a couple of digits and messing with the rope. "It's okay. I feel pretty good," he called, grabbing the next holds. "I think I'm going for it, man." Indeed.

On the ground we were just standing around with our necks crunched back and our hands shading our eyes. The show would be over one way or another in a couple of minutes—you don't hold on for long on that kind of terrain. From where we were the wall looked smooth and yellow like the hardwood floor in a school auditorium—if that floor was rearing up and about to fall on your head.

Marc was fighting but still making progress as we began to lose details with the distance and the angle. In his black tights, he looked kind of like an animated Rorschach blot against the upper wall. Down below, we were into it, barely breathing. This was all symbolic on some level. The rope was toaster-wire orange in the strong light.

Now Marc had stalled out near the top. His last piece was... let's call it a "ways," below him at this point. Hurriedly attempting to arrange a nut six or seven meters short of the finishing chains, he needed to move on before his guns were gone and he peeled. He was obviously fading quickly where he hung, quivering as he poked at a crack trying to line up the placement. Shep started getting agitated. He began dancing excitedly, muttering under his breath.

"...leave the pro," he said to no one in particular. "He should just forget it and go." He flipped at the rope and spoke to us and the air and the world in general.

Then he leaned back and addressed Marc directly and authoritatively. "Forget the pro, man! Leave it! Just go for it! You can do it!"

Above, Marc was definitely shaking as he tried to pull up enough rope and maneuver for the clip.

Seeing that Marc was ignoring him, Shep got emphatic.

"FUCK THE PRO, MAN! FUCK IT! GO FOR THE CHAINS! GO! GO! GO!"

The rest of us looked at each other in alarm. We began to move around a bit, each trying to wonder unobtrusively about landing areas and where we were standing and such, just in case anything should happen to go wrong up there, and like, you know, pull or something.

"FUCK THE PRO! THE CHAINS! YOU CAN DO IT! GO NOW!"

To us on the ground, it seemed that Marc was flickering and vibrating like an old movie print as he finally pushed the rope through the 'biner. Instantly it was home, he made a step, a stretch, a lean, and he was there, hanging back from the station as the rest of us clapped and shouted and Tuzo barked the birds out of the trees.

Later, when things had calmed down again, I picked up Simon's rope and tied in. It was my turn to have fun.

For sure. Back of the Lake on a Sunday in August. It's just gotta be the best place in the entire whole world. 🍂

VII   BIG WALLS

"Big walls" is a term of art in mountaineering writing. It refers specifically to climbs of steep rock walls, usually over several days, which require techniques not usually necessary on smaller crags. Big-wall climbing was once indelibly associated with "aid climbing," a controversial topic. Aid climbing is necessary when a climber needs more than his hands and feet to ascend. If there are insufficient holds, or if the climb is simply too steep or too hard for the climber, it becomes necessary to insert protection into the rock and to pull up on it, or to clip a sling ladder (etrier) into it and stand on that, rather than on a natural hold. Protection is inserted either by hammering (pitons); drilling and hammering (bolts, rivets, dowels); or by careful placement of many of the protection devices available today which slot into cracks and other discontinuities in the rock (chocks, friends, stoppers, etc.). These last protection devices are generally made out of aluminium alloys, and the simplest of them are carefully machined wedges, slung with wire, that are placed in cracks by the lead climber and removed by the seconding climber. "Protection" or "pro" is what makes high-angle climbing possible; by inserting protection devices on the way up the climb, the climber reduces significantly his risk of taking long falls, as the rope is clipped to protection using carabiners—aluminium snap locks that can be snapped into the protection. Thus a climber falling two metres above his protection will have two metres of rope between him and an anchor point and will fall only four metres—two metres down to the last piece of protection and two metres below it.

The most famous of the big walls are in California's Yosemite Valley, and every climber knows of the great routes on El Capitan and Half Dome. In Canada, the Squamish Chief is the best known of the big walls. In the 1960s and 1970s, the heyday of big-wall climbing, extensive aid was used to surmount these huge cliffs; today the emphasis is on using as little aid as possible.

Canadians had a significant role in the development of traditional big-wall climbing. The Grand Wall on the Squamish Chief, climbed in

1961 by Jim Baldwin and Ed Cooper, was the third of the big walls to be overcome in North America, after the Nose of El Cap and the Northwest Face of Half Dome in Yosemite, and Jim Baldwin, a pioneer Canadian wall climber, helped establish the third route on El Cap, the Dihedral Wall. Canadians were also notable in making early repeat ascents of many of the most difficult Yosemite walls.

The major development in alpine climbing in the 1960s was the extension of climbing techniques learned on the big walls to large and sometimes remote alpine faces. "Turret's Way," included in this section, is an example of this trend in which the mountains of Canada—particularly in the Bugaboo group of the Purcell Range and in the Rockies—played a leading role.

Today, the distinction between big walls and large alpine face climbs has largely disappeared.

~ Bruce Fairley

TURRET'S WAY

Pity the poor adjective. He (she?) is the unwanted Georgian cousin of today's writer; a slightly old-fashioned relic of the past whose presence is somewhat embarrassing and whom one hesitates to introduce to friends. Ernest Hemingway and his followers destroyed the love of the adjective in English; it has never recovered. "Use adjectives as little as possible" is the credo learned by all of today's aspiring writers.

In Michael Down, however, we have a writer who cares not a whit for the credo. Exuberant language is the hallmark of his mountain writing, and the unwanted adjective comes alive again in his pages. In "Turret's Way" the senses are aroused to dine more fully than in any other piece in this anthology. The feast begins with a vista of the "blazing copper skin" of the west face of Turret and concludes with one of the most vivid descriptions of a great electrical storm to be found anywhere in literature. One of the problems of metaphoric and "poetic" language was thought to be that it robbed prose of energy. "Turret's Way," however, is an illustration of how carefully chosen sensual language can add both drive and precision to an essentially narrative piece.

An issue that arises often between editor and writer deserves some comment here. Where does editing stop and rewriting begin? Just how far should an editor go in altering a manuscript to conform to her/his own literary values or tastes?

A number of the contributors to this volume, when contacted about the republication of their material, sent us their original manuscripts, urging us to re-edit them, and complaining of rough treatment at the hands of earlier editors. In all cases, including this one, we preferred the edited versions to the originals. The editing was fairly liberal in "Turret's Way"; a couple of paragraphs were omitted entirely and the last crucial paragraph was vigorously torn apart and reassembled. We felt, however, that the excluded material was extraneous to the main line of the story, and hindered its forward drive; and that the revised last paragraph better sounded the appropriate final note.

Probably the author has never lived who enjoyed seeing his work edited down, however, we feel that the 99 percent contributed by the author and the one percent contributed by the editor have made "Turret's Way" into a stirring tale that will be well-appreciated by both climber and armchair mountaineer. In the end, Mike Down sent us two versions of this piece and invited us to choose. We chose the version as edited by Moira Irvine, and thank him for his indulgence in allowing us to make that choice.

~ Bruce Fairley

Turret's Way

Michael Down

The wall soared above, aloof and austere, its blazing copper skin barely blemished by the wrinkles of time. From our immediate vantage point the south face of Turret looked blank. But as the sun traversed the sky changing nuances of light and shadow transformed the wall's outer shell and cracks and corners became discernible. As eyes screwed to adjust to the new reality, cardboard cut-outs of great huge flakes asserted themselves from a retreating backdrop of flawless granite and a route connecting them began to take shape.

After hours of contemplation with the glasses a line was linked up. But the network of flakes appeared loose and insubstantial, with blank sections only hinting of nailable cracks. There was the question as to how a fortress of overhangs guarding the upper headwall would be surmounted. And a disturbing lack of bivouac ledges, save a broken sill bisecting the breadth of the 2000-foot-high conical-shaped wall, pressed on our minds. Nonetheless there was only one way to find out if this magnificent and neglected wall would go.

The first pitch surprisingly gives way to deft footwork and goes free on broken, uncut diorite. Then the first of a series of expanding arches. Out come the aiders and in go the pitons. Only 40 ft out I pop a nut behind a creaking flake and take a flight, leaving bits of knee and elbow behind. Before reacting to this state of affairs I meet Scott's piercing eyes. They say one thing—we can't afford this sort of ignominious behaviour. I tacitly agree but there is some reluctance on the part of the psyche. Still too much anxiety to entirely immerse myself in the wall. After an age of switching from one thin corner to the next, I'm up.

The next pitch turns out to be the crux. After mixing it up in the corner of a pillar and a lanky tension traverse, Scott gingerly moves into a curving arch pinched flush to the wall. He becomes totally absorbed. Every placement, every movement takes on remarkable quality; direct, uncomplicated, effectual. Riveted to the belay in a beating sun, my vision animates as Scott fastidiously taps his way up the pie-crust-thin corner. He becomes a sorcerer with hammer and piton, the image of a Don Juan Warrior: one who leads an impeccable existence, making every action count. I follow with incredulity, pulling out a string of knife-blade stacks with a few taps and tugs. We pause for a moment at the belay to soak up the power of the wall and tune in to the vertical way of being.

Just before nightfall I watch Scott, silhouetted against the mysteries of the headwall looming above, place our only aid bolt. This transfers us into a shallow corner that opens onto an unexpected gift of a ledge. It's real narrow but long enough for one and a half bodies. We share the goodies, eating slowly while flecks of lightning dart about in the distant Monashees.

We wake engulfed in chilling mist. I drift upwards in the vagueness of early morning, following a discontinuous shallow crack that splits off the ledge in a triplet. Small nuts, tied off blades, lost arrows, and a pendulum lead into a solid corner that negates the remaining blank section. Then we're off again into the expanding flakes. Hard aid never relents until Scott slips on EBs at the base of a corner jammed with loose flakes. Seemingly unencumbered by the rack of iron, he stems and jams with meticulous precision, his rhythm free, fluid, only perceptibly shifting when the corner narrows to finger tip width and must be nailed. This delivers us onto a sloping, boulder-strewn ledge that takes some engineering to make habitable. We send a stream of boulders crashing into the swirling void and carve out a niche for the night. Before retiring I ease up another manky seam and fix the rope for the morning on a bolt drilled in a horizontal quartz band underlying the headwall. We spend the night struggling against gravity and each other, stuffed sideways in a bivi sack secured to hold us back from rolling off into space.

The dawn comes up on our eyrie cold and clear. Sir Sanford's frozen rump is in full view and dominates the ice-locked landscape stretching south toward faraway Sir Donald. Again possessed of unwavering purpose, Scott nails up a thin, elegant dihedral on a series of novel placements, consuming what remains of our dozen or so bent and broken knife-blades, then breaks left through the overhangs and onto the headwall with an ingenious mix of questionable aid pins and tight chimneying. Cleaning is awkward but the struggle fades to insignificance as the exposure reaches an exhilarating climax. The wall falls away in tawny sheets, its swooping lines funnelling to a dramatic focal point within the imagined depths of the Austerity Glacier way down below.

Above, another thin crack splits through one last bulging shield of monolithic rock. As I nail and nut ephemeral voices drift past on sporadic updrafts of crystalline morning air. Then we see them—Rob and Tom clambering up the bottom of the south-west buttress in sharp coloured contrast to our muted granite world—as sharp as if seen through an eagle's eye. A wave of nostalgia sweeps over me. Those had been warm-hearted days shared in the fragile shelter of our storm-lashed camp, savouring Rob's gourmet cooking while ritually preparing haul bags, racks, and energies for the journey ahead. With the summit another three or so pitches to go, chances are we'll revel in that camaraderie again tonight. But the descent is uncharted territory. Probably several rappels down a headwall that rears up from a huge snow gully filling the south-facing gap between Turret and Austerity, then a steep plunge down to a cavernous bergschrund. And a front of towering black thunderheads are boiling up fast to the west.

The first wave of storm pinned us in the base of a groove that ran with torrential hail. For hours we stood in etriers as if paralyzed. Only thoughts were wildly active as ribbons of white flame cracked open the obscured sky and licked at the surrounding array of granite towers, sometimes connecting with an explosive thud. After a bitter soaking, the vast conflagration of mountain and storm subsided long enough for us to hangdog our way up the final corners in a driving flurry. The summit offered no refuge; descent was imperative.

We had just begun the headwall rappels when a great mass of ink black cloud, stirred alive by convoluting folds of steely grey, clawed its way up the glacier at a reckless speed. The Blackfriars, overshadowed and clear cut in a great smoothness confounding ice and sky, appeared suspended, purple-black in the encroaching blur of darkness as ghost-curled fingers of the evil black cloud scratched out the failing light. In moments a feeling of foreboding, of physical as well as psychological discomfort, came over us. We could feel, indeed almost taste, the palpably oppressive, heavy sensation of a powerful electric field—a curious tickling, almost a crawl up the spine or brush across the cheek. Then we were engulfed in a smothering blackness, like the fearful primitive darkness of a total eclipse blotting out an ancient battlefield. The hail began to fall again; first with an incessant bounce, then with a heavier flow thickening into a smart perpendicular downpour. Soon the wall was a streaming sheet and the expansive couloir cloaked in the murk below became a canyon roaring with a spring-swollen river. Muffled up in toque, helmet and hood, I pulled off the latter for a moment to relieve the constrictions around my head. But the roar of hail and gravity was too intimidating. Just then the electric wind released its tremendous tension. Great claps of lightning crashed into the summit we had just departed, exploding blinding white light in our faces and sending chattering vibrations through our bodies. Scott and I exchanged a hint of desperation; talkative resolution lapsed into grim silence. We were swallowed up in the immense indifference of the world.

With uncompromising resolve Scott led the way down the rappels, applying his technical ingenuity to the maximum in rigging hanging stations behind expanding flakes. Each set of anchors was a horror that had to be ignored in itself. We'd rejoin for a few token words and fumbling with carabiner brakes then off he'd go down again into the impenetrable obscurity preceding another round of reverberating thunder.

Great sheets of white-hot flame continued to burst upon our en-shrouded world, revealing in a macabre flash the ongoing seriousness of the descent. Shattered rock bands blocked passage down the steep couloir filled with deep potato-flake snow, and a labyrinth of ice runnels coursing with hail would have to be traversed without crampons if we were to negotiate the schrund at its shallowest break. But when confronted with imminent death one becomes keenly aware of and detached from the situation. Decisions are final and therefore all powerful; there is no room for regrets. One chooses, then performs with the utmost of a tempered spirit lusting for life, accepting the ultimate responsibility for every action. Will and patience were with us—we could see the way out. ❧

THE IRON BUTTERFLY

The non-climber tends to assume that climbing is a fairly straightforward, if difficult, affair: you gather up whatever ropes and equipment you need, start climbing at the base of your chosen mountain or cliff, and climb until you reach the top. In fact, particularly in the case of big walls, many climbs are done piecemeal—sieged—rather than conquered in a single charge.

In the early years of big wall climbing it was common for climbers to make their ascents in siege style—climbing a pitch or two, descending (with ropes left fixed to the high point), then returning when time, energy, and psyche permitted. As wall climbing matured, climbers came to accept that an ascent made as a single push from top to bottom, with no fixed ropes, was a worthier goal, and siege climbing fell into ethical disfavor.

But not into disuse. Big walls are an entirely different cup of tea from any other form of climbing, and some walls are just bigger, scarier and more dangerous than others. The technical extremes of wall climbing have been reached in California's Yosemite Valley where the sound rock, good weather, and the possibility of rescue in the case of difficulty, have made single-push ascents of difficult routes almost routine; but there are places where remoteness, bad rock, and bad weather combine to up the odds against success to the point where a siege seems to be the only sane approach.

The Iron Butterfly, as Jeff Marshall and Steve DeMaio named their route on the north face of Wind Tower, was such a place.

~ David Harris

The Iron Butterfly

Jeff Marshall

The van, full of sixteen-year-old boys, was in a typical state of pandemonium. Mrs. Brown had once again volunteered to drop us off at some trailhead for yet another backcountry adventure. When the van approached the Pigeon Mountain overpass, one of the youthful spirits withdrew and focused his attention to the south. There it was; dark and ominous; real, yet intangible. The North Face of Wind Tower. The young man could never understand his urge to scale the face as the mountain would seemingly beckon him to grow and become a challenger.

The years passed and the young man grew through a number of harrowing experiences. He met people; wild people with a flare for adventure and an acute lust for life. The young man's appetite for climbing was becoming voracious.

Every time he saw the face the urge to climb it grew stronger. His pilgrimage was nearing. In the throes of ambition he had learned that the wall was unclimbed. Reports from previous attempts were that the wall overhung and was quite impenetrable, but this didn't matter for he had learned the quality of believing. Believing not in the words of others, but in the driving nature of the internal beast.

*   *   *   *   *

In the spring of 1986 I met Steve DeMaio, and we hit it off right away. He was talented, courageous, safe and overwhelmingly keen, not to mention extremely attractive. Coming from an Ontario, one-pitch rock climbing background, he was keen for the unclimbed big walls of the Rockies. I thought—at last—a catalyst.

I showed Steve the wall and explained to him the spell that it had put on me. He was into it. A few weeks after that conversation saw us hiking up the Wind Pass drainage armed with enough gear for a one-day effort. Little did we know that we were about to embark on the three-year Wind Tower experience.

As we hiked along the base of the wall, I was overcome with a great feeling of anxiety. Every time I looked up the wall was overhanging and, for the most part, featureless. Eventually we reached a point directly below the summit and Steve found what seemed to be the only access to the wall.

I remember that it was cold as I tossed rocks and belayed. He was on the pitch for a long time and the weather was taking a turn for the worse. When he reached the belay he informed me that the climbing was 5.11 and that the rock quality was somewhat dubious. The Kid was not impressed.

Seconding the pitch was memorable but not enjoyable and at the belay my level of ambition was at a low ebb which coincided nicely with the weather. That gave us a good excuse to head down. Leaving a fixed rope, we hiked out; two very humbled young men.

We visited the wall two more times that year and managed another pitch-and-a-half. In the meantime a number of other projects were completed and so the summer was not a complete write-off. The days were getting shorter and the temperatures were getting too cold to climb technical rock. It became apparent that we were getting involved in a big wall experience and that a different approach would have to be taken. The lines were strung tight and left to the winter.

First thing the following spring found Steve and I, in company with Geoff Powter, up for round four. On this attempt Steve completed pitch three and was rarin' to go for more. Meanwhile Geoff and I had been freezing our asses on the belay due to a rather large arctic front that had moved in and was forecast to be with us for a few days. Needless to say, enthusiasm at the belay was on the wane. At this point Steve got pissed off and laid down the ultimatum: "Either we continue or I'm off this project." A strong proposition indeed, but alas the cold won out. Steve rapped down, cleaning as he went. In the interim, Geoff booted Steve's sleeping bag off the ledge. We watched as it bounced down the scree. I said: "It's OK son, the exercise'll do ya good." Upon reaching the base, Geoff went for the bag and Steve and I sat and had a long chit-chat about the route. Steve was finally convinced of the genius of coming back on a warmer day.

Our next attempt was with a somewhat less than meek and timid Irishman by the name of Choc Quinn. Choc volunteered his services as porter and guinea pig. Porter to help cart gear, and guinea pig to jumar the first line. The first jumar is quite free hanging and it is hard for me to recall seeing anything as comical as poor Choc freight-training a big pack off his harness, spinning around in space, trying to figure out how to get this jumar business to work in his favour. My stomach still hurts. On this attempt, Choc stretched out on the second belay ledge and watched as Steve and I jugged to the next station. This day was a real breakthrough as I spent hours thrashing on the fourth pitch and managed a remarkable fifteen meters. So down we went again. If this is starting to sound like a siege it is only because it was.

The very next day, Steve and I hiked up, jugged up and finished the fourth pitch. Not without mishap however. Whilst nailing my way off into the wild blue yonder, the tied-off knifeblade that I was standing on, in a string of many, popped.

Yowsa! Fifteen meters later the Kid is upside down, staring at Steve. Steve asks: "You OK son?" I say "Fuck!" Steve ties me off, sits back in his belay seat and howls.

When I woke up the next morning in my apartment, I was fascinated that my right arm wouldn't move. At the hospital I was diagnosed as having torn shoulder ligaments and was told that I should spend the next six weeks drinking and chasing girls. I found this to be a reasonable recommendation.

Six weeks passed and it was time to try again.

Phone call: "Steve, let's go for it." Steve: "Sorry, James, not into it." "Oh well, just have to go for a solo I s'pose."

Glenn heard this and in an effort to save me from myself, offered to go. We scheduled three days off and got packed. Glenn took the first jumar while I did the ground work. He had never jumared before but soon had it figured out. Twenty feet from the belay he noticed an inconsistency in the line. Upon closer inspection he discovered that there were three strands between him and the ground! The rope had been chopped by rockfall. Half of the station had been destroyed. Glenn was hysterical.

Eventually this all got straightened out and we continued to the second belay for a bivy. Wow, my first night on the wall. The next day we jumared to the high point and put in pitch five. At the belay, after eight hours of gymnastics, I informed Glenn that a hammock bivy would have to be set up due to rapidly approaching dusk. He informed me that a hasty retreat was in better taste. He had done well so I granted him this request. He had absolutely no experience in wall tactics so I felt a big responsibility to take care of my little friend. When I back-cleaned the pitch and reached Glenn, it was getting dark. We only had one headlamp so I gave it to him since he had several knots to pass and numerous places where he would be clipping in and out of things. I belayed him and lowered the packs on one line, while he rappeled on the fixed line. Halfway down the first rappel, I lowered the packs too quickly and heard Glenn say "Fuck!" I watched the headlamp spin down in the dark. This was frightening because the rappel was on a diagonal and if he came off, he was going to swing way out into space and end up hanging off me. All went well, however, and we spent the night on the ledge. When I reached the ground the following morning, I found Glenn on his hands and knees, kissing the ground.

A week later Steve and I were up for a very serious attempt. Day one produced pitch six. Steve woke up on September 15 to cloudy skies and his little buddy singing happy birthday from his hammock. That day we put up pitch seven and half of pitch eight. We awoke the next morning to below-zero temperatures and new snow. The season was at a close and the wall had resisted for another year.

On June 19, 1988, we were back up, equipped with 30 kg packs and quiet determination. Steve finished the eighth pitch that day after an intricate series of A4 placements and a fall onto a hook which miraculously held. I managed to rip the entire traverse while jumaring. A great way to start. June 20 put us one pitch below the summit. While leading the tenth, Steve dislodged a rock from 30 meters above. It was a direct hit. I went black as the structural integrity of my helmet was dramatically altered.

We woke up on the 21st to an ocean of ground clouds and a stunning sunrise. By 10:00 a.m. we both stood on top, elated but strangely feeling empty. It was over. Apart from the fact that seven-and-one-half pitches of fixed line had to be cleaned, the experience had ended. We named our new route *The Iron Butterfly* because it was visually elegant and graceful, requiring a delicate and patient hand to get close to it and touch it. On the other hand it was an omnipotent force that was firmly opposed to human passage.

Three weeks later I went up with my good friend Matt Groll, cleaned the lines, and ended the story. 🦋

ZODIAC WALL

For many years Canada's best known big walls were on the Squamish Chief overlooking Howe Sound at Squamish, British Columbia. The first ascent of the main wall of "The Chief" was made by Canadian Jim Baldwin and American Ed Cooper in 1961. Big-wall climbs were a novelty in those days and the ascent developed into a media spectacle that attracted crowds, sponsorship and controversy. The climbers spent more than 40 days working their way up the wall, coming down most days after gaining a few more metres. The style attracted criticism from some climbers, but it was good for the tourist trade—one weekend cars backed up for kilometres to catch a glimpse of the daring heroes.

Climbers attempting later ascents of The Chief, either by established routes or new lines, sought to climb more quickly and efficiently; but few of the teams who tried the face in the 1970s could match the pace of Hugh Burton and Steve Sutton, who had begun rock climbing as teenagers and were among the most committed wall climbers in the world at the time when big-wall climbing was in its Golden Age. Both Burton and Sutton made significant contributions to wall climbing in the mecca of Yosemite, where they learned to endure long runouts with poor protection, risking long falls to establish new routes.

Zodiac Wall is located on the north side of The Chief. The original ascent was made by Americans: Fred Beckey, Alex Bertulis and Eric Bjornstad and Leif Patterson, Norwegian born. Like similar climbs of that period in Squamish, it has suffered from declining interest in big-wall climbing, and sees almost no ascents these days.

This piece describing the second ascent is evocative of the era in which it was written and of the conditions under which big-wall climbs were made in the days when the true measure of a climber was the number and quality of his big-wall routes. The most prolific of the big-wall climbers at Squamish tended to take some pride in being social outcasts from respectability. They enjoyed the reputation of being hard-drinking, rowdy, party types who specialized in breaking up bars and climbing while stoned.

Rock climbing today has lost some of the unreality of that era; committed climbers today are just as likely to think about vitamins or training as about beer and marijuana; and there is probably no turning back from the onslaught of ever more difficult free-climbing, which has displaced aid climbing almost completely in the public imagination, and even to a large extent on the big walls themselves. Still, it is nice to look back, even perhaps with some nostalgia, to a time not so long ago when big-wall climbers were a rare breed, practising a mysterious craft far from the madding crowd, on silent, lonely heights.

~ Bruce Fairley

Zodiac Wall

Hugh Burton

Stumbling up the North Gully trail we just barely managed to dump our not-quite-big-enough load of supplies on a huge boulder at the base of Zodiac Wall. Staring into the darkness and leaning over backwards, we could see nothing but the summit rim. It didn't matter. We didn't know where the route went, only where it started. We figured it would be obvious. Knowing nothing about a route is like the first ascent in some ways; there's no apprehension about hard nailing and unprotected free climbing. You take everything as it comes. The first ascent party (Fred and Leif and others) called it a six.

Rumours of expanding blocks in roots flashed through our minds next morning as we again stumbled up the trail, looking up instead of down. An unnecessary bolt fifteen feet off the ground confirmed that we were on route. Enjoyable free up a flake system ended at a ledge. Fantastic? A gallon of water from the first ascent to add to our one. Hesitating for some strange reason, I glance down at the mouse floating belly-up therein. No longer thirsty, almost sick, I fire it off into the gully. It explodes on a flat-topped boulder and shatters the ominous silence.

Steve works up and left in a huge awkward downward-hanging flake system. After several strenuous mantels onto moss ledges he reaches the end of his rope. Leaving his station in a steep corner, a well-formed crack led left under the ten-foot triangular roof above. A couple of hook placements, a few bolts and then a beautiful system of thin face cracks leads into the first bolt ladder.

The sun pierces the damp clammy gully. It comes closer and closer until its warmth flows over us. The peaceful valley of the Squamish River is a welcome change from the usual view of town and mills so familiar to Chief climbers. Steve leads on; strange free climbing—ramps, small grassy ledges. A small grassy nook marks the end of the lead. We laze in the sunshine—peaceful and quiet.

But again it's time to move. Iron rack cuts into shoulders. Climbing quickly (another bolt ladder). Mantel off the bolts into a cold eight-inch crack. After thrashing around for a while, bongs in lengthwise get me started. More jamming until the rope stretches tight behind me. Thirty feet of easy free gains the monstrous Astro Ledge.

It was unreal. Huge pine needle and sand beds and a gallon of good water greeted us. A warm breeze swept the wall, the pine trees swayed and we were very much at ease.

A hundred feet right of where we had gained the platform, a large overhang served two purposes: a roof for our bivouac, and a way to the top. Up its inside corner, a series of stumps marks the route. The dead stumps were uselessly loose now, the rock fractured, and several stumps on the ledge awaited Steve's fall as he tried to pass the section. It didn't come, and in thirty feet the crack became bombproof once more.

The sun now setting, the brilliant red sky beckoned us to watch. Back to the ledge. Our new system of bivouac food, proven in the Valley a few weeks before, was again put to the test. Bags of popcorn, chips and Coke flooded from our haulbag. So confident at our progress the first day we left one chocolate bar, a bag of popcorn, and some water for a summit refreshment. Darkness swept the valley as we did our dessert.

Another cool quiet crystal-clear morning dawned quickly. Steve continued his lead around the lip of the overhang as I half belayed, half packed the haulbag. Suddenly he was flying toward the ledge. I grabbed the rope and stopped him forty feet from the ground. A phenomenal mantel onto a moss ledge was finally accomplished. Passing his bad belay, a huge low-angle groove led on. It was really thick, like a steep jungle. Huge soft ferns grew in the back. Chimneying, jamming and easy nailing led to a bolt halfway. Steve continued, a similar pitch ending in a squeeze chimney with some pins placed in a huge tree root.

Constantly joking until now about the lush vegetation and route markers (stumps), two cracks shot off in different directions over a huge overhanging wall. No stumps visible, they were beautifully clean. No pin scars—no way of telling which way. Following our usual procedure, we followed the easy-looking one. Sixty feet up and left, it became obvious it was the wrong choice—the crack petered out. Lowered off my top pin I hung and swung by my waist in mid air. Finally I was able to touch the rock, and got a pin in another system. Ten feet later several good pins marked the end of the lead.

Steve passed me and, nailing discontinuous cracks, was soon twenty feet above. While placing a pin in an expanding system of flakes there was suddenly a horrifying explosion. Spurred on by the thought that my station might be falling out, he was up another twenty feet and onto a tiny ledge in about fifteen seconds! Looking to his right, in the direction of the alternate crack system, a beautiful line of bolts rushed towards us, ending in a small pendulum to his stance. A beautiful jam crack to a sloping shelf ended his lead.

Sun setting and no ledges. Fearing another belay seat bivouac I started to lead through the maze of overhangs and corners. Slings on spears of rock led around a roof and onto a small ledge. Darkness pressing, but we knew this was the last lead. Passing a fixed pin confirmed we were on route. Ten feet later I was lost. Tying off a huge root that was hanging down, I followed fifteen feet to the tree it belonged to. Cleaning a little moss away revealed a standard angle crack.

Disengaging myself from the wretched tree after a ten-foot fall I came to the conclusion that the crack expanded like all shit. Chockstones became a necessity and soon I had twenty feet, another twenty to the top. Everything blanked out here, partially because it was pitch dark by now! Ropedrag created an impossible situation. Just pulling up slack provided enough extra force on my pins that they started shifting down. Tying off the haul line and checking the rappel three or four times, I did a bodywrap rappel in my T-shirt, totally overhanging in the blackness. Fortunately I hit the small ledge.

Steve did a spooky overhanging jumar. The ledge was really small—no room to put the haul bag. Removing our summit refreshments, we ate the little that was left. Some more dessert and again everything seemed pretty adequate. Cleaning the ledge of some of the larger more exciting boulders we confirmed that "Zodiac Wall is a one-bouncer."

As the tremendous crashes subsided, we again felt very alone. The peaceful night passed very slowly, both of us sitting up, legs dangling, totally exhausted and content. Tremendous white columns glowed eerily in the darkness scarcely a hundred feet away. Thankful for our small sanctuary we rested easy until the very first hint of dawn.

The weather was rapidly deteriorating. I quickly packed the bag as Steve cleaned the pitch to the ledge. After jumaring back to the highpoint, a couple of unlikely moves to the right and up gained a huge ledge. And what a place! Huckleberry bushes fully ripe greeted our thirsty throats. But no need—it had started to pour.

Two mostly third-class pitches up and right and we were on a huge forested ledge just beneath the summit. Walking through the waist-high bushes soaked us to the skin. Finally we were up—on the spongy carpet of moss crowning the Chief, with clouds swirling all around us. ❧

VIII CANADA, ETHICS AND ICE AXES

Most mountaineers are like amateur cooks: they have one recipe that they use on guests over and over again, taking security from a formula that they know will work. In the case of mountain writing, the formula is the blow-by-blow account of the climb. Magazines devoted to mountaineering are heavy on the pictures, short on really good prose. Mountaineers themselves are people of action, but their writing often plods. It is especially rare to find an essay in the field that rises above personal soul-searching, investigation into the efficiency of equipment, or diatribe against the latest perceived ethical transgression.

Climbers are generally younger folk—people who do. Some of them become outstanding writers, but few ever delve too deeply into the issues of the sport when they turn pen to paper. As a form, the essay is more developed in British or American mountain writing than in Canada, where there are fewer publishing opportunities available and the genre is little appreciated. Reprinted below are some exceptions to this scarcity. It is hoped that as the great climbing generations of the 1960s and 1970s turn from climbing to more sedate pursuits, some of them will pick up their pens and enrich the stock of mountain essays born of this country and its climbing traditions.

~ Bruce Fairley

OH, CANADA

In 1970 the tide of history finally caught up with Canada's only really important climbing periodical, the *Canadian Alpine Journal*. Astonishingly, from 1907 to 1969 the journal retained the format established by its first issue. The cover, of course, was green; the size suspiciously akin to that of the revered *Alpine Journal* published in London, England. There were pictures—scanty and poorly reproduced ones—but the emphasis was on tradition and safety. Events recounted in the *Canadian Alpine Journal* took on a theological tone; the peaks were for spiritual fulfillment and the keynote was reverence. In addition, it was clear that among mountaineers no one ever exhibited poor taste, argued or swore.

All that changed in 1970. The pictures in the new, larger-format *Canadian Alpine Journal* leapt out of the page: bold, striking and sharp. Photographs of Bugaboo Spire or Mt. Robson seemed to throw down the gauntlet and say, "Climb us—if you dare!" For the first time the journal showed not only where climbing in Canada was at, but where it was going: out onto the huge walls of vertical rock and thick, dripping ice, onto the massive ramparts of the Squamish Chief and the treacherous north faces of the biggest peaks in the mighty Rockies.

It is fitting that this essay, "Oh, Canada," should have been the lead-off article of that wonderful issue. Its author, like many of the innovators in Canadian mountaineering up to that time, was an import from an older tradition, a climber raised in the post-war climbing scene in Great Britain, which produced so many outstanding climbers from the British working class. Coming to Canada from the crags of Scafell and Borrowdale, where a new army of youngsters was climbing everything in sight, MacDonald sprung from a renaissance, when mountaineering was rediscovered in Europe and made for the first time into a popular sport.

Nothing like this had happened in Canada. Climbing was institution-bound and conservative. Almost no great climbs had been done since the Second World War, and this was especially true in the Coast Mountains around MacDonald's new home town of Vancouver. No wonder MacDonand felt, as he sat through slide shows of flora and fauna at the monthly meetings of the Alpine Club of Canada, that he had stepped backward into the reign of Victoria.

By 1970 much had changed, yet the tone in this essay is wistful; for MacDonald the Canadian renaissance came too late. The climbers leading the way on the Squamish Chief were a younger university crowd, and MacDonald never became a part of their circle.

But what an insightful piece this is to anyone who knows anything of the climbing history of those days! MacDonald understood completely why climbing would appeal to a technological generation. He knew too that good company was essential to the health of the sport and was a barometer of its strength. And there are many other sly observations here, not the least of which is a professional summing-up of the career of one unique climber himself, who brought a great sense of history and climbing development to his shrewd observations on the Canadian climbing scene.

MacDonald would, I am sure, be pleased to think that the younger generation that revitalized Canadian climbing shared many of his own sentiments. They were, as well, mainly a home-grown crowd, particularly in the Coast Mountains, and in ways not dissimilar to the khaki-clad youth of MacDonald's salad days in Britain: poor, not too elegant, but with enormous drive and appetite.

This is my favourite mountaineering essay.

~ Bruce Fairley

Oh, Canada

Les MacDonald

The climbing scene in Canada has been for me a long-simmering love-hate affair, taking me on the one hand to the depths of despair, and on the other to heights of ecstasy.

Coming from a post-war Britain, where climbing had rapidly emerged from the easy pre-war period of the Harris tweed knickerbocker set, or the rather nice affable middle class England, to the new wave of shipyard workers, miners and Lancashire mill workers with a common uniform of commando vibram boots, camouflaged windproof pants and an ambition to climb everything in sight, the Canada, or more specifically the British Columbia of that era, was for me a rather dismal discovery.

You have to understand that climbing in that period of the after war years was exhilarating heady stuff. It was a sport and with it went all the discipline and rigor of training, and of course suffering, to get in shape. We spent a month of concentrated calisthenics before the assaults on the Central Buttress of Scafell, a dedication known only to the fanatic members of the colliery soccer team in my town before that.

Our heroes were Buhl the roofer from Austria, Cassin the carpenter from Courmayeur, Joe Brown the plumber from Preston, and quarryman Jim Birkett from Langdale. Intertwined with the modern heroes went equal veneration for the giants of the past, long and not so distant. From Whymper and Mummery down to Jones, Kelly, and Colin Kirkus of the home front variety, to the strange sounding continental types like Knubel, Lochmatter, and Ravanel.

There were other folks who ventured into the hills in those days, who, unknown to them, we held in awe. The remnants of the pre-war school, they carried gigantic rucksacks, wore tricounis and clinkers, and dressed in anything but the ex-army garb of the new army which was us. The exalted members of the Alpine Club, the Ladies Alpine Club or the Fell and Rock, they never quite seemed to accept, or forgive, the momentous flood of young people, who after the dark years of the war had discovered "their" mountains.

I recall vividly at the age of fifteen, sheltering from a Lakeland downpour along with my partner in the deserted drumhouse at the top of Honister Pass, being questioned rather patronizingly by two old gentlemen as to why we climbed and where we came from. Our monosyllabic replies were accompanied by the sighs and "ahs" familiar to anyone who has ever been patted on the head by uncles, aunts, and schoolteachers.

For them, from their comfortable homes and warm offices of the week, the weekend trek to the hills in a Jaguar or Armstong-Siddeley resembled more a pilgrimage to Lourdes. Their rope-festooned figures and bellowing guffaws could often be glimpsed and heard in the "Select Saloon" on a Saturday night, sipping whiskey and gin through the inevitable mustachioed lips, men and women alike!

For us, the discovery of the hills, the sun-warmed rock, the mists, rain, and streams of North Wales, Glencoe, and Skye was a revelation to dream about during the interminable hum-drum week down the pit, in the fab. shop of Vickers Armstrong's, or in the rusty skeletons of new laid keels, along the stocks of Clydebank.

Our weekend pilgrimage to the hills was more of a full-scale cavalry charge than a trek; carried there by overloaded ex-W.D. Ariels, B.S.A.s, and Nortons, with the luckless rearguard of the infantry hitch-hiking resolutely behind. Not for us the comfort of a Clachaig Hotel or a Dungeon Ghyll, rather the tent of Sty-head tarn, which on some Saturday evenings resembled a Bedouin Camp, and the twinkling candles from the cave on Scafell, a troglodyte commune. But at least it was ours, for the Christian Temperance League and all the rest of them always descended to the valley of an evening to quaff their half and halfs, and leave us to our Horlicks and the guardianship of the hills.

They often accused us of a lack of real love and respect for "their" mountains in the hallowed pages of their periodicals. The accusations were slipped innocuously between the umpteen glossy plates of Alpine flora and their daring exploits on the Monte-Rosa, the Via Appia and the bars of Gstaad. We'd never last they said, the temporary phenomena of the war-babies, that was us!

We knew differently, and our love and reverence for the steep walls of Pillar Rock and the alpine pennycress in its crannies, voiced in the nasal vernacular of a scouse or a geordie was of an earthiness and an ardor that was philosophical light-years away from the dry academia of a Geoffrey Winthrop-Young, and one they could never hope to understand.

The mountains brought other rewards; to have a friend who lived in Wigan and one in Carlisle was a cosmopolitan accomplishment unequalled by any member of my immediate family in all their history. Yes, climbing was not only a sport, a love, a new phenomenon, for us it was akin to liberation.

The same development and enthusiasm had also swept the continent, but our luckier brothers from Lille, Lyon, Munich, and Stuttgart had a greater swath of mountains, real mountains, to pick from. The airy cosmopolitanism which came with a friend in Wigan called Bert, knew no bounds after trips across the channel had gained a Jean-Pierre in France and a Rudi in Austria, after hectic days together on the Chamonix granite had cemented the life-long bonds peculiar to the mountaineering fraternity.

Although news from the Alps was slow coming through, the weekend adventures of Cunningham and McInnes in Glencoe, Brown and Bonington on Clogwyn or Dolphin and Birkett in Borrowdale were always old news by about mid-week.

The extra curricular activities of the Creagh Dhu were always a source of wonderment and envy. How to beat the system, cock a snoot at the climbing establishment, and still put up hell-fire routes most weekends. Hamish McInnes with some of the boys roaming the Highlands looking for big game on the Laird's property with a bunch of stenguns liberated from the Glasgow armories had a touch of the romance of a latter day Rob Roy or Che Guevera. A feverish night on the deck of a swiftly moving truck after hitching a ride, cautiously rolling up a gigantic tarpaulin and kicking it off the truck near King's House, to be picked up later on as the new roof for the Glencoe bothy, was an experience good for at least 6 months in Borstal.

At the age of 17 I knew the stations of the "Jungfrau Bundesbahn" better than the Pope knew the stations of the cross, and still no entry stamp in the pages of the stiff shiny new passport. What we lacked in sophistication and funds we made up for in audacity, this reaching its nadir after the official British expedition had climbed Mt. Everest, the Creagh Dhu launching a Himalayan expedition in retaliation. For Cunningham and McInnes, it ended in near disaster at a high altitude camp when they lost all their weekend camping and climbing equipment in an avalanche. Cunningham, the west of Scotland wrestling champion, became the bread-winner, challenging the local wrestling champs around the Garwhal in order to win some food.

If that was a Chaplinesque low point in the movement's quest for realisation, the high point and eventual official recognition was surely Joe Brown's inclusion in the Mustagh Tower expedition, and his feats there, which are legendary now.

European expeditions suffered no such Victorian hang-ups in their recognition of Solda or Buhl. The French Nanda Devi expedition of 1951 included two of the most advanced climbers of that period, Roger Duplat, leader, and Gilbert Vignes, the latter being a specialist in artificial climbing.

By the fifties the nouvelle vogue of paratrooper windbreakers and boots had turned into a fast flowing tide, wearing the latest in Le Trappeur boots and Terray duvets. Italian hemp had given way to Viking nylon, a triumph of British cunning, which could be sold for twice its price at the guides school or sports store in Chamonix, two years before the French found out how to make it!

My only feeling of kinship with the old school gushed through me one afternoon as I watched a Keswick youth skip nonchalantly solo up the FOUR main climbs on the vertical Kern Knotts. A feeling of anger tinged with possessiveness I guess would describe it. Kern Knotts was almost hallowed ground for us, we had sweated with fright and found the holds the hard way, in clinkers, overcoming the dire warnings of the guide book along the way. Now young kids, clad in the new P.A.'s with steel supported soles and no traditions or even ropes behind them, romped up and down our routes. The feeling of kinship was somewhat satanic and not easy to exorcise! We all meet our nemesis in change.

Being used to waiting an hour on a rainy Sunday in the line-up to do the Napes Needle, the Lions from my garret window in Vancouver didn't seem possible. With all haste that Sunday morn, my first, I sped through Stanley Park on foot, and across the bridge. I tried to figure out how many routes they'd have on those two choice monoliths, and how many of the boys must be swarming up them this beautiful day.

After climbing a great fence and fighting through the primeval jungle, I found them deserted, with no sign of serious route cleaning having ever been done. What a find, after an eight year apprenticeship on the crags of Britain with but 3 accredited first ascents on a 60 foot crag in remote Northumberland! Here was a limitless expanse of rock by comparison, and all of it seemingly virgin!

The next days were spent tracking down the climbing community and eventually finding them in the Art Gallery, a bad omen, after a bizarre false start in the "Alpen Club" on Victoria Drive, the latter evening spent alternately downing beer from Steins and trying to converse in fractured Deutsch about climbing with a tableful of soccer players who were more interested in Herman Dienst than the Kaisergebirge of Anderl Heckmair. By comparison the austere, polite, but soulless atmosphere of the Art Gallery, appropriately overlooked by Emily Carr's dark green rain forests, confirmed my worst fears.

Like Scrooge confronted with his Christmas past, I felt somewhat unequal to a confrontation with yesteryear. It was a curious reincarnation of the cosy Victorian middle-class mountaineering species which I thought I'd left behind forever. I felt that purely as a clinical observation, not with any antagonistic feeling. Curious Canada, the paradox of the new struggling with the past, more Union Jacks and portraits of the Royal family than I'd ever seen before!

I sat through slides of flora and fauna, pack horses, raising of the flag, and church services at camp, followed by picture postcard scenes of scenes of lakes at 6 different times of the day, and clusters of climbers clad in what could easily have been imported regalia from Zermatt, circa 1926! Speakers made occasional reference to pitons much after the fashion of ministers of the Scottish Kirk talking about sex. No wonder the Lions still retained so much of their virgin rock!

Official, as opposed to private trips could be ponderous, relieved albeit by the enticing walls and slabs of the mountains themselves. Ice axes; yes axes, always axes; cherished, fondled, crooned over, carried to the top of the Camel in July, and most as blunt as old nick. I suppose I voted with my feet, like so many before and since, shortly after that. Particularly after being ordered to tie into a rope for a slog up a pile of stones by a stentorian leader who wouldn't hear any nonsense about walking up hands in pockets.

John Dudra was a lone beacon in those days, leaving the trail of orange peels and candy wrappers that led to the easy summit, to search out the new. His loss was great for B.C. mountaineering. In this regard, the crusade for one new route after another is another lone saga. The inability to share the joy and pleasures of new climbs with other parties, to rekindle experiences with others who have willingly passed the same way, and vice-versa, was a deflating process which whittled away at the urge to try the new and difficult. But there were heights of ecstasy also, as I said in the beginning; the dozen or so routes I put up on Camel with my wife and best man over a honeymoon long weekend, marred only slightly by an irate water board official chasing us down the path to Grouse, his threats gradually fading away as we left him behind; the cliffs of Pt. Atkinson we ran through like the plague one set of summer evenings, until we eventually ran out of enthusiasm and piscatorial names.

But many changes have taken place in Canadian mountaineering whether we agree with them or not. Those who thought that the new highway to Squamish meant that it would be possible to climb Garibaldi without taking the motor boat up Howe Sound anymore, didn't consider the point of view of the young. They were more interested in the Chief's walls than the grandeur of Garibaldi. Most weekends one can find many parties of competent climbers on the Chief. The days when one could count the number of people who could lead good grade 5 on the fingers of your hands are gone. Contrary to some opinion, the parties on the Chief aren't simply rock gymnasts. Most know their way about high mountains, and difficult ones, equally well.

One glaring difference from their counterparts in Europe though, is that they are generally unattached to any mountaineering organization at all. The fidelity of their confréres abroad to their respective clubs, whether on the continent or in the British Isles, attests to a skilful leadership which has managed to keep pace with modern mountaineering trends and ideas. As a result they have kept the adherence of the younger generations. Unfortunately we can't say the same thing here in Canada.

Now we could rationalize our way out of the awkward question by blaming the young themselves; a set of cliches comes easily to mind—"shiftless, undisciplined, irresponsible"—but that doesn't help much. The task of turning the existing mountaineering clubs, particularly the Alpine Club, into strong healthy organizations with the kind of spirit which would attract young people could be a rewarding job for the 70s.

Surely the demise of the clubhouse in Banff symbolises the end of an era; a history of CPR-imported Swiss guides, of attempts at ersatz Swiss villages, of attempts to import a whole style of mountaineering which, although it had its moments and its Conrad Kains, was really quite alien to the Canadian scene.

If it succeeds in nothing else next year the leadership of the ACC should plan an expedition abroad. I don't mean the Cooks' Travel variety costing the weight of the Aga Khan in rubies for safe passage, but a real serious Canadian mountaineering expedition of and for the young climbers who are doing such great things these days.

The growth of a sizeable, energetic, Canadian climbing fraternity is a fact, and harnessing its latent energy and vitality for all our benefit is a task that needs doing, and soon. ❧

MOUNTAINEERING AND THE ETHICS OF TECHNIQUE

No one who reads modern mountaineering journals can miss the passionate debates over questions about what is reprehensible and what is acceptable in modern mountaineering practice. Climbers use the term "ethics" to describe the largely unwritten codes that have evolved to determine where lines should be drawn that cannot be crossed. The concept first arose from the sudden popularity of climbing. Pitons, the metal pins that were driven into the rock to protect a lead climber from a fall (and then usually removed) were destructive of cracks; each time a pin was hammered in and withdrawn the crack was enlarged and scarred. On the well-trodden crags of Britain or Yosemite in California, it became clear that such continual destruction of cracks would ultimately destroy many climbs, and that even minimal piton placement altered the nature of the climb for the next party. Chocks were introduced into North America in the 1960s from Britain. These were aluminium wedges that could be inserted by hand and without hammering, and removed as easily, and within a matter of years pitons had disappeared from short, established climbs.

Possibly because the modern ethical discussion began with this debate about undesirable protection, it never seemed to progress much beyond it. The most sharply contested issue has always been the use of bolts—anchors that are placed by drilling a hole in the rock and hammering in a pin or dowel that cannot then be easily removed, and is intended to be permanent. The introduction of bolts meant that any rock face in the world could be climbed by those who had the patience and stamina to drill the anchor holes. Bolts drastically lowered the notion of the impossible. Climbers have still not finished arguing about when their use is justified, how many per pitch are acceptable and how many simply destroy the sense of adventure. Pick up a British or American climbing magazine today and you are still likely to find the topic under intense scrutiny.

Coming from a part of the world where hard rock climbing was not the basis of the mountaineering tradition, I found the so-called ethical debates myopic in their focus. They concentrated so intensely on the question of what protection was fair and right that few other issues received any attention. In part this was because the best writers on the subject were mainly rock climbers. Even if they climbed extensively in the mountains, these writers went there from Yosemite, Tahquitz Rock or Cloggy in Wales.

The debate over protection as it emerged in American climbing magazines demonstrated that many participants were not as rigorous in their thought as in their climbing. Climbers spoke frequently of the style in which a climb was done as an ethical issue. The style of a climb refers to the form demonstrated by climbers during their ascent. If a climber comes to a difficult move, inserts a piece of protection above his head and pulls up on it in order to overcome the difficulty, he would be using poorer style than a climber who was able to make the moves on his own, without the aid of yarding on the "pro." Clearly, as long as techniques that damage the rock are not involved, no ethical issue arises. (Had the climber driven a piton, the situation would be different; the next party up the climb would find a slightly larger crack where the piton had been, which might make the move less difficult.) In often failing to distinguish between style and ethics, many American climbers showed that they were using the ethical debate in an unethical way, and as a form of one-upmanship to put down weaker climbers and glorify the stronger. This attitude put them close to the position of Thrasymachus, which Socrates mercilessly debunked in the first book of Plato's *Republic,* that the values of the stronger are the good.

All ethical philosophy begins from the question, "What is the good?" But classical philosophy, as the great American thinker Leo Strauss showed, recognized that this was a question that could not be finally answered. It was the constant search for the good that thus became important. The essence of philosophy lies in the inquiry. The most searching thinker about mountaineering ethics would recognize that the essential ethical question in climbing is whether the activity serves the good. This is a much wider line of inquiry than the question of whether a hundred bolts on a mountain wall is justified.

It was in order to reflect upon these larger questions that I wrote the essay that follows. Mountaineers tended to talk about ethics as if they had invented the subject. There was no attempt to relate the ethical squabbles to the larger issues of philosophic inquiry. Positions tended to be adopted without consideration for the fact that we live in the mass age, where a popularized sport impacts on many beyond the participants. I have heard frequent travellers to Nepal deny, for example, that mountaineering has had any destructive impact there. My view is that this attitude shows that ethical philosophy is not hard enough at work among mountaineers.

Developments in the climbing world since I wrote this essay in 1983 have tended to confirm my conclusion that modern mountaineering technique has become autonomous. I hope that mountaineers throughout the world will take time over the next few years to look at what is happening to our shrinking and choking planet and to reflect on their role in it.

∿ Bruce Fairley

Mountaineering and the Ethics of Technique

Bruce Fairley

In the summer of 1983 John Baldwin invited me to join Jean Heineman and him on a climbing trip to the unfrequented section of the Coast Mountains which lies between Bute and Toba Inlets. This was to be another in a series of long and original traverses out this way which John has put together over the past few years and it was intended to feature his preferred mode of access. We would be walking in and out. Rob Driscoll, a young climber from Vancouver, also joined the party.

We began with a sopping two day bushwhack up the Orford River. This was followed by two more days of drizzle and fog, and a further two days of wallowing in heavy snow as we plodded on towards our first air drop, in admittedly better weather. We did little actual climbing, nothing whatsoever of a technical nature.

Rob and I chafed a little under this inability to grapple with the peaks. We wanted to get onto some steep rock or ice and put our technical skills to work; it was slightly frustrating to have to pass by possible challenges because there wasn't really enough time and we had to keep moving. But John and Jean seemed almost indifferent to weather or poor snow—they cheerfully stormed ahead no matter what the conditions.

One night we had a discussion about those who love mountains versus those who love only climbing. The conversation induced a slight feeling of guilt in me. I wondered if I was worrying too much about achievement, losing the sense of beauty in the mountain environment through an obsession with technique. I thought of the early explorers of the range who had cheerfully invested weeks just to climb one remote peak.

The explorations of John Clarke were also much on our minds during the expedition for he had pioneered some of the ground we were going over. My attitude to this enigmatic climber had always been ambiguous; I wondered if he was missing the point by not concentrating more on technical ascents. But John's and Jean's conviction that Clarke was the real exponent of true mountaineering ethics in the Coast Mountains set me reappraising my conclusions. For Clarke it was simply being in the mountains that mattered.

Issues in mountaineering ethics have occupied my thoughts for some time since. The narrow scope of the debate carried on sporadically in the journals aroused my fascination. In the mountains climbers of outstanding promise were dying by the score. One need only count the toll in the English speaking world over the past dozen years: Ian Clough, Leif Patterson, Gary

Ullin, Escourt, Haston, Patey, Al Givler, McKeith and Lauchlan, Unsoeld, Burke, Boardman, Tasker, Grassman, Jotterand, Alex McIntyre, Sorensen, George Manson and his companions.[1]

The price of climbing in the forefront of modern alpinism has now become the willingness to risk one's life in the pursuit of greater and greater difficulties. In the American Alpine Journal we now have a new category of reportage to accommodate the statistics: "Ascent and Tragedy," and two to three dozen climbers are reported as dying in the Himalaya each year, while in the European Alps the fatality rate is reportedly close to 1000 deaths per season.

Yet in the journals this commitment to extreme boldness does not seem to have provoked much comment or reaction. The situation may be contrasted with the willingness of writers in an older tradition of mountaineering to see a moral failing in such total commitment. Writing in 1954 James Ramsay Ullman labelled the first climbers of the Eiger North Face as individuals with "more luck than sense." Speaking of the situation which prevailed in the Alps during the thirties he wrote: "Competition was everything; competition literally to the death… seldom has there been an unhappier example of how hysterical and perverted nationalism can infect even the most unpolitical of activities."[2] And Henry Hall, returning from Waddington in the thirties, discouraged any attempt on the main tower as foolish and likely fatal.

One would expect that such a staggering expenditure of brilliant talent and human potential in the modern expedition game might at least provoke a little intelligent soul-searching in the journals. I have been unable to find anything of this nature taking place. The hotly contested ethical question is still the use of the bolt.[3] I wondered if this was right.

1. Not all of these individuals died in the pursuit of extreme alpinism; they are included because their names are recognizable. Anyone who doubts that mountaineers are dying in unprecedented numbers is referred to the last few issues of the AAJ or any of the journals which treat climbing in the European Alps.
2. Modern climbers tend to belittle much of Ullman's writing partly, one suspects, because he was not a hard man. Also his style tends towards the eulogistic; modern readers prefer the grimmer school of "warts and all." My purpose here is simply to use Ullman as an example of ethical thinking evident in North American mountaineering at the time of his writing. The fact that he was chosen as the official historian of the American Everest Expedition shows that his values were those of the mountaineering establishment of his day, at least in the U.S. Quotations from *The Age of Mountaineering*, JB Lippincott, 1954, pp 76, 73.
3. See, for example, most recently the debate in AAJ 1982 and 1983 or the re-emergence of the question in *Mountain* issues 91 and 92. Since this manuscript was written the article by Martin Boysen, "The Reason Why" (*High* magazine, No. 10, July 1983), has come to

A second question concerned me. What relationship exists between modern alpinism and our society's publicly held sense of values? Are modern extreme climbers to be regarded as iconoclasts, rebels against the stifling mediocrity and boredom of technological existence? Climbers often seem to take precisely this view of themselves. Or are they, in fact, representatives of technological society—those who have assimilated completely the public beliefs of western society? I thought that the second question might answer the first.

Before going any further, however, I should explain my use of the word "technique." Climbers refer to a climb as technical when it is seen to involve difficulties which require the use of artificial protection beyond ice axe and rope. A broader use of the word however will be more frequently employed in this essay. In this sense technique is an attitude, a way of perceiving and organizing our lives. In his book *The Technological Society* Jacques Ellul uses the word in this way and I am accepting his definition. The concept is a little elusive. Ellul's definition was "the totality of methods rationally arrived at and having absolute efficiency (for a given stage of development) in every field of human activity."[4] What Ellul distrusted was the complete ascendency of the standardized programme, the agreed upon procedure, the flow chart—in short mechanized thinking—to achieve results which had been predetermined. Technique is the enemy of the spontaneous and irrational, the casual and the carefree. It seeks always a better way of doing things and works toward the eradication of disorder through system.

Climbing literature has used technique in both senses of the word. In North America the issues have been framed around practices in the field of rock climbing, most specifically with regard to the legitimacy and use of various kinds of protection, to a lesser extent with the validity of certain routes. Concerns over guidebooks, first ascent fever, aircraft access, commercialism, publicity and soloing are also part of the debate.

Commentators have zeroed in on questions of 'pro' so completely however, that many see ethical issues materialize the moment one reaches for a chock. John Lauchlan for example, writing in CAJ 1982, spoke of relief at not having to follow the "ethical" lead of a climber who was attempting to lead a difficult ice pitch without resting on his tools.[5]

I fail to see that any truly ethical issue was involved here. A decision to use non destructive aid may be crucial to the question of style, but not to the

my attention. The article catches Boysen in a mood of reappraisal; without being judgemental he canvasses many of the issues raised in this article, concluding: "It is natural that a new generation of climbers will attempt ever more ambitious routes, but only if these can be accomplished safely will climbing truly advance."

4. J Ellul. *The Technological Society*. Knopf, 1964.
5. J Lauchlan. "Aggressive Treatment." CAJ 1982:37.

rightness of human conduct. Ethical standards arise from interaction between persons. Royal Robbins explains the point in the second volume of *Rockcraft*:

> Although a climber may set as a personal goal the ascent of a route in as good or better style than the first ascent party, it does not follow that others should feel constrained to follow that example…it is a bit much to expect anyone to climb for any reason other than his own pleasure. If someone wants to use aid on the normal route of Higher Spire, that surely is their business and no one else's. Let everyone climb as they please, *as long as they don't interfere with the right of others to do the same.* [my emphasis][6]

Issues of clean climbing are not the same thing. To widen a crack by the use of pitons is unethical in that others are affected by the act; it makes the climb easier for them, different in character from the first ascent.

While these distinctions are easily accepted by most modern climbers, the more interesting question is the relationship between the developing rules of protection and our public sense (as climbers) of what is valuable and important in our sport. The argument for a rigorous code of protection, for example, runs somewhat along these lines: avoiding questionable practices (excessive bolting, placing pro on rappel, etc.) keeps standards of climbing high, prevents the over-development of cliffs with its consequent trivialization of the finer lines, and maintains the quality of the experience.

Yet thoughtful writers have questioned that it is somehow intrinsically better to climb at the highest standard. Andrew Gruft, writing in CAJ 1973, observed that it could be more rewarding for a weaker climber to struggle up a peak in mediocre style than for a stronger climber to climb it in fine style. And in a brilliant essay called "Mountaineering's Real Values" Dick Sale suggested that the modern obsession with difficulty threatened "the basic roots of climbing." "We are led to believe," he said, "that only the opinions of the leading climbers are relevant…the net result is a pervasive impression that hard climbing is all important." Sale rejected the idea that mountaineering values could be founded on technique; like Gruft he plumped for the sum total of the experience. He compared the literary treatment of Hermann Buhl and Dougal Haston:

> The exploit of Hermann Buhl on Nanga Parbat was impressive, not because it was an ascent of awesome technical difficulty, but because it required an inner fire that most of us cannot hope to emulate. In the years since

---

6. R Robbins. *Advanced Rockcraft*. La Siesta Press, 1973. p 82.

Buhl's climb we have had commentaries on his life, and they have usually touched on the human aspects of his ascents. But, if his death had been more recent, would he have received such a tribute? Or would he have received, as did Dougal Haston, merely a catalogue of climbs, as though that was all life comprised…When I read his obituary, I was left with the vaguely hollow feeling that his life had amounted only to a handful of climbs, with no human significance.[7]

Conclusions one reaches about these ethical questions follow from the assumptions one begins with. It will be useful here to outline some of the assumptions behind my arguments.

Like George Grant and Jacques Ellul, on whom I am drawing heavily for this discussion, I assume that a fairly homogeneous sense of values exists in western society; most people believe in roughly the same things. George Grant identifies this shared ethic as the belief in liberalism, which dictates that man's essence is freedom and that therefore his business is to overcome and shape the forces of nature which restrain him from doing as he wishes. This belief is obviously a long way from ancient or Eastern philosophy which views man as part of a larger order, not essentially affected by human action. The chief tool in the shaping of the western world is technology but so pervasive is the spirit of conquest over the irrational and random that technique becomes more than just machinery or applied science. Life itself becomes in essence a search for efficiency and results. The highest form of human activity becomes that of problem solving.

Many social critics looking out over the phenomena of crime and terrorism, the decline of political institutions, cultism, "the flight from feeling," and the exhaustion of workers, have condemned the liberal ethic as too inward looking to ever produce a whole or healthy society.[8] I am not going to elaborate these criticisms because the complaints against technological society are quite familiar. What is interesting however is the extent of the conviction among climbers that, in the mountains, they can transcend these problems. Yet the record of modern extreme alpinism may well testify to the opposite conclusion.

Consider the problem-solving aspect of Himalayan mountaineering: the logistic and organizational burdens which bury spontaneity (it is rumoured that the recent Russian ascent of the south-west face of Everest in-

---

7. D Sale. "Mountaineering's Real Values." *Mountain* 58, 1977. p 42.
8. A recent discussion is found in C. Lasch, *The Culture of Narcissism.* WW Norton & Co Inc, 1979.

volved 1000 persons); the obsession with results and tendency to measure achievement not in human terms but in technical progress; the exaggeration of difficulties to attract and publicize sponsors.

The equating of mountaineering conquest with spiritual victories is seen as somewhat old fashioned and even embarrassing. Yet Herzog's account of the French ascent of Annapurna remains a masterpiece in the literature of mountaineering precisely because of the spiritual victories accrued. Herzog wrote:

> Together we knew toil, joy and pain. My fervent wish is that the nine of us who were united in face of death should remain fraternally united through life.
>
> In overstepping our limitations, in touching the extreme boundaries of man's world, we have come to know something of its true splendor. In my worst moments of anguish, I seemed to discover the deep significance of existence of which till then I had been unaware. I saw that it was better to be true than to be strong. The marks of the ordeal are apparent on my body. I was saved and I had won my freedom. This freedom, which I shall never lose, has given me the assurance and serenity of a man who has fulfilled himself. It has given me the rare joy of loving that which I used to despise. A new and splendid life has opened out before me.[9]

Somehow this passage has a ring of truth which is missing from Messner's "the higher I climb the deeper I see into myself." I do not wish to denigrate Reinhold Messner, a man of immense courage and one of the world's greatest climbers. But I wonder if he has ever achieved the kind of spiritual victories that Herzog found (thinking in particular of Herzog's very full life after Annapurna). There is something terribly abstract and cold at the heart of Messner's climbing philosophy. For some the break with Habeler was sad and unfortunate. The break of course was necessary to an ethic which regards technique as the ultimate pole of value—a solo climb of Nanga Parbat satisfies the thirst for "absolute efficiency" which I have suggested has become a measure of "the good" in modern times. Yet it is possible to feel slightly disturbed at any credo which suggests that solo climbing represents the ultimate mountaineering experience.

This is a point of view which men like Geoffrey Winthrop-Young would not have understood since it was "the ideal social fabric" of the halcyon years—in other words the friendships—which he believed gave

---

9. M Herzog. *Annapurna*. EP Dutton and Co Inc. 1952. p 12.

especial value to mountaineering exploits. And it was Tom Patey's dictum that "good climbing and good company often go together; each is essential to the enjoyment of the other."

If we are not to view ascents as mere technical achievements we must have an ethic and a vocabulary with which to judge them. At present the standards focus on results and grow out of the ideology of technique: was the summit attained, was the difficulty extreme, was efficiency high? The question, for example, was any garbage left on the route, is seen as slightly ridiculous; the issue does not enter into the question of success in any way. Two avenues deserve discussion.

The first concerns the value distinction George Grant draws between science and the attitude to knowledge in western civilization when he speaks of modern scientific investigation as representing the victory of "power over wonder."[10] This distinction is invoked by Royal Robbins in the fascinating interview published in *Mountain* following the Harding/Caldwell ascent of the Wall of Early Morning Light in Yosemite. Robbins' original objection to the climb stemmed from its technical emphasis; he felt that El Capitan had been bolted into submission and that the technical thrust of the climb over-shadowed the spiritual qualities shown during the ascent—the stubborn perseverance of spending twenty-seven sometimes stormy days on a wall. In contrast Robbins offered Peter Haan's ascent of the Salathe, by then an old route in Yosemite—a solo climb by one who had never done a grade five route. Obviously the climb represented no "technical" advance (Robbins had already soloed El Cap) but, as he said, "the whole climb turned on a question of the human spirit."

Current mountaineering literature does not seem to regard "wonder" as sufficiently valuable however unless it is harnessed to "power." Writing in CAJ 1982 Geordie Howe finds Paddy Sherman's book *Expeditions to Nowhere* unsatisfactory simply because the climbs are not impressive enough. Mountaineering books today are expected to describe extreme ascents; the human story is insufficient. There is no attempt to relate Sherman's travels to earlier traditions represented by the likes of Shipton and Tilman.

The trend is exemplified especially in the journal of the American Alpine Club which now publishes little other than the cream of the world's most spectacular technical mountaineering accounts. The commitment to history, science or poetry is small. One ferrets through 247 pages of the 1983 version to discover an exceedingly brief account of the alpine adventure story of the year—Peter Hillary's brilliant ten month traverse of the Himalaya. Did the editors fail to pursue the author for a fuller account of this grand journey because Hillary did not solo any grade six alpine walls en route?

---

10. G. Grant. *Technology and Empire*. House of Anansi, 1969, p 116.

Attitudes to the human dimension coalesce around the issue of death on an expedition. Although at times continuing the climb following a fatal accident may be the ethical thing to do (undoubtedly Harlin would desperately have wished Haston and Kor to realize his dream on the Eiger), the drift of current practice is to consider death as simply one of the challenges to be overcome on a route, something akin to a piece of overhanging ice. The leader of the Canadian Everest Expedition expressed this view as clearly as anyone. "A death on the mountain is simply an event, a logistic problem—just as getting up a tricky rock band is."[11] Here is the ethic of technique in its most naked manifestation. But if death is simply "a logistic problem," then human relationships at best are non-committal and utilitarian, and the act of continuing a climb despite fatalities affirms that the passing of friends makes no difference to our goals or aspirations.

Related to the traditions of wonder is, secondly, the idea of simplicity. Here Chouinard has some thoughtful comments to offer in his handsome volume *Climbing Ice*. How, Chouinard asks, can we maintain the challenge of modern ice climbing given the degree to which technology has advanced? He observes:

> Modern man, enslaved by his technical imagination, is shovelling coal to a runaway locomotive. But technology should set him free, opening choices instead of dictating them. Declining a possible technology is the first step toward freedom from this bondage—and returning human values to control. The whole direction of climbing moves against the technological gradient. Here personal qualities like initiative, boldness, and technique are supported rather than suppressed by the tools of the trade... This is the technological inversion: fewer tools applied with increasing delicacy. I was rewarded for walking this edge by seeing more sharply what was around me, and I felt more deeply what comes boiling up from within.[12]

Although it is tempting to comment on the recent Canadian Everest Expedition in the light of these criteria, my comments are really directed at the big expedition game in general. It astonishes me how the participants in such exercises misconstrue their activities. They seem not to realize that large scale ventures of this kind are essentially organizational exercises, with radio calls replacing office memos, supply build-ups mocking corporate strategies, and problems along the way being sorted out through bureaucratic procedures. To expect the human dimension to shine through in such

---

11. "Everest, The Expedition Chronicle." *Equinox*, V 2:7, January, 1983. p 84.
12. Y. Chouinard. *Climbing Ice*. Sierra Club Books, 1978. p 188.

circumstances seems naive in the extreme. Nor does it seem accurate to me to suggest that problems or unhappiness on a venture like the Canadian Everest Expedition can be laid at the door of the expedition leader. In such a game the methods of technique provide the real leadership. Climbers are there to achieve a predetermined end by applying the methods of efficiency. The expedition is a success if the summit is attained and the technique applied was efficient in the eyes of modern climbing technocrats.

Who can look at the death toll in modern alpinism and deny that objective danger is now a necessary feature of "important" climbs? How can this be reconciled with the claims of "freedom" or spiritual transcendence which mountaineers invoke in support of their activities? To me the trend seems much closer to the pursuit of record breaking which trivializes modern international sport.

Nor are such climbers "free" in the most limited sense of choosing to go or not go. A British climber today hoping to establish himself as a professional is simply not free to turn back from the objectively hazardous. Witness Bonington's candid comments in *Everest, Southwest Face* as he agonized over the decision to remain in the International Expedition of 1972.[13] Yet Bonington knew the climb was doomed from the start and could only be a disaster in human terms. His agony was over the commercial situation; the impact the wrong decision might have on his career.

Before I leave the subject a word on the vogue for so called "alpine ascents" is in order. While these ascents are in many ways simpler than large expeditions, the decision to use or not use alpine style does not seem to me to be crucial to the question of whether technical or human values will be emphasized on a climb. Technique is not simply bolts and Friends and fixed ropes; it is a whole way of perceiving experience. One can be just as bound up with the ethics of technique on a small endeavour as on a massive expedition. On a recent alpine style ascent of McKinley the party chose to go for the summit, leaving their companion who was suffering from œdema, at high camp and to his own devices.[14] It would be fatuous indeed to praise such climbers because, after all, they did not use siege tactics.

The wisest words I have heard on this topic came from Peter Boardman:

> It is the vogue nowadays to praise small, compact expeditions. Nevertheless, the self-appointed, armchair guardians of the ethics of Himalayan climbing should show more tolerance in their judgements. Actions, in climbing,

---

13. C Bonington. *Everest, Southwest Face.* Penguin, 1975. pp 30–44.
14. AAJ 1982: 141.

speak far louder than words, but people do get killed with appalling ease in the Himalayas when ambition drives them to follow lines on photographs. It isn't always necessary to achieve a stylish ascent that can be related historically to the advancement of standards in the sport. The Himalayas, 1,500 miles long, and with countless objectives, offer one of the last spiritually expansive areas of modern mountaineering. Here, you can really feel that you are going where your nature leads you, instead of being pressurized in your ambition by ethical squabbles. In the Himalayas, the star to follow should be the attainment of a sense of personal satisfaction and enjoyment, and the sole guideline should be the preservation of the identity of the area and its inhabitants, by avoiding insensitive invasion and preventing desecration of the area's sanctity with litter, bulldozers and bolts.[15]

I must conclude with some defence of my own status, for some may feel that this kind of discussion should be left to those who have the most at stake—the hard men themselves. Don Serl criticized Anders Ourom as a "dilettante" when he sought to enter the debate over the mounting of the Canadian Everest Expedition.[16] The argument would be that only first-hand experience of life on the extreme edge can render one competent to discuss these questions. The point has some validity. But my point is equally valid—how many of the best climbers have read Jacques Ellul or F.H. Bradley?

It might be asked what answers I propose for what I have characterized as an ethical dilemma. Are modern climbers supposed to stop taking chances? I do not suppose that this is likely to happen, or that the spate of spectacular ascents (and their resultant "tragedies") is about to abate. These days men would rather be famous than live to grow old. And as I have tried to show, the drive behind the behaviour is a part of a larger social ethos which enwraps our age. Climbers are driven by more than they realize. Who could ever rationally consider the umpteenth ascent of a mountain worth lives expended? Who could ever say that increased efficiency in climbing a rock wall was an object worth dying for? I have no comprehensive answer to propose, beyond a tentative suggestion that climbing literature needs to represent a greater scale of values than it presently does.

---

15. P Boardman. "Changabang Commentary." *Mountain* 55, 1977. p 27.
16. Wrongly, in my opinion. Ourom may not have climbed in the Himalaya but he had been a regular contributor to *Mountain* and as such was well appraised of the "ethical" questions involved in large scale mountaineering undertakings. The Serl/Ourom debate may be found in the letters section of the *Vancouver Sun*, February 1982. I have been too lazy to go and look up the precise dates.

Whether modern alpinism is ultimately an expression of "the good" is also a question I must reserve at present. If it is good that human society be ordered along principles of technique then the ascendency of such principles in even so trivial a field as mountaineering can be seen as a step in the right direction. The difficulties of judgement in this area cannot be minimized. Many wise and compassionate men have believed that the world's most pressing problems—starvation, poverty, illiteracy—can be overcome by the application of the methods of efficiency and organization. It may seem obvious that my sympathies lie with an older tradition. But there are ultimate questions involved in this debate which it would be pretentious to try and answer.

"I have learned that the mountains and death are irreconcilable," Don Serl wrote to me from India, shortly after leaving the Canadian Everest Expedition. At the time I was unsure of what he meant, beyond the commonplace. But as I have tried to show, the extreme spirit of modern alpinism seems to obviate those values which traditional mountaineering affirmed: spontaneity, idiosyncrasy, exaltation, a sense of belonging to an order which was greater and more meaningful than individual achievement.

Beyond the quest for wonder and simplicity of course, there is also the example of the true iconoclasts: MacInnes and Patey, Tilman and Shipton, Doug Scott, Beckey, Muir, Norman Clyde. Canadian mountaineering is particularly rich in such figures: the Mundays, Tom Fyles, Culbert, Baldwin, Clarke.[17] These determined individuals remind us that it yet remains possible to operate outside the basic assumptions of one's time and still achieve a rare and meaningful significance. ❧

---

17. Some note on the inclusion of these various figures is in order. They have been chosen for widely different reasons: Patey and MacInnes for their completely individual and self-reliant style; Tilman and Shipton for their self-sufficiency and commitment to each other; Muir, Clyde, and Beckey for their exploratory spirit. I include Doug Scott because he has always been interested in climbing with his friends, even when they have not been supermen. The Canadian group are all linked by the exploratory urge and a rejection of the easy way into the mountains—noted bushwhackers all! Also, in an age when technical achievement is most prized, the moderns among them have concentrated their efforts elsewhere. Those who were notable as soloists have soloed for reasons that had nothing to do with "technical" concerns.

FURTHER USES OF AN ICE AXE

Not all mountaineering essays are deadly serious. The extract below shows that humour still lives in Canadian mountaineering. Not surprisingly, the article is from a university climbing journal—the University of British Columbia's *Varsity Outdoor Club Journal.*

~ Bruce Fairley

Further Uses of an Ice Axe

Steve Grant

Most climbing manuals do not mention the versatility of the ice axe. An extended awareness of the capabilities of this versatile tool will surely enhance one's enjoyment of the great outdoors.

Golf

The ice axe may be used in the fashion of a putter. In this way one may have the pleasure of a round of golf in the alpine meadows. The pleasure is increased if one remembers to bring golf balls, as rocks are a poor substitute. The aspiring player is cautioned not to engage in this sport in open crevasse areas unless the ball is roped up.

Tent pegs

Besides being a good tent peg by itself, the ice axe is also useful for levelling tent sides and hammering regular pegs.

Road work

Removing boulders, filling holes, drainage works and digging mud are operations facilitated by the enthusiastic use of someone else's ice axe.

Car repair

Many car repairs necessitated by logging road travel are made easier by an ice axe. Examples include straightening the jack sockets and removing broken shock absorbers from V.W.s.

Axe

Certain ice axes, of the MSR [Mountain Safety Research] Thunderbird pattern, are useful for chopping wood, especially if the pick has been honed to a razor-sharp edge. In addition, the adze is a perfect tool for blazing trees, skimming off a shallow bit of bark, which hopefully isn't as painful to the tree as traditional blazes.

Bog tool

The ice axe can be used to make one's toilet, literally, by digging a hole in the ground. Then the informed hiker drives the point of the ice axe into the ground behind the hole so that the shaft is at an angle with the head over the hole. The hiker can then rest on the top of the axe, tripod-style, and leisurely contemplate the view while relieving himself undisturbed by quivering knees. Stray bits of toilet paper can be recovered in a sanitary fashion, and manoeuvred into the hole with the axe, which is then used to fill up the hole and replace the sod.

It is hoped that these suggestions make your next camp more pleasant. ⚘

IX   HARD ROUTES IN THE ROCKIES

To stand beneath any of the big faces in the Rocky Mountains of Canada and look up is to understand the meaning of the word "commitment" as it is used in mountaineering. These faces present some of the most horrific climbing challenges on the North American continent; steep, draped with gleaming sheets of ice, interspersed with bands of often loose and decomposing rock. The ascent of routes through these complex and frightening walls represents one of the final stages of development in the exploratory stage of Canadian mountaineering.

While ascents of any big rock face can prove treacherous, those made in the Rockies present their own special problems. On the whole, these walls are not as remote as those in the Coast Mountains and considerably more accessible than those in the Yukon or Northwest Territories. They tend to be steeper, however, and the overall quality of the rock can be poor. While some of the great Rockies face climbs, such as the Greenwood/Locke route on the north face of Mt. Temple, have some quite good rock, many of the large faces consist of badly shattered sediments, that offer not only difficult climbing but also poor protection possibilities.

Faces in the Rockies are intimidating and until recently climbers pioneering new lines in Banff and Jasper National Parks mostly left them alone. The important developments in the range up to the 1960s generally took place on the ridges and buttresses that framed the faces, rather than on the faces themselves. A major breakthrough in terms of attitude occurred when a group of climbers led by Hans Gmoser started giving the cliff of Yamnuska, located on the eastern edge of the Rockies near Exshaw, some attention. Gmoser's route *Directissima* marked a significant leap in technical standards and, more importantly, a shift in attitude. Climbers were prepared to start looking at the vertical as their proper abode. Yamnuska is now considered a rock-climbing crag rather than a venue for mountaineering adventure, but it continues to be important in Rockies climbing and has often acted as a bellwether of what can be expected in the greater ranges.

But despite *Directissima,* no figure had yet appeared on the scene who combined sufficient technical ability with the drive and attitude that it would take to venture out onto the forbidding mixed ground of the steep north faces, where one would never know whether to don crampons or leave them off, to cut steps, to traverse to snow—in short to deal with the hundred critical decisions it would take to surmount a thousand-metre wall of ice and rock.

Brian Greenwood emerged in the early 1960s to take up the challenge of these great faces. He was quite possibly the greatest alpinist Canada has ever produced. To be fair, he was born in Yorkshire, England, and learned the rudiments of rope technique there, but he had done virtually no serious climbing when he came to Canada in 1956.

In retrospect one might ask where Greenwood found his inspiration. When he began climbing in the late 1950s an ascent of one of the bigger Rockies peaks by any route was a notable affair. By the time Greenwood hung up his axe and crampons in the early 1970s climbing in Canada's most famous range had been blown open; every climber aspiring to the status of hard man was eyeing the committing routes on the big faces—and most of these climbs were Greenwood's.

Meeting Fred Beckey in 1959 likely helped some. Beckey was easily the greatest active alpinist in North America, and he had a single-minded passion for new routes and a sharp eye for emerging talent. He and Greenwood teamed up a number of times in the five years after they first met to climb new routes in the Rockies and in the Bugaboos (a range of steep granite towers in the Purcells). On the whole, however, the climbs he made with Beckey were not Greenwood's most important. Those climbs for which he is remembered most today were accomplished with a small group of friends who lived in the area around Banff and Calgary, including a carpenter named George Homer, who was himself an exceptional rock climber.

All of these climbers in Greenwood's circle were members of the Calgary Mountain Club, and they tended to view themselves in opposition to the Alpine Club of Canada. They enjoyed passing unfavourable remarks about over-the-hill ACCers who could no longer keep up to the young bloods in the CMC. Much more loosely organized than the ACC, the CMC attracted, in the 1960s and 1970s, pretty well all the best of the Rockies climbers, and the collective achievements of CMC members are mighty impressive. Similar to the self-styled "Squamish Hardcore" on the Coast, CMC members rather made a point of priding themselves on their vulgarity, irreverence, lack of organization and ability to consume beer. It was the kind of close camaraderie and friendly rivalry engendered by the CMC that probably had a lot to do with stimulating people like Greenwood and Homer to pile up the great number of fine climbs they did; and if there has been a "golden age of Canadian climbing" it is certainly the period when the CMC was most active.

Probably the truth of the matter is that climbers like Greenwood and Homer were caught up in a world phenomenon: they lived at a time when the pace of climbing, in common with many adventure sports, moved into a higher gear, as all over the world climbers began launching themselves at problems considered by an older generation to be impossible. The achievements of Greenwood and his cohorts, however, remain especially remarkable because they were made in a country that really had no tradition of technical climbing.

Since that time, the standard of climbing in the Canadian Rockies has continued to advance, but while it is possible to point to Brian Greenwood as the central, driving force of the early days of modern Rockies climbing, there has been no one dominant figure since. Some, like John Lauchlan, have had higher profiles than others, but no one climber has "owned the Rockies." Peter Arbic, Barry Blanchard, James Blench, Joe Buszowski, Dave Cheesmond, Dwayne Congdon, Steve DeMaio, Sean Dougherty, Kevin Doyle, Jim Elzinga, Jeff Marshall, Ward Robinson—to name only a few—have, at various times and in various combinations, all contributed to a phenomenal rise in standards over the last 20 years to the point where it is now safe to say that the hardest routes in the Rockies are on a par with the hardest alpine routes anywhere, and that the best climbers from the Canadian Rockies are on a par with the best alpine climbers anywhere.

$\sim$ Bruce Fairley & David Harris

Hard Routes in the Rockies **247**

KELLOGS

Kellogs was Brian Greenwood's last great climb, and it was made with a strong team. The line chosen was up the brooding, unfriendly north face of Mt. Kitchener, which fronts defiantly onto the Banff-Jasper highway, a monumental nightmare of ice hoses, down which rocks perpetually cascade, and bands of dark, slatey rock. It was these twin hazards of rockfall and rotten rock that made this climb such an epic endeavour.

By the time they came to Mt. Kitchener, both George Homer and Greenwood were old hands at dealing with both of these conditions. On the north face of Mt. Temple, Greenwood had been fortunate in finding some surprisingly firm rock, but on routes like the east faces of Mts. Babel and Hungabee stonefall and poor rock were the order of the day. Nonetheless, the party seriously underestimated Mt. Kitchener, and it took everything they had learned from years of dealing with the less than perfect conditions of the Rockies to bring the team through safely.

~ Bruce Fairley

Kellogs

George Homer

"Have some more cheese man, we won't need all this food. Be up it in a day. It's only 2000 feet, can't be more. We'll be all right. Pass the beans."

The next day we reached the foot of the face. At about nine on that August morning we walked under the considerate groaning seracs which let us past before vomiting a ton of ice across our path. We roped up at the 'schrund and Rob Wood front pointed up the short ice wall. We three down below dodged the endless falling harmonicas, and watched the sun disappear around the east ridge, much to our disappointment.

We mooched up the 'schrund and out onto the snow slope. "Taking a bit longer than we thought, eh! Still, once we get onto that ice, man, be a piece of cake. Up today, you'll see. Pass the chocolate."

At about 2 p.m. we reached the ice. Standing on the rock, we watched the constant barrage as stone after stone fell in joyous liberation to the glacier below, occasionally trying to liberate one of us along their way. Bob Beale caught two on the hand, one breaking his finger. "Er…let's stick to the rock for a bit."

As I eased over one steep wall of poised jumble I thought, "Must be careful here," as about a ton of rock seemed to be held in suspension by one key-stone. Following the pitch, Bob knocked off a tiny rock which trickled onto this key, starting an enormous rock avalanche, totally demolishing the wall we had just climbed. "Good pitch, eh?"

One of our ideas for speed had been that two could jumar and two climb, but on the whole route we found only one place where we considered the belay good enough to do so. We continued to climb the rock alongside the ice thinking we might still go onto it, but the stone fall never ceased. It was becoming increasingly obvious that we had underestimated the size of the face, and that a bivouac was imminent.

We climbed until 7 p.m., the rock never improving and the stone fall never decreasing. Here we found a good ledge backed by a cornice. We soon had a brew on, and we considered our position. Our plans had now changed completely. We could see the ice slope we had planned on climbing, and the narrow ice-choked chimney near the top, continually feeding stone into the slope below. We thanked Christ that we were not over there. Above us rose a tower of shitty-looking rock, with a chimney running through it for about 250 feet. We decided that had to be the way, seeing as we couldn't get back down.

The next morning we tried to hold onto the sun, following it along the ledge until, with a sigh, it disappeared for the day. We ate most of our food and had a luke-warm brew, as the stove ran out of gas. We would be off today for sure, so we saved just one bar of chocolate.

A couple of pitches of almost rock brought us to the chimney. This turned out to be a steep crack. Doffing my sack I climbed it, followed by Brian Greenwood. Rob and Bob jumared, with my fearful eyes on the four pins, as Brian climbed the remains of the chimney. Eventually we all joined Brian. It didn't look too good. Above us was about fifteen feet of overhanging corn flakes. Brian suggested chopping steps in it, but with determination and a lot of luck it was overcome. Easy ground was our prize.

A few easy, rotten pitches put us below a system of steep chimneys. The sun never reaches this depression in the face, and everything was coated in verglas. The chimneys were a last resort so I did a long traverse, chopping steps with my ice hammer. "At least the rock is solid here." I headed for what looked like a line about 300 feet away. Climbing up a rocking chimney, I belayed on a huge chock. That's where the traverse ended; the continuation looked impossible.

Above was a steep corner capped by a roof, wet and verglassed. "You'll be all right up here Brian. Good line," and up they came. Before too long Brian was up the next pitch and I followed, climbing the corner over the grotty roof and up a steep wall. Never have I seen such loose, and potentially loose, rock. We were impressed by that lead, especially Rob, who fell off. And so, of course, another bivy.

We were pretty close to the top, but afraid of being caught in the ice-choked chimney we had glimpsed above. We decided to bivouac. Three pieces of chocolate did little to ease our hunger. A night spent dreaming of cream cakes brought us to a cold, sunless morning. Rob led off into the bottom of a short ice-gully, and Bob climbed this to the foot of the steep icy chimney.

Brian and I, belayed out of sight of the leaders, speculated on when we might reach the top and chewed every one of the six calories out of our breakfast gum. Rob, in the lead, sent down a constant flow of ice, whilst Bob slowly froze into his stance. It seemed we had been sitting cold and still for hours when we heard Rob shout he was on top, and we were warmed with joy. There was no style in any of us when we climbed that desperate chimney. A constant tight rope, with crampons flailing ice, rock and air brought us, tired and relieved, to the top. We fell into the sunlight and shook exhausted, hungry hands. ❧

SMALL WALL

This humourous piece is set among the cliffs and crags that surround Yamnuska, the bluff that is the spiritual home of the Calgary climbing community. Yamnuska can easily be seen from the Trans-Canada Highway a few miles east of the town of Exshaw; it is almost the first cliff one encounters driving west from Calgary. It was on Yamnuska that Gmoser and Grillmair first tackled some of the really steep ground that the Rockies had to offer, established the *Grillmair Chimneys* and *Directissima*, two routes that remain very popular today.

"Small Wall" distills many of the common experiences of wall climbing (with the added dimension of winter conditions) into a clever narrative, well worth re-reading. Interestingly enough, George Homer, who wrote the first selection in this chapter, was one of the two who made the first ascent of the *Iron Suspender* route Ben Gadd found so challenging.

While this is the only piece of technical climbing writing that we could find from Ben Gadd, he has written the huge (nine hundred pages) *Handbook of the Canadian Rockies* (Corax Press, 1988), a superb introduction to the geology, biology and recreational possibilities of the range.

∼ Bruce Fairley

Small Wall

Ben Gadd

Having to be talked into doing a climb makes you uncomfortable. Your lack of confidence shows.

'Um…well, we could probably do it, but it is sort of ridiculous. I mean: a completely artificial looking, unjustified bash-up on mixed pitons and bolts. An 800 ft, two day climb? Ridiculous!' (Not to mention scary.)

Greg won't give up. 'It's only been climbed twice.'

'Only twice? weh-hull; let's go have a look…' Inferior climbers begging for glory.

The first day we manage two pitches. According to our topo you fake the beginning with a carabiner (holding the haul line) taped to a 25 ft pole because the first party climbed it in winter by drilling shallow holes in the limestone and hanging on whittled down cliff hangers, with the odd bolt for protection. Fortunately we have no whittled down cliff hangers. There's also a thin, flakey aid crack off to the right that's supposed to be A4—only I'm fairly certain (at the time) that nobody's climbed it.

So—all being fair in love, war, and direct aid—we squandered most of the good style we brought with us and cheated the first pitch. Besides, the previous successful party did it that way, and they were ace climbers.

Second pitch: overhung again; bolts, nuts, cliff hangers, and the odd piton. The battle axe approach, but we take pride in doing lots of it on nuts, especially a big expanding flake that would have been awful on pitons. As usual, Greg isn't taking enough pictures of me.

In the gathering dim, we buzz down long free rappels to the ground. Big Wall Climbing this: fixed ropes, carabiner messes, jumaring. Greg walks home to Calgary in the dark; must work tomorrow. I get to stay at the hut and dream all night of bolts falling out. Actually, one did fall out on the second lead.

Resting in the valley next day, waiting for friends to come hoodling over the hill for a day of sensible climbing and hiking. Alas, Greg is due to return at midnight or so, laden with extra candy bars and bits of hardware for the inevitable big push—to do only six more leads. But if they're anything like the first two…nonetheless, we are on schedule. The original ascent took about six months; the other party fixed two pitches on the first day, and did the rest on the second. So can we.

Greg arrives in midnight confusion and in the morning we jumar up the fixed ropes in disquieting weather. Strenuous, this jumaring. I have to collect the rope (on account of the wind) as I adrenalin up, spinning, plus I'm wearing a pack, and before long I feel like heaving all over the bystanders. Except there aren't any: all our friends, who promised to come watch, have buggered off somewhere. The bastards. What if I drop my glasses? What if…?

Then, atop the first lead, the predetermined scariest thing must be done. I have to let myself out on the jumars and continue to the top of the second pitch, where Greg is waiting to lead on up. This letting out is committing; after relinquishing the first stance, we likely can't get back to it owing to the amount of overhang in this section of the climb. Then, a thought. The thing to do is to get all set, holding to the belay bolt until the very last moment—like a diver, standing on a high diving board, thinking ahead to the next fraction of a second—and then let go! Done. Swinging out on the end of my long spider line as the wall rushes back. 'YAHOOOOOOOO!' God; it was actually fun!

The whole climb becomes fun. Third pitch: couple of aid moves, then F6 to the ledge. A short lead, to boot. Fourth pitch: the best one. An F6 traverse, then up along a big overhanging technological aid crack you stuff with bongs and big nuts, finishing F5 again to a super-duper belay perch. Hah. It's in the bag. We know what we're doing now.

The thing we've climbed on this pitch is called The Lug. It's a thumb-shaped, mostly-detached pinnacle midway up the face (the only one left; all the rest have fallen off) and at the top of it, you are sitting in the centre of an immense saucer-on-edge, prudently tied to the wall beyond you (instead of the perhaps ephemeral Lug) by several trusty bolts. Finally the route has acquired a purpose: to get to this place.

Then it was Greg's turn, as the afternoon got windier and colder. A long bolt ladder over more overhangs, then cliff hanger moves (the ultimate aid horror) and a weird belay on a skiddish slab that you can't quite sit/ stand/lie on comfortably. A *de facto* hanging stance.

Greg has climbed fast and competently. The weather is going to shit. The light at 8 p.m., is going fast, too. At the end of the next lead we will be off the aid at what is described on our topo as a 'big ledge.' My lead. Up and away over steep, wet slabs and corners, illuminated by occasional blasts of lightning. The hardest free climbing of the day, and it's gone and turned into night. Snowing hard, now; mustn't fall; where the hell is the next hold? Greg patiently shivering at his sodden belay, knowing that I'm going to come off in a few minutes. Later on, we'll think of this as the epic pitch; it's a prideful thing for the idiot who manages to lead one of these.

I get up somehow. Greg jumars in a lightless mass of tangled rope to the belay bolt I've located by feel on the ledge, which is quite large (we discover, after the flashlight arrives) if a bit sloping. To quote John Wesley Powell, explorer of the Colorado river, 'Everything is wet and spoiling.' But we delight in having lived through the worst; opening haul bag for deep interior goodies (we have everything); brewing tea, eating; pulling into our Mexican bivouac sacks—plastic garbage bags—and watching the snow fall till morning.

The last two leads are F5 nothings to competent climbers in the sun; quite awful to us in the snow plastered rottenness and cold. We struggle up; a fall, a stuck rope, a summit. A minor limestone buttress has been climbed again. Nonetheless, we find the long stagger down to the hut exceptionally pitiful, especially grunging along under the haul sack. Next time we'll pull it up attached to a wagon.

Our friends tell us at the hut that they worried all night. And they help us carry all the weary, scuffed-up gear back over the hill to the cars. We appreciate it, in our sullen way. ૐ

AGGRESSIVE TREATMENT

John Lauchlan has already been introduced in two previous selections: "Gangapurna Stories" and "The Third Party". In this description of a fierce winter ascent on the ice of Snow Dome in the Canadian Rockies he again demonstrates why he was one of Canada's greatest climbers and greatest mountain writers.

⁓ Bruce Fairley

Aggressive Treatment

John Lauchlan

"How can you break both front posts with one kick?" "I don't know, but I just did. I'll send them a letter, maybe they can explain it." "Do you want to bag it?" "Naw, I'll just lash 'em on and keep going." Dwayne and I soloed on while James fiddled with his crampons. It seemed a bit presumptuous, carrying on. We were attempting a new route in winter on the east face of Snowdome. We were on the next gully system left of *Slipstream* but the character of the two lines couldn't have been more different. While the ice of *Slipstream* shone blue and inviting to our right; the smear above us was malnourished and anaemic. In fact, a lot of the ice above us was rock. Oh well, we're supposed to know what we're doing...I read it on an Everest poster.

Picking our way through the rolling water ice steps of the lower benches we finally broke out onto the alpine ice that leads to the bottom of the 'real' climbing. James catches us just as we arrive at the base of the first pillar. We don't pay a lot of attention to it. It's quite steep but only about 30 ft high before it kicks back. We've all spent the winter teaching ice climbing and have gotten pretty cocky about soloing around on the steep stuff.

"Want a rope for this?" "Why don't you drag one up for me...just to see how my crampon stays on." I grab the end of the rope and clip it onto the back of my harness. I mean, it's not like I could actually fall off something like this...I'm not so used to having this hulking great pack on my back, but then...it's only thirty feet.

I start off. James fiddles with his crampons. Dwayne stares out at the valley as he feeds out the rope on automatic pilot. No problem here...up a short fan, around onto the steep stuff, up alongside a little rock corner, tools over the top and we're...Aaaaaahhh!!! I drop about half a meter as both tools and both feet cut through the ice simultaneously. As I fall I dart my foot out to the right and catch myself in a precarious bridging position. "THIS IS VERTICAL SNOW!!!!" Having broken through the surface of the ice my left foot and hand tool are pushed through into the rotten depth hoar behind. I am just able to hold myself in position...every time I move slightly the skin of ice that supports me breaks off.

Below there is frantic activity. James hurriedly buries his ice axe while Dwayne tries to decide whether to belay me or untie and watch. "If he comes off, really let him run a long ways before you try to stop him dead." "If he falls that far he probably will be, but better him than all of us." Battling off panic, I try to calm down. I've got to find a way to take the weight off one of my arms so that I can move up. I lean slightly onto my left hand tool. I'm slipping through!! I regain my bridging position just in time. My pack is pulling me over…sapping my strength…better do something. I slowly lean the other way. The rock is slightly overhung and devoid of mitt-sized holds but if I can press my forearm against it the prickly rock might give me just enough friction…I lean. It holds…a little. Very, very carefully I pull out my Chacal and grope for a shaft placement. I manage to fiddle the axe in sideways behind the skin of ice and, after a series of swimming and bridging manoeuvres, pull over the bulge.

"Had a little problem down there guys." "We hadn't noticed." My heart still racing, I climb up to the base of the next steep section and bang in three ice screws. No more foolin' around. The others, clued into the technique, make short work of the pillar. Much to my disappointment neither of them falls off. The pitch above looks like the real thing, finally…beautiful blue pillar, nice and steep, the better part of a pitch high.

"I'd like to do this one." "Thought you were worried about your crampons." "They seemed just fine on the last bit. Besides, I've never had a chance to lead something steep like this with a big pack on." Dwayne and I look at each other. "OK James but we've got to make a pact. No more fiascos…right?" We all agree so James takes the rack and sets off. Thirty feet off the belay, just into the steep part, he stops to set his second ice screw. "Look at this guy. Just because I told him that I had to rest on my tools on *Slipstream* he's got to do without." "Well I just thought I'd try…it's not that bad actually."

After struggling to get the screw in before his pack gets him, James yells "I'm in," and proceeds upwards. After making about two moves he drives his terrors deep into the ice and hangs back on his umbilical cords. "I'm totalled." "Good," we say, thankful not to have to follow his ethical lead. Fifteen feet higher James stops suddenly and bangs in a Snarg. "Guess what…more vertical snow." He explains that just above him the ice changes suddenly. With no rock corner to bridge to, there is no way to continue up safely. Leaving his pack at the Snarg, he traverses right into a small groove in the rock. The ice is only an inch or so thick there, but at least he might be able to protect it with rock pegs. Half rock climbing, half ice climbing, and extremely slowly James pieces together the groove as we watch expectantly from below. He disappears over the top.

"Got it," he finally yells down. A good thing too, the sun's going down. Manhandling the packs up the pitch we soon find ourselves searching the ledge system for suitable accommodation. Failing to find a berth we are forced to fight for a seat in 'Coach.' Good thing we're all little folk, or the three of us never would have kept our buns on that glorified foothold, let alone got the tent up on it. Anyway the next morning is cloudy, as winter mornings tend to be on faces that catch the early morning sun. I run out the rope from the tent to get a look at the continuation of our gully system. In the hurry of impending blackness the night before I hadn't gotten a look at it. It doesn't look too appetizing. The breakfast menu consists of a choice between vertical porridge on the left, or thin ice on the rocks to the right. Now it is rumoured that unreasonably thin ice has been climbed by comic book heroes and the criminally insane…but even Albi can't put a belay in verglas. We opt for the ugly looking rock corner on the left.

The climbing turns out to be surprisingly good…for a couple of pitches. Dwayne and I swap leads up thin ice runnels tucked into a corner. Very reminiscent of the north face of Les Droites. Of course this can't last forever…this is the Rockies we're talkin' about here.

"My turn!" James forwards as we look up a grotty corner of rock. "Well OK, but I get next try," I say, thankful he's been aware of his place in the rotation. James does his fingernails-on-the-blackboard imitation for the better part of an hour while we make jokes about the belay. He's forced out to the right of the corner and soon yells down a cheery, "No belay. No cracks." Fortunately we have carried our courage in my rucksack so I send him up the 'Bold' kit on the haul line.

Actually it wasn't James' fault about the bolt. The kit was kind of buggered up and he'd only used it once before…and Rockies rock being what it is…I'm sure none of us could have put it in any better. It is unfortunate that it had to break though, the handle I mean…before he could try a second one. I follow slowly up the awkward rock, crampons flailing, to arrive at James' island of insecurity. This belay is even funnier than the last one…except this time it's my turn. We decide to leave Dwayne down below. If I come off maybe one of these belays will hold!

The next pitch was extremely frightening and I'd rather not talk about it. I will hint however, that it goes straight sideways, features a thin crust over crud rock, two tied-off blades, and three terrified climbers. It ends, finally, with a buried axe belay. James and Dwayne whimper across the traverse and we crawl neurotically up towards the final fiasco…the serac. We hadn't actually formed a plan for getting through this thing. Yesterday we were brilliant alpinists, you remember—capable, competent, all that stuff. Now we just want to go home.

Arriving at the end of the ice section of the serac, we put in all our remaining ice screws to hang back and look at the twelve meters of overhanging snow that loom over us. I gather together all the ice tools in anticipation of aiding over the stupid thing on axe shafts. "Jeeze, this is going to take all bloody night." Have you ever noticed what amazing things fear can do for creativity? Since it turns out to be my lead, I look frantically for an easy way out. To our right a crevasse cuts into the serac—maybe I can bridge up that thing! I crawl onto the wind roll below the overhang and pick my way over to it. No way... the thing's just as overhung as anywhere else...but what about...I chimney back into the crevasse, five, eight, ten meters...ALRIGHT! A pale blue light shines through the snow above me...we can burrow our way out!

An hour later, in the pitch dark, three soaked and shivering figures pop out of the Snowdome Glacier and bumble off home. Like hypothermia, swollen heads respond only to aggressive treatment. 🏔

THE WILD THING

Writing about hard climbing is difficult. Words can describe the physical appearance of mountains and rocks and the positions into which bodies can be contorted; but no words will ever convey the experience of serious alpine climbing to someone who hasn't been there. But for anyone who has been there, for anyone who has climbed (or ridden or driven or paddled or fought) their way out past the edge, for anyone who has crossed the dark frontier, "The Wild Thing" conveys the experience, and the addictive need to seek it, with unparalleled intensity.

In the years since the death of John Lauchlan, Barry Blanchard has become Canada's most important climbing writer. To some extent this is because he took part in many of the most significant climbs of the 1980s, but to a much greater extent it is because he is just as willing to explore new ground with his pen as with his ice axe. Where Lauchlan lifted the lid on the Pandoran box of the personal/emotional side of climbing and peeked inside, Blanchard has ripped the lid right off and dived in head first. His writing is an unflinching exploration of the human side of the climbing experience—he examines himself and his partners without shame and without false modesty.

It is easy to overdose on that kind of bare-wires honesty though. On anything other than a solo climb there is more than one set of emotions involved and I have always felt that the major weakness of mountain writing is its first-person point-of-view: however well climber-writers manage to convey an image of themselves, they invariably do a bad job of characterizing their partners. But in "The Wild Thing" Peter Arbic's earthy empiricism provides a perfect anchor point for Blanchard's extended, angst-twisted metaphor and we finally get to read about a climb on which more than one of the climbers is real.

It is the juxtaposition of the two voices, the counterweighting of one by the other, that makes this story work so well. That and the transcendence of emotion. Anyone can write about tenuous crampon placements or gnarly fingerjams, but to convey in words the joy of testing yourself in the company of people that you love and respect and trust... That is surely what climbing writing should do, but so rarely does.

This is, no contest, my favourite piece of climbing writing.

∽ David Harris

The Wild Thing

Barry Blanchard & Peter Arbic

BLANCHARD

She is beautiful. Her face is smooth and white. She watches me climb through pale gray eyes. Her expression never changes; it is tranquil, powerful and compassionate, but mostly it is calm: detached and calm. The white mist hangs from her body like silk and the sweep of her limbs is all grace and balance. The white lady can draw me up and fulfill me or she can be death's mistress.

I lock my elbows and stare into the mirror. Ten years of climbing have reaped their toll on my body and soul. A patch of scar tissue marks the fragmented bone in the bridge of my nose; a souvenir from the North Face of Les Droites in 1980.

There was a full moon illuminating the Argentière basin that September night so Kevin and I climbed without headlamps. The next morning, one hundred meters from the top, Kevin sheared out a frisbee-sized piece of ice with his left crampon. He didn't sense it, and therefore didn't call it. It fell fifty meters gaining speed and rotation. I looked up and took it in the face. I saw black and then blood: red blood splashed across blue nylon. Nauseated, I hacked and staggered my way up to Kevin. "It looks bad," was all he could say. I waded through the rest of the climb wondering if I would be scarred, ugly.

My fingers are stroking the bridge of my nose; it didn't scar too badly. I watch as my hand moves down over the drag of my two day stubble, across the nakedness of my chest to the three inch ridge of scar below my left nipple. My knife wound from Joshua Tree, 1981. A blade was clenched in a greasy fist that slashed upwards from the asphalt and dust. I should have had stitches but I couldn't afford them and so I kept climbing. The cut healed open from the constant stretching.

The latest addition is still fresh: six months fresh. I look at it now. It is part of my left hand. A one hundred and twenty-five meter slide down a forty degree snow slope left two people dead and me with a thumb that doesn't bend much and has two pieces of wire holding it together. It is my new companion now. My old thumb doesn't exist any more, just this new one and how it came to be.

Don't think about that Blanch. It will only wreck another day. Have there been two consecutive days that you haven't relived it? SUFFER machine. Thank Christ for Jill. Those were her arms that held you, healed you after your white lady gave you a flick of her dagger instead of a caress.

The beautiful white lady with the red dagger. She's given you the few moments of euphoria that you've known, but not love. Only a real woman can give you love.

I look into my own brown eyes reflected in the mirror. The lady is calling me again, and I know I'll go. But I'm going to follow her hands with a sober eye. I'll watch for the dagger.

Starting

The North East face of Mount Chephren rises for fifteen hundred meters above the Mistaya River. It's a wedding cake draped over with black satin. Long ridges and gullies slice through horizontal bands of snow and rock. The face is similar to other big walls in the Rockies and the Alps but, like a human face, the union of all its parts creates a distinct pattern. There are no duplicates; it is an individual.

ARBIC

Staring at Chephren that day got me fired. It looked to be in shape, if such a thing was possible, with a little something left for the imagination. A week later Ward is on the phone with a promise from lying Ralph (the weatherman): cold and clear for four days. Ward has the same itch I do. The plan is set. When Barry agrees to come everything seems to click into full party mode.

Day One

I can't recall having fallen off while mountaineering before. Nevertheless, I go sailing and a few loose holds continue on over Ward's head. A little higher I fix the ropes, scoping the next two pitches. Then down the lines to our snow cave. God damn, those next two look ugly. Hey Bubba, deluxe digs man!

BLANCHARD

The gas stove hums along producing a steady blue flame. I chip pieces of snow from the sidewalls of the snow cave and stuff them into the contoured aluminum pot. Snow turns into water and the water is converted to food and brews.

Do this well I tell myself. It is important. Divide out the hot chocolate, but get more snow on before you drink. Only boil what you need. Keep checking. Make sure the water always has snow in it. Don't waste fuel, you may need it.

Peter and I are shoulder to shoulder at one end of the cave with Ward's feet wedged between us. We need the least amount of space this way and will sleep the warmest. Our ensolite pads overlap to form a large mat which covers the whole floor. The walls and ceiling are glazed from the heat of our bodies and the stove. Small grains of snow no longer sprinkle down on us with every movement. The musky smell of hashish oozes around us like incense burned with a lover in the sanctuary of a bedroom.

She's here now. She hovers. She doesn't need our technology to sustain her but she does need us. We are important to her, her lovers. I close my eyes and a stroke of white silk caresses my face.

It's my turn on the Walkman and although I can't hear Peter and Ward, I catch occasional glances from vibrant eyes as they putter about arranging their wombs for the night. She's been good to us today. We climbed four fifth-class pitches and 600 meters of third-class ground. I'm excited and content. This is how humans were meant to be.

Day Two

Somewhere high in the atmosphere, air is converging and descending: high pressure. A stable, cold airmass creates a cloudless sky over the Rockies. In the human zone it is calm and crisp. The air is like cold water. Clear and refreshing, you can taste it on your teeth when you breathe.

ARBIC

Ward is out there trying to be delicate across a slab on front points. His tool searches for something to hook across into the corner. Three meters up the corner a piece pulls. Barry and I giggle as Ward swings. Scary business eh! Ten meters up and Ward comes slamming down to the base of the corner in a flurry of pin popping. His axe goes winging off in the general direction of the truck. A very real moment.

BLANCHARD

The motion stops and Ward screams "Fuck! Fuck! Fuck! How did I pull so many pieces?" We don't answer. Ward pulls it together and starts back up the pitch. I turn to Peter: "God, I'm shaking, man. I think I'm more scared than Ward is." "I don't think so," Peter replies. Over the valley I see the lady's dagger slicing away.

ARBIC

I swing around in my harness to get my face out of the way. Barry scrapes around for something to stem. He gets scrunched up under the roof of our little alcove, working for some gear to move out on. A couple of tie-offs, a couple more maybe, and he's gone. I turn up "The Clash," strum a few bars and grin at Ward. You gotta love it, this kind of situation.

BLANCHARD

Performance time Blanchard. So the last two years have been tough. So what? Everybody suffers. Maybe you're not as good as you were four years ago, but you're here now! Do what you can do. It's no one's fault but your own that you're not climbing as well as you used to. Yeah: no one but injury, failure and death.

Cut the shit; you're hesitating. No asking Peter or Ward to take the pitch. Ward's shattered. Shattered like you were in '83. Same fall, same fear, same burn. We all have only so much to give. Do what Kevin did for you then: grab the rack, jump in and fire.

I bridge out my left foot and hook my front points onto a small ledge. Snow falls and Peter shifts his face away from it. I reach for her hands and step into the dance. Be nice darling, be kind.

Two hours later she leaves me. It's been intense. I've trembled and reached and hauled. She drew me on through my fear. Those gray eyes; that long and perfect body. I wanted her. She's gone now and I'm standing on a small horizontal island a thousand meters up. The ground falls away before me. Behind, I'm anchored to a system of pitons and chocks. It's cold. Ice crystals are hanging in the still air that is a sparkling haze around me. I'm immersed in silver water.

Where is she? Why has she left me? I risked for her.

Ward arrives, then Peter. Ward pulls up onto the snow ledge. He runs the rope to an anchor at the base of a steep chimney. Peter goes at the chimney and I rap down to dig the cave. I hack out squares of frozen snow and think of her.

ARBIC

Somewhere below I must be beaning somebody. Barry has wisely retreated to dig a cave. Ward is stuck at the base of the corner holding me. The spindrift separates us and makes it easier to chuck off the loose holds. Waves pound over for the longest time. I imagine what various sizes of rocks will feel like. I finish the pitch howling at the stars. Ward cackles back.

Day Three

The last pitches were magic. I marvelled, jugging the lines and cleaning. Up into Ward's niche, another screw in and clip. Barry comes up and I stem out over the stance as he tries to jam himself out of harm's way. A polished tongue of clear ice hangs above. I can hardly believe how good it is. At the top a long blade rings into sound rock. Somebody laughs again and it seems to ring a little longer here.

Shit, it took a long time to get this anchor. Half a dozen pins shift as Barry starts to jug. I add my weight behind them. I'm a bit freaked, with twenty minutes of light left and maybe one pitch to true love. I pin my heart on my sleeve, hand over the rack and shoo him off. By the time Ward arrives I am beginning to suffer a little. Barry calls down that he doesn't think it will go. We poke around for a bivi but prospects are gloomy. Look Bubba, get up that thing right fucking now! As he works we suffer a little harder.

"Wild thing, I think I love you,
But I gotta know for sure."

BLANCHARD

This is hard. It's dark now and I'm alone. My hip is cramping and my calves have turned to stone. I know I am tearing muscle tissue.

WHERE ARE YOU?

I'M AFRAID.

I'M GOING TO FALL.

IF I FALL I WILL DIE.

The cold, sterile blade of the dagger is pressing against my flesh. The flat of the blade is searing into me from breast to groin. The edges are hungry. One more pulsation and they will bite. My strength is being devoured. My heat is being conducted from me. I want out. PLEASE! I want to wait for the sun. I want to be with you. I need you.

Ward and Peter shout to me from the darkness below. We must finish tonight. I can't quit. I press my fingers into the shafts of my ice tools, my forearms vibrate and strive upwards.

The ice vein is thin now. I'm bridged between snow and rock trying to hook my right tool above the chockstone. Dust falls into my face and I am blind.

The pick holds and I pull up into the final alcove. A number three Friend bites securely behind a frozen block. One more hard press and I step out on the south slopes of the summit of Mount Chephren.

She's there waiting for me. Wind pulls the white dress tight to her body. I strain against the ropes of my mortality. I enter her embrace. She is power and benevolence. She has let me in and the dagger is sheathed for now. 🌶️

HIGH ANXIETY: THE LIMITS OF TECHNICAL DIFFICULTY

One can be sure neither Norman Collie nor James Outram ever thought about doing chin-ups or running stairs prior to heading out into the Canadian wilds for another adventure. If you had pressed the point with them, they would probably have called themselves "sportsmen" rather than athletes; in any case they would have been a bit baffled by any attempt to separate the climbing of a peak from the train journey, the packhorse trip and the wilderness camp-out that preceded it. For these early climbers, it was all one. Mountaineering was something you did on your holidays; it wasn't something you trained for. If you needed some extra technical know-how for the climb you had in mind, generally you went out and hired a guide.

Also, the idea was to keep yourself out of danger, not to court it. Written accounts of the pioneers often emphasized the dreaded abyss and vertical upthrust; in fact, the essence of mountaineering lay in route-finding your way around such horrors.

How things have changed. Norman Collie would no more have understood Jeff Marshall's pursuit of the "deadly game" of solo ice climbing than Marshall would be willing to invest days with packhorses travelling to some remote snow slog. The sense of obsession that Marshall brings to his dream of back-to-back ice climbs would have been regarded as unhealthy by the pioneers, a fundamental misunderstanding of what the game is about. But today the game is about technical challenge, and no-one can deny that solo climbs of fiercely vertical frozen waterfalls meet the criteria. And climbers such as Marshall are serious athletes whose focus is on pushing physical and mental abilities to the ultimate, not on achieving some holistic communion in the good companionship of like-minded "sportsmen."

Unless you were a guide, for the men and women of Collie's generation climbing was always a firmly recreational pursuit. For Jeff Marshall, climbing has become something more. The dream he achieved on the frozen pillars of *Polar Circus* and *The Weeping Wall* demanded his attention for weeks before he actually went out to attempt the routes. Climbing here has gone beyond something one simply does in one's spare time. It becomes a demand, a craving that must be fed, a need that overpowers the more mundane aspects of daily existence and comes to dominate one's psyche.

Some critics of mountaineering literature have lamented that the humanistic vision of the pioneers has passed on with them, and that technical excellence has come to dominate mountaineering thought. The victory is one of power over wonder. Indeed one might take exception with Jeff Marshall's premise that having reached the "limit of technical difficulty" the only way forward for the modern climber is marathon or solo climbing. But few could argue that the quest for technical achievement has led to some mighty impressive displays of audacity and cool, precise control of one's craft, operating at the highest level. This article alone gives ample proof of that.

~ Bruce Fairley

High Anxiety

Jeff Marshall

In late March of 1985 during the drive home after a climb, my partner and I got into a discussion of the future direction of waterfall climbing. It appeared to us that ice climbers had reached the limit of technical difficulty. After all, water can only drop so vertically, and ice can only be so rotten before it can no longer support the weight of the climber. So what was to be next? We were able to come up with two alternatives: climbing several waterfalls in a day, or climbing the big ones alone.

Marathon climbing would be an exercise in applying peak levels of fitness, proficiency and determination in a wilderness situation; an Olympic event, if you will, in an uncontrolled environment. Solo climbing, on the other hand, would be a deadly game involving painstaking precision and ultimate mental control. There would be absolutely no margin for error in that most unforgiving pursuit. As with any activity, some participants take it more seriously than others; this is the story of the modern-day extreme.

In November of 1985 I began training for what would prove to be the wildest day of my life. The vision first came to me in the form of a climbing marathon in B.C.'s Yoho National Park, an area containing some of Canada's best ice. The plan was to combine both Twin and Takakkaw Falls in a single day effort. This translates to roughly forty-five kilometers of skiing and thirteen hundred feet of ice. Having tried this once before and having failed miserably, I realized that the idea far surpassed my physical state at the time.

I began doing chin-ups and running stairs in an effort to turn this fantasy into a reality. At this stage of the game, with the goal so desperately far away, it became a constant battle to either simply quit, or endeavour to persevere. As I grew stronger and faster, another vision came to me, oh, the curse of ambition! Polar Circus and Weeping Pillar are two Grade Six climbs that are within two miles of one another on the Banff-Jasper Highway. The idea became to solo Polar Circus and climb the Weeping Pillar with a partner in a single day.

Every so often that winter, I would go out and solo an easy climb just to give my mind a gentle stretch. March was nearing, and by now the training had turned into a blur of relentless chin-ups and endless flights of stairs. At this point I was cranking out roughly six thousand feet of stairs, and nine hundred chin-ups per week. Of equal, if not greater importance, was the belief that it was going to happen. I had seen the video of success in my mind many times while training.

March arrived, and the dates had been set. The excitement was intense. I had already done my first rock climb of the season in an effort to release some pent-up energy. On the evening of March 8, my partner and I drove to the Twin/Takakkaw trailhead. We enjoyed a few hours sleep before the alarm went off, and the tour began. The plan was for me to ski in and climb Twin Falls alone, ski back to Takakkaw, climb it with Ian, then ski out together. We said our goodbyes then parted company. At 6:30 a.m., I was standing at the base of Twin, ready and waiting for the seven o'clock light.

The dawn comes; the dance starts. Everything goes well, and I kiss the three hundred foot Grade FOUR after rappelling back down to its base. I change into ski gear and head back down to Takakkaw at a whirlwind pace. Ian is waiting there, keen and fresh. The thousand foot Grade FIVE sits quietly and takes its cold, calculated beating. After several rappels, we reach the ground at dusk. We ski out the remaining fourteen kilometers by headlamp and arrive back at the trailhead at 9:00 p.m., after nineteen hours of non-stop action. The drive home is a nightmare as Ian sleeps and I battle fatigue, trying to stay awake.

Ian had also agreed to accompany me on Weeping Pillar. Three days of complete rest, much eating and no communication passed. Then when I contacted Ian, he was feeling ill and couldn't make it. Backing out or waiting for another partner was unthinkable; it was too late, I was possessed. The cruel ultimatum had been made for me.

I jumped into the truck after work and drove north into a stormy horizon. In a moment of weakness, I granted myself one last chance for partnership. On the way I pulled into a Youth Hostel that a friend was minding and tried to talk him into accompanying me. He wouldn't have any part of it. I jumped back into the truck, drove the remaining hour to the trailhead, and crawled into the back for a few precious hours' sleep.

The alarm goes off at 4:00 a.m. By 4:30 I am at the base of Polar Circus, ready to climb. The first placement is made and the volcano erupts. I climb the first half of Polar Circus by headlamp, stopping briefly to contemplate John Lauchlan's fate on the slope that took his life while he was attempting the first solo ascent years earlier. Dawn comes, the ice is good, and in no time the big waterfall is mine. After what seems like an eternity of down-climbing and rappelling, I arrive back at the truck by 10:00 a.m. Looking back up at the route I told myself, "It's been a good day."

"But it ain't good enough…"

A quick drive up the road brought me to the pull-out for the Weeping Pillar. The climb is notorious for its consistently bad ice. At half height, a big snowfield separates the two five hundred foot vertical pillars. I am apprehensively looking up at this giant, with the knowledge that it has never been soloed before.

High clouds block the sun; the ice should remain dry and frozen. I whack up the first pillar. The ice is plastic, the placements are good, my mind is sound. But the upper pillar is in typically rough shape.

"It has been a good day."

"But not good enough."

I start touching my way up the delicate, lacy temptress. High up on the pillar, the ice goes from bad to worse while the angle of the ice remains uncompromisingly vertical. Thirty feet from the top I run into big trouble. I can't get my tools to stick in the fragile glasswork. The ice is terrible. The exposure is horrendous. Progress looks bleak; retreat is impossible. I have one tool out ahead, probing. In a flash, the ice mushroom that supports both feet is gone. I'm off, except for one tool that is ripping its way through the ice. After six inches it stops. I have to get back on. This is a time for High Anxiety, and demands all that five years of ice-climbing has taught me. The concentration is intense. This is no longer climbing; this is the real thing—survival. With the utmost care, I slowly pick my way to the top.

At the top, I can see how badly shaken I really am, and have a headache from the stress. This incident will cost me a week's sleep, waking up in a cold sweat as the tools rip again through the ice of my dreams. Rappelling back down is done with great care and patience. Reaching the snow ledge, I turn outwards and let out a thunderous howl that rocks the entire valley.

A quick run down the slope and a few more rappels brought me to the ground. I arrived at the truck feeling completely satisfied after eleven hours of mind games, and recall asking myself, "So son, was it a good day?"

Laughing and howling, I jumped back in the truck, cranked the tunes and headed for home. ❧

X   THE CULBERT ERA
IN THE COAST MOUNTAINS

Dick Culbert was, for the 15 years between about 1960 and 1975, the most famous and prolific climber in the Coast Mountains. He began his remarkable career while still a teenager, in the Howson Range, disappearing into this unmapped country for two months, enduring incredible hardships and privation in the name of exploration. Later, Culbert studied geology at the University of British Columbia, and during the field season, which he inevitably spent in the Coast Mountains, he was able to continue his program of exploration while pursuing his field work. At UBC he met kindred souls, particularly Glenn Woodsworth; they discovered a federal government grubstake program and for two summers, backed by these admittedly small government grubstake funds, along with friends Arnold Shives and Ashlyn Armour-Brown, they tore up the unexplored regions of the Coast Mountains while compiling research notes for the first guidebook to the range. The guidebook was published in 1964. It remains to this day probably the finest achievement in mountain guidebook writing ever accomplished, for it sought to outline the access and climbing routes for one of the greatest mountain ranges in the world—starting from scratch. Its publication marked the end of Culbert's first phase of climbing development.

Culbert had joined the BC Mountaineering Club in 1956, and he joined the Varsity Outdoor Club at UBC when he enrolled. Thanks partly to his drive, these two clubs became the major force in exploring the Coast Mountains during this time. As Culbert's ability improved, he became more interested in the technical aspects of climbing, and though he never lost his love of exploration, capped his career by putting up a number of very fine rock routes in the Coast Mountains.

~ Bruce Fairley

THE COAST GUIDES

There probably never has been and never will be North American climbing guides as well-loved as Culbert's guides. It is impossible for anyone who was not climbing in the Coast Mountains in the 1970s and early 1980s to appreciate the tremendous regard in which they were held. This was partly because Culbert had finally opened the door to greater recognition of the Coastal climbing community in Canada—there was pride in the local hero involved—but mostly it was because of who Culbert was and what he had done. We all admire people who have led exceptional lives, and Culbert's life of exuberant exploration of the great peaks—and also the nooks and crannies—of the Coast Mountains was an amazing life, and inspired an entire generation of mountaineers. Culbert was also a man possessing a very fine sense of judgment. His lack of self-aggrandizement and thoughtful approach to what he did combined to make his pronouncements on the state of Coastal mountaineering definitive.

I discovered climbing as part of the generation nurtured on Culbert's guidebooks, and even today, many years after I first opened those volumes, I still get a special excitement when I pull down one or another of Culbert's guides from the shelf and thumb through it, recalling the sense of astonishing discovery, the great adventures that every page promised, the life of greatness those books called us to. Here finally was something worth doing, and in poring through those pages we saw opened to us a lifetime of boundless possibility.

The following introduction, from Culbert's first coastal guide, is included partly by way of tribute, though it also speaks directly to those qualities that have always made Coastal mountaineering, at its finest, unique. And, of course, the piece also contains some of the finest advice on wilderness travel to be found anywhere, from one who was a master.

～ Bruce Fairley

Introduction from A Climber's Guide to the Coastal Ranges of British Columbia

Dick Culbert

GENERAL

The vast majority of people living in the Coastal Ranges, and all but a few of the mountaineers, reside within a half degree latitude of the 49th parallel. Even within the region easily accessible to this population, the logging roads are opening access faster than climbers are exploring the surrounding summits. In recognition of the fact that the unknown is still the essence of much of the attraction of the Coastal ranges, many roads and trails have been described which are as yet part of no established route. On somewhat similar grounds, the reader should remember that many routes outlined in this guide have been done only once, and any group which repeats such an ascent and returns agreeing in all ways with the viewpoints of the original party, may consider itself a rarity.

SOURCES OF INFORMATION

A word of caution might be inserted regarding maps of the Coastal Ranges, as the older ones especially should never be completely trusted. It is not uncommon to find creeks flowing the wrong way or non-existent, or valleys which are thousands of feet out in elevation. Glaciers are often missing or spread across a complex mountain area in the appearance of an ice cap. Seasonal snow is very commonly mapped as glaciers and conversely cases have even been known of forest cover maps marking light forests over a glaciated region. Summit heights should be trusted by neither absolute nor relative elevations, even when these are given to four-figure accuracy (e.g., 9614 rather than rounding number off to 9600). This uncertainty is reflected in different maps giving different elevations.

GENERAL MORPHOLOGY

North and east faces are, on the average, steeper and more glaciated than south and west exposures. Coastal Range peaks which lie along the eastern edge of the mountain chain and adjacent to interior plateaus, tend to be high, barren, and gentle in nature. Summits along the coast, although of lower average altitude, are more precipitous.

Glaciation has played a major role in shaping the mountains of the Coastal Ranges. Typical glacial features are hanging valleys and truncated ridges, the results of ice deepening pre-existing valleys to leave adjacent to-pography hanging a few thousand steep feet above the new valley floor. This effect is most pronounced near the coast and may make difficult the task of finding a route down into a major valley, especially where cloud, trees or convex slope prevent view of the valley side from above. Along the north coast, gouging becomes so pronounced that the majority of difficulties in a climb may lie in finding a route to the 4000 or 4500 ft. level.

ROCK

Contrary to some popular opinions, the Coastal Ranges are by no means all granite, nor does granite necessarily mean firm rock. Few general rules connecting rottenness with rock type are obvious. In the Howson Range for example, the volcanic rocks are fairly stable while the granite is rotten, but the reverse holds true for the Garibaldi Lake area. Recent volcanic rocks are almost always loose.

WATER AND CREEKS

Creeks and rivers constitute one of the most common barriers throughout the Coastal Ranges. Even streams marked as intermittent on maps may in fact be unfordable. (Conversely, tributaries descending into a major valley often sink under the alluvium along the edges and never reach the main river, which makes things difficult if hunting for a tributary.) Crossing streams is an art which must be cultivated. Some climbing-oriented comments might be that ice axes are very poor for felling trees, that nylon ropes are poor for making rafts or handlines and that a raging torrent is not the place to discover how much a climbing rope stretches on a Tyrolean traverse. A safety rope during a river crossing is a tricky arrangement at the best of times and should never be worn if traversing above a snag. Some people use a tumpline when fording to be free of pack if they slip, but this setup can be unstable when the wearer is not used to it and could conceivably injure the neck in a fall. Attempting to swim under a pack is nevertheless an unpleasant alternative if footing is lost. Sweepers and partial log jams are typical of coastal rivers and should always be approached (when fording) from downstream, never from above. If you must fall off a low log, make it on the downstream side. (A log which sags under a person's weight to touch fast water will throw the person on the upstream side.) Ice axes are always handy in fordings, but are invaluable in the opaque waters of glacial streams for depth probing.

Most creeks of the Coastal Ranges are of a tender geological age, and many have cut canyons typical of young streams. The combined effect of gorges and bush make valleys rather unpleasant routes of travel. Small creeks often have their trenches criss-crossed by windfall. Larger streams may have boulder beds with flanking bars which make good travelling when not flooded, but these streams have the nasty habit of winding to cut a bluff out of one valley side and leave an opposing gravel bar. As bluffs alternate along a valley, a party may be in for tough going if following a stream too large to ford.

Flash floods are rare on the coast, but a difficult crossing may nevertheless become impassible in a matter of a few hours. Glacial streams will naturally rise during a period of hot weather. During spring runoff, air temperature above snowline is the important factor as this controls direction of heat radiation and hence melting. Freezing level altitudes may be obtained from the weather bureau.

In many coastal valleys the creek has cut through glacial till (a clay and boulder mixture). Where this is steep it can be both treacherous and deceptive.

Tributaries and even major river valleys are often considerably deeper than maps indicate.

Only on the high barren ridges bordering the interior plateau is lack of water likely to be a problem in the Coastal Ranges.

A few of the broader valleys are plagued with beaver ponds. For some unknown reason the beavers tend to build chains of dams along the main river and flood the adjacent regions rather than choose strategic damsites on streams. The result is truly ugly swampland when the ponds get silted in and it may be necessary to walk miles of ancient beaver dams along the rim of a river. As yet there have been but few reports of quicksand from climbing parties.

ROADS AND TRAILS

The most important feature of coast trails and access roads is their transient nature. Parts of some trails may grow over completely in a single summer, while others which have remained in good condition for years may suddenly succumb to an epidemic of windfall. Forest fires also take their toll.

As a rule of thumb, few trails on maps are in existence, and few of the trails which do exist are on maps. Animal trails are common, but have the bad habit of fading out where needed most. Moose trails especially should be treated with suspicion as they commonly lead to swampy areas and often include rivers or swamps as part of their route.

Drivable roads are even more short-lived than the average trail, unless maintained. Logging operations account for the vast majority of access roads in the Coastal Ranges and these are seldom built to last. Once an area has been logged the grades are abandoned unless timber still farther back is to be reached, or the Forest Service decides to do maintenance work. Conversely, a dilapidated road may suddenly be rebuilt for logging an adjacent timber stand. Road owners have a habit of barring access with locked gates to avoid theft of equipment. Most companies will loan keys on request for weekends or periods when their road is not in use by logging trucks and when the fire hazard is not too high. Which company controls which gate is not always easy to determine, however, and ownership changes are commonplace. Most maps do not show many of the logging roads, although recent issues on the 1:50,000 scale are improved in this respect.

Bush

Coastal bush at its worst is as impenetrable as jungles anywhere. Experienced parties have been known to be held to two miles travel in a day of backpacking, but this is rare. A party in good shape when route finding and backpacking through average bush conditions requires about an hour for every mile travelled, plus somewhat less than an hour for every thousand feet elevation gained.

Bush is light near the interior and generally increases on approaching the coast. Timberline is about 5500 ft. along the southern coast but is usually controlled here by topography rather than altitude. On the northern coast (say Prince Rupert region) it runs about 4500 ft. Below timberline, light green foliage is a good thing to keep away from. On hillsides it usually means burned or logged regions with second growth, or tangled berry bushes. Light green foliage in valleys generally indicates deciduous trees with their associates the devil's club and willow thicket. The worst sign is the light green ribbon marking an avalanche track through the timber zone. This is the domain of the slide alder, and as the runs tend to fan out on the valley floor they can make travel very unpleasant. One compromise is to traverse about 100 ft. above the valley bottom to avoid the widest part of the fans yet not be inconvenienced by the valleys of tributaries.

Wildlife

The Coastal Ranges have an average quota of pack-robbing rodents and unpleasant inhabitants. Unlike those of national parks, the coastal bears are not accustomed to people and are usually timid unless wounded, surprised or with cubs. There have been some exceptions to this rule, however, and the word 'unpredictable' is perhaps the best single adjective. The cougar or mountain lion is almost never troublesome and generally keeps out of sight. The moose mating season is in fall, and this is one case where it is best not to try scaring off an intruder by shouting.

About one out of every hundred camps which are left unattended for a day in the Coastal Ranges is going to get pulled apart by bears (which, incidentally, seem quite at home on glaciers). Local mountaineers seldom bother to take precautions on weekend trips but important expedition caches should be hung by wire. Porcupines and assorted other pests occasionally chew pack-straps for salt. In some areas it will be found advantageous to use one's pack as a pillow so as to awaken when some "snaffle-hound" starts on the food.

There is no fish, bird or mammal in the Coastal Ranges which is poisonous to eat. The easiest emergency meat within the scope of rocks and an ice axe comes in the forms of porcupine (quill pigs) and grouse (fool hens). A fishing line is good survival gear. Parties which do not intend to spend most of their time hunting for food should not depend on game for supplies.

There are a few rattlesnakes in the valleys adjacent to the Okanagan region.

Mosquitoes, black flies, deer flies, no-see-ums, etc. are not confined to the Coastal Ranges and it will suffice to say that precautions should be taken. Some repellents on the market are of little value and it is best to become familiar with a brand before depending on it for an expedition. Ticks are found mainly in the southern interior portions of the range and are most active in the spring. They do not carry Rocky Mountain spotted fever. There are no poisonous insects which a climber is at all likely to meet, the most unpleasant encounters being with wasp nests which plague some localities in hot summers.

Ice worms are often abundant on the larger snowfields.

WEATHER

As the Coast Range is the first obstacle in a major storm path from the North Pacific, bad weather is to be expected. On the Northern coast especially, blizzards are common year-around occurrences above 6000 ft. Parties not experienced in navigation under storm and white-out conditions might try a little practice work in poor weather, with mixed rock and fresh snow climbing, before an expedition to high peaks of the Coastal ranges. Parties which are out to climb something (as opposed to being out for enjoyable climbing) may have to settle for making ascents in spite of blizzards, and should come prepared for this. Groups of less violent purpose might consider such items as chess or crib boards and pocket-size books.

Both summer and winter temperatures are more extreme on the interior side of the Coastal ranges but major storms are less common. Thunderstorms, on the other hand, are more frequent.

Weather forecasting, on the coast especially, is somewhat of a nightmare. In periods of unsettled weather, little faith may be placed in forecasts even for populated lowlands, and climbers attempting to extrapolate forecasts to nearby mountains should realize that they are doing little better than playing games. 🍂

FREIGHT CHRISTMAS

Most climbers have a fairly recreational approach to climbing. Objectives are selected from a guidebook and the adventure consists of following written directions—little thought is given to how the routes "got there," and even less to how the guidebook came to be. But guidebooks don't come from stores any more than routes come from guidebooks. Guidebooks, like climbing routes, are the result of an incredible amount of hard work and dedication; unlike climbing, though, guidebook writing has spawned no literature.

Well, almost no literature.

"Freight Christmas" shows that guidebook writing can be just as difficult and dangerous as climbing.

~ David Harris

Freight Christmas

Dick Culbert

Although the party which spent the summer of 1963 digging up guide-book data in the North Coast Range managed to track down most of the people they were after (and some they weren't), two major contacts were absent and it was decided that a winter trip to the Skeena was required. Glenn Woodsworth and myself hence climbed into freight-riding outfits on Boxing Day and were dropped off in Squamish. A skeleton yard crew, however, informed us that no freights ran Boxing Day and no drag north until early next morning. That night we huddled under a streetlight in light snowfall and tried to ignore a small crowd of Indian kids throwing a mixture of questions and jeers—a most noble beginning. I was still a little mad at having slept through a freight's arrival and departure in Williams Lake a few months earlier and awaited this ride with open eyes—it pulled in at three a.m. There was some doubt as to whether the run would stop, due to no business in Squamish Yards, but it had to stand down for the plutocrat (passenger), and we caught the only thing hungry—a flatcar. It was a cold and clearing piece of the next afternoon when the two small mounds of snow on the wooden deck shook the powder from around the mouths of their sleeping bags and observed that deceleration this time marked Quesnel Station. A friendly engineer here invited us to be unnoticed in the second unit and the rest of the lap to Prince George was loud but warm.

At Prince George that night it was thirty below, and as we had from midnight till dawn to survive, we retreated to the laundromat. This particular form of all-night-warmth-with-seats has taken much of the kick out of freighting and may explain why I saw so few people in the railside jungles this summer. A very cold, bitter dawn found us in an empty grain car well on the way to Vanderhoof. Powder snow billowed in through one door and the game was to keep the door from sliding open, but never entirely close same (otherwise you don't get out). The door won hands down. It was a good hop, though; for in fourteen hours we were unfreezing our sleeping bags in a Prince Rupert Laundromat, and preparing to sponge a warm room for the night off our good friends Jim Baldwin and family. It had been forty-eight hours since we had eaten anything significant. The best way to travel with freights is in a stupor.

The next two or three days were standard but successful data interviews, interspersed with rounds of free coffee and a hitch-hike hop to Terrace.

The region most under consideration lies between Skeena and Terrace Rivers and West of the Kitsumkalum. A recent hoax in a climbing magazine (re: Reisentein Pks.) had focused attention on this rather unexplored piece of the Coast Range as demonstrated by a raft of letters from the States.

All too soon we were waiting once again in a blizzard at night adjacent to Terrace Station. I have never once seen a drag leave Terrace on time, and this was no exception, but eventually through the immense cloud of wind-borne powder snow which enveloped our resident flatcar, we watched a clear dawn on our old friends the Seven Sisters. We got sided at Smithers, but managed to board the second unit. This, however, proved a mistake as a CNR unit is a much bigger animal than its PGE[1] cousin. You can scream and not hear a thing even inside your own head. As we leaped next midnight into a snowbank at Prince George yard entrance the sudden absolute silence was more shocking than the cold. We spoke in the open air and it sounded as if standing in a great hollow drum. One of Glenn's ears was not working at all. These effects persisted next morning, but we heard enough at the PGE yard to find that no freights ran south until after New Years. The remaining option was to hitch and this we did—both hitting good going and celebrating New Years midnight by walking homeward through Vancouver. What a hell of a way to write a guidebook. ❧

---

1. Pacific Great Eastern railroad

THE CAT'S EARS

The Cat's Ears was an historic climb; it marked the end of an era of climbing in the Coast Mountains of Canada. Like most such ventures, this significance was not appreciated at the time; it became apparent only later that this would be the last expression of a powerful mountaineering trio.

Dick Culbert, Paul Starr and Fred Douglas were undoubtedly one of the strongest teams the Coast Mountains will ever see, physically powerful, technically solid, and highly motivated. In 1970 they had trekked some 50 kilometres over rugged and largely unknown ground to complete the first ascent of the East Ridge of the Devil's Thumb, a huge tower anchoring the Panhandle ranges on the boundary between British Columbia and Alaska. From the Thumb they saw the weird pinnacle of the Cat's Ears shooting up from the rock and ice to the south in one striking column capped by two triangular spires. Their 1970 route on the East Ridge of the Thumb is now considered one of the classic climbs of North America. But no one has ever repeated the Cat's Ears.

In retrospect, one might wonder at such a strong party travelling so far to climb such a delicate object. But Culbert's generation seemed captivated by pinnacles as no other generation has been in Canada. Great towers meant clean, finely jointed vertical rock, and the discovery that such near-vertical ground could be climbed with the proper equipment and technique came as a revelation. The generation of the 1980s, in contrast, proved more interested in the problem-solving aspect of threading a line up huge and complex mountain faces.

In the carefree Starr and the solid Douglas (a titan who had been known to pack charcoal and an hibachi on weekend trips), Culbert found ideal companions when he turned from pure exploration to emphasize the technical aspects of mountaineering. The quality of the friendship among the three is caught nicely by this selection; Starr has done a fine, robust job of capturing the devil-may-care attitude and disdain for bureaucracy which allowed the friends to roll past all difficulties with a wink and a chuckle. For the 10 years following the publication of "Culbert's Guide" this trio dominated Coastal climbing, culminating their achievements with the climbs on the Devil's Thumb and the Cat's Ears.

To help put those achievements in perspective, especially for those readers who have never climbed the routes put up by Culbert and his partners, it is worth noting that they were grading their climbs in something of a vacuum. As the generation which followed found out the hard way, many of their routes were ridiculously undergraded. What they wrote up as "stiff fourth class" often turned out to be mid-fifth (and was often unprotectable into the bargain), and "5.6" just as often turned out to be 5.8 or 5.9. In the 1960s this was not far off the standard of the best rockclimbers on sunny lowland crags, and Culbert and company were doing it with mountain boots and heavy packs, in some of the wildest, most remote terrain on the continent.

It remains something of a mystery, even to those who know him, why Culbert gave up mountaineering so completely after this climb. Perhaps Starr's article contains hints. After a time even the hardest climbers begin to reflect on the number of chances taken, the avalanches escaped, the persistent rockfall, the feeling of being stretched to one's limits. On this climb the trio had seen their bivouac site of a night previous nearly devastated by tons of rockfall.

One cannot help but notice in the many articles by Coastal climbers of the time a relish for the harsh conditions of the mountain environment they had set themselves the task of exploring. While deprivation and hardship make for exciting reading, there is no doubt that such punishment exacts its toll. In this delightful piece, however, what one remembers is infectious enthusiasm and gusto.

~ Bruce Fairley and David Harris

The Cat's Ears

Paul Starr

It was one of those trips in which nothing seemed to go wrong—except for the McKinley tent we had borrowed. After putting my finger through the fabric of the fly, I decided it was time to borrow another, perhaps slightly newer, tent. Then there was the advantage of starting in Seattle… You see, last year's BCMC[1] St. Elias expedition got into hot water with U.S. customs for importing supplies from Woodwards to be flown to Yakatut via Seattle. In other words, they had to pay duty! But we were clever; we bought most of our food in Seattle because the State of Alaska has a fine ferry system between Seattle and Haines which takes walk-on passengers. Dick Culbert, Fred Douglas and I caused a minor disturbance by showing up that sunny Friday afternoon with about twenty boxes of food and other goodies (especially considering the ferry rules stipulate hand luggage only!), but we persevered. When the ferry finally steamed away only one hour late, we were well ensconced in the "slums" of the *Malaspina*.

Now let me explain. On the top deck of the *Malaspina* is a large, open-air patio with a translucent roof and nice green indoor-outdoor carpeting. This patio is furnished with reclining chaise lounges which, in fact, make very comfortable beds! However, since this area is open to the air, only the hardier walk-ons sleep there. And what a crew! Before we left I had thought that we were destined to be attractions of a sort (and we were, eventually), but we were by no means stand-outs. Hitchhikers of every description abounded (all headed for the wilds of Alaska). Among them were two young divorcées with an assemblage of children you wouldn't believe, and an older couple right off a Hemingway book jacket. So we made ourselves comfortable among the riff-raff, contributing greatly to the general aura of disarray as we gradually brought up all twenty boxes of food and equipment from the car deck. Occasionally the purser would show up and shake his head. A little later a crew member would arrive with a vacuum cleaner and start vacuuming. But we gloriously resisted all attempts at tidiness. When cabin passengers appeared we would all stare while they sat uncomfortably on the patio's fringes. After about five minutes they would leave.

The voyage lasted fifty hours—Friday evening to Sunday evening. On Sunday, we spent the day packing our air drop, arguing about what iron we needed, hustling boxes… By this time we occupied almost one quarter of the *Malaspina's* "slums," and had become minor celebrities after spreading

---

1. British Columbia Mountaineering Club

out over fifty pitons and seventy 'biners all in a row. The weather, which had been fine all the way up the coast, became predictably poor in the Panhandle region. At Wrangell, Dick and Fred got off the boat to phone Chuck Taylor (our pilot two years ago) and ran into Fred Beckey! He was on his way to climb a mountain east of the Stikine called Hickman, and he was noticeably taciturn when we told him of our destination. Then we were in Petersburg, and it was raining.

I should mention that the BCMC ran a trip into the same area west of the Stikine River in 1970. That year we flew from Wrangell to Shake's Lake. Then we trekked thirty long miles to the Devil's Thumb which we climbed (1971 CAJ). This time we three had no intention of repeating that ordeal. On the very nice topo maps (one inch to one mile) that the Americans provide for their remote regions we noticed a fairly large lake about ten miles west of the Thumb. Although the contours were steep, we had a photograph from 1970 which showed one side of the pass which would have to be crossed. It looked quite feasible.

On Monday morning we showed up first thing at the Alaska Island Air office, although there was no question of flying that day in the heavy ground fog and light rain. We wrote letters, dried our sleeping bags which were wet from the night before, and generally killed time waiting for the weather to break. And break it did—in the afternoon the fog lifted and we began to see mountains. By six it looked good enough to fly.

It was a glorious flight. We broke through the last clouds and the entire ice cap lay before us. In the centre stood the Devil's Thumb, which lives up to its name. Lesser peaks abounded everywhere. We circled the Thumb. Our gentlest surprise was the overall lack of snow. Two years previously our efforts had been greatly hampered by the snow which plastered everything. This year the great north face (six thousand feet high) was virtually snow-free. This meant that the glacier snow would be well consolidated, a fact we much appreciated.

On the circumnavigation we also got a good look at our objective, the Cat's Ears. It looked even worse than we feared. A full thousand feet high, quite vertical, and with obvious difficulties in getting to its base. The pilot didn't spare any breath in expressing his opinion of our sanity.

We dropped into the Witch's Cauldron, a huge depression in a fantastic glacial valley just west of the Thumb's base. Tributary glaciers flowed in from every direction, but there was no outflow. We were going to traverse this valley and planned an air drop and base camp at its head. The valley is, to say the least, abrupt. Its walls are either granite cliffs or icefalls averaging three to five thousand feet in height. No more than a mile wide at its head, it was with some trepidation that we flew up it.

The air drop was exciting too. I was jumping up and down on boxes slightly too large for the rear hatch of a Beaver, while we flew just fifty feet above the glacier. Every now and then the whole plane would shudder as an unexpected downdraft came in from an icefall. Upper Scenery Cove Lake was our landing. The pilots had been sceptical when we told them where we wanted to land. When we flew into the valley we soon realized why. The entire head of the valley consisted of smooth granite cliffs and hanging glaciers. Since the valley floor was at 1000 ft and the highest peak was 6200 ft, we were naturally impressed by the area's alpine nature. The only feasible route out of the valley looked like a vertical green jungle, but we had no choice.

The pilot let us off at the mouth of a small creek. We were soon engulfed by slide alder, attacked by swarms of mosquitoes, and it was 9 p.m. With two hours of daylight remaining we decided to forge ahead up the creek in spite of heavy packs. Fortunately we found goat trails through the alder, although the steepness almost made it advisable to rope up. But in two hours we had reached tree line (2800 feet at this latitude) and made camp on some heather-covered boulders.

The following day we hiked ten hours to the air drop. The weather was good, the scenery magnificent, but the hike was miserable because of our heavy packs and moraine in the Cauldron. We found the air drop strewn over one mile of glacier; some of the boxes had burst open, one was in a swamp. We recovered all the boxes, losing only our Shreddies and some cookies in the box that got wet. Established at 2500 feet, base camp seemed much higher in elevation because of the immensity of our surroundings and the continuous roar of falling ice.

Getting out of the Witch's Cauldron to the upper slopes below the Cat's Ears looked bad. We had a choice of steep slabs or a broken serac field. The following day (Wednesday) was destined to be a recce combined with load carrying. The slabs turned out to be two fourth-class leads, followed by straightforward heather and steep snow slopes. We dumped four days of food and all our iron at 5000 ft and returned quickly to base camp. The weather was holding magnificently, and we would have to begin an attempt on the Cat's Ears the following day.

Thursday, 20 July was another beautiful day. Quickly we climbed to our cache at 5000 ft and spent an hour dividing up food and iron. Our climbing packs ended up being close to fifty pounds each, what with bivi gear, three days of food, three ropes, forty pitons and fifty carabiners (we were ready for extensive aid, just in case). Beyond the cache was a reasonably well behaved crevasse field, which was only mildly obnoxious, terminating in a schrund which was quickly passed over in one half lead and a few chopped steps. Fortunately the bottom was filled with collapsed ice. We were now in a broad, steep gully at about 6000 feet elevation. About seven hundred feet above us on all sides rose rock walls. In the centre, two ice gullies (one draining each side of the base of the Cat's Ears) came together and spewed rocks down the broader gully we were in. Their course was marked by a deep, black trench and many shallower troughs. By this time the sun was very hot and the snow very deep and steep. As we neared the base of the ice gullies the sun hit them. The cacophony of stone fall was most sobering! Having sat down on a rock ledge, we ate and discussed our next move.

The centre ice gullies were out of the question, and the rock cliffs didn't look too inviting either. We decided that the far cliffs towards the south face of the Thumb looked somewhat better, but that necessitated traversing under the barrage of stone. We unroped and crossed singly, trying to run in the soft snow. I for one was exhausted when we reached the opposite side. We hauled out some of the iron and I immediately went on aid because the only place we could reach the rock easily was overhanging and slippery. But a couple of moves brought us out on easier ground and we continued up doing easy fifth class for three leads. We then discovered why the Cat's Ears is such a stupendous pinnacle, and why the ice gullies resembled bowling alleys. The entire cleft between the Devil's Thumb and the Cat's Ears was a shear zone of softer rock which was slowly crumbling away!

We were now forced onto an extensive area of loose rock, and sand overlying slabs. It was steep, and almost impossible to climb. We unroped of necessity (because of all the loose rocks) and went up for three to four rope lengths. This was by far the most unpleasant part of the climb! A short lead above this section brought us out onto a sloping sandy ledge leading directly back to the right ice gully.

It was now fairly late in the afternoon, but we were at approximately 7500 feet and right at the base of the Cat's Ears proper. It was a very airy place indeed, and looking back down over our route was not particularly re-assuring! We decided to bivouac on this ledge, and to fix at least two pitches of our climb for the next day.

To get into the notch between the Thumb and the Ears, Fred led out across the ice gully, chopping huge steps so we wouldn't have to use crampons the next day. On the other side of the gully the Cat's Ears were extremely foreshortened; the bottom lead or two looked easy, but after that it was anybody's guess. We elected to go to the notch first. Perhaps that place had some unknown attraction for us all! It took two full leads of cramponing to climb up the fifty degree gully; the last ten feet were the worst because the ice disappeared, leaving a pile of loose rubble with the belayer directly beneath. Dick managed somehow, and I followed him. The notch was quite a letdown. I have never seen such a desolate place. It was very abrupt, giving no reasonable routes out. By the time we rappelled back to Fred it was time to bivouac, so we retreated leaving only eighty feet of fourth class fixed.

The bivouac ledge required considerable excavation. Fortunately Fred's monster ice axe turned out to be an excellent prying tool and we were soon quite comfortable despite the sand. Although the ledge was fairly wide, we tied in. Maybe the airiness of our position was affecting us a bit.

The following morning we inevitably overslept. The barometer fell considerably overnight—we were reading nearly five hundred feet too high. Except for some high clouds, the weather still held. We elected to leave all our gear behind, except for down jackets and a bit of food. No one could see how we were going to do any serious climbing with the loads we had had the day before. Needless to say, we brought all our iron with us. We consolidated into two packs so that the leader wouldn't have one.

The day we climbed the Ears remains an incredible jumble in my mind. Lead followed lead and I remember being very exhausted at times. For instance, Fred did one lead which probably wasn't any harder than 5.6, but it was overhanging, and the exposure was out of this world. Following, I was dragging the rope for Dick, and between my pack and the horrible rope drag I felt like crying. The overhanging section made me feel like the rankest beginner, and I still don't know how I got over the thing. Then there was the time that Fred was following Dick over one of the hardest moves (probably 5.7) and he pulled out the key hand-hold and pendulumed forty feet. We ended up jumaring that part.

From a purely statistical point of view the climb went quite easily. We did 11 leads, all but the first being 5th class. Although the cliff was basically vertical, it was exfoliating in large slabs, forming ramps that were easy to climb. Difficult climbing was encountered when changing from ramp to ramp, and route finding became a problem of deciding which was the best ramp to climb. Nearing the top the ramps became steeper, until two hundred feet below the top they became vertical, and formed corners and chimneys. The climbing averaged between 5.3 and 5.6, with the odd move reading 5.7. We used fifteen 5 aid pins, ten in a single lead. Except for frost-wedged loose rocks, the rock was good and piton cracks were frequent. Near the top the climbing became very airy. The crux lead was difficult because protection cracks disappeared, and some hard (A2-A3) nailing ensued, followed by an unprotected chimney. The final lead was the finest of them all, with Fred leading on good holds (one of which was the summit ridge itself) on absolutely vertical rock. The summit was gratifyingly small, but a large ledge ten feet below gave us the luxury of basking in the evening sunlight. While we were on the summit a float plane flew by a mile or so to the north of us. We waved and danced, but much to our disappointment no acknowledgement came.

Then we thought about the descent. It was nearly 8 p.m. and the key was speed. Somehow rappelling down seemed to be even worse than climbing up. Maybe I had read too many reports about the dangers of rappels, but it just wasn't the same as in the local mountains. Eight double rope rappels of varying lengths brought us back to our bivouac ledge by midnight, in the last vestiges of daylight (the best part of northern climbing is those long summer days). On the way down we watched several tons of rock collapse just above our bivouac ledge and roar right by our sleeping area, fortunately missing our equipment. A sobering sight to say the least. But as there was nowhere else to bivouac, we passed a somewhat nervous night in spite of the success of the day.

Four rappels and some downclimbing brought us back to the snow gully, well before the sun hit the ice. We were by this time rappelling on bolts and flakes, having used up fifteen pitons in climbing the Ears (between leaving them on rappels and dropping them). A short rappel took us over the schrund, and we raced down the glacier, pausing only momentarily where our tracks had disappeared in a collapsed snow bridge. We cleaned out our cache and proceeded more slowly to the slabs and on to base camp.

We were now in a quandary as to what to do next, having climbed and descended our main objective in the first six days of a two week trip. The Witch's Cauldron was an unpleasant place to climb from. All peaks were much more difficult from that side, and more dangerous. We considered returning to the pinnacles left of the Ears or even the Thumb itself, but our iron supply was somewhat decimated, and, more important, none of us felt like going back up. We also vetoed climbing the fine 8000 foot peak at the head of the Oasis glacier, because it was two miserable days away and perhaps a bit more than we had time for. We finally resolved to pack out back to the Scenery Lake cirque, where we had seen quite a few lower but very steep peaks on the way in. Here, there was a pleasant heather bench about two thousand feet above the valley floor which would make a perfect campsite, except for the bugs.

From the campsite we climbed a 6400 foot peak we named "Shelob." It had two leads of fifth class, and several of fourth up a sharp south ridge. Our retreat was a minor epic, racing against darkness and swirling fog. Unfortunately, we climbed the wrong route—there turned out to be an easier one on the other side! Just above our campsite was a peak, we named the "Troll." It looked like an overgrown West Lion and was only 5600 feet high, but its slackest ridge turned out to be six leads of reasonable fourth and fifth class mixed. Our descent was notable in that an earthquake hit the west coast of

Alaska just as I was taking off en rappel. The whole ridge swayed in a sickening way (it reminded us of the ferry) and we were certain the whole rubble pile was going to collapse. But neither a rock moved nor a chunk of ice fell, and we continued on down.

In the interval between climbing these two peaks there were five days of storm. Anticipating a storm day for this purpose, we made a quick dash back to the Cauldron to recover some equipment and food left behind as our packs were just too big.

The final day of the expedition was spent attempting to climb the 6200 foot peak at the head of the cirque. "Scenery Peak," as we called it, defied our somewhat desultory effort with such obstacles as an ice gully, a knife-edge ridge, and at the base of the peak itself, another steep fifth class ridge. The day was too nice for such heroics, so we climbed a slightly lower satellite, and gawked at all the unclimbed peaks.

The expedition ran out of steam shortly after our successful climb of the Cat's Ears. Our desire and the good weather ran out just about simultaneously, and we never really got going again. The area, however, is magnificent. It revels in fine, unclimbed peaks and huge granite walls. Unfortunately everything is dwarfed by the Devil's Thumb, the main magnet that attracts climbers. Two years ago we saw nothing but snow peaks and long, flat glaciers. This time we entered what seemed to be a completely different area, consisting of mainly fairly low but relatively difficult peaks, even by their easiest routes. One measure of difficulty could be the fact that we did over thirty double-rope rappels even though we climbed only three peaks! The whole area both east and west of the Stikine River deserves consideration for future expeditions. ❧

XI   TRIP REPORTS

Trip reports are the office memos of mountaineering literature: doomed to be read once and then forgotten. Dashed off by amateur mountaineers from all walks of life (usually on the day before a deadline) they are published in local club newsletters that are rarely seen by anyone outside the club. Yet the very reason why participants write such reports is what makes them appealing. They are written because one person found something challenging, companionable, adventuresome, memorable or stimulating about a week or a weekend spent in the mountains.

Because they are so concise, packing a whole story into a few paragraphs, trip reports are mountaineering's "light" literature—breezy, quixotic and neighbourly. The examples we have chosen here illustrate that even a well-crafted short sketch can be memorable.

Dick Culbert, the great climber of the Coast Mountains, was introduced in the previous chapter; here are a few words about the other two authors in this chapter.

Ralph Hutchinson was a frequent climbing companion of Paddy Sherman and Fips Broda, and participated in the trip to Huscaran described in the chapter "Canadians Abroad." He is a judge of the Supreme Court of British Columbia and has climbed extensively in the Coast Mountains of British Columbia.

Tami Knight is a well-known rockclimber living in Vancouver. She put up many hard routes at Squamish in the 1980s and made the first female ascents of several difficult climbs, including *Astroman* in Yosemite. She has published several books of climbing cartoons.

~ Bruce Fairley

The Golden Hinde (7,217´) August 17, 1974

Ralph Hutchinson

In the dead of winter, I was summoned to the phone by an urgent call from Dick Culbert. Breathless from this unexpected exertion, I panted silently while being importuned to lead a climb to Vancouver Island's highest on a two-day weekend in August. In my feeble state, I agreed, and gratefully returned to the fire and the brandy I had reluctantly left. It was not until two hours later, on recovery, that I realized such a trip was impossible—three days was the minimum, even allowing for a full bottle of brandy.

Thus it was that the pre-climb write-up in *The Rucksack* suggested a minimum of three days. I fondly hoped this would deter all sensible mountaineers, and I was correct. Two days before the trip, one BCMC member contacted me, and was dissuaded from this rash venture. Unfortunately, the Island Mountain Ramblers had decided I should also lead the same trip for them. Twenty-eight of them (all insane) gathered at midnight at the Ralph River Campsite on Buttle Lake, behaving like Bilbo Baggins after he had a whiff of Smaug.

The Golden Hinde is in the centre of Strathcona Park. It was named (as we all know) after Sir Francis Drake's flagship of one hundred tons. Drake had a flair for the dramatic, and when he set out from England on his voyage, his ship had been called the *Pelican*, a name that was not destined for great things. On Vancouver Island we are constantly thanking that buccaneer for changing the name of this ship.

Strathcona Park runs down the centre of Vancouver Island, and contains the highest mountains of the Island. This park had the distinction of being the first of Her Majesty's parks to permit, simultaneously, logging, hunting and mining within its boundaries. These pursuits have continued unabated for many decades; the advent of twenty-eight climbers to Burman Lake was a shock it could well endure: it is not that long since the B.C. Hydro Commission attempted to create a mini-Kemano by reversing its flow to the Wolf River. Fortunately this venture failed: the mining, logging, and hunting have all been successes: so is the climbing.

In brilliant weather, the multitude gathered at the South end of Buttle Lake on the 17th of August, 1974 to be ferried in to Burman Lake by a recalcitrant Husky (plane, not dog). Of the twenty-eight, four had been or were members of the British Columbia Mountaineering Club, namely Val Humphreys, Alf Meninga, Maisie Flanagan (Primrose to those who remember her from 1954) and the intrepid leader.

At Burman Lake, the last load arrived at 10:30 a.m., and by 11:00 a.m. we were sweltering on our way to the peak. This was reached without much difficulty, except for the members, by 2:30 p.m., and all managed to reach camp before dark.

The balmy weather looked so settled that a few had arranged for the plane to pick them up on Sunday at noon. The rest of us set off for the two-day slog out to Buttle Lake, and by 11:00 a.m., we were on Burman Peak, sniggering gently as we watched the clouds swirl in from the Pacific. The few spent a hungry three days waiting for the weather to clear, and the plane to return. Our trip out was the normal ridge walk with mixed bush en route and a gully or two for variety. The whole trip was made more fun by the mist which reduced visibility almost to zero for a day, and consequently when we heard the concentrator at Western Mines, we allowed ourselves a small pat on the back for negotiating the ridges successfully. We were back at the cars by late Monday afternoon.

In summary, this is not a two-day trip, but an enjoyable three-day trip. The British Columbia Mountaineering Club really should put it on their schedule one year, and climb it. ໒

Misadventures in South America, Spring 1966, Cerro Cuerno 18,000

Dick Culbert

Plaza de Mulas has real atmosphere. Perched at 14,000 feet on the side of Aconcagua— indeed too little atmosphere! A point of view I would have gladly subscribed to that evening, having just back-packed 50 lbs. for 18 miles up the desolate valley of the Horrones to this Plaza. I had then made the foolish attempt to pack to 20,000 feet next day. That was a mistake. Now, however, as I acclimatized at this little shelter amid the confusion of Argentine army mules and climbers from a dozen countries, I had a chance to savour the many unique flavours which Plaza de Mulas does offer. Mule dung fires, for instance, over which little groups of colourfully-robed men were cooking unimaginable brews; and the constant flow of strange languages, strange customs, strange equipment and strange foods among the various expeditions passing through or acclimatizing.

Aconcagua country looks very much like the Rockies. Ridges are fairly gentle (except for a few faces), the rock banded, colourful, and draped in talus. Casting about for something to do while acclimatizing, my attention was soon focused on the abrupt form of Cerro Cuerno which dominated the head of the Horrones valley. Its southwest face looked like it needed a route put up badly. I had sprained a finger trying to do an ice-axe arrest down a collapsing gravel terrace the day before, but felt in reasonable shape.

Basically, this was a plan born in ignorance. To begin with, I didn't know about *penitides*. Entire glaciers were made of these things—unbelievable forests of needles and ridges from about two feet to ten feet high. Getting through this mess at that altitude absorbed much of the day, and most of my energy. Finally the face—and Yikes! Cuerno means "horn" and if I'd seen the route in profile I wouldn't have tried it alone, especially without a rope. Then there was the rock, which consisted of surprisingly unstable downslab. It was good luck (combined with considerable searching), and not good management which eventually turned up a route never going above class 4 difficulty. Finally the summit, where cairn records showed that this was indeed a new route.

Now about this getting down. As far as I could interpret from Spanish and German scrawls in the cairn, the usual approach was via an obvious glacier. Of that nonsense I'd had enough; especially as both *penitides* and crevasses were at their prime at that time of year. Instead, I trundled off into an oncoming storm along a ridge joining with the scree slopes of Aconcagua itself. The ridge soon became knife-edged, with unstable class 4 pitches.

Weather grew rapidly worse, and by the time my way was blocked by a totally impassable tower, a fully mature Andean blizzard was in progress. To make a long story short, this proved the most desperate position I had met in the last couple years of climbing, and it was finally solved by a very long traverse across very rotten, very windy, very icy, very class 5 faces. Getting through was mainly a direct function of good luck.

My luck had just run out with this episode, however. Perhaps it was the mule driver's food with which I was stretching my own rations, but from somewhere I contracted amoebic dysentery. Instead of pushing on up to Aconcagua, I spent two days crawling like a sickly snail down the wind-blown gorge of the Horrones and two more returning to Santiago in Chile. As if this ending were not sufficiently ignoble, the bug stayed with me throughout the month I spent riding local buses in Patagonia, and it wasn't until I was up into Bolivia and Peru that energy for further mountaineering was available. 🏔

Perspective: A Winter Ascent of Diedre

Tami Knight

A weekend skiing in Black Tusk meadows! And what a weekend! Clear, cold and incredible snow conditions. And nothing had gone wrong yet! Five minutes out of the van and one of our party complains of cold. We look at her. Pack askew and gasping and wheezing coming from her told us she shouldn't be going on, so we turned back. I was so mad I could have crapped tacks.

Peter piped up. "We could go ice climbing at Squamish? We could drive back to the city, pick up our gear, etc, etc, come back out and beat ice tomorrow!"

Craig agreed. "Ya, lots of ice there—perfect winter conditions although a tad minimal." I reluctantly agreed. After all, today was short so might as well do something worthwhile tomorrow.

So we went back to the city and got our gear and drove back out to Squamish that night. Next day we thought about what to do. Slabs at base of the Badge? Naw. Hey, What about Diedre? Not too horrendous, besides if it is, then Peter can lead. We roped up for the first pitch which in summer is quick third class. Peter edges up the 5.6 slab to an arch full of snow. He clears it away and slams in a peg. Pins in Diedre!!! An ATROCITY!!! But sure is fun! Besides nuts don't do so well in the ice-filled crack. Pete frictions across (horrendous) then more pro and then up to easier ground. Soon he's at the tree at the base of the Diedre corner. Craig follows the pitch and I come up third.

We stomp our feet to warm them and wonder what we're doing here. The pitch looks more horrendous than horrendous. The ice streak looks bomber but if you climbed that there'd be no pro. So Peter opts for the corner which was weird climbing but at least protectable. So he scraped up, bridged out, laybacked off ice tools in the crack, pounded in another pin, kick kick and more ice showers down on Craig and me. Rock climbing in crampons is manky. Craig follows the way Pete goes and I get to climb the lovely ice streak on the right.

Craig leads the next pitch. He steps out onto the ice streak and starts poking his way up it. Fifty, sixty feet. Hey Craig! Why don't you put in some pro? Huh! I can't! Then more climbing and off belay! I'd say that pitch was fairly hairball, a hundred feet with not a piece of protection!!!

Two more pitches of beautiful ice and snow climbing and the final moves to the top—small bulge—place the tools high—feet up high—and then the usual Squamish finish—Lunge for the Tree!!!

We trundle down through the snow and slink over the boulders at the base of the apron and back to the van. On the drive back we gloat over the route. A classic! Fantastic! Totally recommendable!

Next day it poured rain and all the ice fell down. Hee Hee Hee Hee... 🖋

XII PERSONALITIES

Included here are a few sketches of figures who have played some role, however brief, in Canadian mountaineering. It is surprising, really, how little of such material is available. The scarcity is likely due to the absence of a periodical for Canadian mountaineering; gossip and thumbnail sketches tend to be the fodder of the magazines, and Canadian journals have taken a loftier tone. It will undoubtedly surprise some to learn that Edward Whymper had a hand in several Canadian ascents, while the inclusion of the other selections certainly testifies to the wide range of diverse characters who have found a home at one time or another in the Canadian mountaineering community.

Of the authors in this chapter, Arthur O. Wheeler and W.D. Wilcox have been introduced in earlier chapters, which leaves Edward Feuz and Murray Toft needing introductions.

Edward Feuz lived for many years in Golden, British Columbia. He was one of the Swiss guides Canadian Pacific brought to Canada as part of their program to promote climbing and skiing in the Canadian mountains. Feuz built an impressive record of first ascents in the Rockies and the Selkirks, and vies for honours with Conrad Kain as the greatest of the Canadian guides.

One of the finest Canadian mountaineers of his generation, Murray Toft began climbing in the Rockies at an early age. He has an impressive list of first ascents, including the north face of Mt. Victoria and the first winter ascent of Mt. Chepren. He is an instructor in outdoor pursuits at the University of Calgary.

~ Bruce Fairley

Some Memories of Edward Whymper

Arthur O. Wheeler

Edward Whymper was my friend. I first met him on the main street at Banff in the Canadian Rockies and recognized him from his pictures. I introduced myself and challenged, "I hear you have come out to Canada to climb Mt. Assiniboine." He replied, "Not so. A man does not climb mountains like Assiniboine after he is sixty years old." This was in the spring of 1901 and Assiniboine still a virgin peak, although attempts had already been made to reach its summit. The first ascent was made later in the year by James Outram, accompanied by the Canadian Pacific Railway Swiss guides, Christian Hasler (senior) and Christian Bohren.

Whymper came to the Rockies under the auspices of the Canadian Pacific Railway, presumably to report upon their attractions to travellers interested in mountains and the many phases of scenery, climbing, science and art they present. If an official report was published I have not seen it and any knowledge of his doings was conveyed to me by the published newspaper reports. I rather fancy he came with the intention of discovering the Canadian Rockies and found they had already been discovered.

He brought with him four Swiss guides and for part of the time had James Outram as collaborator and guest. Most of his major climbs were made by Outram or his guides, who reported to him. It must not be forgotten that when he came, Whymper was beyond the age for strenuous climbs.

Whymper was of a very precise and imperious character and strongly objected to interference in his premeditations. An amusing anecdote is told of his first arrival at Mt. Stephen House at Field, B.C. In those days the trains did not carry dining cars on account of the heavy grades and meals were served at the Company's tourist hotels along the route. The train had stopped for dinner. Whymper was busy collecting and checking his many boxes and express parcels and paid no attention to the dinner bell nor to the departure of the train. Miss Annie Mollison, manager at Mt. Stephen House, well known to all visitors to the Rockies in the early days, a Scottish lady of determination quite equal to Mr. Whymper, sent a page boy to tell him his dinner was waiting. He paid not the slightest attention. A second time the boy was sent, but without result. Miss Mollison became annoyed and said to the boy, "Go tell Mr. Whymper that if he is not here in one minute he will get no dinner." Whymper arrived on time and ever after a mutual respect and friendship grew up between them.

Of the many parts of the region he travelled, near the railway, he seemed specially attracted by Ice River Valley and camped in it for some time. It is likely the real attraction was the blue sodalite to be found in

Sodalite Valley, a tributary of Ice River Valley. He seemed much impressed by this mineral, which is somewhat of the nature of lapis lazuli and susceptible of a high degree of polish.

While camping and exploring in Ice River Valley, his transport was handled by an outfitter, that dry, humorous old stick, Tom Martin. Whymper had a habit, when thinking things out, of marching back and forth along the trail, with his hands behind his back, à la Napoleon. On this occasion a log had fallen across it and every time, to and fro, he had to stop to step over the log. Eventually he became conscious of it and it got on his nerves. He called, "Martin! come here." Then, "Martin! cut that log." Martin, chewing a straw, gazed at it reflectively for a few moments and then said, "Wall! Mr. Whymper, I've been up and down this valley many times and every time, that log has been there, and I'm thinking, Mr. Whymper, that if you want that log cut, you'll have to cut it yourself." Whymper exploded, "Martin! you're fired" and stalked off to his tent. Presently there was another shout, "Martin! come here," and Martin who had been fired several times before, duly appeared; and there was the Chief with a bottle in one hand and a mug in the other: "Martin! have a mug of beer."

Much of Mr. Whymper's supplies were put up in the form of concentrates, tablets and capsule. While his guides seemed well in hand, this was anathema to the packers and pony boys, who were accustomed to sizzling rashers of bacon, hot cakes and syrup, washed down by fragrant black coffee, and nearly led to desertion. Later, Whymper confessed, almost with tears in his eyes, that the Canadian methods were the best and most satisfying for pack-train travel in the Canadian Rockies.

The following is indicative of his conservatism. Several years later he again came to Canada and, en route for the mountains, put up at Braemar Lodge, Miss Mollison's nice little hotel in Calgary, where mountain lovers were always welcome and well taken care of. She had retired from Canadian Pacific Railway service and was now on her own. I then lived at Calgary and the morning after Mr. Whymper's expected arrival phoned Braemar Lodge. Advised that he had arrived, I said that I would like to speak to him. Presently the voice came back, "Hello! are you there?" Assuring that I was, the voice continued, "Mr. Whymper says he does not like the telephone and will not come." It sounded discourteous, but was ameliorated by an invitation to breakfast with him the following morning. On inquiry I found his breakfast time was eleven o'clock or later. By that time my days, pretty busy ones then, were about half over, so I did not see him before he left for the mountains.

Our next meeting was in London, in 1907, at the rooms of the Royal Geographical Society. It was set for 4 p.m. by his appointment. You know how it is; strangers cannot get about London as quickly as the inhabitants and I was one minute late. He was sitting in an easy chair by a bright, log fire and his greeting as I entered, after an interval of six years since I had seen him, was, "Well! I was on time!"

I was then President of the Alpine Club of Canada and had travelled to London to attend the Jubilee dinner of the Alpine Club as the Club's guest. At the dinner I listened with much enjoyment to the very fine and witty address of the President of the Club and Chairman at the dinner, the Right Rev'd the Bishop of Bristol. I was particularly struck by what he said about Mr. Whymper. He said,

> ... Therefore you have thoughtful, imaginative, strenuous, virile literature as the natural literature which comes from the Alpine Club. [Hear, hear.] It has been—I was going to say, my duty—my pleasure to look once more at some of the literature which Alpine Club men have put forth to the world, apart from descriptions of mountaineering efforts. I have been very much struck indeed with one of the earliest of the important works to which I refer; I mean Mr. Whymper's great book on the Andes. [Hear, hear.] That book is a marvellous collection of archaeology, history and science of all kinds—geology, petrology, entomology, and all sorts of things; excellently put as literature, and accompanied by abundant evidence of, I suppose about the most skilled power of illustrating man ever had. [Hear, hear.] There is nothing like Whymper's illustrating, I think, done by the mere hand. He makes noxious insects much more real than life. There is one standing prominent in the middle of a page, the most dangerous, poisonous, mischievous beast that is to be found in the whole of the Andes. I regret to say that the natives call it the 'Bishop.' [Laughter.] A few pages on, he describes another formidable stinging beast, evidently only less bad than the 'Bishop.' That the people call the 'Devil.' [Laughter.] The libel stands in the latest edition.

A fuller résumé of the Bishop's address will be found in the 1908 issue of the *Canadian Alpine Journal,* page 299. In 1908 Mr. Whymper proposed the writer as an Honorary member of the Alpine Club.

It will be remembered that at our annual camp for the year 1909, held in the Lake O'Hara meadows, the veteran Edward Whymper was present. He came from England especially to attend the camp, stayed there with us for three days and then returned direct to England. His address to the annual gathering is an outstanding record of the *Canadian Alpine Journal* and is given, in full, in the 1910 issue, page 214. It was his last visit to the Canadian Rockies.

The foregoing incidents are illustrative of the downright and imperious character of the man, but to his friends he was kindly, humorous and distinctly human. In later years he married a French lady and they had a little girl. He used to write me about her funny little ways and the pranks she would play upon him.

He presented me with a number of signed photographs. One, of the ice tongue of the Yoho Glacier is now of special value as it shows the grand ice-fall and the cave in it from which flowed the initial source of the Yoho River. Owing to the great recession of the ice in the past twenty years this ice-fall has melted and gone, and now is replaced by the ragged rock ridge over which it used to tumble. Another, is of the Kicking Horse River falls, below the railway near Leanchoil. At my summer home at Banff I have one of his beloved Matterhorn and of the Hero, himself.

A great mountaineer, a notable scientist, a prince of illustrators and a master of terse and graphic literature, to which his books *Scrambles Amongst the Alps, A Guide to the Valley of Zermatt and the Matterhorn, A Guide to Chamonix and the Range of Mont Blanc,* and others, now classics, bear witness. I shall always feel proud to know that he included me among his friends. ❧

Bill Peyto

W.D. Wilcox

While dinner is preparing and the delicious odour of frying bacon blends with the pungent smoke of the spruce-wood fire, there is time for a little study of our packers and cook. Who are they and whence did they come? Perhaps no more interesting character has ever appeared in this region than my old packer Bill Peyto. I made my first excursion to Assiniboine with him and have travelled several hundred miles under his guidance. Bill is very quiet in civilisation, but becomes more communicative around an evening camp-fire, when he delights to tell his adventures. His has been a roving life. The story of his battle with the world, his escapades and sufferings of hunger and exposure, not to mention the dreams and ambitions of a keen imagination with their consequent disappointments, has served to entertain many an evening hour. Peyto assumes a wild and picturesque though somewhat tattered attire. A sombrero, with a rakish tilt to one side, a blue shirt set off by a white kerchief (which may have served civilisation for a napkin), and a buckskin coat with fringed border, add to his cowboy appearance. A heavy belt containing a row of cartridges, hunting-knife and six-shooter, as well as the restless activity of his wicked blue eyes, give him an air of bravado. He usually wears two pairs of trousers, one over the other, the outer pair about six months older. This was shown by their dilapidated and faded state, hanging, after a week of rough work in burnt timber, in a tattered fringe knee-high. Every once in a while Peyto would give one or two nervous yanks at the fringe and tear off the longer pieces, so that his outer trousers disappeared day by day from below upwards. Part of this was affectation, to impress the tenderfoot, or the "dude," as he calls everyone who wears a collar. But in spite of this Peyto is one of the most conscientious and experienced men with horses that I have ever known.

In camp, Peyto always goes down to see his horses once or twice a day even if they are several miles distant, and I have even known him to look after them in the depths of night when he thought they might be in trouble. When the order to march has been given the night before, our horses are in camp at dawn. Quick and cool in time of real danger, he has too much anxiety about trouble ahead, and worries himself terribly about imaginary evils. He sleeps with a loaded rifle and a hunting-knife by his side. "Bill," said I, one night, upon noticing a row of formidable instruments of death near me, "why in the mischief do you have all of those shooting-irons and things here?" "I tell you," said he, with an anxious look, "I believe this country is full of grizzlies; I heard a terrible noise in the woods this afternoon, and besides that, they say the Kootenay Indians have risen. They may come into the valley any night."

A picture of a train of horses crossing an angry stream comes to my memory, and one animal has put his forefoot through the head-rope and fallen helpless as he is swept away by the torrent. Suddenly a man leaps from his saddle, and with a sharp knife in hand, rushes out into a foaming swirl of waters whence it seems impossible for anyone to return alive. A flash of steel in the sunlight shows the rope has been cut, and after a struggle the horse regains the shore, dragging the man after. It was Peyto! On another occasion a fast freight, coming suddenly around a curve, surprised two pack-horses at a few yards' distance, but Peyto struck one on the head, and seizing the rope of the other, pulled the beast from the rails as the engine rushed by, while everyone else stood immovable in a paralysis of fear. ✺

Viscount Amery

Edward Feuz

Viscount Amery came out on political matters [in 1929]. He had to give a lecture in Edmonton, but in the meantime, he wanted to climb these mountains. He was quite a climber in his young days; he was out with Mummery and all kinds of climbers. So I got orders from [CPR] headquarters in Montreal to be ready for Colonel Amery.

Amery was a lovely person, a small, little man, didn't talk very much, very nice to travel with. We were out a whole month together. Mr. A.O. Wheeler, the organizer of the Canadian Alpine Club was there too. He was trying to be the boss like he always had. We were on the way to the mountain and Wheeler wanted to camp—I don't know how far away. So I had a row with Mr. Wheeler. I said, "Do you have to climb the mountain with Colonel Amery or do I have to climb the mountain with Colonel Amery? I'm going to camp where I want to camp." I had been there before, and I know exactly where to camp you see. So we went up there, and we climbed the mountain. But that's some story.

We started up 3 o'clock in the morning with the lantern on the Alexandra River. Going up through the trees, we could see the weather was threatening. The clouds were down and the weather was going to be bad. But I kept on going. I thought, "Well, we're still in the trees. If it comes on bad, we can still go back." So, I kept going, kept going. The weather didn't improve. We got above timber line and I looked up at the mountain and I said, "Well Colonel, it doesn't look to be a very nice day. I think we should go back. We should have a nice day going up there on the first ascent. You can't see very well, and it's not much pleasure."

But the Colonel, he turned around and said, "Edward, yes, but we don't turn around in Switzerland, when we climb the mountains, do we?" he said in a nice English way. I said "Yes, we don't turn around. We go there. But in Switzerland you see signs ahead of you all the time where you should climb the mountains. I've never been up this mountain before. I've got to find it first. It's a different thing, Colonel, but if you insist to go, I can stand as much as you, Colonel, so say yes or no." He said "Let's go."

So I went. And do you know it got so bad we finally had to crawl on top on our hands and knees. The snow came down so fast in your face it stuck right to the eyelashes, and you couldn't see more than ten or fifteen feet ahead. I said "Well, we come to the top, Colonel." I made a stoneman. And the Colonel was lying stomach down, out of the storm, to rest his face.

Down in the valley, it was all black. Off we went, down, down and down, slow in that storm. When you're up that high, you can't go very fast.

You've got to make sure of your handholds and your footholds, so that nothing happens. But everything is slippery. We went down, and when we got into the first trees, it was pitch dark. So I took my little folding lantern that I always have and I shoved a candle in. I kept it at the back for the Colonel, so he could see where he stepped in the trees. He was so tired, the poor chap, that he could hardly lift his feet any more. So we walked in the trees for an hour. I said "Colonel, I think a good idea would be to stop here for the night and make a fire and then go home in the morning. You're tired and it's very slow going. We'll never get there tonight. We'll have to walk all night. I've been out lots of times in worse places than this—right up in the rocks, and tied on to the rocks all night. Here we can make a fire and be comfortable."

Amery turned around and said "Oh, no. We don't do that in Switzerland. We go right down to the hut." I said "Yes, but in Switzerland, you have a trail to go right up to the hut. You can see your little trail where people walked before. Here we have nothing. I can't see where I'm going, and you're so tired you can't move." "Oh, I think we'll go on, Edward," he said. I said "All right, Colonel, we go on."

It wasn't fifteen minutes after he said "Edward, I think your idea is a splendid idea." "All right, Colonel. When we get down a little further and I hear some water, we'll stop there and I'll make a fire and I'll make you a lovely cup of tea, and I'll make you comfortable and we'll stay there for the night." "Very nice," the Colonel said.

So I went down there and started the fire quick. I made him a bough bed next to the fire with branches, and by that time the kettle was boiling, so I gave him a cup of nice tea. And before five minutes he was snoring away. I had to wake him up to eat, and he ate, and he went to sleep again. And then he had a great smile on him. As soon as it got a little daylight, I woke him up and said, "Colonel, a cup of tea, and we'll be started for home."

The next day was a rest day, and then we pulled out. We were going to climb Mount Bryce. We went up there and the weather started to get bad. So we camped at the ice field and it snowed a foot overnight. Climbing was doomed.

So the Colonel said, "Edward, we can't do anything today. I'd like to have a bath. How can we arrange that?" "Oh," I said, "that's very easy, Colonel. We just make a hole in the ground. I've got a very nice tarpaulin and we put that in the hole. I get the cook to make lots of hot water in the pails and we put it in there, and you just slip out of your tent and jump into your pool and have a little bath right out there in the open, right amongst the snow." "Wonderful," he said. So we fixed it up for him and he had a wonderful bath.

The same evening it started to clear up. I could see that something was bothering him. I said, "Anything wrong, Colonel?" "Well, you know Edward, when we got onto my mountain it bothered me a little…this bad weather we had and…" "Do you think we weren't quite on the top? Is that bothering you?" He said, "Yes, exactly. I was worried we weren't quite on the top." I said, "Well, we'll fix that. It's going to be a nice day tomorrow. Let's climb Mount Saskatchewan. It's right opposite your peak, just across the valley. It isn't a very hard climb. We better just go there, and I'll show you the stoneman. You saw me build the stoneman on top, didn't you?" He said, "Oh, yes."

So we went up Mount Saskatchewan, which is over 11,000 feet, and it was a glorious day. And when we got to the top I said, "Now sit down here. Here is the glass. Look right across. You see your mountain now, Mount Amery, over there." He took the glass and smiled and said, "You're right, Edward. It's right on the very top." ❧

Eckhard Grassman

Murray Toft

Every once in a while a CMC'er[1] asks me how I got the scar on my right cheekbone. For those of you I strung along for years, what follows is the straight goods. Gospel.

To begin with, this was my best epic with Eckhard. It was February in either '68 or '69 and I was becoming interested in winter climbing. Having done some ridiculous ski tours with Urs [Kallen] and Eckhard on a pair of old twisted planks, I listened to Eckhard's great tales with amazement. I was especially impressed with his winter epic on the north face of the Dent D'Herens where he claimed to have lost bits of toe and ear. At that time he seemed to have used up about seven of his nine lives already!

So when I became enthused about trying the Wind Tower ridge, Eckhard was asked to be my mentor. He hadn't been in Canada very long and was full of enthusiasm for exploring new areas. Especially since he had just bought his legendary red Land Rover. The Land Rover, we thought, was going to be our key to success for it would eliminate much of the approach. Little did I know....

So, off we went on a perfectly normal February day. Temperature minus twenty-five, no heat in the Rover, Eckhard raving about some past epic, wearing a T-shirt and an anorak....

The foot of snow on the old road to the Wind Tower presented some challenge to the Red Blare-on, as we later christened the Land Rover. Arriving at the top of some of the hills it would just simply run out of energy and roll back down. This only antagonised Eckhard. Racing the engine and popping the clutch, he thought he was Juan Fangio as he roared up the hills again and again to eventually make it. I was beginning to wonder by this time if it wouldn't have been a lot faster to just get out and ski.

We eventually arrived at what was to be the major challenge of the climb: a small dam in the creek. On the other side we could see the roadcut continuing in the direction we wanted to go.

Eckhard jumped out and thumped his foot on the ice a couple of times. Assured that it was solid enough to drive across, he backed the Land Rover up and took a run at it. The trajectory of the ton-and-a-half of Land Rover hurtling across the ice was just enough to put it roughly in the middle of the dam. Unfortunately, that's where it stopped.

The next thing I heard was an incredible booming as the ice started to crack under the passenger-side wheels. I couldn't believe what my eyes were

---

1. Calgary Mountain Club

seeing. It was like the sinking of the Bismarck. Slowly the ice tilted down under the weight and the Land Rover listed right thirty degrees. With a peaceful sigh it slipped in slow motion into the waters of Wind Tower Creek.

By this time Eckhard was on the roof, fucking God, the world, me, the dam, his jeep, Canada, in a style of profanity only he could scream.

It was an incredible spectacle. Like a picture postcard of a winter wonderland: snowcapped mountains and trees all around, a beautiful creek running through the mid foreground, and that little touch of red to set things off. In this case a red Land Rover up to its window and air filter in the creek. Little pieces of ice floated in and out of the windows.

After about twenty minutes of outrage, Eckhard cooled to the point of realizing that we were in a bit of a pickle and that all further progress to our objective would be delayed until we got the jeep out of the dam. In true undaunted Grassman style he took the bit between his teeth and produced an insignificant come-along hand winch from the dripping luggage area. Immediately upon coming in contact with the below-zero temperatures it turned into a frozen pretzel. So, while Eckhard hacked away at the icy tangle of cable I proceeded to anchor one end of the climbing rope to the nearest good-size tree. It was Eckhard's plan to winch the jeep back up onto the ice that hadn't broken yet, and drive off into the sunset singing German beer-drinking songs. He was in his element that day.

Well, really creative Eckhard winched for a good hour and eventually took the forty-eight feet of stretch out of his climbing rope. At this point the jeep took one enormous lunge back on to the ice, but only for a second. The weight was too much for the ice to bear, so back in the dam again.

This performance was repeated several times, each time the jeep moving back into deeper water, the ice getting only marginally thicker. After the third attempt Eckhard was really working up a lather. He was literally dripping sweat from every pore. His thin cotton anorak was totally encased in an icy mantle of frozen sweat.

"Er, Eckhard, do you mind if I give it a couple of goes for awhile? You're getting really knackered, man."

So it was that I politely accepted my fate. Two cranks of the hand winch later I was flying through the air, propelled by the snapped winch cable. Eckhard had narrowly missed having another epic himself—his amazing Karma had me in his place with only seconds to spare. He had lucked out again.

The whole winching system had been stretched tighter than a G string. My two cranks were all it took to break the camel's back, so to speak. When it snapped, the cable sounded like a rifle shot, but I didn't know if it was from the snapping of the cable or its connecting with my cheekbone. At any rate I didn't care much, for I was concerned about the rate at which my duvet, knickers, and the snow were turning red. In the background I could see stars and hear Eckhard profaning again. He was hopping around on one foot, then the other, with his fingers stuck in his mouth like a child ready for a spanking. He didn't know if I had been decapitated or not. There was blood everywhere.

Eventually I gained consciousness enough to remember my first aid kit and directed Eckhard into creating a gauze pad to stop the ooze. Stacks of butterfly bandages and gauze later I managed to split for the highway. I got a ride with a psychoanalyst going to a convention.

When he asked me why I climbed in winter I was really short for words. ⚜

XIII   TRAVERSES: MOUNTAINEERING IN THE HORIZONTAL MODE

If you took down from the shelf any of the classic books of mountaineering from the last century, such as *Scrambles Amongst the Alps*, by Edward Whymper, one fact that would immediately catch your attention is that many of the "climbs" described were not climbs at all as we understand the term today. These accounts from the "golden age" of mountaineering are just as often about new crossings of cols or traverses of mountain country where no peak was actually attained. In that century, traverses were the backbone of a well-rounded mountaineering résumé. Today, however, mountaineers have been overcome by the vertical, and traverses, while not quite out of fashion, tend to excite less interest than formerly.

It is partly because traverses no longer attract the prestige of more glamourous ascents, such as those of the Himalayan giants, that Canadian mountaineering has not been particularly well understood outside Canada. Because the traverse remains an important ingredient in the recipe of Canadian climbing, commentators from the United States or Europe have occasionally belittled Canadian accomplishments in our own mountains. Typical of this attitude is Chris Jones's account in *Climbing in North America*. Although this book is billed as the only comprehensive history of North American climbing, there is almost no mention of mountaineering in the most extensive mountain range on the continent—the Coast Mountains of British Columbia— nor is there any satisfactory account of mountaineering in areas of the Canadian north such as Baffin Island. And a good part of the reason for this omission is that in the Coast Mountains and on Baffin Island the traverse has been, until recently, the dominant form of mountaineering expression.

That is not to say that Canadian climbers are not also present in the front rank of climbing as the sport is popularly conceived—Canada has produced its share of world-class alpinists and rock climbers—but rather that those whose main love is the traverse of mountain country are not generally known or appreciated.

Traverses represent the horizontal mode of mountaineering and the objectives of traverses necessarily differ from those of other forms of mountaineering expression, such as face climbing. For example, it is often difficult on an extended traverse to carry significant amounts of climbing hardware simply because the weight of food and fuel prohibits the carrying of too much else. Therefore, technical ambitions must be down-scaled in favour of other rewards—the viewing of extensive tracts of mountain scenery; the exhilarations of finding a route through unknown country; or the satisfaction that comes from being self-reliant in the mountains over an extended period.

Nor are traverses necessarily without technical mountaineering challenges. Many of the long traverses done in the Coast Mountains by John Baldwin and his companions, and lately by Alex Frid and Pierre Friele, have included significant technical climbing and skiing—all done with little or no climbing equipment and all on cross-country skis.

And of course not all traverses are confined to the glacier paths and the cols. A challenging alternative is to link together a number of summits by starting at one end of a chain of peaks and working one's way through to the last summit in the line—climbing all the peaks en route. It is that kind of traverse which is described in Don Serl's article "The Traverse."

Historically, traverses have been closely related to mountain exploration, and they will continue to be important in the fabric of Canadian mountaineering, partly because this country still offers stretches of relatively unexplored country; but also because traverses will continue to appeal to those whose quest is for new experiences—the exploration of unknown country both in the mountains and within themselves.

 ∼ Bruce Fairley

FROM TELLOT LAKE TO KNIGHT INLET

From 1974 to 1985 I was the sole editor of the *Canadian Alpine Journal,* the journal of record for Canadian mountaineering. Submissions to the *CAJ* arrive in anything from great wodges to barely discernable trickles—most in the mail, a few by hand. Each manuscript, even if arrival is in wodge mode, is an individual. First categorizing can range from "Think about"; to "Acknowledge and file—deal with (i.e., read) later"; to, for some sad creatures, "No."

A few have a look about them. One time the author is known, another time, the title attracts. Sometimes there is no easily identifiable reason. The manuscript just looks interesting and must be read immediately.

Even more rare is for the memory of that first reading—the excitement, the pleasure—to endure. Sara Golling's "Tellot Lake to Knight Inlet" is from the 1974 *CAJ,* the first of the 13 journals I edited. I had to read it right away, and, even today, more than 15 years later, I still remember the fun and the thrill.

∼ Moira Irvine

Tellot Lake to Knight Inlet

Sara Golling

July 1 Nabob Pass is snow-covered except for islands of heather, lakes of reflections, scattered garbage and long-forgotten caches. Our tracks decorate the snow from above Ephemeron Lake (known to our pilot as Tellot) to Nabob Pass, and separate there into seven curious lines wandering from heather island to flat rock to lakeside to garbage heap and back.

July 2 Seven weirdly bulging creatures in shouting colours, hooded, flapping and wet, weave between crevasses to gain the uninterrupted snow in the middle of the Tiedemann Glacier. Dull grey the world, and small; nothing exists but fog, snow, rain, wind, and six other grotesque forms, soddenly plodding.

July 3, 4 We peer out of our three tents at the base of the Rainy Knob, see the grey world unchanged, hear the continual speckled sound of rain.

July 6 It's hot. Fred, Eric, Erich, Jennifer and I each struggle to remove one leg from the wet cement we're mired in, thigh-deep, so we can sink again one step closer to the Claw hut [the Plummer memorial hut]. We try crawling; a cry of despair bursts from one who has suddenly sunk in to the tops of his legs.

July 10 Eric, Erich and Fred climbed Serra III yesterday, while the rest of us explored less ambitious peaks: Dragonback, Eaglehead, Tellot, and Argiewicz. We looked from our sunny cirque to the Serras, and saw swift-swirling mist tumbling toward us. Today we are trapped. The hut shudders, windows whistle and moan, and candle flames flicker. The hut's aluminum sheathing ripples thunderously.

July 11 On the peak of Heartstone it's warm enough to sunbathe... until the wind begins to blow. Roland, Fred, Jennifer, Ellen, and I bask under the intense blue of a storm-washed sky.

July 12 There is a little pool of water at the very edge of the summit of Claw Peak but one could suffer vertigo drinking from it. Jennifer and I must be the most exhilarated pair ever to sit here; neither has done much rock climbing at all, and this was the first leading either of us ever tried. We look westward to the massive form of Waddington; so long hidden from view it now draws our eyes as irresistibly as it has drawn our thoughts. The boys are all out climbing Serra I. We hope they aren't blown off.

July 13 We've all known about this since Roland and Ellen came up to the hut on the 7th and told us. Now we're looking at it: an avalanche that buried and scattered our cache at Rainy Knob. So we dig, and dig, and dig... "Yahoo! Found the kitchen!" "Yippee! Here's the toilet paper!"

July 14 Roland is halfway up the face of a serac, waist-deep, shovelling with his hands. Avalanches roar down the rock faces just north and the sun is now shining full on the eighteen hundred feet of icefall below, softening it to a deep mush. Without a shovel we can't go up any further…we two are in the icefall between the Arabesques and the northern bulge of Munday. The other five are investigating Munday's northeast ridge.

July 16 "Oh, let me go first," Ellen offered, "I've never fallen in a crevasse before." Five minutes later, only her head and arms were visible. "I can't touch anything with my feet!" Eric pulled her out and we trudged the rest of the way to the Bravo-Spearman col, camped, and hiked up Bravo. We started from the base of Rainy Knob this morning with supplies for a week and took a long time to wallow through the soft deep snow between gaping blue crevasses in the Bravo Glacier. When the headwall stopped avalanching Fred and Eric put a handline up it, using all our ropes—and it reached down almost to the bergschrund; not quite.

July 17 We've all climbed Spearman now and our camp is set up in the Spearman–Waddington col. We can see our other airdrop site at the lower end of Glacier Island.

July 18 "ICE" I yell. Four helmets duck, chunks of ice and rock smash down. We check the ropes and keep climbing…. On the main summit of Waddington I look about amazed; it's so tiny, the drop so sheer. I saw this blade of rock broadside from the Claw and it was massive; now its slenderness astonishes me. Fred, Jennifer, Erich and I perch and eat and gaze for too long.

The other three climbed the Northwest Peak today; straddled huge, rotten ice feathers at the summit and returned to camp at a sensible, sunlit hour. Our descent is slow—ropes tangle, further down they snag. At the Notch blackness creeps up from the shaded eastern side and a bitter, icy wind howls and buffets. We are cold, fingers numb and stiff, and we move with great deliberation, darting beams from our headlamps down the jagged rock. Back on the snow we still operate in slow motion with the exaggerated caution of drunks. We are drunk. Finally at camp in the Spearman Col we see traces of pink in the east.

July 19 Everyone but me slept most of the day and now, at dusk, we are hurriedly packing up camp. Weather has moved in today—wisps of cloud streak past. We haven't enough food for a prolonged siege so we move— with regret; Roland and Eric wanted to climb Waddington too. The crust breaks and bruises shins. Half a moon provides illumination until flying clouds blot it out…the Tiedemann winds sinuously down the valley far below and in a dream we see lights there gleaming at us, winking, glimmering. Pools of water mirror the moon. Snow bridges solid a few days ago hang sagging and tattered over wider crevasses. Further down a spectacular dawn lights our way. We arrive at the Rainy Knob camp around 8 on the morning of the 20th.

July 22 We are camped high on the Munday plateau in thick fog and freezing wind. We left Rainy Knob for the last time late yesterday afternoon and gained about thirteen hundred feet on the north east ridge before carving tent platforms. Trail-breaking was heavy and there was no compensating view.

July 23 Frost feathers—on everything! Blue patches! We all make tracks up the highest peak of Munday and stand there drinking in the view then pack up camp and head down to set it up again in the Munday–Agur col. Snow slopes from between the two eastern summits provide a quick and easy route down. Later, all but Ellen and me traipse up into the mist shrouding Agur.

July 26 Erich and I are sitting on top of Jester feeling slothful. The wind carries voices clearly from the west—Fred, Eric, and Jennifer are energetically climbing all four peaks in this group today. We strain our eyes to see Roland and Ellen's tracks—they have trekked away to see Fury Gap and Mt. Chris Spencer.

July 27 Returning from Mt. Repose I scrambled up some steep gravel on the southern side of Glacier Island (where we have been camped since the 24th) and find a miniature garden of rare beauty; a tiny stream sparkles brilliantly down a bed of dense emerald-green moss, clusters of alpine flowers bloom, their soft colours vibrant in the sun.

July 29 A muffled, thundering roar issues from a small, bottomless hole in the bare ice of the Franklin Glacier. A powerful river is flowing beneath us. We walk beside a noisy stream rushing along on blue ice. Then it becomes a moulin, plunging into a hole six feet in diameter to join the main river below. We left Glacier Island this morning, followed the south-east margin of the Franklin until we were below Icefall Point, then worked our way through disorderly crevasses toward the middle of the glacier. Here the travelling is straightforward. Getting off the glacier is less pleasant. We traverse slopes of unstable gravel, mud and boulders covering glassy black ice; rocks teeter and boom around us. We camp on sand above the boisterous new-born Franklin River with grit in our hair, grit in our eyes, and grit in our mouths.

July 30 At this time of year, there are few sandbars to walk on. We are forced to climb over a noticeable bump of rock and slither down a gully on the other side before we find any. Then there are a few brief encounters with brush and one odoriferous little bog before we get to an old logging road and begin to develop blisters.

At the logging camp that evening there are rows of sleepy-eyed men leaning on bunkhouse railings to watch us straggle in on our aching feet. One of them mutters a comment to the man beside him and the warm evening air carries it to our ears: "Hey, those wimmin ain't wearin' any brassieres!" ❧

THE TRAVERSE

The title of this article carries a hint of pretentiousness—*"The* Traverse." Yet to anyone who has seen that mighty horseshoe of peaks that surround the Tiedemann Glacier in British Columbia's central Coast Mountains, the title is justified. The traverse from Mt. Waddington at the head of the Tiedemann to the peak known as Serra I is almost certainly the most spectacular of such undertakings available in North America south of the Yukon and Alaska. The peaks are technically challenging but generally feature good rock. Snow and ice techniques must be called on as well as rock-climbing skills. The scenery simply cannot be beaten and the traverse is long enough that an element of risk always lurks—it would be difficult to escape quickly to easy ground once one had committed oneself to the traverse of all the peaks.

The climbers who undertook the first traverse of the dominant peaks of the Waddington massif formed one of the strongest teams ever to go into the Canadian mountains. Peter Croft (his story "Pickled in Yosemite" appears in chapter 15) is generally recognized as the finest North American rock climber of any period and was just hitting full stride at the time of this story. Greg Foweraker is generally unknown outside the British Columbia coast, but was one of the strongest rock climbers of the day and had partnered Croft in the first free ascent of the Squamish Chief's University Wall (and would later be involved with Don Serl in the first ascent of the West Face of Mt. Bute). Don Serl, the writer of this piece, has been, since the retirement of Dick Culbert, the technical climber in the Coast Mountains who matters most, a station he has held now for almost 15 years. The list of serious routes he has to his credit in the range is unequalled and demonstrates an astonishing appetite and commitment. Serl's thoughtful voice is pre-eminent in most matters where technical climbing in the Coast Mountains is concerned, and he is frequently called upon for advice by visiting climbers. This article is taken from the *Canadian Alpine Journal*, to which he is a regular contributor.

                                                   ∼ Bruce Fairley

The Traverse

Don Serl

The helicopter whirled by the peaks a final time and spiralled steeply down toward Fury Gap. Tensions and doubts welled up. Should we put down in the col? What if the weather didn't hold? How would we do on Serra V? Could we deal with these packs? The skids settled into the gloaming, sacks and boots hit the snow, the power came up, and we were on our own. Ahead lay the most magnificent string of peaks in the Coast Mountains, nine great summits of 11 and 12 and 13 thousand feet. We hefted the packs, settled them onto our backs, and started uphill.

The traverse of the Waddington Range had been the subject of speculation and the object of desire amongst Coasties for years and years. Several attempts to traverse the Serras at the eastern end had failed—Serra V always seemed very nearly insuperable. While the climbing problems were easier to cope with, almost attractive, from the west, access and the commitment of tackling the project from the far end was a deterrent—the prospect of getting to Serra IV or V after two or three days and of then getting caught in bad weather remains most unappealing. And now here we were, on our way, the weather fine, conditions excellent, plugging up the initial slopes of the north-west ridge on Waddington, full of fears and fire, committed!

The evening darkened into night, rock led to snow, crevasses loomed and disappeared, an arête led on into blackness, the boreal glow and sudden meteors shimmered and flickered overhead. That night I seemed to be travelling alone, barely aware of the others, getting used again to the kinesthetic pleasure of working muscles and the bite of crampons and the creak of the pack straps, communing with the spirits, a bit awe-struck, I suspect, by the enormity of where I was and what I was (we were) confronting. Somewhere nearby I sensed the spirit of the Mundays moving with me, up this great ridge that they had discovered and ascended so many years ago. I felt on hallowed ground, my feet in their steps, my senses absorbing their memories.

Four hours and most of the ridge disappeared. We found a snug spot in a flat little col and erected the tent. A very short two hours later Peter was brewing for brekkie—early travel is fast travel! Half an hour up the ridge we emerged into the sun as we wound down into the bowl at the base of the Angel Glacier. The snow was perfect, the morning air crystalline. Geddes, then Bell sank beneath us. The Klinikleen shone in the distance. A few more steps—the vast trench of the Tiedemann yawned below our toes—we sat and ate. Just a couple of hundred meters away the rocks of the summit tower warmed in the sun—how many times had I tried this mountain? We cramponed down to the 'schrund with nearly two thousand meters of air beneath our heels, found a way around its end, and quickly crossed to the base of the Tooth. Shattered but firm rock led to the Notch. Greg and I sorted gear—Peter mumbled a few words and was gone—we stuffed the ropes and a handful of hardware into the packs and followed. A spray of ice crashed down, with Peter safely in the back of the chimney, then he was over the second chockstone and out of sight, moving up fast. We started the chimney, then traversed onto the dry blocky face to the right—I was starting to think "Maybe. Maybe this time." A ledge appeared. A gully opened around the corner. The rock suddenly started to get badly shattered and snow filled the depressions. We moved out onto the righthand arête, opening the exposure onto the Tiedemann again, and suddenly, there it was: a stubby pyramid of snow, sky beyond, the top of the Coast! We grinned and chuckled and had a bite and took a few photos, then I lazed back and basked and basked and basked as close as I could comfortably get to that elusive top. Life could be no better!

The next morning we retraced our steps from the bivy site on the ridge to the Angel Glacier, then found a way through the crevasses and ran below the ice cliffs to reach Combatant col, relieved to have behind us the only really objectively dangerous section of the traverse. As the sun climbed, we crunched up the western slopes of Combatant and scrambled the ridge to the top of the north peak. There we passed four lazy hours (something about letting the sun go off the east face delayed us) making water in hollows in the slabs, eating huge amounts of our seemingly infinite food supply, sleeping, and trying to hide from the searing glare of the sun! Ah, the rigours of alpinism!

Our enforced rest over, we quickly topped the main summit, regained our packs in the notch between the summits, and descended snow slopes into "Chaos" col. The 'schrund at the base of the west face of Tiedemann was awkward, but once across it we found easy snow slopes and superb rock leading us reasonably easily to high on the mountain. In a scene that was to be repeated several times along the traverse, Peter tossed a rope down from above to belay us up one short difficult section and we scrambled to the top just as the sun blinked out in the western distance. Two surprisingly complicated hours farther along the ridge we found a pleasant flat prow and stopped.

A strong breeze pushed up the south face all night but it swept on upwards above us and left us comfortable in our bags until the first rays of the sun roused us. The relaxation dissipated quickly—the sky was pallid and layered and Greg was sick, curled in an uncommunicative fœtal ball, occasionally colouring the snow with gastric juices. He came around a bit and we coaxed some tea into him. Meanwhile Peter and I vigorously attacked the food stocks—we still had far too much along and eventually we abandoned a dozen or so Saimins and a couple of big bags of pasta that we just couldn't figure how to consume for breakfast. To add to the troubles the stove was starting to burn poorly. An earlier mix-up had lost us some fuel so we had replenished with remainders from the King's hanger. Now this old fuel was clogging the stove and we were without a pricker. Repeated fiddling with a knife kept it running, albeit poorly, until we reached the hut.

Finally we got packed and set off slowly. Greg, while very low on energy initially, perked up rapidly as we down climbed and was displaying a reasonable appetite by the time we took a short break below Asperity. A fine snow arête, some solid scrambling, and a short belayed step flowed quickly past and we found ourselves on the summit by mid-morning, only two hours from the bivy. The big peaks were done—now for the Serras! Onward!

A clattering above jerked my head up! Two-thirds of the way down the ice slope skirted the glacial cliffs on the north-east side of Asperity—danger! A swarm of ice chunks spewed out of the mixed ground onto the snow. The biggest piece skipped and slid a couple times and then, its momentum building, flipped up on edge and started for me. It was immediately apparent…well, as my mind put it at the time, that "That fucker's got my number on it!" On it came, whirling fast, bouncing a bit, angling very gently across the grain of the slope, true on course. Would it deflect? Might it bounce over me? I took a good grip on the tools, crampons firmly set, eyes riveted, nowhere to run, waiting. Whir-r-r-l-l-lll- now!—body flung sideways—dull awareness of a great blow on the back of the forearm, eyes scanning fast for followers—number TWO spins by to the left—duck the helmet against the ice to take the shards as the wave of pain crashes into the consciousness, buckling the knees and tearing a long deep groan out through the teeth…. A couple of minutes pass, hunched on the slope. Breath rasps in and out, in and out. Raise the head—slowly straighten up—not broken— flex it—aaaahhh! Easy…this still has to work…still gotta get down. Voices! The others appear, angling in through the seracs. A few words, then down again, slowly, tentatively, in pain but in control. Find a way across the 'schrund and plug across to the rocks in the col, weary from aching and tension and adrenalin let down. Peter brews while Greg and I drift in and out, recuperating. An hour passes…two….

Mid-afternoon, time to go. The dullness of the sky was as strong a spur to action as the tower above us was a lure. We belayed the first pitch past an old fixed pin, then a second up and right through corners and ramps and walls with ice smeared everywhere but always with enough rock exposed for uncomplicated climbing. Peter ran out the third rope length up steep slabs and through a clean-cut chimney on the arête while I brought

Greg up. One final rope length to the exact summit and, twenty-one years after Dick and Glenn, we had the second ascent of the hardest peak in the Coast Mountains in the bag!

Their summit note, written late in the day as an impending storm broke, ends, "Now how the hell do we get down from here?" We were wondering a bit of the same sort of thing, as the eastern walls of Serra V drop vertiginously into the IV/V col. We scrambled down to the north-east and found a good block, then Peter set out into the unknown. He rapped into a little notch, scrambled out its far side, clipped a directional anchor into the ropes, and continued down the arête on the outside of the pinnacle which was formed by the rotten gullies that met at the notch. Nearly at full ropes, he found a fine incut ledge which was easily made quite comfy by tipping out a couple of big blocks. Anchors were hard to come by, but eventually a couple of pegs and a nut or so got placed and he disappeared downward again. A disturbingly long time later we heard his shout and slid down to the next stance, a horrible affair of loose blocks and plaques of mudstone vaguely attached to the cliff. While the story didn't come out until later, he looked pretty pale—his troubles with finding anchors had been preceded by having a flake snap off beneath his feet, penduluming him into a corner and momentarily causing him to lose control of the rap. We were all hurting.

While the anchor blocks seemed passably well wedged Peter said that everything had been expanding when he had tried a pin placement, and we were seriously worried that the wall below was so steep that the ropes would not touch back in. In that case, all Peter could do would be to prussik back up and we would tie both ropes together and abandon what we had to in order to get down. He disappeared over the lip below and we waited quietly. Cold winds gusted out of a steely sky. A hammer rang, echoing off the walls, then long silence descended again. Finally the ropes slacked and a shout drifted up from below. My turn.

I clipped in and started towards the lip a few meters below. As I poised at the edge, worried about knocking loose fragments down onto Pete, Greg stepped down onto the blocks which I had just vacated to ready himself to follow me. There was a grating as the two big blocks lying under the ropes directly above me started to slide out from underneath his foot—my heart froze, the world stopped—the blocks wedged against each other and held—Greg oozed back onto a higher ledge—I gingerly tensioned the ropes off the blocks and moved to the side. We had a problem! The blocks would have to go, but where was Pete? Would they miss him? I started to climb back up to the anchor but within only a couple of moves I pulled another big block out of the wall above me and only just managed to hold it teetering in place while I stemmed hard to keep myself on the rock. This was beginning to seem a bit serious! Still, there was not much debate about the options. Greg tossed me the end of a prussik to clip myself off with and I worked the rap rig off the ropes. We shouted the tale down to Peter and had him tie himself off to the ropes and clip back to just one carabiner attaching him to his stance so that he could pendulum out of the way as a last resort. Meanwhile Greg tied off both strands in case one got cut. Then, with hearts pounding, we tipped off the blocks, giving them as much of a shove out and left as we could in the hope of avoiding Pete. They hurtled down into the col below, exploding off our wall to smash themselves against the slope opposite. Peter remained safe on his ledge, his guts curdled by the sound of these passing monsters. We joined him, feet barely skimming the wall, then one more rappel took us to terra firma where we jabbered, jittered, and ate convulsively, the ancient animal in each of us unquenchable in hunger for life. It was quite some time before we calmed ourselves enough to notice, metaphysics imitating reality, that the evening sky was clear, limpid, and blue.

The final day of the trip was definitely an anti-climax after this paroxysm of danger. We had burned up some of our nervous energy by constructing a huge tent platform against the base of Serra IV, and consequently we slept long and soundly, secure, safe, out of reach of the wind and cold that haunted the col that night. In the morning we quickly hopped up onto the fine blade of Serra IV's summit and then traversed the ridge to Serra III. Our spectacular rappel off the summit took us to the easiest ground we had seen in some time, but one more rappel further down was necessary before we reached the II/III col. At last we could leave our packs behind and the climb up the lovely walls and arête to the summit slabs was real pleasure. We regained the col then two long raps deposited us into the soft snow of the Tellot Glacier and to all intents and purposes the traverse (THE Traverse!) was over!

One little detail remained. Peter (by rock) and I (by ice) nipped up the north side of Serra I to ice the cake while Greg waited below. Perhaps he was pondering my earlier jesting question to him, "So, how do you like alpinism so far?" Judging from the smiles which lit our way down through the slope to the hut, I reckon we all had much the same answer. ❧

ARCTIC LOBSTERS

In spite of its soft and comforting name, the Penny Highlands is actually one of the harshest and most austere ranges of mountains in the world. Huge spires and cathedrals of golden granite rise out of endless sheets of ice in an arc that starts at the Arctic Circle and sweeps northwest for a thousand kilometers along the coast of Baffin Island. It is immense, empty, and stunningly beautiful.

One of the early visitors to this range was Doug Scott, an Englishman who has since become legendary for his exploits in the Himalayas, but who at that time was more of an alpine rock climber and big-wall specialist. His pictures of the area set me on fire, and for the next several years my life revolved around my need to see those mountains with my own eyes, to feel that granite under my own fingers.

My wife shared my crazy dream and in 1979, having decided that the only trouble the two of us were likely to have was in finding an alpine wall big enough to satisfy us, we headed north.

The reality, of course, is that it is easier to be a big-time climbing hero on the cliffs near Vancouver than in the mountains of the Canadian Arctic. It is seriously cold up there in early May, and the mountains are enormous; so we spent four weeks ski touring, exploring, climbing a few easy peaks, and making plans to come back some time in the future, with extra courage and ability.

Two years later, in late April 1981, we were back. Instead of extra courage and ability we brought along Ryan Shellborn, and with his help we managed to leave tracks on a lot of glaciers that hadn't had tracks left on them before, and even put up a new route on a big mountain.

We did nothing very grand in the way of technical mountaineering, but particularly on the first part of the trip—the traverse Ryan and I made from Coronation Fjord to Summit Lake—we were walking an alpine highwire without any kind of safety net. We took the absolute minimum amount of food and equipment and highballed the route in five days. Several years later when a party with considerable Antarctic experience did a similar traverse—gaining the icecap from the next fjord northward, which added about 40 kilometers to the route—it took them 37 days.

In retrospect what we did can be seen clearly in its historical context. We were part of a general movement away from large-scale expeditions, toward a fast and light approach to the mountains—an approach where safety lies in speed and flexibility, rather than in extra supplies and back-ups for everything.

But at the time I didn't think of what we were doing in any context other than that of need. I *needed* to go there, so I went. And every night, as I sat in my tent, wrapped in my sleeping bag, I wrote about what had happened to me that day.

~ David Harris

Arctic Lobsters

David Harris

21 April: "Here we go, round again." The Second Red Lobster Mountaineering Club Expedition to the Cumberland Highlands has somehow managed to survive four days of partying in Montreal and Frobisher Bay, and Ryan and I are now securely bivouacked in the Parks Canada garage/warehouse in Pangnirtung.

Pangnirtung is the usual blend of seal carcasses, twenty-four-hour-a-day skidoo races, and friendly people. We spent our time today running around doing all the things that have to be done when someone says "You're leaving tomorrow morning" and you thought you weren't going to leave for three days.

But we're packed and I'm happy. I'm full of curried chicken and I've just come back from a too-good-to-be-true call from Vancouver. Corina's voice was fractured and delayed as it rebounded from the satellite, but the message was clear. The doctors have given her a clean bill of health and she can come after all. We agreed to meet at Summit Lake in about a week, and I returned to our warehouse bivi whistling.

22 April: Today Ryan and I were rodeo cowboys. We straddled the loads lashed on the komituks and the skidoos blasted off over the rough sea ice at about mach 2. The komituks bucked crazily and I was glad we had had a day off from the partying. About noon we reached the falls at Windy Lake and spent a few sweaty hours getting the loaded komituks (they weigh about two hundred and fifty kilos each) up and over. The falls are still frozen but the weather is unusually warm and no one seems sure when they will melt out. Two days from now we probably wouldn't have made it through.

23 April: Being a cowboy for an hour yesterday was kind of fun. Today we did it for about eight hours and it was no fun at all.

We reached Summit Lake fairly quickly and left a big cache of food and equipment at the warden's hut and then carried on north. As soon as we entered Owl valley the snow changed and our broncos started bucking again. Early afternoon saw us on North Pangnirtung Fiord and the ride got even lumpier.

When we finally turned west up Coronation Fiord our punishment took on a new twist. Between the ice and snow was a layer of slush, and every so often the skidoos would break through and slap our faces with a great rooster-tail of freezing, salty mush. Finally the skidoos could penetrate this bog no further so we said goodbye to Pat and Peter and skied off up the fiord into the murky twilight, mostly staying on top of the snow, but occasionally sinking almost to our knees in the underlying slush, and trying not to think about how thick the ice could be if everything on top of it had turned to porridge.

We made about four kilometers and are now camped on the solidest-looking snow we could find, eating another big meal of curried chicken and thinking peaceful thoughts about the pleasant days of skiing that wait for us in the coming month.

24 April: We are camped a few kilometers up the Coronation Glacier after a day of terror and exhaustion.

We slept in a bit this morning, to recover from the two days of komituk riding, so it was not until 11 a.m. that we started skiing. The Coronation Glacier flows right into the fiord and presents a solid wall of ice hundreds of meters high and over a thousand meters across and we had decided that the best way up onto it would be at its extreme left margin. With about a hundred meters to go to the end of the fiord I saw two sets of fresh bear tracks going up the moraine to our left. We dropped our packs and I skied out from the shoreline to see if I could see where the tracks went. I looked up, but instead of tracks disappearing into the distance, I saw a little white cub staring down at me from only thirty meters above.

Fear blanketed my mind. We grabbed our packs and began skiing away along the wall of ice toward the middle of the fiord.

Twenty meters and look back. The cub was still there. Another twenty. Now his mother was beside him.

"Oh Christ, no!"

Twenty more and they were still watching. We were getting closer to the most broken area of the glacier—the only place that wasn't a wall of vertical blue ice rising straight up out of the fiord—but the mother was starting to descend toward us. She was huge.

"No, no, no, no."

We could only ski in slow motion, sinking to our knees in a porridge of snow and slush, mired by our heavy packs, and by the time we had made another twenty meters and she was down to the fiord.

I knew that within the next thirty seconds a polar bear was going to kill us. She had been denned up all winter and must be ravenous. I hoped that there would not be too much pain, and reflected that in my dying I would become part of the food chain. This thought was strangely comforting and my fear was no longer such a terrible thing.

Salvation appeared in the form of the cross-section of a crevasse that provided an entry into the icefall. Ten meters of bottomless slush and then we were clambering over the first ice blocks. Off came the skis and we began a tottering dance through blocks of ice with just a thin covering of snow.

We were stumbling and falling, slipping down between little blocks and sliding off large ones, making virtually no progress. We needed crampons and ice tools and all we had was cross-country shoes and ski poles—and each other. Ryan held me when I slipped, and I helped him when he needed a boost, and soon the cubes that we were grovelling over hid us from her view.

During the next hour the crescendo of fear gradually diminished. Only to swell again as we realized that we were trapped in a glacial maze. At first it didn't seem too bad. We were skiing the bottoms of crevasses not more than twenty meters deep and rarely less than two meters wide and we were both still so strung out, expecting the bear to round a corner behind us, that neither of us considered the impossibility of a huge icefall composed of shallow little crevasses with nifty ski trails at the bottom. Then I punched a ski pole through the floor and was looking straight down into the dark blue forever.

Our brains started working again and we realized that crevasses do not have wide level floors, and that perhaps we ought to put on the rope. Then we realized that since we were already in a crevasse, a rope wasn't likely to help much if the floor gave way.

We spent many terrified hours wandering around in an icy labyrinth, expecting the bottom to drop out at every step, but eventually found a ramp that led to the surface and a safe route out of the icefall.

25 April: Last night I had the shakes so bad that I couldn't finish writing, and I'm still not completely over yesterday's terror. *Ursus maritimus* is the complete predator, has no natural enemy, and is afraid of nothing. I have no idea why we weren't killed then and was never sure we wouldn't be killed today. Or whether we will be killed tonight. We saw tracks several times today and since early afternoon were traveling in a whiteout. We would have to have been within fifteen meters of a bear before seeing it.

At least we've got enough Valium to get us through the night.

*26 April: I feel safe fo*r the first time in three days. There might have been a bear around last night's camp, but there won't be any here. We have reached the point where the Coronation Glacier flows down from the Penny Icecap—about forty kilometers from the ocean and well out of bear territory.

The whiteout continued through the day, allowing only occasional glimpses of huge walls looming out of the mist and we took turns telling one another how outrageous the view would have been if only there had a view.

Skiing by compass is the shits, but we didn't really have any choice—I pulled the wrong fuel can off the komituk and we've only enough gas to last a couple more days.

27 April: We woke to a cold blue morning and our first view of the valley in which we had spent the last three days. It is a narrow canyon stretching almost forty kilometers to the fiord-head, with clean granite towers and walls rising over a thousand meters straight up out of the ice on both sides.

We plodded steadily uphill with the Coronation walls slowly shrinking behind until we were in a vast sea of rolling white hills and skiing by compass again even though the sky was blue and visibility unlimited.

At one point we could see a huge rock wall a few kilometers to the west but when we tried to locate it on the map, we couldn't. The maps of this area aren't great but we didn't believe a feature that big could be missing. Were we completely lost? A careful recheck of map and compass reassured us that we were still on course. So where was this mountain? There wasn't anything but ice on the map for way over ten kilometers.

My sense of the scale of the place readjusted with an almost physical lurch and everything clicked into position. The peak we were looking at was on the map alright, but all I could think was "If it looks this big from twelve kilometers, what must it be like to stand beneath it?"

Eventually there was no more uphill and we were looking across at the north-west flank of the Tête Blanche group, a massive and complex array of faces, walls, and ridges through which there was no obvious passage. We turned left and skied another two hundred meters up onto a knoll which turned out to be the eastern summit of the entire icecap and which gave us the view we needed.

In addition to the Tête Blanche massif we could now see the mountains on the east side of both the Weasel and Owl Valleys, a whole range of unnamed peaks to the north, and dozens of peaks to the west of Mt. Asgard. Some view. Eventually we sorted out our exact position and began looking for a way down to the Highway Glacier.

It was a twelve-hundred-meter descent and from a skier's point of view the choice of routes varied from stupendous to orgasmic. We chose the southernmost route and managed to get most of the way down unroped. There were occasional crevasses and one small icefall higher up, but always a way around. A few hundred meters from the bottom though we were confronted by a band of crevasses that seemed to go all the way across. Our decision to rope up was made as, side by side, we slowly sank into a loosely-filled hole.

We made camp on the Highway Glacier and are now sitting in our tent, secure in the knowledge that we can get to our cache tomorrow in any weather.

During supper we tried to catalog the climbing potential of the areas we'd skied through in the last few days, but that potential is too vast and we were too tired. It's time for some sleep.

28 April: We had planned to make a short trip up the Highway Glacier to have a look at the northernmost route down from the Penny Icecap (which we hadn't been able to see from above) but a combination of whiteout, sloth, and my desire to see Corina again, soon had us heading down-glacier.

It was an ugly journey. The Highway Glacier was four-and-a-half kilometers of trap crust, Glacier Lake was a horizontal mogul field, and Summit Lake an increasingly icy skidoo track. The wind reached gale force, and the light was so flat that the limit of visual discernment was about two meters.

And when we finally reached the hut, the fucking lock was frozen shut and we couldn't get in. After a lot of cursing and door kicking we finally roasted the lock with the MSR stove and got the key turned before it froze again.

Chocolate cookies. No wind. Fifteen-centimeter foam mattress. And Ryan had the courtesy to move out to the emergency shelter when Corina arrived late in the afternoon.

29 April to 6 May: Low-key, adrenaline-free touring. We explored a new ski route to the west of Summit Lake and added several hundred more entries to our catalog of "climbs waiting to be done". As far as I know we are the first people to visit this area and that added a certain effervescence to our days.

This traverse was on the same scale as the one Ryan and I did last week, just as remote, just as beautiful, but without death breathing down our necks it seemed more like a holiday than an adventure.

7 to 9 May: We skied through some of the area to the east of Pangnirtung Pass and further thickened our catalog.

12 and 13 May: After a couple of days of R & R at Summit Lake, Ryan and I set out to climb Mt. Bredablik. We finished the climb on a buttress above the precipitous south-west face with four pitches of technical climbing on rock to 5.7 and ice to 75°.

14 to 17 May: We took our time on the walk-out to the fiord-head. Most of the snow has gone from the lower Weasel valley and the first buds are appearing.

I wish I could stay up here forever.🏵

XIV RUCKSACK

Here are all those selections we found indispensable, but which did not comfortably fit in any other category.

〜 Bruce Fairley

The Millionaire Guide

Conrad Kain

"The Millionaire Guide" is Conrad Kain's best-remembered story, told by him in the Altai, in New Zealand, and at many Canadian campfires. It is pure invention, Kain never having ascended the Gross Glockner. Professor R.M. Algie, of Auckland, N.Z., supplies this narrative which Conrad wrote for The Press (Christchurch) in 1915. A dialect version was published later by P.A.W. Wallace in his book, The Twist and Other Stories (1928).

$\sim$ *J. Monroe Thorington*

Having been a guide for a couple of years, and having travelled in different countries, and meeting many different people, I always wished that the time would come when I could "play" the gentleman myself; meaning by this, when I could hire a guide and act like "an elephant in the heights." I say "elephant" because, really, some of the tourists are as helpless on the mountain side as an elephant would be on the back-stairs.

The year 1907 had been my best climbing season, and I had made plenty of money, and so could afford to play the tourist myself. I was on my way home from the Alps when this longing for adventure came upon me again. The weather had been grand, and the mountains looked very inviting.

In Innsbruck, the capital of Tyrol, I had some time to wait for the next train. While walking around the streets and looking in the shop windows, I took a great fancy to a fine Norfolk suit displayed in one of them. I may say that it was the first decent suit I had had, and therefore I felt very happy, if not proud, in it.

Seeing myself in this new suit, I thought here was my chance to travel as a tourist, and I at once made up my mind that I would climb Gross Glockner, which is one of the highest mountains in Tyrol, but by no means the most difficult. It is, however, a good climb for a gentleman whose feet are all thumbs.

I started immediately to make plans for the trip. I thought, first, I must forget that I am a mountain guide, and secondly, I must forget the climbing of the Matterhorn, Monte Rosa, Mont Blanc, Meije, Les Ecrins, Grepon, and many other well-known mountains in the Alps. It is very difficult for a man who has been born, brought up, and made his living by mountain climbing, to forget it all, but the spirit of adventure made this possible.

I had to change my program a great deal on account of being unable to get a new pair of boots, as my old ones were almost worn out, and told tales of mountain climbing.

At Zell am See I left the train, thinking of, and planning, my trip. I wandered up to the high village called Heiligenblut which is the starting point for the mountain on its easiest side. I stayed at one of the best hotels, and asked the hotel-keeper if he knew a guide named Schultz, and where I could find him. This hotel-keeper was a most obliging fellow, and sent for the guide at once. This guide was a member of a well-known and highly-spoken-of guide family, and I found his name registered in different huts and hotels in the Alps, but I had never met him personally. However, I was sure that he knew my name. After a short time a really fine specimen of a man stood before me, he was finely built, and his well-cared-for beard gave him the finishing touch necessary for a typical mountain guide. He made a respectful bow, as is the custom, and I laughed to myself when I thought of what he would say if he knew that I was a guide like himself. I asked him if his name was Schultz, and he said, "Yes, that's me." I then asked him if he could take me up Gross Glockner, as if so, I would like to make the trip in as comfortable a manner as possible, and I told him that this would be my first mountain-climbing expedition. When I had finished with this, he said, "I am at your service, Sir."

I then asked as to the difficulties of the climb, and if there was any danger; also as to how steep the climb was, and then the weather question! This is the most difficult question to answer. Many tourists have an idea that a guide knows, or ought to know, all about the weather, and one is often forced to tell untruths in order to satisfy them. He listened to all my many questions with what I call a guide's patience, until I asked him about the hand-holds on the south wall over which people talk so much. I wanted to know how many hand-holds there were and the distance between them. That was more than any guide could stand, and he said in a loud sharp voice, that if there were none he would make some. He also said, "You will be quite safe, I will look after you. Don't be afraid, you can do it all right; an old lady sixty-seven years of age went up the other day and had no trouble whatever."

I said, "Oh I am not afraid with you, but I hope you will be very careful." I then explained that I had climbed quite a number of rock peaks, but had never been on a glacier or ice mountain, and that I was always a little worried when I thought of how my poor old mother would miss me if anything happened to me. My voice got quite weak with the desire to laugh, and I was very glad when the guide said, "Good night, Sir."

The first act was now over, and I considered myself quite an actor. I celebrated with a few good long glasses of lager beer, and while enjoying this I had the pleasure of spinning some yarns to my neighbor at the table and the waitress. After a few glasses of beer and this boasting, I really quite forgot that I was a simple guide. During the night I completed my plans about the climb; I was really afraid I should not be able to keep from giving myself away on my holiday. After much thinking I got confidence in myself, and in the morning I could face the guide, the mountain, and the wide world without any fear.

My guide was waiting for me, and I asked him to have breakfast with me. I ordered the best things I could think of, in order to make a good impression on him. I told him he could take as much wine and provisions with him as he wished, and he said it was not necessary, which showed me that he was an honest fellow.

The trail from Heiligenblut to the hut was a really good one, and as we got well on our way and out of sight of the village we began to talk about different things. I told him that I wished to go very slowly in order to enjoy the view. I knew quite well that he would not believe this, as this excuse is used by many tourists when it is necessary for them to rest, and when they are short-winded. Talking and at the same time going up hill do not agree with the lungs very well, so, as I wanted to ask many questions as to the life and living of a mountain guide, I used this excuse in order to get an opportunity to do so.

I can only give here a very small part of our conversation. I commenced by saying, "You people in the mountains certainly have a wonderful and a free life, but I suppose there are drawbacks to it as there are to everything else. However, nobody can take away the fresh air from you, and that gives you health and a good appetite." At times, I would take a deep breath as though I was storing up the fresh air in my lungs for the days in the city when I was working, and where the air often feels so thick.

"What do you do in the winter?"

"Work in the woods at all kinds of work, if I can get anything to do," he replied.

"I suppose you make so much money in the summer that you can live in the winter even if you have nothing to do?"

He answered by saying, "There is a great difference in seasons, but in spite of it I did very well, and I did not come across a cross or unkind lady or gentleman the whole time. They were all most generous and kind." I stopped him here and said, "Do you mean that some of them are unkind? I do not understand this, as very often the life of a tourist depends on his guide," and he answered, "Yes, Sir, you would not believe the selfish people we meet with even among holiday-makers."

I am sorry to have to say that my guide spoke the truth in this regard. I could remember many men, and rich ones, too, who had made bargains with me, and tried to get my services below the tariff prices set by the Government, and had been very pleased with themselves when they had been able to do so. I did not continue asking him questions as to this, as I knew so well the characters a guide met with among the mountain climbers. My guide then told me that, generally speaking, one could make a living as a guide, but not a fortune, as even if there was a good summer, the winter was always long, and generally in the spring he was "broke," which comforted me, as it showed me that I was not the only guide in this condition in the spring.

I tried to get him to tell me some of his experiences with tourists, but with a smile on his face, he said: "I don't think it is wise to talk about the tourists," and I thought he was a very wise man, as telling tales as a guide is a dangerous game. Still I kept on asking him, and said I was sure he must have some very good tales to tell. However, I could not get him to tell me any of his yarns so I asked him many questions, which he did his very best to answer, and thus I was able to get a great deal of information.

Just then a couple of women passed us, and I asked him what he thought of them as mountain climbers. "Well," he said, "sometimes it is surprising what some of them can stand, and I have seen some who are tougher than the average man." I then asked him whether he would sooner go on a climb with women or men, and he said he really preferred men. I then interrupted him, and said, "I don't believe that," and pointed out to him that it was only natural that ladies from the city should take a fancy to the guides, as they are so fresh looking compared to the city men, and also so natural. I then added that they did not have polished manners. We mountain guides very often have to listen to this sort of nonsense, and must not kick when the tourist "pulls our legs." There is a great pleasure in "pulling someone's leg," and as this was my only day as a tourist I wanted to have that pleasure. This conversation gave me no difficulties whatever, as I was just repeating to the guide what I had heard from many tourists myself, when on climbs of this kind.

"I am a married man, Sir, and that is the end of it," he said.

"What difference does that make?"

"It makes all the difference in the world, as when you are acting as guide to a lady the first question she always asks is: 'Are you a married man?' and if so 'How many children have you, and do you love your wife?'"

I then said to him: "Do you think it is always necessary to tell the truth?"

"Yes, it is better; with a lie one does not get very far." This saying he then illustrated with the following story:

"Not so many years ago one of the guides from —— found out how far one could go with a lie. He had a very charming young lady to guide. I did not see her myself, but was told she was a lady no one could help liking, and, of course, she asked the guide the same old question, 'Are you married?' The guide was, but he said, 'Nein, Fraulein' ('No, Miss'). After a few days' climbing the young lady took a fancy to her guide. I might say here that the fellow was a very handsome-looking man, and besides this, he was quite a humorist, and one could not blame the girl for falling in love with him. They got on very well together until the fifth day, when they met a party on a summit, and one of the members of the party, knowing this guide well, asked him how his wife was getting on. Of course, you can understand how both the guide and the young lady felt."

"Well, that was bad luck," I said, but the guide did not agree with me as to this. He thought it might have been much worse, as the young lady might have reported him, and he would have then lost his guide's license, at least for a considerable time.

We took many rests on the way, and in one of these the guide looked at my rather worn-out boots and made the remark, "It seems your boots have seen their best days, Sir." Whenever he said "Sir" to me an indescribable feeling came over me. I wished to speak a little more about climbing to him, so said, "You have done quite a bit of climbing in the Alps?" "Yes, Sir, I have." He told me about great climbs on the Matterhorn and many other mountains around Zermatt. "I suppose you know also the Chamonix district (Mont Blanc range)?" "Oh, yes, I do; I have tramped quite a few times up that snow hill." He had the same opinion about Mont Blanc as many other guides, including myself, that it is a very tiring snow tramp.

"How do you like the Dolomites?"

"I am sorry I never had the chance to visit them," he said.

It was now time for me to tell some tales about climbing in the Dolomites, and about the gambling one does with one's neck when doing this. I think I "put it on pretty thick" like the man lecturing, and ended by pointing to my boots and saying, "This shows the effect of climbing in the Dolomites, the country of sharp stones."

"Did you climb without a guide?" he asked me.

"No, never without; I believe it is not wise to go without one, and risk your neck on climbs of that sort. I made all my climbs there with Conrad Kain. Do you know that fellow?"

"Oh, yes, I know him; that is, I have heard a great deal about him. He is one of those cold-blooded lads. Personally I have never met him. He has been travelling. Last year he was down in Corsica with a gentleman I used to travel with frequently. A friend of mine met him this summer in Kaisergebirge with a lunatic."

I laughed and said, "I'm glad you did not say in the Dolomites, because I was there and I would not like anyone to take me for a lunatic." We spoke a long time about the climbs and guides there. Fortunately he spoke very well of me, Conrad Kain. He made a remark about the Dolomite guides, which is rather common amongst climbers, "those fellows must be like monkeys." The conversation about guides and monkeys if continued would have caused me to laugh, so I spoke again about the beauties of Nature and the fresh air. Speaking about these I forgot that I was a tourist and not a guide, and spoke in my dialect so fluently that the guide asked me where I came from.

"You are from Vienna, are you not? What is your business, if I may ask, Sir?" I stopped and looked him in the face without a smile, and said in a low voice, "My dear friend, I excuse you, but at the same time must give you warning to remember never to ask your men about their business. A man from the city comes to the mountains to get the good air to freshen up his tired brain, to get new life and strength for the rest of the year and when he is on his holiday he tries to forget his daily life at home. He does not like to remember it. He wants to enjoy the golden freedom which he has only when he is in the mountains for a holiday."

My guide looked rather ashamed when I had said this, and answered, "Yes, it might be so, Sir; I beg your pardon"; but I reassured him by saying, "Oh, never mind, don't worry. I don't mind your asking. I can tell you what I am and from where I came. I am an officer of the Post Office in a country town in Lower Austria. I have been born and brought up in the country."

"I thought so, because you speak almost the same dialect as I do," he said.

A short distance from the hut we met a party, and my guide stopped to talk with the guide with them. I went on slowly, and later was glad that I had done so. I was almost past the hut when someone called out from a window, "Conrad, what are you doing here?"

I rather feared the game was up, but I was a little ahead of my guide, and I looked around and recognized a gentleman with his wife, for whom I used to be a guide around my home. Quick as an avalanche I threw him a sign with my finger, like you throw a kiss to a lady, but to a gentleman it means "shut your mouth." Then as I came close and we shook hands, I said:

"Don't call me by name. I am travelling as a tourist like you are."

He looked queer and said, "What is the matter? Are you travelling as a tourist with a guide?"

I answered, "That is just what I am doing; for two days I am a gentleman, don't spoil the fun."

He turned away to hide a laugh.

After supper in the hut I went to the guides' room, where I talked to all the guides, and asked them how they were getting on, and how they liked being mountain guides. To get a little bit more fun in, I ordered a couple of bottles of wine for each table, and in a short time everyone in the guides' room was in good spirits, and we had a really good time until about two o'clock in the morning, when the guides raised their hats and thanked me for the wine, and very happy and satisfied I went to bed.

At six o'clock next morning the guide came to me. He made his usual bow and said good morning, and asked me how I felt.

"Oh, very well, thank you. How are you this morning? Have you a headache?"

"No, Sir, I never drink in the evening before I climb. I suppose you feel a little tired from sitting up so late."

"Oh, no, I am used to it, you know. I must often sit up very late in the Post Office."

I left it to him to take what provisions were necessary for the trip, and I told him that if he liked to take a little wine or whisky along it would be all right, but he would not consider taking any, so I had to take it myself. We started out from the hut with the other party I have already mentioned. They had made the climb a couple of days before, but they went up with us for the fun of seeing me act the greenhorn.

A short distance from the hut we came to the glacier which had to be crossed. Here I asked the guide very seriously if there was any great danger of dropping into the crevasse, and he told me not to be afraid, as he would look after me, but I must step nicely and as rapidly as possible. "Just put your feet down one after the other, and they will take you safely across the ice. Don't put your whole weight on, and take your foot up as quickly as possible, in order to avoid sliding, and, above all, don't think of slipping."

I said, "Well, that is easier said than done," and I tried my first step on the ice. I think I really acted the real greenhorn. My feet went in all directions and would not stay where I had put them. If I had a good place for one foot, and wanted to bring the other up to it, I pretended I could not find it. It was very hard work. After all it is not very easy to act as a greenhorn if you are not one, and I would hate to be a "gentleman" all the time. I acted as though I wished to sit down to be more safe, and once I really fell when I did not want to, and hit my head on the ice. I saw stars then, and decided my guardian angel had fallen in love with someone else. I looked so sad that the guide said:

"If you are afraid, you had better take the rope."

And I said, "Oh, thank you," and looked as though I was thinking of my poor old mother.

He gave me a rope and put it on me. I looked at the way he was making the knots, and said:

"What do you call these knots?"

He said, "Don't you like them?"

"Oh, yes," I said; "but I should be glad to be able to make them."

He then said, "I suppose the Dolomite guides make another kind of knot for rock climbing, but the one I make is all right for snow and ice."

I asked him if he would let me try to tie the knots, so he took my rope and gave it to me. I twisted it around and around and once more around, but could not make the knot. He was very patient, and again showed me how to make it; so I took the rope again and made a knot that looked like an octopus and a big snake having a fight. It was good enough to hold an elephant, but he said it was too big, and tried to teach me once more.

"You take the rope, so, and so and so!"

After that I took the rope, and tied the knot properly and the guide looked rather surprised, and said:

"You have tied this kind of knot before?"

I said: "Why, how can you ask, when I have never been on a glacier before. The only kind of knots I have ever made are those on the mail bags in the Post Office."

He was very much pleased when he heard this, and said: "Well you pick it up very quickly."

At this point the gentleman and his wife laughed out loud, and I gave them a sign to stay behind.

This mountain is climbed almost every day in the season, and there is a good trail, so that a man really has very little trouble but as I had never been on a glacier before, I had to see and learn as much as I could, and also I asked the guide where he had to cut steps. He told me it was not necessary to cut any, as there were old ones. However, I asked him if he would show me how to cut ice steps, anyway, which he did. Then I tried it myself, and handled the axe helplessly, and after I considered the steps were good enough, I told him to try them. He put his foot in and said: "That's no good. When you cut a step in the ice you must cut it so that it slopes towards the mountain, and then it must be far bigger than this."

So, I made a second attempt, and let him try again, and he said: "That's far better, but you have to cut the steps more on the slope on the high side, because when you go down the steps must be big enough to put your foot on comfortably. He then showed me how to use an ice-axe. "Don't keep your hands so stiff. Swing them as though you had nothing in them, and place your thumb on the handle, and then give it a twist with the other hand. Don't use all your strength, it is not necessary."

I then tried a third time, and the ice was so good that I forgot I was a "gentleman," and with a few blows I had the steps well made. He tried them, turned around, and looking sharply in my face said:

"Oh, Sir, you must be fooling me; you have been cutting steps long before this."

"Why," I answered, "I have never been on a glacier before. But I am very good with an axe, because as I told you before, I come from the country."

"Well," he said, "if that is so, you are one of the best pupils I have ever had, as you pick things up so quickly."

At this point the gentleman and his wife, who had been listening, coughed, and I turned around and waved my hand to them, in order to tell them not to give things away.

We then continued with the climb with many short rests, and much conversation about the beauties of Nature, until we reached the summit, where we shook hands. I thanked him for his good guiding and for the pleasure he had given me, and looked around at the many mountains, and pretended I had never seen such a sight before.

"The Post Office," I said, "is not like this. How I envy you, guide, with nothing to do in the summer but climb mountains and enjoy the beauties of Nature." I thought to myself that after this remark he would surely know I was a "gentleman," which was so, for he said:

"Yes, Sir, if one could have a kind and considerate gentleman like yourself to guide, the life would be the finest in the world."

Meanwhile, the gentleman and his wife could not help laughing, as I spoke to my guide in a loud voice, in order that they might hear me. The guide wondered what was the matter, but they only laughed the more and said: "Oh, there was too much pepper in our lunch."

To make a long story short, we got back to the hotel in Heiligenblut, and as I was in a hurry to catch the train, I settled with the guide right away. I gave him what he wished, and a little more, because he had given me a good time, and had believed I was a gentleman. He then gave me his book, and I wrote the very best recommendation I could think of, and signed my name, "Conrad Kain, Naswald." Now a guide never looks in his book before a gentleman, so he put the book away and said he hoped I would not forget him when I wanted a guide for longer trips and we shook hands. I was very glad he had not found out who I was.

I then said to myself that the whole holiday was over, and that I must pack up my things and leave before he looks in his book and finds out who I am, but I was not quick enough, for in a few minutes he came back quietly, and said:

"You have fooled me. Why did you fool me?"

All the people looked at us, and wondered what was the matter, so I said:

"What is wrong? Did I not pay you your fee, and write a good recommendation in your book? What makes you think I am guying you?"

The hotel-keeper then came out to try and quiet the guide, but he said:

"Du Himmel Sacrament, you fool me. You asked me if I knew Conrad Kain, and I told you lots about him, that he is a lunatic and monkey, and can stretch himself. And here you are yourself."

I really felt very badly to think that it had all come out this way, as all the ladies and gentlemen at the hotel had been talking of my big climb, and I had felt very proud of it, and now they all knew I was but a guide myself.

The gentleman and his wife I have mentioned before began to laugh, and told the whole story of how I pretended to be a greenhorn and a gentleman, and hired a guide in order to take the trip. It was impossible for me to leave at once, because they all wanted me to stay and have a good time, and all the guides crowded around and said:

"What a man. When he is a mountain guide, he hires a guide to climb that easy mountain. He must be a millionaire."

I stayed there that night, and told the guides many stories of my climbs in Dauphine and Corsica. I really did boast a little that evening, like a real Dolomite guide. The guides could not forget the joke, and laughed about it a lot, and I often heard them say "The Millionaire Guide."

Next morning I went off in great style, with much waving of handkerchiefs, and everyone wished me the best of luck:

"Auf Wiedersehen, millionaire guide."

Quite contented, I went home and climbed the mountain to my home. I had never returned from a trip so happy, and I told my mother all about it, and said:

"Oh, mother, I am happy. I have had such a fine time."

She said: "Oh, I know the kind of time you mean; you will get into trouble if you are not careful."

"Don't worry, mother," I said. "There is nothing wrong. I only travelled as a tourist and hired a guide, and was a gentleman."

To my great surprise she did not see the joke, and was very angry, and said:

"Stupid, I always knew you were a fool, but I had no idea you were such a big one!" &

The Old Camp of 1911 Revisited in 1940

A Survivor

Only a few things remain, the dining table and camp fire site, and a few odds and ends, if one looks very close. One could only tell where the large tent had stood, by the remains of a few tent pegs, and a pile of mineral specimens, collected and left there by the late Billy Gray.

The dining table was a heavy affair, like everything else in that age, but it was strong and durable. For some forgotten reason the head of the table had to point northward. This Druidical masterpiece had not fared well, the elements having brought about its downfall. Perhaps the savage rites performed upon it had something to do with it.

Close to the table were the charred remains of the camp fire. Around this faithful servant and companion, the camp life was centered. If it could only record its impressions of camp life, and especially of aspiring cooks, it would indeed have a tale to unfold, which would be interesting, and I am afraid somewhat embarrassing, as more than once it had been invested with human attributes, especially when the cooking was below standard, which, alas, was more often than not.

The camp was pitched as close as possible to Garibaldi, the distance being in an airline not much over a mile. The party in camp consisted of thirteen climbers, a good half of the club membership at that time, and nearly all of its active members. Only three are now with the club, four are dead, and the remaining six are scattered all over the world. We were all novices in the art of mountaineering. What we lacked in climbing ability, we made up with determination and hard work, and all were set to explore the district and climb its major peaks.

The two weeks camp cost $130.00, including pack-horses, boat fare, and some camp equipment. This sum was paid by those attending camp, which means it cost each member $10.00. The pack horses brought the supplies from Brackendale, to about the 4000 ft contour, or edge of Round Mountain meadows, they were then back-packed to camp about two miles.

The food was rough, consisting mostly of flour, beans, bacon, oatmeal, rice and cheese. The luxuries were tea, coffee, sugar, jam and dried fruits. Two half-pint bottles of Bovril were reserved for emergency. Everybody took turns at cooking. Mixing and baking the bannocks in a reflector pan was trusted to only one or two artists at this craft.

There was only one tent and fly in camp, which had to accommodate everybody, and everything. Sleeping bags were only just coming into use, there being but a single homemade one in camp. The climbing equipment consisted of three or four ice-axes, two ordinary ropes, and a variety of homemade alpenstocks. Only a few members had real climbing boots with edge nails.

Out of the twelve days, six were spent away from base camp, on two three-day trips, to Mamquam and Castle Towers, the latter being its first recorded ascent. Only two of the thirteen in the party were Canadian born, the remainder being from the Old Country, mostly England. In the camp sports English Football (Soccer) was played at every opportunity. The football field was so hilly, that the two goalkeepers could not see each other. In many ways the camp was a great improvement of the first club camp (1910) held on the same ridge, but at the other end, which of course gave us the advantage of shorter distances to our objectives, which was most noticeable in our climbing and exploration trips.

Leadership of camp naturally fell on the shoulders of a native son of Vancouver, a cigar maker named Billy Gray, who was about twenty years old. Billy was a natural born leader, showed excellent judgment in climbing, camping, and exploration problems. He possessed a well-balanced mind, full of native intelligence. He was keenly interested in geology, and had he lived, that would have been his life's work. He was drowned a few years later, whilst on a geological survey.

These brief and sketchy notes will give some idea of the B.C. Mountaineering Club's evolution, which more or less coincides with the progress of mountaineering.

—One of the three survivors. ❧

Air-Drop

Roland Burton

For a trip into the bush of two or three days duration it is no hardship to carry your own food, as well as the usual equipment. For longer trips, or trips involving many people, it may be cheaper to fly in ordinary food instead of carrying in expensive freeze-dried food. The flight over the area permits a preview of the route, which may be handy for navigation later.

Helicopters are very nice, but at present they cost $155/hour for a machine with a six-hundred-pound payload, and you pay flying time from wherever they are stationed, which may not be near where you want to go. Besides, what are the four of you going to do with six hundred pounds of food, anyway? So we usually use airdrops.

To organize an airdrop, you proceed as follows. First find somebody with a private pilot's license and a mountain endorsement; offer to rent the plane for him. Next, get the expedition crew together and spend several hours packaging the stuff to be dropped. Some advice on this is included below. Finally, get as many maps of the area as you can find, and look for suitable drop sites.

The choice of a drop site is governed by two considerations. You would like the packages to land gently, and you want to find them later, on foot. If the pilot is good, he will fly fairly close to the ground over the drop site. This is not so the packages will land gently, because they are travelling at least at the plane's speed, but so they will not be spread out over too large an area. With practice, a dozen or so parcels can be dropped in a five hundred foot diameter circle. There shouldn't be any trees around to catch the wings of the plane. A wide snowy pass above timberline or a glacier free of crevasses seem to be the ideal sites. A frozen lake is alright if it's frozen hard enough. Snow is the softest thing we have found to drop things on.

We don't use parachutes because they cost money, and because you have to fly high up to give them time to open, and consequently where they land can not be accurately predicted. Also, the possibility of a makeshift parachute wrapping itself around some important part of the little plane seems to discourage most pilots.

There are two disasters which may befall your airdrop after you have dropped it. It may be buried by a fresh snowfall, or it may be eaten by the local inhabitants of the area (chipmunks, wolverines, etc.). Metal containers stop these snafflehounds; but all you can do about snowfall is use a drop site at a low elevation, remember exactly where the drop site is with respect to topography, get to the drop site as soon as you can, and don't go anywhere when it's likely to snow. We are experimenting with dropping bamboo wands with weights on one end, so they will land upright and mark the drop site.

About packaging: Remember that the package will be travelling at speeds between 90 and 125 miles per hour when it hits the ground, and this is faster even than the average automobile accident. About the easiest thing to drop is bread (not sliced) because it is nearly impossible to destroy. Similarly, oatmeal, raisins, tang, Jello, packaged soups, cheese, sausage, fruitcake, and hard candies are hard to destroy if they are put in small plastic bags. Bottled goods, such as instant coffee, do not survive, and broken glass contaminates everything else, like shrapnel. (Put instant coffee in plastic bags, or even better, take tea bags.) We dropped some stoned wheat thins on the Squamish-Cheakamus this spring and although they landed on the only rock in the drop area, for some reason they were totally undamaged. This fall, on our Naden Pass-Cheakamus Valley caper, we again dropped SWT's, and although their box was undamaged, every single cracker was broken into myriad tiny pieces, the largest being about a quarter inch square. Conclusions???? Tin cans may be dropped if they are packaged very well. Jam tins should have their lids soldered or epoxied on, then wrapped with wire. Small tins survive better than large ones. When a package containing tins lands, the tins try to keep going. If you provide some crushable material around them, they will happily burrow into it. If this is newspaper, O.K., but if it's instant potatoes, oatmeal, tang, nuts, or raisins, you will have an interesting stew.

Dropping white gas for cooking provides an interesting problem. In dropping standard five gallon drums, we found the drum stops but the gas keeps right on going, through the bottom of the drum. The smaller quart tins, wrapped in newspaper in heavy cardboard boxes, survive a little better, with about half being recovered intact. The best solution is to drop the quart cans packed tightly inside Styrofoam acid boxes, obtainable from the local Chemistry Department. On impact, the tins burrow through the Styrofoam and emerge intact.

It takes no effort at all to drop a hundred pounds of goodies, but if four of you have to recover all of this, that's 25 pounds each, which is no fun to carry. You might have to camp at the drop site for a couple of days and eat your way through the food. The ideal aircraft for small drops seems to be the Cessna 172 with jump door, which opens upward out of the way. If you can't get an aircraft with such a door, a regular door will do, but as it is not designed to be opened in the air, you have to push on it very hard indeed, and it opens only abut six or eight inches. At any rate, make sure you can get your packages through the door of the plane, even when the wind's blowing 90 mph. outside the door.

And finally, some assorted Pearls of Wisdom:

- Don't count on recovering every package, i.e., don't put all the meat in one package.
- Expect the white gas containers to burst; don't put food with the gas.
- Some time during the spring, with six inches of soft now, around two in the afternoon, conditions are ideal, and we once dropped twelve cans of beverage protected only by their flimsy cardboard carton, recovering all of them.
- If you drop a climbing rope, mind it doesn't get caught on the landing wheels.
- Please clean up your drop site. Burn cardboard, paper, etc.
- If your honey and your comet cleanser get mixed, don't despair; spread the mess on the skis of somebody you don't like. 🙠

Logan Bread

Bill Lipsett

And now for something completely different. Here is a recipe for a tasty bread that has been extensively field tested on many trips and always found to be in great demand.

1 cup water
4 cups whole wheat flour
¾ cup brown sugar
3 tbsp. milk powder
1½ tsp. baking powder
½ tsp. salt
½ cup liquid honey
¼ cup molasses
¼ cup and a bit oil
⅜ cup wheat germ
¼ cup sesame seeds (optional, or add your own ingredients)

1 Mix dry ingredients in a large bowl
2 Add wet ingredients and mix together well
  NOTE: mixture should be moist but not too runny. If it is too dry add a bit of milk.
3 Pour into buttered 8 inch loaf pan
4 Bake approximately 1 hour at 350° F [One of our proofreaders suggests that in his experience, 1½ hours gives better results.]
5 Use toothpick test to see if it's done. Stick the toothpick in and if it comes out clean the bread is done.
6 Air dry overnight. ❧

Of Rurps and Nursery Rhymes

Matt Scott

One night, while sipping draft in a west-coast tavern, an acquaintance of that evening said to me: "Ever used a rurp?" I shook my head. "Never needed to." He snorted. "You call yourself a climber?" I was annoyed. "I am a climber. I climb. But I have never used a rurp."

My acquaintance of the evening, who obviously used them every weekend, ignored me. I felt he would like to be able to kick footholds in solid rock.

I should explain, before going on, about rurps. The initials stand for "realized ultimate reality piton." As the words suggest they are only used on severe climbs. They are designed for direct aid, not for safety belays.

The reason I had never used one of these matchbook-sized pieces of hardware is simple. I am not normally a wall climber. I hate the tangled jingle of artificial climbing; remembering which rope has who or what on it.

I felt unfairly penalized for a preference for free climbing.

I peered into the soul of the man across the table. Egocentric. What climber isn't? Unsure? Ahhhh, here we have it. Good old one-upmanship. That's it.

I thought back to an earlier time, in Halifax. A railway cut surrounds the south end of the city. Cliffs ranging from ten to forty feet grace the excavation, and although I have a horror of dynamited rock, this stuff was extremely sound. On Saturday afternoons I taught the basics of rock technique to a few young men. One of them got into difficulty half way up a simple pitch. A few of the onlookers made jibes and admonished him to get up or else. The result was unfortunate. Before I could shut up the loud-mouths the poor fellow made a futile, desperate lunge for a hold he didn't understand. He peeled and felt the rope. He never climbed again.

Back in the tavern I relate then to now. I seldom climb walls and don't use rurps because I don't understand that aspect of mountaineering. The tussles between stamina and gravity are exciting, even beautiful. They are the climber's food. But to bolt and rurp one's way up two thousand feet of granite? Not for me. Rather the free-moving ascent of a complete mountain.

In my experience such an approach often raises eyebrows. It shouldn't. I have no doubt that wall climbers derive enormous pleasure and aesthetic satisfaction from their esoteric efforts. Theirs is a great feat. Yet the John Muirs of the world should not be relegated a lesser position. They are simply different. Some of us are tigers of the rocks and some of us are just men of the mountains.

I turned back to my acquaintance of the evening. "Can you recite the complete Mother Goose backwards?"

He stared at me for a moment, incredulous. "No."

I smiled. Obviously he had never spent six days stuck in a high altitude tent. 🙢

The Great Siwash Fiasco, January, 1968

John Rance

Part I

A Sunday afternoon scramble on Siwash Rock in Stanley Park provided several voc'ers[1] with a close-up of Vancouver's finest in action. Five climbers, John Rance, Gary Gustafson, Mike Miles, Ralph Sayles, and Chris McNeill were perched upon the top of the rock when a police cruiser arrived on the scene. We were climbing in direct defiance of a sign prohibiting such things but past experiences of previous climbers told us that we had little to worry about.

The police, who must be running out of real criminals, disregarded precedent and decided that the only way that five experienced climbers with rope, slings and carabiners could get off the rock was with the aid of a very large fire truck, an inhalator, a police cruiser, ten firemen and two policemen. I had been watching a particularly beautiful sunset when the policeman's voice came booming up to destroy my reverie. "Don't move, we'll get a rig to get you down!" Wow! I thought as my mind blew apart and the ecstatic vision of God expressing himself in the sunset disappeared. After I had sufficiently recovered my senses, I thought that the best thing to do would be to communicate intelligently with the officer. "We're good climbers," I began, "we have ropes; we know what we are doing." The officer refused to listen and after a few minutes of noncommunication I decided to rappel down. "Don't move, that is an order!" warned the officer.

While awaiting developments we discussed possible means of escape, such as rappelling off the back and swimming away. However, after deciding that the water might be too cold, we resigned ourselves to our fate and sat down and discussed the non-function of bureaucracy.

Soon the conversation changed to more real things like whether a huge ladder truck could possibly get down to the rock. We all decided it was probably impossible but we were soon proved wrong when the biggest thing the Vancouver Fire Department owns appeared on the seawall. The drivers are pretty good but we cannot say much for their hoist operators. They had difficulty lining up the ladder and finally needed our directions to get it in place. After the ladder was in place we started down but this was not what the firemen had in mind and so we were told to get back to the top. Up came a fireman. I told him that I refused to suffer the further indignity of being carried down the ladder on his back. The fireman, being a reasonable man, agreed that this was unnecessary and we descended under our own power.

1. Varsity Outdoor Club, of the University of British Columbia.

Now came the little name and number exchange with the nice policemen. Discussion was impossible. To my claim that we were perfectly capable of getting down by ourselves came the classic reply, "Tell it to the magistrate." At the same time Ralph was discussing with the other officer just how good we were, how the sign was hard to see and poorly placed and how Dick Culbert's guidebook said that it was okay to climb the rock. Gary, meanwhile, was congratulating the firemen on the fine piece of driving while Mike was trying to discover the name of the informer. Well, that about ended it. The next chapter will be written in court, after we receive our summons.

Part II

"Yes, they were voc'ers," read the blackboard in the clubroom. The moment I entered I knew our disgrace had been well advertised. Radio, television and newspapers carried the police version of the story. "Five youths rescued from Siwash Rock" and "Fire Department saves stranded climbers" were typical headlines that accompanied our story. Surprisingly, *The Sun* reported the correct facts. It erred only in affiliating us with the "Open Air Club," a ruse which was originated by Mike Miles.

Part III

"Unlawfully did you use land in Stanley Park where signs have been posted forbidding such use," read the court clerk. The off-duty police in the front row seemed amused. The judge, confused, asked the prosecutor if there was any information supplied by the police officer who was at the scene.

"Yes there is, Your Honour."

"Read it," commanded the judge. The information, detailing all possible data including the height above water at which Chris McNeill was first spotted (ten feet) and the fact that a diver once dove from the rock and was killed, was read.

Gary Gustafson was called to the front of the court. The judge was interested in climbing and questioned Gary about outdoor activity in general. Gary pleaded guilty as charged and the judge gave him a suspended sentence. Things were going to be all right and we sighed in relief.

Mike Miles was the second to the front. The judge, now in fine form, asked more questions about climbing. The police were enjoying the judge's off-hand jokes immensely. Mike pleaded guilty as charged. "Young man, you are in this court because you have broken the law." The smiles and chuckles ceased and everyone listened intently as the judge proceeded. "The law says

you may not climb in Stanley Park so you ought to know better than to diso-
bey the law. If you were hanging around pool halls and smoking cigarettes
like you should have been you would not be in this trouble now."

The police, the prosecutor, the gallery and the accused all erupted in
laughter.

Mike was given a suspended sentence as were the other accused climbers. In this manner the story that began a month before amid frustration
and anger on the slimy pinnacle of Siwash Rock ended amid gales of laughter in a crowded court room. &

Sometimes You Know—Sometimes You Don't

Jim Sinclair

I knew it was the crux. It had taken two days to get here, in some ways much longer. I was sixty feet out from Chris, between us was a tied-off knife blade, a small part of it into the incipient crack. The rest of its length protruded out and down, but it would have to do. It was like walking down Granville Street with every neon sign selling the same message…"It won't hold a fall."

I tried to calculate it. I'd drop twenty-five feet if the pin held, and I could extract myself easily enough. But if it didn't, I'd go one hundred and twenty feet, probably hit the ledge thirty feet below Chris and at best be seriously hurt.

Perhaps fifteen minutes had gone by and I hadn't moved; nineteen years of rock climbing was working in my head—I just didn't know if I could get over this last bit or not. There was no bolt kit, no crack—not even a cliff hanger helped. It was free it or go down. Going down was tricky but no major problem. But could we go up?

There seemed to be a microflake at knee level on the steel wall. Was that another six ft above it? Eyes inches from the rock, the hand caresses over it. Yes! A ripple perhaps a thirty-second of an inch…but a ripple! Somewhere in the deepest being the pros and cons of justification are being weighed. "You've stood on as small things before," the pros say. "I know, I know," you tell your other self. "But this could lead nowhere. I wasn't facing death then, or maybe I was. I don't know. But that was then, this is now. World do I love life! Why do I come up here anyway? There stupid, up there, above the right hand." The demon pros never let go. The judgement must be exact, precise, infinite. I stood on tip-toe feeling very secure on the half-inch ledge I was standing on. Strange, when I'd first reached it I was apprehensive about stepping onto it. Now, twenty minutes later, it felt like a ballroom floor. I was safe, if only I didn't try to use the microflake.

Yes! Yes! It was there—a little finger hold. I wouldn't quite reach it from the ledge but it was there, inches above my reach. The years of climbing, worn out kletterschuhe, discarded ropes and the voice of judgement convinced me it was there. But I couldn't quite reach it.

This was no boulder problem, no jump off and try again game. It was the ability to move up and judgement of whether you can or not. You get one chance in the game. You judge right the first time or you don't play again. The left foot went to the microflake and immediately skidded off. "How you doing up there man?" Chris secure on his ledge, two comfortable pitons for a station and basking sunshine. "It's HAIRY buddy, I just don't know about this." No answer, then—"How's that pin?" "The shits," I call down…no answer.

Again, for reasons unknown, the left foot creeps toward the microflake. Slowly ease my weight to it and even get a few pounds off the right foot before retreating back to the ballroom floor. It had held! Incredulously my left foot had held!

I lit a smoke, trying to get the green taste out of my mouth and waiting for it to happen. What a beautiful thing a horrible thing like a cigarette was at a time like this. Far down in the valley a crow glided. Below him little toy cars weaved their way through the forest following a white line that never ended. The cigarette finished, with no conviction to do or die, but rather attracted as to a magnet, I again brushed off the little hold. The left foot went up, weight eased over just right, right hand reaching for the sky. I touched it, tips of fingers deep into its ripples. The right foot is 10 inches from the ballroom floor…fifteen inches! Don't come off now left foot. Please don't come off now. The neon signs are exploding in the head and you know, absolutely, that the piton will not hold a fall. You're committed, it's only fifteen inches to the ballroom floor but there is no getting back.

To the onlooker you are suspended there, climbing to nothing, defying gravity to the extreme. Perhaps a suicidal maniac with a death wish, at best a misled youth surely to die. The tricouni set would call you an engineer, safe on your ladder of pitons and hardly climbing at all. You reach a state of near total fusion with what you're doing. Every fiber of the body is instinctively controlled to place the fingers a few inches higher to the hold that must be there. To breed your left foot with the microflake, to seduce it and so to be a part of it. No longer is anything done consciously. The years of training have taken over. The instincts are in control of your body, mind, nerves and soul. They creep your fingers upward even as you know you're moving off, you're on the brink. There is no time but the minute part of the second difference in which is first, the left foot coming off or the fingers touching the ripple above. There is no distance but the fifteen inches back to the ballroom floor. There is no problem in life greater than the placing of a finger an inch higher. Then it's there, the left hand goes out, a good hold, mantle up…it's over.

We were on easy terrain, moving fast to the top and I wondered. What if we'd climbed to the crux and retreated off? Did we climb to the crux or were we leading up to the climb? Did we do a two day route? A two-hundred-foot wall? Or did we do a one hour climb, fifteen inches high? &

THE PITON

The descent of the south face of Mt. Sir Sandford following our winter ascent in early March of 1989 was probably the most intense four to five hours of my mountaineering life. The south face was virtually unknown ground and I was with two friends, Jeff Dolinsky and Marvin Lloyd, with whom I had never climbed before and neither of whom had ever driven a piton. Both proved to be very steady mountain companions, but we had little gear, the weather turned for the worse, and once we were in the gully we had chosen to descend, great rivers of spindrift snow would cascade down, burying us up to our knees. The snow was light enough that it did not even knock us off our feet, but we retreated in fear that a huge build-up of snow higher on the face would avalanche into the gully and obliterate us. To this day I can remember each piton placement, each rappel station, vividly. But one moment in that descent stands out for me above all others.

∼ Bruce Fairley

The Piton

Bruce Fairley

Apprehensively I belay Jeff Dolinsky down the steps to where Marvin Lloyd is crouched 50 metres below. Jeff's voice carries a note of despair as he shouts up to me, "This is a terrible place, Bruce; we're just sitting on a pile of snow. There's no protection; no cracks. I'm going to try a bit further toward the gully." I watch as my two friends move off to the right, casting about for some island of security in this ocean of white. Jeff shouts up again, "This isn't much better, but I'll sink my axes in and you can come down to me, Bruce. The slab is real thin and you'll probably slide down for a bit. Sorry about that."

I start down, keenly aware that there is no protection in place between me and Jeff's belay. And a couple of ice axes buried in spindrift is really no belay at all. The condition of the snow is terrible. I back down a steep slab covered by the thinnest layer of loose powder. Suddenly I know the snow will not hold. "I'm going to come off here!" In an instant the snow evaporates beneath my feet. I plunge six metres down the steep slab, startled, amazed at the cold rock flying by, landing unhurt but shaking and buried in a pocket of spindrift.

The fall crystallizes my thoughts. That morning as the sun rose we had set off boldly up a direct line to the summit on Sir Sandford's great south face. Initially the snow was good for step kicking, but a few hundred metres up the climb we hit slabs devoid of protection cracks and thinly covered with loose snow. These we climbed like marionettes, gingerly picking our way up, wondering if the snow would give way at any moment and send us on a whirlwind ride to the bottom. It is the thought of those slabs that haunts me as I regain my feet and consider the huge expanse of face we must yet descend. A fall there might be impossible to stop in this treacherous snow. It is a risk we must not take.

We strike off across the face, traversing towards the great gully that gashes through the west edge of the wall. There we will hopefully find the cracks and blocks for the rappel stations we will need to get down the face safely.

At a point where the rock beneath me steepens, I stop and sweep the snow with my mitt. The gully is below us; two rappels should take us in. As I brush the powder from the rock a beautiful pin crack emerges, grinning from beneath.

I have four pitons on the rack. Those four pitons, a few ice screws, some slings, and the skill acquired from many bad days spent on rock and snow must now get us down 800 metres of unknown ground. It will soon be dark; grim phantoms of cloud are scudding across the sky. They mean us no good—we will be lucky to get off this face without a storm. Taking a standard angle from the tiny rack, I reach for my pin hammer, slot the piton, and give it a tap.

There is a special sound that a well-driven piton makes. As the first blows of the hammer strike, only a dull thud results, but as the piton bites into the rock the clanging rises in frequency, becoming a musical "ping." Only one who has climbed and been in a desperate, tottering spot can know the exultation that comes with the rising sound that tells a climber, "The piton is good." And this piton was good. Never have I heard such a clean, confident ring as the ring of that piton high on the south face of Sir Sandford as darkness dropped down and the wind rose.

* * * * *

As I finish driving the piton and sling it for rappel, I know that we are going to be all right. The anxiety throbbing in my brain begins to abate. There is still tension and worry there, but it is good tension, and good worry. We still have 800 metres of face to descend and almost no gear. Every rappel will need to be selected with utmost care. We will have to carefully nurse our tiny stock of pins and screws and like misers hoard at least one pin until the last possible occasion; hoping that enough weaknesses will appear on the walls of the gully to make the descent go; hoping that when the rack is finally exhausted the chasm will not plunge into a sudden precipice. It will be tense and it will call for careful, meticulous discipline. But the piton has sung; there is rock on this face that will take a good pin after all.

As I rappel off down through the swirling snow to the next station, a huge block that can be easily slung, it comes to me suddenly, like a vision, that this darkness, this storm, this terrible uncertainty of outcome is going to be fun. 🌣

XV CANADIANS ABROAD

Canadians arrived on the international climbing scene late in the game and have been hurrying to catch up ever since. The Canadian Everest Expedition of 1982 was the splashiest attempt at asserting an international climbing presence; the Everest team might be forgiven if they appeared at times to be carrying the burden of establishing Canadian legitimacy in the great ranges of the world. The tone of much of the Everest publicity was: "We really can climb with the best of them."

Infrequent visits to the Himalayas by Canadians had been made long before 1982. E.O. Wheeler discovered the Rongbuk Glacier, Earl Denman made a credible attempt to solo Mt. Everest in the 1940s, and Dave Jones was recognized internationally, if not at home, in the late 1970s. But, for the most part, Canadians tended to make their mark in Peru, which was a great deal closer, and cheaper to reach, than Nepal. The first comprehensive guide to the Cordillera Blanca and Rosko (the most popular ranges in the Peruvian Andes), for example, was produced by a Canadian, John Ricker. Leif Patterson, who could be considered at least partly Canadian, visited Peru numerous times in the 1960's and was one of the outstanding figures in climbing new routes there. And Vancouver Island climber Joe Bajan stormed a number of impressive Peruvian walls in the 1970s.

In the more recent past, a group of Canadians based in the Calgary/ Canmore area has come to prominence for their record of hard alpine-style climbs. Barry Blanchard, Kevin Doyle and Ward Robinson are recongnized world-wide for applying the alpine skills they honed in the Rockies to some of the biggest faces of the Himalayas.

In the world of big-wall climbing, Canadians have been at the fore-front since the late 1960s, when a group of typically rowdy and disreputable climbers, mainly from the Vancouver area, made first, second or fastest ascents of many of the hardest big walls in the Yosemite Valley; and lately Peter Croft has been a world leader in both hard free-soloing and in the speed climbing of big walls.

$\sim$ Bruce Fairley

HUASCARAN

The article that follows describes the first ascent of an elegant rib on the highest peak of the Cordillera Blanca, Huascaran. The account is unusual in that it was not written by one of the summit party. It is, however, a highly readable tale and typical of the sort of casual mountaineering which many Canadians enjoyed abroad, without fanfare, before nationalism hit North American climbing circles in a big way.

Canadians take their cue from the British when it comes to mountain writing. Understatement is preferred to heroics. This account takes a familiar line—a group of bewildered amateurs suddenly find themselves, despite all their happy bungling, face to face with a foreign culture and with all the bureaucratic rigour and tangle necessary to transport themselves and their equipment to the scene of a great adventure. The tone recalls the dry humour of the British travel writers Evelyn Waugh and Eric Newby; the unflapable sahibs are always able to muddle through, even if it does take a bit of good luck (not to mention rum).

Paddy Sherman has already been mentioned in the introduction to the article on the first ascent of Mt. Logan. As the author of *Cloudwalkers,* he was at one time Canada's best known mountain writer, but he was also one of a small group of Vancouver climbers who consistently demonstrated an interest in international expeditionary mountaineering throughout the late 1950s and the 1960s.

In this article Sherman's friends are portrayed as a fun-loving and well-balanced set of chaps, just as interested in having a good time as in making it to the summit. Many readers will likely find their own happier climbing experiences reflected here. Those going to Peru today, however, will find some things quite changed; Huaraz is no longer the charming town it once was, for it was never properly rebuilt after the great earthquake of 1970. And a recent expedition to this part of the world endured the horrific experience of violent interrogation by guerillas of the "Shining Path" movement and were subsequently caught in a cross-fire between guerillas and police!

But the combined joys of fine weather, exhilarating challenge and the glory of the high and majestic Cordillera are great magnets, and they will no doubt continue to draw many climbers to this unique region of the world's mountain landscapes.

~ Bruce Fairley

Huascaran—The First Ascent of the Western Spur

Paddy Sherman

It would be tempting to tell in dramatic style of the vast amounts of planning and determination that went into our party's new route up Mt. Huascaran, at 22,300 feet the highest point of the Peruvian Andes. But it would also be a pack of lies, even when retrospect has properly steepened the slopes and sharpened the difficulties. For in truth the whole affair was so cavalier and casual that we were embarrassed even to mutter that overworked word "expedition."

The paternity of our venture is still a trifle dubious, with several putative parents. But my recollection is that it began after a drink—as so often happens—following the 1967 Yukon Alpine Centennial Expedition. It was idly mentioned that the following year I would be forty and thus ready for a long run downhill. Foolishly I said that I should therefore start as high as possible in order to ensure a long runout. Five minutes later we were soliciting friends for a trip to Peru. We didn't really fancy the time and money involved in the Himalayas; and Peru seemed as remote; for practical purposes as high—yet we could be in Lima overnight from Vancouver. And Huascaran—well, we knew less about it than we knew about Everest, and the object of the exercise was to avoid finding out much more until we reached there.

We got some thirty-year-old maps, thought of calling it all off when we read in National Geographic that an avalanche from our peak had killed five thousand people in a few moments of 1962, and held even greater doubts of our wisdom when we read a booklet prepared by a Seattle party that climbed the peak in 1964. What organization! What effort! It was positively frightening.

However, by resolutely avoiding training together, by rigidly refraining from buying standard 'expedition equipment' or doing much research, we gradually regained the appropriate disorganized attitude. We reached a pinnacle of sorts when we arrived at Vancouver airport to find that the plane was delayed four hours and nobody had told us. A mild complaint to the airline brought on vicious retribution. We were ushered into the VIP waiting room and given so many free drinks that some of us were still splendidly disorganized when we landed in Lima on May 31, 1969.

Membership in the party had fluctuated in the year before we set out, but the seven who finally took part were: Fips Broda, Ralph Hutchinson, Skip Merler, Bob Paul, Bernie Segger, Dave Wessell and myself. Our ages ranged from thirty-five to forty-nine, and the only real question on our minds was whether or not a group of Elderly Gentlemen could find true happiness in the wilds of the Peruvian Andes. The answer was so thoroughly affirmative that some of us are going back again in 1971.

That weekend we found Australian climbers who had been waiting three weeks to get their gear out of customs, and others from France who had been there even longer. But since we were disorganized and had taken everything with us rather than ship it, we got our stuff out Monday morning. On Tuesday, June 3 we headed out in a small rented Mercedes bus for the four hundred kilometer drive to Huaraz, in the Santa Valley beneath the Cordillera Blanca.

The road was a masterpiece—first 190 kilometers of blacktop through coastal desert, then 210 kilometers of dirt through lunar landscape to Conococha Pass, which is above 13,000 feet. Our driver, accustomed to Lima's sea-level, had trouble urging his German beast up the passes. We spent a lot of time walking, between 10,000 and 11,000 feet. As Dave said, it was the first time he had seen a Mercedes with its Benz down. His puns declined as we ascended. So did our driver. As we stopped at Conococha, he passed out. His wife, who had taken the spare seat for the great adventure, took one look at him and dutifully did the same. Since Fips knew the language and could instruct a faulty Mercedes properly, he took over and charged headlong down into the Santa Valley, just as the equatorial sun went out at six as if switched off.

Our disorganized luck served us well in the dark and we landed at the Monterey Hotel, a hot-spring resort with two swimming pools, splendid food and unbelievably low prices. Since it was the middle of winter and the elevation was over 9,000 the place was empty, and there was nobody to watch us training on beer and sunbathing on the terrace.

Huaraz is a delightful town, and we bought everything we needed to complete our supplies before setting out June 5 in a Land Rover and Jeep driven by Herr Klimm, the hotel manager, and a friend. The Seattle party had made elaborate plans to hire mules for the trip from the village of Musho (10,000 feet) to base camp at 14,000 feet. When we reached Musho we hadn't even decided whether we'd take mules or carry everything up in two trips. But weakness triumphed over virtue when we found that Pablo Beltran and his son (age eight) would provide five burros at a reasonable rate. Away we went, starting in the midday equatorial sun with packs on our backs, heading up four thousand feet that we didn't know were waterless.

Disorganized was the word for this episode. We carried no drinks and lost most of our throat linings before staggering into the campsite where our gear had been dumped. Fifteen minutes later the sun was switched off. It was dangerous staggering around the campsite in the dark, because numerous cows had spent a lot of time here browsing among the tree-sized lupins.

Next morning was June 6—D-Day, and we all felt rather like survivors of the first assault as we staggered out of bed and compared headaches. Fortunately they faded as we ambled leisurely up the very steep trail leading to the edge of the glacier at 15,000 feet. We cached some gear, and decided to put Camp One here next day. As we moved up next morning, impressed by the beautiful peaks of Huandoy just to the north, we alpinists were properly put in our place. As we rounded a corner at 14,800 feet, a cow stood admiring the view and quietly suckling a calf.

While the others went down for more supplies, Fips and I prospected through the gigantic crevasses until we found a good campsite at 16,250 feet. We levelled it, revelled in the views, and looked rather apprehensively and in vain for an obvious route to the saddle (Garganta) between the North Peak and the South Peak, which was our goal. All were in bed by 7 p.m., rather weary, and despite sleeping pills nobody slept well. It is rather difficult to know the validity of such impressions, however, when darkness lasts twelve hours and you are in the sack for most of it. Even if you get eight hours of sleep, the other four of thrashing convince you that you haven't slept a wink.

At 7 a.m. on June 8, five of us took thirty pound loads to Camp Two. Bob was feeling very unwell, and Ralph was having trouble where his toes had been before he lost them all on McKinley. Rain had frozen on the tents overnight, and the coolness made moving up quite pleasant. But when the sun hit us at 9 a.m. we promptly boiled and sped back down for a lazy day washing, curing headaches and eating. Next morning, more loads up to Camp Two, with Bob staying in bed until the second trip when he would take only his personal gear, thus giving him a better chance to acclimatize. But when I returned from the first trip, he seemed almost in a coma. He was unresponsive to questions, his pupils were pinpoints and his eyes out of focus. At once I set out to get him down to base, hoping that he would improve at lower levels. He didn't, and at first light June 10 I rushed back up for the oxygen cylinders and valve, which were split between the two higher camps.

Bernie met me halfway, and fortunately had a rope with him. Since Bob wasn't in any condition to climb down the small cliff above base camp, we'd slept on a ledge above it. Now Bernie and I could get him down after a couple of hours on oxygen which, to my dismay, improved Bob while he was taking it but produced no residual improvement the moment he stopped. Only his great and subconscious drive kept him going until we reached the valley where a construction crew provided a free jeep for the forty kilometer drive to Huaraz. At the good free hospital there, a doctor pumped him full of drugs and sent him to bed. A good friend at the hotel undertook to care for him until he recovered, so on June 12 I set off back up the peak.

The walk back to base was much easier this time, but made dismal by rather sodden thoughts that there was now no way I could get up the mountain. I could reach 16,250 on my own with little risk, but it was unlikely I'd find anybody near enough to join me. To my astonishment, Ralph and Dave were at base. Dave too had become ill, and Ralph escorted him down from Camp Two. Fortunately Dave was already mending and could be left at base. Suddenly the world seemed brighter when Ralph said quietly: "I'd like to go back up."

On Friday the Thirteenth the pair of us set out, slowly and comfortably. I counted twenty-five paces to the minute at 15,000 feet, and fifteen breaths. In training on the Grouse lift track I often take twenty to twenty-five breaths per minute. We spent a comfortable night at Camp Two, fascinated as always by the sunset, in which clouds changed shape and color so quickly that the whole thing might have been a display of time-lapse photography.

The temperature was twenty-four degrees at breakfast, and Ralph said he had never felt so good so high. We took heavy packs, but left the tent standing. If we found a tent at Camp Three (17,400 feet) we'd use it; otherwise we'd return for this one. Travel was perfect as we headed south, to the right of the huge icefall beneath Garganta. We had no intention of climbing it, but if we could climb steep slopes around a knoll to the right, then we could do a long high traverse left into Garganta, we thought. Just before noon we reached Three, and found the tent collapsed, without a centrepole. Since the nylon flysheet was also missing, the other three had obviously decided to bivouac from here on. Two axes, three bamboo wands and some knots I remembered from the navy twenty years before, and the tent was soon like home. If you like living in an oven.

Avalanches peeled from the ice-cliffs above, the biggest one passing within two hundred yards, but we were well protected. The temperature went way above one hundred in the shade of the tent and I felt a strange heady sensation. As I lay there, I decided to take the next horsewagon down to get a beer, and the notion seemed entirely rational. Instead, we packed our loads up next morning, which was anything but rational. It was just above zero with crisp snow as we began climbing. Soon we were in a gully right of the rock knoll. Higher, it was full of avalanche debris, including smashed bamboo wands left by the three ahead. But we were still in shade. Next, 150 feet of steep ice that took some hacking then a huge schrund with a small bridge. Once above this, our good luck with conditions ran out.

The snow became swimming stuff, unconsolidated, and I went in thigh-deep at every step. We swam slowly on. Then at 18,600 I saw some trampling of the snow at the edge of a big crevasse. Obviously Fips, Skip and Bernie had stopped there for lunch, which wasn't a bad idea, since we were four hours above Camp Three. But as I peeped over the edge, there was the McKinley fly pitched on the crevasse floor, with powder snow drifted heavily all around it—and no sign that anybody had been near for at least twenty-four hours. Now what? Suddenly the whole caper began to sound a little crazy and I began to curse myself for an idiot. Oh, the things that could have gone wrong...

We enlarged the snow-hole, brooding, and scanned the slopes above. Garganta seemed miles away in the soft snow, but the slopes directly above looked frighteningly steep. On the right, a triangular snowface soared for a thousand feet. On the left was a badly broken ice-fall with numerous ice-cliffs. Between them wandered the delicate line of the western Arête. Airy, not to say scary, before it fell back and led more gently in a direct line to the summit.

At 2.45 p.m., we spotted the three of them in the chaos of ice above. My heart sank because it looked so chaotic that they couldn't get out before dark. We shouted back and forth, and Fips came out to the head of an ice-cliff to ask the best way down. We told him, and he hammered in an aluminum stake for a rappel. Then I almost died of shock when a red figure came over the edge, hurtled headlong down the rope and lay still on the ice beneath. Move damn you. Don't lie there. If you're badly hurt, you'll be be-nighted. If...

Strangely, there was no shouting. Finally my telephoto showed three figures still on top of the cliff. The 'body' was a pack, and my relief was al-most hysterical.

They made it down a few minutes before dark, and as we lay in our bags with snow drifting around us, we heard of their astonishing feat. Like us, they'd decided Garganta was too far in those conditions, and when Bernie suggested a direct route up the unclimbed Arête, they all agreed. De-spite the fact that Fips had collapsed from the sun's heat on Friday after-noon, they had left at 6 a.m. Saturday with bivy gear and headed up the ridge to the right of the ice-fall. Fips led for 11 hours, including Grade Five ice-climbing with one 170-foot lead-out, and a ridge so narrow that often one foot was on each side. Skip took over the lead, and darkness caught them at 21,200 feet. It was still too steep for comfort, but they chopped out platforms. Bernie sat alone, the others using a plastic bivouac tube, and they settled down to some constructive shivering. The temperature was about ten below, with a brisk breeze.

Nobody tried to cook next morning, Sunday, June 15. They set out at 6 a.m., taking at first four breaths per step, and later five. The lead changed every 150 feet and at 9 a.m. they were on top, feeling good enough to eat a little, and for Fips to blow his harmonica.

Nobody proposed returning down the Arête. They retraced their steps to the bivouac, then headed right (north) and logged their way through the ice-cliffs, making long rappels. One of them Fips finished upside down. In another, Bernie's pack came off and capsized him. But at last they were back with us tired, but safe.

Obviously they had to go down next morning. Ralph and I didn't fancy the long slog into Garganta with only two of us. And the new route up the arête didn't sound the sort of thing to be repeated with nobody left on the mountain to help in case of trouble. So reluctantly we all headed down, and two days later were down in the valley, facing nothing more arduous than a round of parties laid on by friendly local people.

The only thing needed to perfect our trip was the sight of Bob in action when we flew over to inspect the lost city of Machu Picchu. The pointed peak of Huayna Picchu overlooks it, so naturally we had to climb it. Bob demonstrated his complete recovery by racing up so fast he had time for a sleep on top before we joined him. ❧

DHAULIGIRI IV

Most of the climbs described in this volume are about successes. This story is different; it is about a strong party which both failed to reach its summit and saw two of its members die. The story is of historic interest: Chic Scott was the first Canadian to participate in a modern Himalayan expedition that selected a serious technical route as its objective.

Much of the grim reality of Himalayan climbing comes across in this piece; weather, altitude and poor snow conditions can wreak a devastating toll on even the most highly motivated team. This particular article probably had a lot to do with educating Canadian climbers about the conditions they would encounter when they took up an interest in Himalayan climbing. The route the expedition chose was finally climbed by a Japanese team in the late 1970s.

Chic Scott has remained a familiar figure on the Canadian mountaineering scene, although his involvement with the Himalayas largely ended with this venture. Prior to leaving Canada for a number of years of successful guiding in Europe, he was best known for a number of long ski traverses in the interior ranges and Rocky Mountains, including a winter tour from Jasper to Lake Louise, and for a couple of important first winter ascents, including those of Mt. Hungabee and Mt. Assiniboine.

Most recently he has returned to guiding and thrown his flair for organization into the Canadian Himalayan Foundation, the Calgary Climbers Festival and a new journal of international mountain writing called *Alpinism*. And as his recent success on the huge 2,500-metre face of Mt. McArthur (in the St. Elias Mountains of the Yukon) shows, he is still climbing big routes.

~ Bruce Fairley

Dhauligiri IV, an Attempt from the South

Chic Scott

Dhauligiri IV (25,133 ft) is the fourth highest peak of the Dhauligiri Massif. Despite a number of attempts from both the south and north it was still unclimbed in the spring of 1973 when I was invited to join a strong British team attempting the mountain from the south. The northern approach is long, low angle and not particularly technical except for the final thousand feet along a thin, rocky ridge. It has been attempted once, in spring 1973, by an Austrian party. The southern approach, as well as being extremely long (ten to twelve miles ground distance), is technically very difficult. It involves a two-mile-long narrow ridge, requiring fixed rope throughout, and a five- or six-mile-wide glacial basin to the foot of the peak itself. The summit pyramid of five thousand feet presents a steep ice face and a very long, thin summit ridge. The southern route has a history of tragedy—five Austrians and one Sherpa disappearing mysteriously from a col at 22,500 ft in 1969 and four Japanese dying during expeditions of 1971 and 1972. Our attempt was sadly no exception.

On 19 November 1973, Alan Dewison, twenty-seven, was killed in a fall of fifteen hundred feet from a col on the south west ridge of Dhauligiri IV. Four days later Raju Pradhan, 'Little Kansa,' was buried in an avalanche several thousand feet above base camp. After forty days and nights of privation, exhausting work and constant danger it was virtually impossible to feel anything. All emotions drained, I simply felt ill and a little more numb. The black cloud hanging over the expedition from the beginning had burst and taken two of our finest and most innocent. Quiet, inoffensive Alan and laughing 'Little Kansa.' The question whether it was worth it, the loss and the sacrifice, no longer had any meaning. Everything had lost meaning.

From the beginning the expedition seemed 'an exercise in unreality.' Underestimating the magnitude of the undertaking it departed Britain leaving behind a massive debt and bringing barely sufficient resources to deal with essentials: Sherpa and porter wages, peak royalty, etc. Partially through lack of information our equipment and stores were only just adequate to conceive tackling a route such as the south side of Dhauligiri IV.

Misfortune in the form of an overdue ship followed by a dockworkers strike in Bombay, delayed most of our food and equipment until well into October (the Japanese reached the summit of Everest this year by mid-October). Alan Dewison and Scotsman Allen Fyffe festered five weeks in India, sifting through dust-covered offices, entertaining themselves watching the rats through their hotel window.

Living on rice, dahl soup and an occasional egg or chicken curry, four of us—Richard McHardy, Ian Rowe, Roger Brook and myself—went on ahead with two Sherpas and an absolute minimum of supplies (air freighted at the last minute from Britain or borrowed in Nepal) to try and get things underway. We slogged thirteen days in the monsoon rains under sixty pound packs through streams and rice paddies, up and down hills in the mud, contending with leeches for our blood, through jungles with never a view of the mountains behind the clouds, and finally to the base of the mountain in a drizzling rain.

Bypassing the site of the previous Japanese and Austrian base camps we located ourselves a thousand feet higher on a steeply sloping moraine between two 'slumbering' avalanche cones (one a thousand feet across). Above an eight-thousand-foot rock and ice face.

Then the deluge came! We had been told that the end of the monsoon was signalled by the snow level descending. That it did. Four days and nights it poured. The moraine was awash, streams six inches deep ran through our camp. The avalanche cones were alive—silent, wet masses, a hundred feet across, pouring down from thousands of feet above. We began to move camp across to a safe position a quarter mile away, ferrying loads across the gullies, balancing on blocks of snow and ice, climbing in and out of monstrous avalanche channels; one eye always uphill, watching for the white, churning cascade.

Fortune still frowned upon us. One of our members had suffered from epilepsy for several years. He had overcome this and maintained his high standard of climbing, doing such routes as The Pillar of Freney and El Capitan's Salathé Route. It was hoped that he would be able to cope with the rigours of an expedition as well but the turmoil of the walk in and of base camp began to show. During the storm and the havoc of shifting base camp Richard was discovered one morning in the throes of continual seizures. For a minimum of six hours (they may have started during the night) he suffered one every ten to fifteen minutes. After filling him with phenobarbital we took turns sitting with him in a swimming tent during our frantic work of carrying loads across 'between avalanches.' During this time a boulder 18 inches in diameter tumbled past our cook shelter crowded with people. Several days later the weather cleared and Richard recovered sufficiently to begin the long trek back to civilization. Ian Rowe accompanied him leaving only two of us, Roger and myself, to try to make some ground towards the elusive peak.

The following day (about 7 October) Roger, Sherpa Wongyll and I moved up to establish and occupy camp I (ca. 16,500 ft). Where a week previous there had been no snow there was now enough to dig a snow cave. The clouds rolled in and it began to snow again. For three days snow piled up and soon our tent, sagging on a broken ridge pole, was in a six foot hole. When the weather showed signs of worsening Roger quite intelligently decided to descend to base: Wongyll and I opted to stick it out another day. Late in the afternoon we peered from the tent. The clouds were clearing! The fifteen-thousand-foot face of Dhauligiri I appeared pink in the evening light through a white veil of mist. Wongyll and I danced and sang for joy. This was our first view of the mountains. In our perch high above a sea of clouds it all seemed more than worth while.

For three days the weather was superb. It seemed as though the fury of the monsoon was spent. In chest-deep snow, surrounded by a world of radiant peaks, we fixed the first four thousand feet of rope up the immense ridge towards the basin. Not to be forgotten, Nature once again showed who makes the rules in the Himalayas. It stormed—4 a.m. and a ghostly howling morning found us digging out the tent again. The snow turned to sleet and soaked us, digging furiously in our down gear. My respect for Wongyll (age twenty-one), already substantial, increased tremendously as he scorned our small shovel and bailed with his bare hands for an hour in our little white hell. Unable to clear the tent as rapidly as it was buried, we retreated. In zero visibility we felt our way along the ridge and wallowed down the four-thousand-foot avalanche slope to the relative comfort of our bamboo shelter and wood fire at base camp.

By this time our food and equipment had reached Pokhara. Attempting to recover from the delay, it and the remaining members were air lifted to base by helicopter. Weight limitations imposed by our pocketbook limited what could be transported. Amongst many other items, twenty-five of our fifty high-altitude food boxes were left behind—to our ultimate disadvantage.

Roger, Wongyll and I were once again established at camp I when the others began arriving. In slowly improving weather we continued up the ridge towards a large serac barrier and an ice plateau three thousand feet above. Despite friable rock the climbing was excellent: narrow snow arêtes, short steep rock steps and chimneys, traverses on steep snow and ice slopes—over a void of many thousands of feet into the dark and sombre jungle below. With clear weather, and support materializing from the rear, there seemed some point to our endeavours. Once again we felt there was a possibility of success.

As our fixed rope stretched further and further we established a temporary camp II on a small ledge beneath an overhang, on a vertical wall. The corner of the Whillans Box dangled in space and the view through the tunnel door seemed straight down seven thousand feet to base. One clipped one's jumar on the fixed rope from the tent door and one's first step was onto the caving ladder hanging against the wall. The elevation was about

18,500 ft. Four very exciting days were spent here (I took my first sleeping pills at this camp) until, after a total of eighty-five hundred feet of rope, we reached the plateau above the seracs and established a permanent camp II.

From the plateau the sunlit view stretched from the massive walls of Dhauligiri V and I across to the many summits of the Annapurna Massif. The final challenge of our ridge, a lovely thousand-foot ice peak, stood above camp. After several carries from below to stock the camp we continued upwards in the now very Himalayan atmosphere. Camp II was 19,500 ft and Roger and I, having acclimatized well, were feeling much the same as on any alpine ascent. The presence on the mountain of the rest of the team, the radios and the equipment provided the much needed security (as we were now edging towards 10,000 ft above the almost invisible dots which were base camp).

Beneath blue sky and frozen peaks raking the jet streams we cramponed our way upwards. After fixing another thirteen hundred feet of rope we front-pointed the last pitch, fifty degree hard snow with short vertical steps, into the wind and wisps of cloud onto the summit. The basin slowly appeared—far across on the other side the monolithic pyramid of Dhauligiri IV. We shook our heads as we studied the scene and realized the peak was a minimum of five to six miles away. To reach it involved angling twenty-five hundred feet down a steep snow slope and crossing the monstrous basin surrounded by more icefalls and hanging glaciers than I had ever seen in one place. It really looked like the end of the world. We became aware of the almost continuous roar of falling ice. Above towered a peak which would be a challenge to any climber in the Alps. The familiar afternoon storm clouds began to roll in as we began our descent. The joy of that day still shines through and remains a prized memory—perhaps my most enjoyable day on the mountain.

By this time Ian Rowe and Allen Fyffe pushing hard and suffering the effects of altitude, were catching up to relieve us. We spent several more days ferrying loads up from below and began carries over and into the basin while the Scotsmen acclimatized with us. Then we descended. It was storming, we had spent about twenty-five days above base and were more than ready for a rest. As well it was only fair to hand over the lead to someone else. All the other members except the doctor, who was acting as base camp manager, were now on the hill at camp I. Through storm and fresh snow we plowed our way down the fixed ropes, stopped for tea and a cigarette in the snow cave at I, then continued down to base. Smoking cigarettes (Gitanes!), drinking gallons of tea and listening to the exotic Eastern music on our radio, I spent several days simply staring into space. I had very nearly forgotten that there was a world beyond the snow and ice of the mountain.

After four or five days luxuriating we moved up the hill again. Alan Dewison and Tony Johnson had joined the Scotsmen out front. I chose to carry loads and bring up the rear while Roger continued up to provide some additional manpower. Over the radio I attempted to follow progress higher up. Camp III had been established at about 20,000 ft, just beyond the peak which Roger and I had climbed a week earlier. Wongyll and I made five carries over the next five days; then, under mammoth seventy pound loads, climbed up the ropes to camp II. Supplies running short, we began a series of carries next morning over to camp III, moving up ourselves in several days. Here we were joined by Allen Fyffe who, experiencing chest pains, had dropped back for a check with the doctor who had now moved up as well and was occupying camp II.

For some added security at camp III Wongyll and I carried into the basin and across the glacier to camp IV at about 18,000 ft. The following day Allen, Wongyll and I, joined by Geoff Tabbner, moved to IV with the final supplies. In the sunlight we laughed and joked as we soloed down the steep slope under heavy loads. Beneath it all there was some apprehension. Occasional cirrus and particularly some cotton batten cumulus, forming during the past few days at about 25,000 ft, indicated a possible change in the weather. It would be an epic retreat, perhaps impossible in a storm.

After a night at camp IV serenaded by collapsing seracs, Allen and I continued up, still under heavy loads. Wongyll Sherpa, a 'young tiger,' was visibly less than happy at being left behind. The route up was all new ground and since food was so low and time so short it had been minimally charted. Bamboo wands ended between III and IV, ropes had been fixed only where absolutely necessary.

From IV we continued across the glacier, through ice blocks and rubble from the seracs above to the base of a five-hundred-foot cliff. Once again on fixed rope and ladders we jumared up, impressed by some of the rock climbing which must have been involved. The cliff led into an icefall. In the early afternoon clouds and mist we groped our way upwards. Grotesque forms looming from the mist led us to a solitary fifty-foot ice 'needle' marking the start of a 'bowling alley'—a chasm of thousands of blocks of ice surrounded by tottering towers of ice cubes. Halfway up this creaking nightmare Allen hollered asking if we were on the right path. In the shining blue ice there were no marks so all I could reply was, "I don't know, but I'm not stopping." After belly-crawling across ice bridges and climbing a wall of moving blocks overhung by shattered seracs we arrived at the top of the icefall to be greeted by a thundering avalanche from another higher icefall. In the afternoon shade and cold, dreading the return trip, we threaded crevasses to camp V at about 20,000 ft. This was definitely becoming a bold route!

Roger and Ian were having a rest day. Realizing how extended and poorly equipped we were they had made an unbelievably bold attempt on the summit. Starting at 3 a.m. they had climbed up the five-thousand-foot, shining, blue ice face of the peak to over 22,500 ft then retreated feeling the route and the venture too dangerous. Further up the basin towards the col on the south west ridge, Tony and Allen pitched a temporary camp, hoping to carry it to the col the next day. Over the radio that evening our plan was made—all six would carry to the col in the morning, Ian, Roger, Alan Dewison and myself remaining there. Carrying one more camp higher up the ridge, Roger and Ian would make a summit bid with Alan and myself in support. In our sleeping bags that night Roger and I decided that all four of us might as well go for it, having one cramped night.

Thin sunlight, 7 a.m.—we began climbing up the glacier through some crevasses towards the fifteen-hundred-foot, forty-five to fifty degree wall below the col. Feeling strong, Ian and I were soon sitting at its base waiting for Roger and Allen who were feeling poorly. High above Alan and Tony soloed, heavily laden. The clouds boiled over the basin's surrounding walls, unusual for so early in the day. The other two arrived, we reassessed our situation. Reluctantly we agreed we were dangerously extended in view of the changing weather. We could not risk being trapped in the basin with barely two days food and a monstrous route to retreat across and down. Clouds filled the basin as we made our way back to camp V. It was 19 November—the weather had held for over a month. Back in the tents we radioed Alan and Tony who had now reached the col. They agreed with our decision. After dumping their loads they would begin making their way down.

A few minutes later I looked from the tent. There was only one figure near the top of the slope. I looked again fifteen minutes later—still just one dot, much lower, climbing fast. I knew what had happened. The face was steep, all were very tired and undernourished, the day getting late and cold and ropes were being ignored in favour of speed.

Several hours later Tony rushed into camp, gasping out the sickening news. Alan had fallen near the top of the face for some never-to-be-known reason. When Tony reached him he was dead: multiple fractures, abrasions. Tony spent thirty minutes searching for hopeful signs but there was no pulse, no breath and a pair of glasses pressed to his mouth remained clear. In our semi-paralysis we tried to conceive of anything we could do. It was suggested we climb back up to Alan in hope for the impossible but sobering we realized it was nearing 5 p.m. Return meant three to four hours across the glacier and a night out in -20° F at 21,000 ft. The risk—complete disaster. We accepted Tony's appraisal of death.

Dinner was several spoonfuls of potatoes and a cup of peas split five ways with sugarless tea heavily laced with sleeping pills. We attempted to sleep, to forget the icy tents, the tragedy. Next morning we began our way down the glacier and through the icefall. The streamers reached out horizontally from the summits above.

Four days later, attempting to carry some food up to Allen and Roger retreating last down the mountain, a small avalanche carried away 'Little Kansa.' Under the stars, by lamp-light, the slopes above heavily laden with several feet of snow, we dug his body from beneath two feet of snow. After four days the weather cleared. Huge avalanches poured down as Kansa was cremated under a sparkling blue sky. We began our slow walk through the jungles and foothills, homeward, leaving two more inscriptions at the base of the mountain.

The storm had broken two days after our decision to retreat. Had we continued we would have found ourselves descending the summit ridge in the holocaust, exhausted, with sugarless tea and perhaps a handful of porridge to take us down seven thousand feet, across five miles of glacier and icefall then up twenty-five hundred feet to the top of ten thousand feet of fixed rope. It is not surprising that we did not manage to climb the mountain. What is surprising is that we made it as far as we did.

Back in London, I sit in a house where I spent ten days this spring. I am cut off, isolated—a different person. I have changed too much to be able to reconstruct my past life—what I was and did and felt. I sit and do nothing and feel nothing. The Himalayan cold permeates more than the body. I suppose I will laugh and feel joy again but I have learnt the truth of the statement, "In the Himalayas there are no conquerors, only survivors." ❧

PICKLED IN YOSEMITE

It is difficult to think of one adjective that can do justice to Peter Croft's ebullient style of describing his climbing adventures. Perhaps irrepressible comes closest, for the words leap and flash off the page at you like exuberant children, full of mischievous and untiring energy. Few other Canadian mountain writers have such unrelenting forward rhythm to their prose, and Croft has already spawned imitators. There is a dash of the poet in his language, and he has taken metaphor and made it a central fabric of his storytelling. All Croft's writing has drive to match his bold solo accomplishments, which are now famous throughout the world. Yet the man himself is modest to a fault; he made a rare appearance in print recently to chide *Climbing* magazine for overstating his achievements.

And the achievements are mighty impressive. Of particular note in a sensational climbing career are his solo traverses of the Stuart Range in the Cascades; his day out in the Bugaboos when he did four major routes; his ground-breaking solo ascents of incredibly difficult, long rock climbs in Yosemite, and his "enchainments," the most talked about of which are a one-day ascent of both the Nose route on El Cap and the Northwest Face of Half Dome in Yosemite (accomplished with the American climber John Bachar), and a one-day ascent of the Nose and the Salathé routes on El Cap (with Dave Schultz).

But lately Croft has been heard from in print less than previously; perhaps a reaction to the publicity that has come his way as a famous climber. It is to be hoped that he will find the urge again to tell some amazing stories, for his pieces have enriched the literature of Canadian climbing significantly, and, like his great climbs, his writing talent is a rare gift.

$\sim$ Bruce Fairley

Pickled in Yosemite

Peter Croft

There's water literally falling out of the sky right now and it reminds me of Yosemite in spring '83. When I arrived some of the locals said that the weather was the worst remembered. But given that the drug-addled memory span of some of these boys was on the order of two or three days I wasn't too impressed. Still, there was evidence of a lot of moisture; waterfalls bellowed and running shoes blew bubbles and made noises that weren't nice. It couldn't last I reasoned. Nowhere in California does Goretex stay wet longer than a month. But it did last and sleeping bags grew moist, fungus was rampant, and the Valley's energy level was that of a moist flame. The Valley pub scene, though expensive, helped some but they closed it every night so we had to resouse our runners and sprint, heads reeled in tortoise-like, to the parking lot. Here we scampered gingerly to avoid the ponds but inevitably one of us would hit the black wet and rapidly tiptoe knee chin, Jack Lalane style, to the tents. I soon realized that a ripstop marination bag was something to avoid. So I whimpered to Roy who had brought me down from Canada and he let me stay in his station wagon. We became castaways, counting the hours by our watches, the days by the nights, the weeks by the Ahwahnee Brunch. Early on I said, "Roy, whatever happens, we must make the Brunch on Sunday." And Roy, who really enjoys his protein, nodded in approval when I said there might be fish. Roy likes fish.

Then came the Camp 4 creature. They said it was a bear but I wasn't entirely convinced after what it did to some of the cars. The Park Rangeroos and Rangerettes were naturally slow to respond as Godzilla pillaged only the climbing peasants. An innocent bear fart aimed at a Winnebago would bring, within the hour, a squadron of heat-seeking F-16's streaking into the valley between El Cap and Middle Cathedral Rock to terminate all bears, dogs, deer, and shaggy vomiting climbers. After about a dozen whacked-out windows and who knows how many bags of Laura Scudders pilfered, the people with the scout hats responded with their version of the Trojan horse: a big corrugated drain pipe on wheels, with pulleys, wires, lids, and wire mesh, baited with an old can of sardines. There had been thousands of dollars damage and probably close to a quarter of a million tortilla chips stolen and the Yosemite National Park Service responded with leftovers from their lunch.

But we got through those times of flood and beast and we went climbing too. This became somewhat repetitious as there were only two climbs that stayed dry. Another was wriggled up a 40 ft stretch of dry rock on

El Cap with a silly wise man in striped double knits from North Carolina called Eric (pronounced Erk) who is very eccentric (no chalk).

Towards evening it would get dark and we would have to come back to the parking lot to sleep. One particularly boggy morning I ran away. I ran and ran up the hillside till I got tired and then I walked back down again, so wasted that I didn't mind the slum. This revelation convinced me to make it a habit. I called this training as it gave me calluses and made me very good at running away from things I didn't like.

My holiday was running out and I clawed at it to slow it down but the wet days flowed through my fingers and in my mind the long routes shrank from too much water. Some friends swept down from Canada about the same time as the blue overpowered the grey and I felt a high-energy urgency to collect some air beneath me, to accomplish something more than just dry socks.

In the end the days were down to one and I fastened my hopes on it. My plan was to be as greedy as possible: *Astroman* with Greg before lunch and *The Rostrum* with Terry after. Both were foaming eager with biceps like loaves of rising bread. And so, the evening before, Greg and I hiked up to the base of *Astroman* through trees dark with monkey shapes brooding. On a shelf scooped from the talus slope we uncurled our bright caterpillar sleeping bags then peeled off plastic, broke into cardboard, unscrewed lids, and ate and drank more than was necessary. Half-way through our feeding frenzy we stopped in mid-chew to gawk across at the high sliced face of Half Dome, where an avalanche bright in the night poured over the edge, roaring panic-stricken like a toppled giant. Soon we were two snoozing babies, bits of bulging belly bared. We woke like smugglers, way before dawn, whispering and packing, pacing and snarling.

Headlamps flashing, we swiveled our heads like owls as we climbed upwards along the flickering and sweeping yellow column. The first difficult section loomed soft and shadowed then grew orange and crystallized hard. I popped a couple of tiny nuts into a black pocket and then, feet high, pasted my fingers into the slitcrack and grappled up to a small ledge where my spotlight bobbed up and down in time to my hyperventilating. To save time I kept moving past the belay and on up the crux corner. Suddenly the light gave up the ghost and the liquid black night slapped tight back up round me. No place to stop so I slid my hands up the crack blindly, hitting against fixed pins every so often till the light coloured rock kicked back and returned some of the starlight. Three beefy knots in the dark and I leaned back secure in the air. A few large stars flickered vainly as Greg arrived at the belay, riding his jumars. The huge sweeping granite curtain came into focus as the next phase filtered in—dawn. Things speeded up to a high pitched hum when I looked up to see the Harding Slot arching over us, drooling water. For a hundred feet I slapped hams into running cracks till we reached the rude, oozing thing. Moments of indecision—despair, apathy, anger, masochistic glee. Twenty minutes later, T-shirt and track pants flapping wet, I popped up out of the Slot's grip like a minnow and arrived at the belay. From there to the top the climbing was dry and with clothes steaming we aped on, reaching the top at a quarter past ten.

While Greg coiled the rope I threw the gear into the pack, tried to thank him, and was off. Racing down ledges and boulder fields, chimp arms high in the air, I felt utterly charged. Terry was at the parking lot and we roared off, he chattering, me imploding his water jug. From the Valley rim we hiked down deep and then slid down ropes to the base; a sort of backwards arrangement. The climbing on *The Rostrum*, as on *Astroman*, is all desserts—perfect fissures of every size. And as the rock sweeps up steeper, the ledges at the end of each rope length become more and more squatonable.

After a powerful pitch leaning out over space with trotters in secure jams I saw dark rumblies (clouds) approaching. Windbreaker whipping and high-velocity sky spit stinging my cheeks, I joined Terry in an alcove amidst chalk, blood smears, and smiles, then led off on the final pitch—a wide crack with teeth. Appendages rattled around inside the cleft, I sanded down another layer of skin, and arrived on top, tender to the touch. Under low shrub trees we stamped up rotting leaves and emerged onto easy slabs to meet a friend. The sun came out and we had sandwiches and beer.

That evening I sat with friends in the Foul Seasons Restaurant, fingers and feet drumming fast to keep up with a metabolism I couldn't crank down. Roy turned to me over his plate of fish and asked with a spreading mustachioed grin, "So Peter, did you have fun?" And I lolled my tongue around in my mouth to keep my smile under control. "Yeah, I had fun." Later that night Roy and I drove down into the simmering Sacramento Valley and headed north, high for over a thousand miles. 🌿

COMING DOWN

Sharon Wood is the first North American woman to have reached the summit on Mt. Everest. Her climb was made as part of the 1986 "Everest Light" expedition, which brought together most of the best climbers in the Canadian Rockies to attempt the West Ridge of Mt. Everest, a long and sustained route that made great demands on the stamina of the climbers involved. Because of the extraordinary explosion of interest in climbing in the Himilayas today, people are more accustomed to hearing success stories, but in fact most expeditions to the Himilayas still fail to attain their objective, and even more fail when one considers human factors. In this latter respect, most of the climbers from Everest Light returned to Canada feeling good about themselves and the expedition, which could certainly be taken as one mark of a successful climb.

Sharon Wood's achievement on Mt. Everest was the culmination of a long and distinguished tradition of female mountaineering and exploration in Canada, which dates almost from the days when the first climbers arrived in the country. The Alpine Club of Canada was revolutionary in permitting female membership from the first (the English Club only relented in 1974) and a number of the most distinguished early climbers in Canada were women, although generally speaking their accomplishments are less well known than those of the men. Outstanding among the early group in the Rockies were Gertrude Benham, who made the second ascent of Mt. Assiniboine; Mary Schaffer, who discovered Maligne Lake; Henreitta Tuzo, who made the first ascent of the seventh of the ten peaks at Morraine Lake; and Georgia Engelhard Cromwell, who made numerous first ascents in the southern Rockies. In the Coast Mountains, the outstanding pioneer was Phyllis Munday, the explorer of the Waddington Range and the Kliniklini Icefield; while the later generation produced Esther Kafer and Elfrida Pigou, both strong technical climbers, and Alice Purdey, the outstanding female climber in Canada of the 1960s and early 1970s who made numerous first ascents both in southwestern British Columbia and in the farther ranges. Sharon Wood likewise had a strong record of outstanding rock and alpine climbs in Canada behind her before she went to Mt. Everest.

"Coming Down," is not the only article Wood published about her famous climb, yet we have preferred this account to those published in mountaineering journals. Perhaps there is a certain inhibition in writing for those who are on the inside. Mountaineers are much more familiar with the world Sharon Wood is describing—the world of cold, exhaustion, life-and-death choices—than the average magazine reader. There is a tendency to be more restrained when writing for one's peer group, who are likely to be more suspicious of anything smacking of heroics.

Yet despite the greater frequency with which the highest peaks of the world are climbed today, no one should consider any of the great peaks of the Himalayas easy. The folly of underrating any of the giants was amply demonstrated in 1985 on K2, when 13 climbers perished, many of them unnecessarily, through not taking the mountain seriously enough.

"Coming Down" is also interesting in that it gives some insight into "life after Everest"—the world of notoriety and the lecture circuit. Sharon Wood writes with a breezy style which largely rises above the banality of journalism. The necessity to condense events into a short article also adds some drama to the story.

Sharon Wood's achievement made many Canadians feel just a little more proud of themselves, and it is fitting that her fine retelling of one of the most successful Canadian expeditions to the far ranges should conclude the selections in this book.

∿ Bruce Fairley

Coming Down

Sharon Wood

A typical day in the life of the girl who climbed Mount Everest: hop into my 1971 vintage Pinto, slam the door twice; still no seal. Stop at the photo shop in Canmore to pick up some slides. The woman at the counter looks at my tab. Sharon Wood. "You're Sharon Wood, the climber? I've been trying to track you down for weeks. Our society is holding a Dog-a-walk-a-thon next…. We're trying to raise money for…. We're looking for high-profile personalities to attract…." Next stop: the Fort Chiniquay gas station for a fill-up and minimum two liters of oil. As usual the attendant visually scans my car; my eyes follow his, reminded that rust is now the dominant color. As I leave the station my front license plate falls off. I stop, scoop it up and throw it into the back seat to share the cluttered space with an array of climbing gear, oil cans, packages of nylons and boxes of slides.

Eastbound again, my foot nears the floor; the noise of my dangling muffler wafts up through the unsealed door to compete with CBC. Ninth Avenue, Calgary, closing in on my destination: a cop pulls me over and gives me a ticket for a missing front license plate. Thirty minutes before zero hour, I pull into the hotel parking lot, eye out for an obscure stall to deftly change from oily jeans to pristine linen suit without notice from any fellow patrons. Twenty minutes to show time.

I stride down the corridor, slides and briefcase in hand. In view of the conference room a flannel-suited man rushes up to me and takes my arm. We walk down the aisle that splits three hundred similarly dressed men, some restless, some bored, all seated, feet tapping, heads nodding, eyes following. My escort hisses distress in my ear; I am exactly one hour late. The platform speaker sighs his relief as he delivers his closing statement. The master of ceremonies is introducing me. Panic begins to seep in and sabotage all my senses. My focus narrows to accomplish my slide setup in less than sixty seconds. Methodically I walk through all my tasks and checks "…and our keynote speaker, Sharon Wood."

The applause is short and tentative as my mind scrambles to form a strategy. Adrenaline is now rushing to my aid. "Good morning." I push the remote button and the first slide fills the screen. I watch their eyes shift from me to the screen where the north face of Mount Everest looms before us. "I thought I had confronted the greatest challenge of my life when I climbed Mount Everest, but then came life after Everest." My audience and I become friends as we sink into the adventure. We all go to Mount Everest.

Spring 1986, Mount Everest: We arrived at Base Camp, 17,000 feet above sea level, in late March. Over the next forty-five days we stretched out nearly three miles of rope to link five camps, staging ourselves higher and higher on the mountain. We had shuttled almost three tons of equipment load by load to supply these camps. By the time we stocked our highest established camp, Camp Five, we estimated that we climbed the mountain an equivalent of seven times. We were mentally and physically exhausted from enduring the severe oxygen debt, brutally cold temperatures, and the raging winds. Our numbers had dwindled to less than six. The sustained stress had taken its toll. There was not enough manpower to install the final camp; we were behind schedule; a summit bid would have to be made now or never.

Dwayne Congdon and I were selected as the first summit team. Barry Blanchard and Kevin Doyle, two of the stronger, healthier members at the time, would help us push through to establish the final camp. Since nothing was yet in place, it would take four people carrying heavy loads to support two people for one night.

May 19, morning, Camp Five, 25,000 feet: I wriggled my body through the snow tunnel entrance until my head came up level with the platform. My first sight was disappointing: Barry and Kevin huddled together looking tired and beaten. No one had slept well that night. We were all spent from running the race for the last two months against the encroaching monsoon. At best we had another week before the bad weather shut us down; at worst it had already arrived.

Some time ago we had entered a second race, our wasting bodies against time. Here we breathed a quarter of the oxygen that one breathes at sea level. For our bodies to continue to get fuel in this atmosphere our muscle is metabolized for energy. We looked like we had spent the last year in a refugee camp. The deterioration rate works faster the higher we get. It is this element that makes Mount Everest almost unattainable to the mountaineer.

We had a hard day ahead of us, the hardest yet, but this felt like our last chance. If we succeeded in getting this camp in place today two of us would push on for the summit tomorrow. Today we had made the decision to start using supplementary oxygen. Each tank weighed twenty pounds; by the time we strapped on two bottles each, on top of the supplies for Camp Six, our packs came to seventy pounds per person. The oxygen we had thought would help instead hindered us. At the oxygen flow rate we set, it was just enough to compensate for the weight difference.

We followed the last stretches of rope out across the face. Six hours of maintaining a painfully slow pace against the ever increasing winds got us approximately a kilometer across onto the face. At 26,500 feet we came to the end of the ropes. This is where the climbing begins by entering a gash that splits the formidable north face right to the summit, a snow-and-ice gully of forty to sixty degrees in angle, sometimes narrowing to shoulder-width and broken by the occasional steep rocky step. Only 2,500 feet to go but over the most difficult terrain and without the aid of ropes. The ropes were our umbilical cord to home, to safety, the last connection to security. We would soon leave them behind. I was first to arrive. I scratched out a perch on the forty-five degree slope and proceeded to busy myself with the task of untangling and dividing up a six-hundred-foot section of very small diameter rope that we planned for use on the difficult sections higher up. Barry arrived and settled in to wait for the others. I gratefully continued to occupy all thought and energy in my struggle with the rope.

Barry let out a muffled cry from under his mask, pointed upwards and dove for the anchor at my feet. Helpless, trapped in my sluggishness, I looked up to see a cascade or rocks ricocheting off the walls of the gully, crashing and bouncing straight for us. There was no time for me to do anything but watch in fear.

The rocks missed us, by some miracle. In those few moments of terror, it seemed like hours of heartbeats and thoughts had rushed by, precious, irretrievable energy lost. Barry and I went no further than to exchange glances. It was just last year on another climb that I had been torn off my feet and had my shoulder broken when I was struck by one much smaller. Now this message from the mountain: commit or go home, but do not hesitate.

Minutes later Dwayne and Kevin arrived. Unaware of the previous excitement Dwayne asked, "What are we waiting for?"

The departure from the ropes was an experience I had yearned for and anticipated for years. It was time to enter that icy gauntlet. I looked up and strained my eyes to focus on some trailings of old rope dangling high on the walls, left there from past attempts. They had been beaten by the wind, and were now barely recognizable, just ghostly tattered shreds. The relentless wind, our constant adversary, tore rocks and snow from the face thousands of feet above and funnelled it into the narrow chasm we were climbing up. We hugged the walls hoping the larger debris would miss us, if the person leading faltered someone else would step in front to keep us moving.

Climbing up through that gauntlet was like crossing thin ice; the only things supporting me were my hopes. All the words of advice and support given to me by friends came pouring back as clearly as the day they were said.

Just a few days ago our leader, Jim Elzinga, pulled Dwayne and me aside. He said, "Just treat that place up there like any other mountain. Don't die for it. No mountain is worth that cost." Later the four of us were fighting our way back up the mountain through a bad part of a storm. I repeated Jim's argument to Kevin. "To hell it is," he replied. "It's a one shot deal. We can't come back tomorrow!" He promptly turned and continued with his teeth to the wind.

That day and the next we rode mostly on Kevin's and Barry's resolve. Their commitment became a great source of inspiration and drive. They clearly made it their goal to get Dwayne and me to that high point, Camp Six, in spite of the difficult and dangerous conditions, and in spite of the fact that they would climb no higher unless Dwayne or I fell sick. This concept of "treat it like any other mountain" has its place, but if the truth be known, one's bearing on limits—the margin one leaves—is altered significantly in a place like this. Mount Everest is the grand arena. Here performance takes precedence over all else. It was this element in combination with people like Kevin Doyle who possessed an overpowering, infectious sense of commitment that caused me to continue.

May 20, mid-morning, above Camp Six, 27,000 feet: Summit day—Dwayne and I cowered against the wind-ravaged cliffs. We had been climbing for hours but making little progress. Jim Elzinga's raspy voice crackled over the radio: "Ya gotta want it!" They could see us. Those words echoed down the caverns of my memory, taking me back one year to a dismal day in Toronto. I was attempting to follow Jim through his regular training regime of running up the thousand feet of stairs of the CN Tower—not once but three times in the same go. No one else possesses the power to motivate and inspire me to such a masochistic act. I could hear his feet pattering up the metal stairs many flights above me. The same words had echoed down the gray cold stairwell, down through the depths of my fatigue: "Ya gotta want it!" Simple but highly effective. Dwayne and I began to solo up through the rock band trailing out a rope and securing it to use later as a hand rail to find our way back down. We knew it would be dark the next time we groped for it. Each step higher involved more and more concentration until we reached a level where the involvement was so intense it prevailed over all else and the fears and doubts faded. This state of ultimate commitment and performance proved to be the most exhilarating experience of the trip.

May 20, evening, thirty feet below the summit: At 29,000 feet, in slow motion, at times reduced to all fours, we made the last few steps. I regretted leaving my ice axe two hours ago. Back there, I had assumed we were only twenty feet from the summit. I had perched myself on a rock, unzipped four layers of zippers and dug into the depths of my clothing to where the radio had been warmly nestled all day. I knew that in just a few feet we would step onto the wind-exposed ridge where the temperature would drop drastically.

I had kept the radio on and turned up to full volume all day, but we had only spoken once. To talk we had to bare our fingers and at those temperatures we would risk frostbite in seconds. When I pressed the transmit button I surprised myself with the sound of my own voice. I then realized how little Dwayne and I had spoken that day. We were so well synchronized in thought, determination and decision that we had not found it necessary to exchange many words.

When I spoke over the radio for some reason I sounded as though we were out for a day hike; I think I wanted to alleviate all the concern I sensed from our anxious onlookers and teammates. After all, it was eight o'clock in the evening, darkness would surely intercept before we got down, forcing a night on the mountain without shelter. I explained that we were doing well and just 20 feet from the top. Cheers of joy and congratulations crackled through the receiver, then the news that for some reason they could no longer spot us. The reason was to become clear just around the corner. Dwayne came up and led through towards the top. What we thought would take us minutes took us another hour as we surmounted one false summit after another. Finally there was no more up. We came together for the final steps to the highest point on earth.

At nine in the evening on top of Mount Everest the sun can be seen setting over an awesome curving horizon. I am sure it was beautiful but to us it meant something very different. We took our masks off and kneeled down, succumbing to the wind, our relief and our fatigue. We were aware we had made it, but there was nothing more. The radio was silent, long forgotten; there was nothing anyone could do for us now.

One nagging concern dominated: here we were on the highest point on earth and the sun was setting; when it set we would be left behind. Encumbered in our multiple layers of insulation and our oxygen apparatus, we managed an awkward embrace.

We stole a brief and knowing glance down upon a peak twelve hundred feet below and just thirty miles away: Makalu, the fifth highest mountain in the world, a mountain we had failed on two years before. We had come so close. To have that experience behind us was comforting. We had learned some valuable lessons there; we had paid our dues. We belonged here.

There was no time, however, to entertain any philosophical revelations; we simply had a job to finish now. Dwayne got out his camera; I got out the flags and we began clicking off the frames one by one. Just as I had unfurled a huge yellow flag, the wind tore it from my grip. I followed its chaotic course down across the knife edge ridge and out over the giants of the Himalayas until it finally disappeared. I felt so small. It could have been a dream.

All time, thought and effort is suspended in a place like this. It took a multiplication of energy and time to do any task, to think out any idea. Of all parts of the body that are compromised by the oxygen debt, the brain is most severely taxed.

Twenty minutes later we gathered all our remaining mental resources and focused them on getting down. It was now a little over twelve hours since we had left our camp. We had allotted a ten-hour budget of oxygen, using it sparingly.

The climb had just begun.

We now measured the oxygen in moments as the daylight drained away. The mountain was oblivious, unsympathetic to our compromised states. I allowed few thoughts aside from the awareness of my partner and the immediate step below me. But periodically a nagging thought would sabotage my concentration: were we really in control.

Of all the experiences a mountaineer fears and strives to avoid on one of these big peaks it is coming down at night after a very long day. On Mount Everest the slightest mistake could have disastrous consequences. Many have had the strength and will to get themselves to the top, but fewer have been able to retrace their steps to safety.

On Makalu, Dwayne's decision to turn around had been precipitated partially by the shock of seeing a Polish climber frozen into the slope beside him at 27,000 feet. It would be so easy to relax into the beckoning arms of that overwhelming fatigue, to remain crouched in rest into eternity as did the West German woman, Hannelore Schmatz, who in 1979 climbed Everest in only thirty-two days but made the tragic decision to bivouac without oxygen on the way down. She and her partner remain on the spot where they died, a reminder that the mountain pays little sympathy to those seeking respite.

I quickly drew in my focus, closing off my tendency to wander in morbid fantasy. I had allowed just enough fear to seep in to keep pushing on down.

Arriving at the first steep rock step before Dwayne, I pounded in a piton and prepared the rope for us to descend. Calm as I tried to be, urgency was of the essence. In these situations where we trust our full weight to the rope, no mistakes can be made. Every detail must be checked and double-checked with speed and efficiency. Some of my anxiety was relieved when I realized we were still quite proficient in spite of our condition. At approximately 10 p.m. the light began to fail and we turned our head lamps on.

The oxygen still came.

Our pace slowed as we concentrated on each step. As the sun disappeared over the western horizon, a full pearly moon rose in the east, casting ghostly white streaks of light across the face. This had to be a good omen.

I thought of our teammates below, following our tiny lights down the mountain. I found solace as I watched Dwayne moving patiently down. At this time in these circumstances, so far out on the edge, I remember feeling secure in the thought that I could not have been matched up with a more appropriate partner. His caution, his experience and his combination of resignation and determination gave me so much confidence. Our grip, our control, was so tenuously bridged over pending disaster.

We were winning so far.

We reached our ropes as anticipated, in darkness. I was grateful for the extra time and energy taken to place them. We had placed over four hundred feet of very small diameter rope over the steepest section, securing it every hundred feet or so. Now we had to separate to descend the ropes one at a time.

I soon lost sight of Dwayne who was above me. Thirty minutes later I reached the bottom and began to wait. Fifteen, twenty minutes, half-an-hour later—my concept of time was lost—still no Dwayne. He should have been no more than five minutes behind me.

I had been waiting in the dark gully, hanging off the bottom of a rope, my visibility limited to the tunnel of light cast from my head lamp. The cold now began to penetrate through to my body core. I only wanted to sleep.

As I leaned against the rock I nodded off and began to dream. I vividly replayed Dwayne's arrival over and over again. I awoke and strained to see his light high above me but slowly I realized it was just another illusion. I dozed off again.

Panic snapped me awake. My mind scrambled to comprehend what was happening. We were coming off Mount Everest at night and I had lost my partner. A nightmare began to take shape. Another part of me believed everything was under control and Dwayne was simply moving slower than I was. I began to climb down.

Once again concentration consumed all the room in my mind to think. It seemed like just an hour later I thought I was within range of our camp, but how close? It was now very dark. I groped for that small alcove where our tent lay, but nothing looked familiar and again the nightmare threatened to return. I tried to think. Had I gone past the camp? If so I was too weak to climb back up to it. But then my light caught a brief flash, the reflection of an old oxygen bottle. I had found the tent.

The tent was empty and full of snow that had been pressed through the walls by the wind over the day. I fumbled with the stove, driven by the need for water. We had not had anything to eat or drink for nearly twenty-four hours.

I was home.

As my senses cleared, scenarios of what might be happening to Dwayne flooded in to fill the gap. I have abandoned my partner. The thought haunted me. When I had left him I had not been aware that I was making this decision. I just knew that standing still on that mountain was going against a very strong self-preservation instinct. I must keep moving.

An hour-and-a-half later, I heard the familiar crunch of a crampon-clad boot on very cold snow. A beam of light filtered through the nylon tent. At 3:30 a.m. Dwayne was home.

He had run out of oxygen shortly after we split, three hours ago. He had had to stop to rip off the mask that, instead of feeding him, had begun to suffocate him. Without the precious gas, his fingers and toes had begun to freeze all that much quicker. He had to stop every couple of minutes to shake the life back into them and collect his wits for another few moves. Now he was safe but his fingers and toes were frozen. I had to take off his crampons and boots for him.

May 21, early morning, Camp Six, 26,800 feet: We awoke with parched mouths, having gotten down little water before the stove blew up in my face. In relighting it in the night we discovered the propane gas had been leaking into the confined airspace of the tent. For once the shortage of oxygen worked to our advantage; the ignition of free gas was spectacular but short-lived. Frantically, we jettisoned everything that had caught on fire; the stove, various items of clothing and most of my facial hair flew out the door and soon hit the glacier seven thousand feet below. We hoped our teammates had gone to bed by now.

Dwayne dug into his pockets and pulled out an aerial he had found near the summit, not realizing it was the missing part to our silent radio. The team had not heard from us since before the summit. The last they had seen of us was our lights inching further and further apart and then disappearing somewhere into the night. No one had slept. We reassembled the radio and pushed the button.

"Hello, Jim? We're coming down." ✌

～

Glossary

aid climbing—gaining height by attaching devices to rock or ice and then climbing the devices rather than the rock or ice. The climbing may be by simply pulling up or standing on the devices. Aid climbing, however, may also involve the use of etriers, short ladders made from sling material, which are clipped into the devices and then ascended.

aid crack—a crack in a rock face ascended by aid climbing.

belay—the system whereby one climber uses the climbing rope and protection devices to safeguard her partner from a serious fall.

belay station—a secure position where one climber anchors himself to the rock or ice with protection devices to safeguard his partner, who climbs the next pitch.

bergshrund—a hole, often large, at the top of a glacier, where the glacier separates from the mountain.

'biner—see Carabiner.

bivi, bivouac—a camp, sometimes unplanned, with minimal camping equipment. Bivis are often made on longer climbs that take several days, where the weight of carrying full camping gear is prohibitive. Forced bivis can be uncomfortable.

blade—a very thin piton – from "knifeblade."

bong—a very large piton – from the sound it makes when being driven into a rock crack. Not often used today.

bridging—maintaining balance and gaining height by having your feet on widely separated holds.

carabiner—a lightweight metal snaplink used to quickly connect two or more pieces of climbing equipment. A climber ascending a rock pitch while roped will typically attach his protection (pitons, chocks, Friends, etc.) to the rope with carabiners.

chacal—a brand of short ice axe used to climb steep ice.

chimney—a large crack usually climbed with whole body inside.

chocks—a form of protection consisting of aluminium alloy wedges or hexagonals that are inserted into cracks in the rock and clipped to the rope using carabiners. In the event the lead climber falls, a well-placed chock will wedge in the crack, protecting the fall (see Protection). Also called "nuts."

cliff hangers—metal hooks hooked over lips in rock faces to provide a minimal attachment to the rock. Used most commonly in aid climbing.

col—a shoulder or low point between two peaks.

cornice—wind-driven snow projecting without support over a drop. An unwary walk on a cornice may lead to death from the cornice collapsing.

couloir—a gully in the mountains, usually steep and containing ice or snow.

crampons—steel spikes attached to climbing boots for use on ice.

crevasse—a crack or hole, often very deep, running across a glacier. Snow on the surface of a glacier may cover crevasses enough for safety or simply hide the danger.

crux—the most difficult or dangerous section of a climb.

EBs—specialized brand of shoe for climbing rock.

etriers—short, light and flexible ladders used in aid climbing.

expanding flakes—a flake of rock with an uncertain attachment to the main rock face. It expands under outward pressure.

fixed rope—a rope usually fixed to a previously attained high point. This reduces effort to regain that high point.

fixing rope—attaching a rope to be left in place for ease of ascending a pitch in future, or to safeguard a return.

free climbing—gaining elevation by directly climbing the rock or ice. Rope and other equipment are used only for safety and not to gain elevation.

Friend—a mechanical device using expanding cams that can be fitted inside rock cracks (see protection).

gendarme—a tower or pinnacle located on a ridge.

glissade—a controlled slide down a steep snow slope.

hardware—metallic equipment used in climbing.

haul line, hauling—a system set up using a rope, the "haul line," to bring up heavy loads of climbing and camping equipment to a high point.

hooks, sky hooks—see cliff hangers.

ice axe—a wooden or metal shaft with an adze and pick mounted on its head. Indispensible for snow and ice climbing.

ice screws—hollow tubular screws inserted into ice to form part of a protection system (see protection).

iron—pitons (see protection).

jug—to climb a fixed rope using mechanical ascenders that clamp onto the rope. Alternatively, a large hand hold.

Jumar—a type of mechanical ascenders used to ascend a fixed rope.

lost arrows—a type of thin piton named for Lost Arrow spire in Yosemite Valley, California.

mantle—to move using mainly arm thrust to gain a relatively flat spot from a much steeper face.

nuts—see chocks.

pendulum—a climbing technique where the climber becomes the pendulum swinging across a steep face at the end of the climbing rope in order to reach easier or more practical terrain.

pitch—the distance between one belay station and the next.

piton—a device hammered into a crack (see protection). Also called pins.

protection, pro—various devices (chocks, Friends, ice screws and pitons) that a climber uses to make attachment to the rock or ice. Together with the rope they are used to form a protection system that limits the length of falls, when done properly, and thus protects the climber.

rack—climbing equipment or hardware organized on a sling to be carried by the climber.

rappel, rap—to use one of several methods to slide down a rope in controlled descent. Called abseiling in Britain.

serac—an ice tower, often unstable and known to fall on and kill unwary and unlucky climbers.

siege climbing—using fixed rope as a secure link between the base of a climb and one's high point. The fixed rope is ascended and descended repeatedly so that climbers do not have to spend nights on the climb. Often considered to be slow, safe and unadventurous.

Snarg—a brand of ice screw.

soloing—climbing alone. Higher adventure and usually much higher risk.

terrors—a nickname for one of the first radical designs of ice axe for climbing very steep ice.

verglas—a thin coating of ice over rock. Difficult and dangerous to climb.

Grades

Grades are indicated by Roman numerals I through VI as follows:

I. An easy route with only a few hours of actual climbing.

II. A moderate route with perhaps half a day of actual climbing.

III. A more difficult route with most of a day spent in actual climbing.

IV. A major route with most all the hours of a long day spent in actual climbing.

V. A very difficult route requiring at least one bivouac en route.

VI. An extremely difficult route involving multiple bivouacs.

Ratings

Class 1   Hiking.

Class 2   Scrambling.

Class 3   Some use of handholds for balance, but rope not required.

Class 4   Most parties will rope up and either travel together or put in belay stations at the start of each pitch.

Class 5.0–5.4   Easy roped climbing, requiring occasional use of protection such as chocks.

Class 5.5–5.7   Moderate roped climbing, requiring good technical skills and considerable protection for most climbers.

Class 5.8   Many mountaineers regard 5.8 as the limit of what can be climbed in mountain boots.

Class 5.9 & up   Difficult, strenuous roped climbing requiring strong technical skills and considerable protection.

A1–A4   Aid climbing, where it is necessary to put weight on one's protection in order to move up.

F5, F6, F7 etc. are sometimes used to refer to 5.5, 5.6, 5.7 etc.

Bruce Fairley began climbing with the Varsity Outdoor Club at the University of British Columbia in 1975. He got off the ground with a climb of the east ridge of Mt. Steele (5,000 m) in the Yukon that first summer. Since then he has climbed in many parts of North America, but he spends most of his time in the Selkirk Mountains and the Coast Mountains of British Columbia. He has established close to 50 new routes in the mountains, including the west ridge of Mt. Gilbert, the east face of Mt. Sir Donald and the north buttress of Wahoo Tower. He has also been the first to make winter ascents of several peaks, including Mt. Sir Sandford, the highest peak in the Selkirks. His book A Guide to Climbing and Hiking in Southwestern B.C. is the only mountaineering guide to the Coast Mountains in print. Bruce is an active member of the Alpine Club of Canada. He has served as chairman of the publications and environment committees and he was vice president of the club from 1990 to 1992. Bruce lives in Golden, British Columbia, where he has his own law practice.

Bruce Fairley stands on the summit of Snowpatch Spire, a great granite tower in the Bugaboos, with the Howser Towers rising behind him. He and his friend Martin Conder ascended via the beautiful Bedayn route. It was something of a cathartic pilgrimage for Martin, who had attempted the route twice before. On Martin's earlier attempt his partner had fallen to his death low down on the climb, probably due to an epileptic seizure.

More Great Books For Those Who Love Adventure In The Outdoors!

Snow Camping: The Complete Guide to Enjoying the Back Country
By Jo Ann Creore

This first book written about winter camping deals specifically with conditions in Canada and the far north. It contains everything you need to know including chapters on clothing, sleeping systems, food, travel and emergencies. Enjoy winter camping to its fullest with help from this informative guide.
5.5" x 8.5" • 224 pages
130 B & W photographs and illustrations
Softcover • $14.95 • ISBN 1-55105-011-0

Ocean to Alpine
By Joy and Cam Finlay

Organized by region, this nature guide to more than 350 places throughout BC satisfies the year-round needs of those who travel in search of wildlife. It sets out the birds, plants, mammals and marine life common to each area and presents striking photographs of the region. Essential directions and information on hiking and accommodation information are also included.
5.5" x 8.5" • 256 pages • 6 maps
54 colour photographs
Softcover • $14.95 • ISBN 1-55105-013-7

Bicycling Vancouver
By Volker Bodegom

This book covers 32 entertaining and well-planned bicycling routes through and around Vancouver. Detailed maps, access and route descriptions, difficulty ratings, road logs, photographs and historical details are included. Let this thoroughly researched book become your essential cycling tool.
5.5" x 8.5" • 224 pages • 39 B & W maps
92 B & W photographs
Softcover • $14.95 • ISBN 1-55105-012-9

Canadian Rockies Access Guide
3rd Edition
By John Dodd and Gail Helgason

The essential guide for exploring the Rockies by car, horseback or on foot. Includes 115 day hikes, plus information on backpacking, boating, camping, cycling, fishing and more. Covers Banff, Jasper, Kootenay, Yoho, Waterton and Peter Lougheed parks.
5.5" x 8.5" • 360 pages • 54 maps
85 B & W photographs
Softcover • $14.95 • ISBN 0-919433-92-8

Plants of Coastal British Columbia
Plants of the Pacific Northwest Coast
By Jim Pojar and Andy MacKinnon

$24.95 CAN • ISBN 1-55105-042-0
$19.95 US • ISBN 1-55105-040-4

This field guide to plants describes 794 species of trees, shrubs, wildflowers, grasses, sedges and rushes, ferns, liverworts, mosses and lichens. The more than 1100 colour photographs and 797 colour maps make this THE most comprehensive botanical field guide for this area and THE best reference of its kind.
5.5" x 8.5" • 528 pages
1100 colour photographs • 900 B & W illustrations • 797 colour maps • Softcover

Coming Soon From Lone Pine!

Hiking the Ancient Forests of Washington and British Columbia
By Randy Stoltmann

Before his untimely death in a mountaineering accident in 1994, Randy Stoltmann embodied his love for the temperate rainforest trails of Washington and British Columbia in this volume. He describes the best walks and hikes in the old-growth forests and includes detailed maps and directions for each of the 31 featured trails.
ISBN 1-55105-045-5

LONE PINE

Edmonton	**Vancouver**	**Washington State**
206, 10426-81 Avenue	202A, 1110 Seymour St.	16149 Redmond Way, #180
Edmonton, AB T6E 2N1	Vancouver, BC V6B 3N3	Redmond, WA 98052
Ph (403) 433-9333	Ph (604) 687-5555	Ph (206) 343-8397
Fax (403) 433-9646	Fax (604) 687-5575	

Or call toll-free 1-800-661-9017